REFERENCE
DO NOT TAKE FROM THIS AREA

Acknowledgments

Special thanks to Traci Cothran, who was the inspiration for this volume; Susan Schwartz, editorial director, and Michelle Fellner, editorial assistant, at Facts On File, for doing an exceptional job of editing and shaping the manuscript; and Joan Atwood, for copyediting the text and for her many helpful suggestions.

No book like this one could have been completed alone. In addition to thanking all of the authors, journalists and civil rights activists whose work is excerpted here, I would especially like to acknowledge the following people who provided me with invaluable assistance and advice: Alfred Baltimore, the Joint Center for Political and Economic Studies; R. L. Beall, library director, *Greensboro News & Record*; Don Bowden and Patricia Lantis, Wide World Photos; Dale Connelly, Sharon Culley, Fred Pernell and Gary Stern, Still Picture Branch, the National Archives; Maja Felaco, Prints and Photographs Division, the Library of Congress; Walter Husman, publisher, the *Arkansas Democrat Gazette*; James E. Jacobson, editor, the *Birmingham News*; Christine Lindsey, the Lawrence Henry Collection; E. Philip Scott, audiovisual archivist, Lyndon Baines Johnson Library; and the many helpful staff members and librarians at the Columbia University Library, the New York Public Library, the New York University Library and the Schomburg Center for Research in Black Culture.

I would also like to thank Gerard Helferich, Carol Jackson, Cynthia Watkins, Edye and Paul Weissler, Alan, Cliff, Gloria and Rebekah Wexler and my parents, Minnie and Nathan, for their insightful comments and encouragement.

Finally, I'd like to express my appreciation to Julian Bond for writing the introduction and to those who contributed to the last chapter by sharing their thoughts on the legacy of the civil rights movement.

The Eyewitness History Series

Historians have long recognized that to truly understand the past we must relive it. We can only see past eras and events clearly when we free our minds from the knowledge of what unfolded between then and now and permit ourselves to experience events with the fresh vision of a contemporary participant or observer.

To stimulate our powers of historical imagination we must begin by immersing ourselves in the documents of the period, so that we can view events as eyewitnesses. The Eyewitness History Series offers readers and students the opportunity to exercise their historical imaginations by providing in a single volume a large collection of excerpts from what historians call "primary sources," the memoirs, diaries, letters, journalism and official documents of the period.

To give these historical raw materials a framework, each chapter begins with a brief summary of the "Historical Context" followed by a detailed "Chronicle of Events." However, the bulk of each chapter consists of a large selection of quotations from eyewitness accounts of the events of the time. These have been selected to give the reader the widest range of views possible. Each has a specific source in the Bibliography to facilitate further study. To further stimulate the reader's historical imagination, a selection of contemporary illustrations is included in each chapter.

Rather than interrupt the main text with lengthy official documents, we have included them in an appendix. Another appendix includes brief biographies of the major personalities referred to in the text.

Eyewitness Histories are intended to encourage students and readers to discover the powers and the pleasures of historical imagination, while also providing them with comprehensive and self-contained works of reference to significant historical periods.

Introduction

The words "civil rights" summon up memories and images in modern minds of grainy television footage of packed mass meetings, firehoses and police dogs, of early-1960s peaceful protestors replaced over time by violent rioters, of soul-stirring oratory and bold actions, of assassination and death. But there were life and death struggles for civil rights long before the words were introduced into American homes on the evening news.

I was a participant in the movement. I teach its history today. Among my students I find many curious to learn about what the movement and its people did, and why, so they can apply its lessons to the racial problems yesterday's movement left unsolved.

A century passed between the Civil War and passage of the 13th Amendment and the classic struggle for the right to vote fought out in the Confederacy's former arsenal, Selma, Alabama, in 1965; those 100 years were the period when the major battles of the movement for civil rights were fought and won. In this volume, the story is told by the people who made it happen, in their words and writings, for behind the larger-than-life figures celebrated today, this was a movement of largely unknown ordinary women and men.

After a long, slow beginning following the Civil War, the movement's pace quickened in the middle 1950s as black demands increased and the courts struck down segregation laws. Southern atrocities, intended to reinforce the segregation system or punish real and imagined transgressors against the racial status quo, horrified the nation and created a national consensus for reform.

But long before a young minister named King helped organize a boycott of segregated buses in Montgomery that would inspire others and create a new method of combatting Southern white power, black and white Americans were laying the groundwork for the modern movement.

Following the Civil War, the decade of Reconstruction represented the first and last use of full-scale federal power to protect the rights of black Americans. Newly freed slaves registered and voted under the protection of federal troops, elected their own to state legislatures and to Congress and ushered in a brief period of reform.

Political compromises in Washington led to withdrawal of federal troops from the South. The rise of white terrorist organizations in the South erased Reconstruction's gains and the freedmen's protections, leaving them nearly defenseless. The Supreme Court ratified segregation and gave legal sanction to the establishment of separate and always unequal societies, divided by race. By the end of the 19th century, black Southerners were returned to conditions that nearly equaled slavery.

During the beginning of the 20th century, the pace of black militancy quickened, and the demand for equality was reinforced. New organizations were born and new strategies developed, each building on the successes as well as the trials and errors of the past.

The movement that followed is generally characterized as a nonviolent protest movement and is remembered largely for its heroes and impressive public displays of bravery in the face of vicious mob action. It should also be recalled as an organizing movement—a series of widespread and anonymous small steps that became larger ones, individual acts of courage and determination that developed into a mass movement.

Behind 1954's *Brown v. Board of Education* was the Reverend Joseph A. DeLaine's tireless petition for equal education in Clarendon County, South Carolina. Emmett Till's 1955 murder struck fear in Southern black hearts, but also planted determination.

I was 15 when 14-year-old Till was kidnapped, multilated and murdered.

Rosa Parks' defiance of Montgomery's segregation laws came not from tired feet but from her life-long civil rights activism. In Little Rock, Daisy Bates demonstrated the obvious—civil rights was women's work, too. In 1957, she faced down an American president, Dwight Eisenhower.

In 1960, in near spontaneous action, sit-in demonstrations erupted in over 100 towns and cities. The 1961 Freedom Rides owed as much to CORE's (Congress of Racial Equality) courage in the face of brutality as to the hundreds who quickly volunteered to keep the rides going. The movements in Albany, Birmingham, Selma and elsewhere had local roots, home-grown organizations and activists who struggled in obscurity for years before they were bolstered by national figures who provided leadership and attracted national attention.

Martin Luther King Jr. didn't speak to an empty field at the 1963 March on Washington or march from Selma to Montgomery alone in 1965. There were thousands marching with him and before him and thousands more who attended tiny meetings, who did the door-knocking and thankless organizing that preceded the successful marches.

And there were others—journalists who balanced sympathy and objectivity, politicians who catered to the mob and a few who defied it, a small band of innovative lawyers, courageous—and cowardly—clergymen and a vast collection of sympathizers, white and black, who helped and opponents who hindered the movement's progress.

The movement wasn't just fought out on Southern streets and dusty roads. It later exploded in Los Angeles, Newark and Detroit. It was written about in the nation's newspapers, argued on editorial pages.

Its battles reached the halls of Congress and the Oval Office. It spilled over into political campaigns outside the South. It elected one candidate president; it defeated another. It colors our politics today. And it gave new life to other movements of the disadvantaged, teaching them the techniques it had refined.

Just as in this volume the movement's history is being rewritten and reclaimed, so is its legacy.

The number of dark faces seen in places where they never dared appear before is one proof of the movement's success. The limited life chances many of those faces represent is sad proof that the movement's victories were not total, that much more remains to be done.

To many Americans, racial conflict may seem to be a national constant. Each day's headlines trumpet clash and conflict. But the history of the movement for civil rights that has occupied most of the 20th century ought to teach us that dedicated women and men can triumph over ancient wrong. They did in the segregated South. They can again today.

Julian Bond

1. The Origins of the Civil Rights Movement: 1865–1948

RECONSTRUCTION: AFTER THE CIVIL WAR

On January 31, 1865, a constitutional amendment, the 13th, passed the House, prohibiting slavery everywhere in the United States. When the result was announced, Republicans on the floor and spectators in the gallery broke into prolonged and unprecedented cheering. Among the spectators who cheered and wept for joy when the amendment was passed were many black Americans. Their presence was a significant symbol of the revolutionary changes that the 13th Amendment represented. For up until 1864, blacks had not been allowed in the congressional galleries.

In 1865 blacks were also admitted to White House social functions for the first time. "For the first time in my life, and I suppose the first time in any colored man's life, I attended the reception of President Lincoln on the evening of the inauguration," wrote former slave, extraordinary speaker and writer Frederick Douglass. As Lincoln approached Douglass in the East Room of the White House on March 4, 1865, he said, "Douglass, I saw you in the crowd today listening to my inaugural address. There is no man's opinion that I value more than yours: What do you think of it?"

Douglass responded, "Mr. Lincoln, I cannot stop here to talk with you, as there are thousands waiting to shake you by the hand." Lincoln repeated his question, and Douglass said, "Mr. Lincoln, it was a sacred effort." The president said, "I'm glad you liked it."

But perhaps the most dramatic symbol of change had occurred a month earlier when, on February 1, the day after the House passed the 13th Amendment, Senator Charles Sumner presented Boston lawyer John Rock for admission to practice before the Supreme Court, and Chief Justice Salmon P. Chase swore him in. There was nothing extraordinary about this event, except that John Rock was the first black

1

accredited to the Supreme Court, a court that eight years earlier had denied U.S. citizenship to his race.

Three months later, the most divisive and bloodiest conflict in American history came to an end on April 9, 1865, when Robert E. Lee agreed to surrender at Appomattox Court House in Virginia. The war to preserve the Union had cost the lives of 620,000 Americans—360,000 Northerners and at least 260,000 Southerners. Of the 180,000 blacks who served in the Union Army during the Civil War, more than one-third of them, 68,178, died. They fought courageously on every front and at sea. Whatever doubts some might have had about the war, blacks knew why they were fighting.

Although four million blacks in the South were now free, their struggle for true equality was only just beginning. Slavery had been abolished by the 13th Amendment, but Southern state legislatures were determined to grant blacks only limited rights and to keep them "in their place," socially, politically and economically. Encouraged by President Andrew Johnson's expressions of leniency, Southern political leaders enacted a series of vicious regulations known as the Black Codes. These were the laws that before the Civil War had applied to slaves; now they were modified to apply to the freedmen (as former Southern slaves were now called). The Louisiana code, for example, stipulated that every black was supposed to be in the service of a white person, who was held responsible for his or her conduct. In many Southern states, blacks were prohibited from testifying against whites in court and could be punished by fine, jail or whipping for any "insulting act or gesture" toward whites, and almost everywhere blacks were forbidden from using the same public transportation facilities as whites. To many Northerners, these Black Codes were regarded as a revival of slavery in disguise.

The status of the Negro became the focal problem of Reconstruction. When the new Congress convened in December 1865, the radical, Republican-controlled body refused to seat the representatives of the new Southern state governments until they met certain conditions. Among these were requirements that each state ratify the 13th Amendment abolishing slavery and the new 14th Amendment guaranteeing civil liberties. After these amendments were ratified, representatives could be elected to Congress. Meanwhile, the South was divided into five military districts under the command of the Army and placed under martial law; and the Freedmen's Bureau, which had been giving aid to Southern blacks before the close of the Civil War, was established as a permanent organization.

The Southern states held conventions to hammer out constitutions that would be acceptable to Congress. Blacks were members of all of these conventions. In none of these state legislatures did blacks have a majority, but they did exercise great political power, and they filled some key positions, such as associate justices of state supreme courts, commissioners of education, secretaries of state, district attorneys, sheriffs and mayors.

The new Southern state governments quickly received congressional recognition and were allowed to send representatives to Congress. Mississippi sent two blacks to the U.S. Senate, Hiram Revels and Blanche Bruce, and eight other Southern states sent 20 black members to Congress. This black representation in Washington dramatically changed after 1876, and in 1901 the last black left Congress. No black was to serve again in Congress until 1928.

Besides passing three constitutional amendments that guaranteed blacks freedom, citizenship and suffrage for the first time, Congress passed two civil rights acts during Reconstruction: The Civil Rights Act of 1866 referred to blacks as U.S. citizens and guaranteed their rights to own property, to engage in contracts and to sue in court; and the Civil Rights Act of 1875 outlawed discrimination in public facilities, such as conveyances, inns or restaurants on the basis of color. However, within a decade the Supreme Court nullified this legislation by ruling in 1883 that the "individual invasion of individual rights is not the subject-matter of the [14th] amendment." The Court held that the 14th Amendment was "prohibitory upon the States" alone, while the

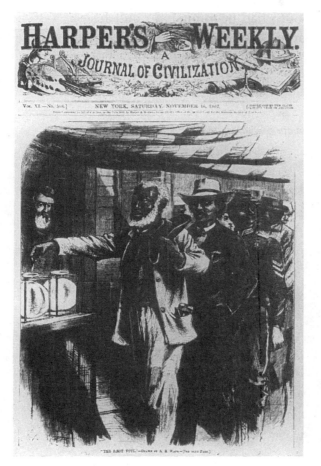

Blacks vote for the first time in 1867. Cover of Harper's Weekly, *November 16, 1867. Courtesy of the Library of Congress.*

Civil Rights Act of 1875 was prohibitory also upon private individuals and groups, and therefore the act was unconstitutional.

Improvement in black Americans' civil status during Reconstruction was in reality more impressive in federal law books than in daily life. Despite the presence of federal troops and the enactment of humanitarian laws by several Southern state conventions, Southern communities varied widely in their respect for the rights of blacks to use public facilities, to testify in court and to even walk the streets unmolested. Bands of hooded white men—Jayhawkers, Black Horse Cavalrymen and the infamous Ku Klux Klan (KKK)—roamed the South at night terrorizing blacks and white Northerners. During Reconstruction thousands of blacks were murdered throughout the South by the Ku Klux Klan, and many more thousands were beaten and driven from their land.

Congress attempted to legislate against these secret societies, but the Ku Klux Klan acts of 1870 and 1871 had little success, and they were later declared unconstitutional. As Reconstruction came to a close and federal troops proceeded to withdraw, the Klan stepped up its terrorism unopposed. By the end of Reconstruction in 1877, the entire South had settled into a pattern of segregation and "white supremacy."

By 1870 Virginia and North Carolina were under conservative Democratic control; and by the spring of 1877, the Reconstruction governments throughout the entire South had been ousted, and the conservatives were back in charge. The South's one-party system was beginning to take shape. Intimidated and frightened, blacks began to

Black Reconstruction congressmen and senators. Courtesy of the Library of Congress.

stay away from the polls in droves. Restrictive legislation was also passed that essentially barred blacks from voting. Other state legislation guaranteeing citizens equal rights was also quickly repealed.

As Republicans became more concerned with the industrial interests in the North rather than with fighting for the rights of the black, Southern conservatives were able to successfully carry out their programs. The matter came to a head in the presidential election of 1876. Rutherford B. Hayes, the Republican candidate, had won the election by a narrow margin over his Democratic opponent, Samuel Tilden. The electoral vote was so close that a special electoral commission was appointed by Congress to decide which candidate had actually won. Hayes succeeded in getting himself declared elected by obtaining the support of Southern Democrats in return for his promise to, among other things, withdraw the last of the federal troops policing the South. The election compromise, known as the Great Swap, spelled the end of Reconstruction. For millions of black citizens in the South, it meant that their civil rights would no longer be protected.

A Short-Lived Alliance

During the 1880s and 1890s, the struggle for black equality appeared to merge briefly with the Populist movement as poor white farmers in the South appeared willing to set aside their racial animosities and work with black landowners to break the economic stronghold that northern industrials had upon the rural South. Although blacks were barred from such organizations as the National Grange and the Southern Farmers' Alliance, they were encouraged to, and did, set up similar organizations of their own, like the Colored Farmers' Alliance.

For only a brief time, from 1892 to 1895, did the agrarian revolt wield any power. Consequently, blacks returned to political prominence in several Southern states. Threatened by the possibility of a powerful coalition between poor blacks and whites in the South, Northern industrialists and their junior partners in the South soon were able to divide the Populist ranks.

Instead of relying on violence, Southern conservative leaders were determined to establish legal and permanent means of depriving blacks of their right to vote. Starting with Mississippi in 1890, Southern states passed laws that set up various restrictive conditions for voting. These included payment of a poll tax and demonstration of the ability to read and explain an obscure section of the state constitution. Although these laws were often applied to black voters, they were seldom applied to whites.

Soon the imposition of Jim Crow, as the South's racial rules were dubbed, became prevalent in every Southern state. All over the South "white" and "colored" signs went up. Trains, buses, barbershops, schools and other public places were segregated by law.

PLESSY V. FERGUSON

Then, in 1896, the United States Supreme Court rendered the famous *Plessy v. Ferguson* decision, which set forth the doctrine of "separate but equal," popularly known as the Jim Crow Car Law. Homer Plessy, a "black man" who was seven-eighths white was arrested for riding on a Louisiana train in a section reserved for "whites only." Plessy had sued on the grounds that a Louisiana statute requiring segregated streetcars violated his right to equal citizenship under the 14th Amendment. Eight members of the Court ruled that the 14th Amendment was not intended "to enforce social as distinguished from political . . . equality, or a comingling of the two races upon terms unsatisfactory to each other." In effect, the decision held that "separate but equal" accommodation laws throughout the South were constitutional. Segregation thus became an American institution, a way of life imbedded in the law of the land.

The lone dissenter, Justice John Harlan, declared, in perhaps one of the most famous dissents in the history of the Court, that "the judgment this day rendered will, in time, prove to be quite as pernicious as the decision made by this tribunal in the *Dred Scott* case . . . The destinies of the two races, in this country, are indissolubly linked together, and the interests of both require that the common government of all shall not permit the seeds of race hate to be planted under the sanction of law."

The doctrine of separate but equal would remain intact for nearly 60 years, until May 17, 1954, when Chief Justice Earl Warren would rule for a unanimous court in *Brown v. Board of Education of Topeka* that in the field of education separate facilities are inherently unequal. The landmark decision would have ramifications for the civil rights of millions of black Americans, especially for those living in the South.

THE ATLANTA COMPROMISE

As the 19th century came to a close, new black leaders who matured during the decades of post-Reconstruction despair were beginning to assert themselves. One of the most influential of these was Booker T. Washington. In 1881 Washington founded the Tuskegee Normal and Industrial Institute in Alabama, where black students were taught vo-

Booker T. Washington, educator and author. Courtesy of the Library of Congress.

cational skills, such as carpentry, mechanics or farming, so they could earn a living. Washington believed that blacks should, for the time being at least, abandon political agitation and seek to get along with whites while concentrating on improving their economic conditions. His views were welcomed by many Southern whites who believed that blacks should accept their status of second-class citizenship and at the same time train themselves in marketable labor skills.

Washington gained national prominence when he delivered a speech at the Cotton States and International Exposition in Atlanta on September 18, 1895. He declared, "The wisest among my race understand that the agitation of questions to social equality is the extremest folly . . . The opportunity to earn a dollar in a factory just now is worth infinitely more than the opportunity to spend a dollar in an opera house." The Atlanta speech was reprinted and distributed throughout the country, and although many blacks resented Washington's eagerness to accept an inferior role, whites hailed the address as "The Atlanta Compromise"—an end to black agitation for equality in return for an opportunity to gain a little economic prosperity.

Soon thereafter, Washington's speech was the target of rebuttals by other black voices, such as John Hope, president of Atlanta University, who said, "If we are not striving for equality, in heaven's name for what are we living? I regard it as cowardly and dishonest for any of our colored men to tell white people or colored people that we are not struggling for equality."

Washington became the government's chief advisor on the appointment of blacks to the few "black posts," such as minister to Liberia and Haiti. He was frequently consulted by Presidents Theodore Roosevelt and William Howard Taft on black affairs, domestically and internationally. Although he did work behind the scenes to fight restrictive laws, there were many blacks who disagreed with his policies. In 1906 the Reverend Adam Clayton Powell (father of the congressman Adam Clayton Powell Jr.) wrote to *The New York Times:* ". . . under Dr. Washington's policy the two races in the South are a thousand times further apart than they were fifteen years ago and the breach is widening every day."

THE FORMATION OF THE NAACP

At the turn of the 20th century, new voices in the black community were gaining attention—and they did not advocate moderation or the status quo. Harvard-educated William Edward Burghardt Du Bois was one of these preeminent new leaders. In 1903 Du Bois's provocative book *The Souls of Black Folk* was published, and in it he charged that Booker T. Washington's philosophy was one of submission and failure. It had resulted in stripping away all black rights. Du Bois wrote,

W. E. B. Du Bois, historian, author, editor and a founder of the National Association for the Advancement of Colored People (NAACP). Courtesy of the Library of Congress.

"Negroes must insist continually, in season and out of season, that voting is necessary to modern manhood, that color discrimination is barbarism, and that black boys need education as well as white boys."

In the summer of 1905, Du Bois gathered together 29 black leaders, mostly professionals such as doctors, lawyers and teachers, at Niagara Falls, Canada, to form what was to become known as the Niagara Movement. Its mission was to reaffirm the struggle for real black equality. Although the Niagara Movement established about 30 branches throughout the country, it gained little ground since money to support black advancement was primarily going to Booker T. Washington. By 1910 it had disbanded. But from its brief tenure sprang one of the most important interracial civil rights organizations—the National Association for the Advancement of Colored People (NAACP).

The NAACP was founded in 1909 "to achieve, through peaceful and lawful means, equal citizenship rights for all American citizens by eliminating segregation and discrimination in housing, employment, voting, schools, the courts, transportation, recreation." A famous Boston lawyer, Moorfield Storey, a white man, was the organization's first president. Its director of publicity and research was W. E. B. Du Bois. Although its original membership list was modest, it included many distinguished Americans, including pioneer social worker Jane Addams, philosopher John Dewey, prominent black Washington, D.C. minister Francis J. Grimke and black journalist and antilynching crusader Ida. B. Wells-Barnett.

By 1914 its publication, the *Crisis*, under Du Bois's editorship, had climbed to a monthly circulation of nearly 35,000, and there were 50 branches of the NAACP in the United States. It also had succeeded in having several federal government agencies rescind their discriminatory rules and regulations. (Today the NAACP has over 500,000 members and 1,800 chapters across the country, and it continues to play an active role in civil rights matters.)

Relying heavily upon the legal process as a weapon for attaining equal rights, the NAACP achieved three major court victories in its first 15 years. In 1915 the Supreme Court ruled against the grandfather clauses that had kept blacks from voting in several states; in 1917 the Court struck down a municipal ordinance requiring blacks to live in certain sections of towns; and in 1923 the Court overturned a murder conviction against a black, because blacks had been excluded from the jury that had convicted him.

One of the early crusades of the NAACP was a campaign for enacting federal antilynching legislation. With the aid of graphic pamphlets, such as *Thirty Years of Lynching in the United States, 1889–1918*, the NAACP exposed a surge of racially motivated, unpunished and uninvestigated lynching in the Southern states. Federal antilynching bills twice passed the House of Representatives in the 1930s, but Southern senators killed them in the Senate.

The NAACP's major role in the civil rights movement of the 1950s and 1960s, including participation in bus boycotts, demonstrations, Freedom Rides, marches, school desegregation and voter registration drives, will be discussed in subsequent chapters.

A. Philip Randolph and the Proposed March on Washington

America's entry into the Second World War resulted in an unprecedented military buildup across the nation and consequently brought nearly 10 years of depression to an end. Industries that had been working at only partial capacity now had more work than they could handle, but the new defense plants, operating with government contracts, refused to hire black workers. According to the 1940 census, there were almost 5.5 million blacks in the American labor force; but of 30,000 employees in 10 war plants in the New York area, for example, only 168 were blacks. The president of the North American Aviation Company explained in May 1941 that despite the firm's "complete sympathy with the Negro, it is against company policy to employ them as aircraft workers or mechanics . . . regardless of their training." He promised "some jobs as janitors for Negroes."

A. Philip Randolph, who in 1925 had founded the Brotherhood of Sleeping Car Porters, saw this situation as an opportunity to force the issue of equality in employment. In 1941 Randolph and other black leaders pleaded with officials in Washington to allow blacks to take part in defense industries. After the federal government ignored their calls for ending discrimination in the defense industry, Randolph conceived of a plan that would later become an integral part of the civil rights movement of the 1960s—a mass march on the nation's capital by tens of thousands of blacks.

In the summer of 1941, 50,000 blacks were organized to march in protest right up to the White House. Shortly before the day of the march, President Franklin Roosevelt met with Randolph and agreed to issue an executive order that declared, "the policy of the United States [is] to encourage full participation in the national defense program by all citizens of the United States, regardless of race, creed, color, or national origins." This directive, known as Executive Order 8802, was the first presidential order for civil rights since Reconstruction. Roosevelt also established the Fair Employment Practices Committee to investigate hiring policies and enforce the program. In return, Randolph agreed to cancel the march on Washington.

Although 2 million blacks did secure jobs in munitions factories, they worked mainly in the least-skilled and lowest-paid positions. Half a million black soldiers served in the European and Pacific theaters, most of them in segregated units under white command, just as their fathers a quarter century earlier had in the First World War.

Even after World War II, the armed forces were still racially segregated. A. Philip Randolph and other black leaders began to make plans for a mass civil disobedience campaign against the draft unless blacks' demands for integration were met. Then in July 1948, President Harry S Truman issued an executive order barring segregation in the military. But it would take nearly a decade for all of the branches of the armed services to become completely desegregated.

TRUMAN'S CIVIL RIGHTS PROGRAM

President Truman also presented to Congress in 1948 a major civil rights program. Although Congress remained on the whole unresponsive, the program was influential in emphasizing the urgency of civil rights and in laying out guidelines for later legislation. In his February 2, 1948 message, Truman said, "The federal government has a clear duty to see that constitutional guarantees of individual liberties and of equal protection under the laws are not denied or abridged anywhere in the Union. That duty is shared by all three branches of the government, but it can be fulfilled only if the Congress enacts modern, comprehensive civil rights law, adequate to the needs of the day . . . ."

Truman's address enraged many Southern Democrats. At the 1948 Democratic National Convention in Philadelphia, the Mississippi delegation and part of the Alabama delegation walked out of the convention hall in protest against the party's civil rights plank. These dissident Democrats, known as the "Dixiecrats," formed the States' Rights Party and nominated Strom Thurmond of South Carolina as their candidate for president. The Dixiecrats campaigned on a platform of racial segregation.

Truman was determined to become the first major party candidate in American history to campaign openly for civil rights. In a surprise victory, he defeated the Republican candidate, New York Governor Thomas E. Dewey, by a margin of 2.2 million popular votes and 114 electoral votes. The Dixiecrat candidate, Strom Thurmond, received 39 electoral votes and a little over one million popular votes.

Truman was the first president to create a permanent Civil Rights Commission and to issue an executive order proclaiming a policy of "fair employment throughout the Federal establishment, without discrimination because of race, color, religion or national origin." Although Truman's proposed civil rights legislation only scratched the surface of what needed to be done, it signaled the growing importance of blacks in American politics, especially in the Democratic Party.

CHRONICLE OF EVENTS

1865

January 31: The U.S. House of Representatives passes the 13th Amendment to the Constitution, abolishing slavery, by a two-thirds majority. It was previously adopted by the Senate in April 1864.

February 1: The first black, John S. Rock, is admitted to practice before the United States Supreme Court.

March 3: The Freedmen's Bureau is established by Congress to aid former slaves.

April 14: President Abraham Lincoln is assassinated while watching a comedy at Ford's Theater in Washington by actor and Southern patriot John Wilkes Booth.

April 15: President Lincoln dies at 7:22 A.M. Three hours later, Vice-President Andrew Johnson takes the oath of office as president.

May 29: President Johnson grants amnesty to the Confederates, with a few exceptions. It is one of the first acts in the long struggle for what Johnson calls "restoration" and Congress calls "reconstruction."

Fall: Black Codes are enacted by all-white legislatures in former Confederate States. The Black Codes forbid blacks from testifying against whites; blacks without work can be arrested for vagrancy; public schools will be segregated. Blacks cannot serve on juries, bear arms or hold large meetings.

December 18: The 13th Amendment to the U.S. Constitution abolishing slavery is declared in effect by Secretary of State William Seward after it is ratified by 27 states.

1866

April 9: The Civil Rights Act is passed by Congress over President Johnson's veto. It grants full citizenship to all persons born on U.S. soil (except Indians). All citizens are to have equal rights to enforce contracts, to sue, to give evidence, to buy property—in effect, to have all the civil rights a full citizen is entitled to.

July 30: Race riot in New Orleans results from effort to introduce black male suffrage into the Louisiana Constitution. Thirty-four blacks are killed, and more than 200 are injured. Four whites are killed; 10 policeman are injured.

1867

January 8: Blacks' suffrage in the District of Columbia is established by an act of Congress over President Johnson's veto.

March 2: The First Reconstruction Act is passed by Congress over Johnson's veto. It is designed to protect blacks politically and economically. Constitutional conventions are ordered, with blacks participating fully in elections.

May: The Ku Klux Klan is formed in Nashville, Tennessee. It is one of the many secret societies organized to terrorize blacks in the South.

Hiram R. Revels was elected to the U.S. Senate from Mississippi in 1870 to fill the unexpired term of Jefferson Davis. He was the first black American to serve in the U.S. Senate. Courtesy of the Library of Congress.

1868

January: Constitutional conventions begin to meet in Southern states, with blacks fully participating.

March 5: The impeachment trial of President Johnson begins.

May 26: President Andrew Johnson is acquitted.

July 28: Secretary of State Seward announces ratification of the 14th Amendment, granting full citizenship to blacks and all others born or naturalized in the United States (except Indians).

1869

December 6: National Labor Convention of Colored Men meets in Washington, D.C., creating a national black labor union.

1870

February 25: Hiram R. Revels, the first black to be elected to the U.S. Senate, takes his seat.

March 30: Secretary of State Hamilton Fish proclaims ratification of the 15th Amendment to the Constitution, which guarantees suffrage to all citizens born or naturalized in the United States.

December 12: The first black to be elected to the U.S. House of Representatives, Joseph H. Rainey of South Carolina, takes his seat.

1871

April 20: The Ku Klux Klan Act is enacted by Congress to enforce the 14th Amendment. It authorizes the president to suspend the writ of habeas corpus and to use military force to suppress disturbances in Southern states.

1872

April 15: Frederick Douglass presides over the Colored National Convention in New Orleans.

June 10: The Freedmen's Bureau is discontinued by an act of Congress, effective June 30.

1875

March 1: The Civil Rights Act is passed by Congress. It states that no citizen can be de-

Joseph H. Rainey of South Carolina was elected to the U.S. House of Representatives in 1870. He was the first black American to serve in the U.S. House of Representatives. Courtesy of the Library of Congress.

nied equal use of public facilities such as conveyances, inns or restaurants on the basis of color.

1877

February: Rutherford B. Hayes makes a secret argeement to withdraw troops from the South in exchange for Southern electoral votes.

April 24: The last federal troops are removed from Louisiana and the last Southern state is returned to control of its citizens. Although Reconstruction helped rebuild the war-torn South, it failed to achieve its primary goal of securing black civil rights.

1881

July 4: The Tuskegee Normal and Industrial Institute in Alabama is founded by black leader Booker T. Washington. It becomes the foremost institute for vocational training for blacks in the country.

1883

January 22: Sections of the Ku Klux Klan Act of 1871, penalizing individuals who conspire to impede provisions of the 14th and 15th Amendments, are declared unconstitutional. The Supreme Court rules that these Amendments apply to states and not to individuals. *October 15:* U.S. Supreme Court declares the Civil Rights Act of 1875 unconstitutional on the grounds that individual business rights to choose their own clientele are violated by giving blacks equal access.

1895

September 18: In a speech at the Cotton States and International Exposition in Atlanta, Booker T. Washington calls for an end to black agitation for equality in return for gaining economic prosperity. His address becomes known as the Atlanta Compromise.

1896

May 6: The separate but equal doctrine is held constitutional by the Supreme Court in the *Plessy v. Ferguson* case, known popularly as the Jim Crow Car Law. The Court rules that as long as facilities are equal, the fact that they are separate does not constitute infringement of civil rights. The doctrine will remain intact until May 17, 1954, when it is unanimously overturned by the court.

1905

July: Harvard-educated W. E. B. Du Bois gathers together 29 black leaders at Niagara Falls, Canada to form what becomes known as the Niagara Movement. Its goal is to reaffirm the necessity for achieving black rights. The orga-

nization disbanded in 1910 due to lack of financial support.

1909

June 1: W. E. B. Du Bois founds the National Association for the Advancement of Colored People (NAACP). He advocates equality and equal opportunity for blacks.

1920

August 26: The 19th Amendment to the Constitution, which gives women suffrage, is enacted.

1931

March 25: Nine young black boys are arrested in Scottsboro, Alabama and are charged with raping a white woman. In the course of three trials, they will be found guilty, but the Supreme Court will overturn their conviction on April 1, 1935. "The Scottsboro Boys" will become a cause célèbre for all determined to obtain justice for black Americans.

1941

June 25: President Franklin Roosevelt establishes the Fair Employment Practices Committee by executive order to prevent discrimination due to race, creed or color in defense plants. It is formed partly in response to a proposed mass demonstration on Washington, which was to be led by A. Philip Randolph, president of the Brotherhood of Sleeping Car Porters.

1947

April: Jackie Robinson signs with the Brooklyn Dodgers. He becomes the first black baseball player in the major leagues.

1948

January 12: A U.S. Supreme Court decision, *Sipeul v. Board of Regents of the University of Oklahoma*, rules that no state can discriminate against a law school applicant on the basis of race.

February 2: President Truman introduces a civil rights package to Congress in which he calls for an end to segregated schools and employment discrimination.

July 15: Some Southern delegates at the Democratic National Convention in Philadelphia walk out in protest against the addition of a civil rights plank to the party platform.

1948

July 17: The States' Rights Party (Dixiecrats) is formed by dissident members of the Democratic Party. Governor Strom Thurmond of South Carolina is their nominee for president.

July 26: President Truman issues an executive order banning segregation in the U.S. armed forces and calls for an end to racial discrimination in federal employment.

November 2: Harry S Truman is elected president in a surprise victory over New York Governor Thomas E. Dewey by 2.2 million popular votes and 114 electoral votes. The Dixiecrat candidate, Strom Thurmond, receives 39 electoral votes and a little over one million popular votes.

EYEWITNESS TESTIMONY

If there is no struggle, there is no progress. Those who profess to favor freedom, and yet depreciate agitation, are men who want crops without plowing up the ground. They want rain without thunder and lightning. They want the ocean without the awful roar of its many waters. This struggle may be a moral one; or it may be a physical one; or it may be both moral and physical; but it must be a struggle. Power concedes nothing without a demand.

Frederick Douglass, speaking in Canandaigua, New York on August 3, 1857, in The Life and Writings of Frederick Douglass *(1950–1975).*

Frederick A. Douglass, escaped slave, abolitionist, journalist, orator and public official. Courtesy of the Library of Congress.

Everybody has asked the question, and they learn to ask it early of the abolitionists, "What shall we do with the Negro?" I have had but one answer from the beginning. Do nothing with him. Your doing with us has already played the mischief with us. Do nothing with us! . . . If you see him on his way to school, let him alone, don't disturb him! If you see him at the dinner table at a hotel, let him go! If you see him going into the ballot box, let him alone, don't disturb him!

Frederick Douglass, to the annual meeting of the Massachusetts Anti-Slavery Society at Bos-ton, speech of April 1865, in The Life and Writings of Frederick Douglass *(1950–1975).*

"The days of bayonets are passed!" is the bullying street-cry of the returned rebel soldiers in Norfolk and Portsmouth, as they fearlessly assume the once-familiar knife and pistol. But Gen. [Oliver O.] Howard, commandant of the small military force retained here, has said, "There is one thing I will do; I will protect the colored people."

Lucy Chase, Northerner who went South to aid the freedmen, newspaper article of June 25, 1865, in Swint's Dear Ones at Home *(1966).*

Well, the war is over, the rebellion is "put down," and we are declared free! Four-fifths of our enemies are paroled or amnestied, and the other fifth are being pardoned, and the President has, in his efforts at the reconstruction of the civil government of the states late in rebellion, left us entirely at the mercy of these subjugated but unconverted Rebels, in every way save the privilege of bringing us, our wives, and little ones to the auction block . . . We know these men—know them well—and we assure you that, with the majority of them, loyalty is only "lip deep," and that their professions of loyalty are used as a cover to the cherished design of getting restored to their former relations with the Federal government, and then, by all sorts of "unfriendly legislation," to render the freedom you have given us more intolerable than the slavery they intended for us.

Statement of the Convention of the Colored People of Virginia, held in Alexandria, Virginia, August 2–5, 1865, in Hofstadter's Great Issues in American History *(1958).*

Congress must create states and declare when they are entitled to be represented . . . We have turned, or are about to turn, loose four million slaves without a hut to shelter them or a cent in their pockets. The infernal laws of slavery have prevented them from acquiring an education . . . This Congress is bound to provide for them until they can take care of themselves. If we do not furnish them with homesteads . . . if we leave them to the legislation of their late masters, we had better had left them in bondage.

Congressman Thaddeus Stevens (Pennsylvania), to Congress, speech of September 18, 1865, in the Congressional Record *(1865).*

In my judgment the Freedmen, if they show patience and manly virtues, will sooner obtain a participation in the elective franchise through the States than through the General Government, even if it had the power to intervene.

President Andrew Johnson, to Congress, first annual message, December 4, 1865, in Richardson's A Compilation of the Messages and Papers of the Presidents *(1896–1899).*

We have worked in your fields, and garnered your harvests, for two hundred and fifty years! And what do we ask of you in return? Do we ask you for compensation for the sweat our fathers bore for you— for the tears you have caused, and the hearts you have broken, and the lives you have curtailed, and the blood you have spilled? Do we ask retaliation? We ask it not. We are willing to let the dead past bury its dead; but we ask you now for our rights.

State Representative Henry MacNeal Turner (Georgia), to the Georgia House of Representatives, speech of 1866, in Meltzer's In Their Own Words: A History of the American Negro, 1865–1916 *(1965).*

Question: What, in your judgment, would be the effect of withdrawing the military and the Freedmen's Bureau from those States, and leaving the freedmen of the south to the legislation and rule of the white population?

Answer: I think the result of such a policy as that would be fearful to contemplate. I fear it would lead to an insurrection, and to a war of races. I think the only way in which the two races can live together in peace and prosperity is by giving the black race the same political rights that whites enjoy.

Rufus Saxtion, assistant commissioner of the Freedmen's Bureau of South Carolina, to Congress, testimony of February 21, 1866, in U.S. Congress' Report of the Joint Committee on Reconstruction *(1866).*

Wherever I go—the street, the shop, the house, or the steamboat—I hear the people talk in such a way as to indicate that they are yet unable to conceive of the Negro as possessing any rights at all . . . To kill a Negro, they do not deem murder; to debauch a Negro woman, they do not think fornication; to take the property away from a Negro, they do not consider robbery. The people boast that when they get freedmen's affairs in their own hands, to use their own expression, "the niggers will catch hell."

The reason of all this is simple and manifest. The whites esteem the blacks their property by natural right, and however much they admit that the individual relations of masters and slaves have been destroyed . . . they still have an ingrained feeling that the blacks at large belong to the whites at large.

Carl Shurz, journalist, to the U.S. Senate, report of 1866, in Du Bois's Black Reconstruction in America *(1936).*

Fortunately, the Constitution of the United States knows no distinction between citizens on account of color. Neither does it know any difference between a citizen of a State and a citizen of the United States. Citizenship evidently includes all the rights of citizens, whether State or national. If the Constitution knows none, it is clearly no part of the duty of a Republican Congress now to institute one.

Frederick Douglass, article of December 1866, in the Atlantic Monthly.

As there seems to be considerable difference of opinion concerning the "legal rights of the colored man," it will not be amiss to say that we claim exactly the same rights, privileges and immunities as are enjoyed by white men—we ask nothing more and will be content with nothing less. All legal distinctions between the races are now abolished. The word white is stricken from our laws, and every privilege which white men were formerly permitted to enjoy, merely because they were white men, now that word is stricken out, we are entitled on the ground that we are men. Color can no longer be pleaded for the purpose of curtailing privileges, and every public right and immunity is enjoyable by every individual member of the public.

Address of the Colored Convention to the people of Alabama, May 1867, in Allen's Reconstruction: The Battle for Democracy, 1865–1876 *(1963).*

The amendment abolishing slavery has been reinforced by another, known as Article XIV, which declares peremptorily that "no State shall make or enforce any law which shall abridge the privileges and immunities of citizens of the United States," and again Congress is empowered to enforce this provision. What can be broader? Colored persons are citizens of the United States, and no State can abridge their privileges and immunities. It is a mockery to say that, under these explicit words, Congress is powerless to forbid any discrimination of color at the ballot box. Why, then, were they inscribed in the Constitution? To what end? There they stand, supplying an additional and supernumerary power, ample for safeguard against caste or oligarchy of the skin, no matter how strongly sanctioned by any State government.

Senator Charles Sumner (R, Mass.), to the U.S. Senate, speech of January 28, 1869, for the 15th Amendment, in The Works of Charles Sumner *(1883).*

We have thought from their organization and from other indications we have had, that the organization, that is, the purpose of the organization, have been to remand the colored men of the country to as near a position of servitude as possible and to destroy the republican party if possible; it has been, in other words, political. We believe it had two objects, one was political, and the other was to hold the black man in subjection to the white man, and to have white supremacy in the South . . . we have evidence of it from parties who have sworn and bound themselves together under oaths, that is, in clubs, to do all they can from year to year, and from month to month, as long as they live, to establish white supremacy in Mississippi, and the disenfranchisement of the black man.

Robert Gleed, Mississippi state senator, to Congress, testimony of 1871, in U.S. Congress Report on the Alleged Outrages in the Southern States by the Select Committee of the Senate *(1871).*

I have spoken of their having the law and the courts all on their side. The juries were made up of Ku-Klux [Klan], and it was impossible for any of the loyal people to get justice before the courts. Not less than fifty or sixty persons have been killed by the Ku-Klux [Klan] in the State, besides some three or four hundred whippings, and there has never been a man convicted that I have heard of. Out of all those that I arrested, against whom there was as good proof as could possibly be given, enough to convict anybody before twelve honest men, I do not think one has ever been tried.

Colonel George W. Kirck, North Carolina state troops, to Congress, testimony of 1871, in U.S. Congress' Report on the Alleged Outrages in the Southern States by the Select Committee of the Senate *(1871).*

The evidence is cumulative. Ruffians in paint and in disguise seize the innocent, insult them, rob them, murder them. Communities are kept under this terrible shadow. And this terror falls especially upon those who have stood by the Union in its bloody trial, and those others of different color who have just been admitted to the blessings of Freedom. To both of these classes is our nation bound by every obligation of public faith. We cannot see them sacrificed without apostasy. If the power to protect them fails, then is the National Constitution a failure.

Senator Charles Sumner (R, Mass.), to the U.S. Senate, speech of April 13, 1871, on the Ku Klux Klan Act, in The Works of Charles Sumner *(1883).*

The [Kentucky] Legislature has adjourned and they refuse to enact any laws to suppress Ku Klux [Klan] disorder. We regard them as now being licensed to continue their dark and bloody deeds under cover of the dark night. They refuse to allow us to testify in the state Courts where a white man is concerned . . . Our people are driven from their homes in great numbers having no redress only the U.S. Courts which is in many cases unable to reach them. We would state that we have been law abiding citizens, pay our tax and in many parts of the state our people have been driven from the poles [sic], refused the right to vote. Many have been slaughtered while attempting to vote, we ask how long is this state of things to last.

We appeal to you as law abiding citizens to enact some laws that will protect us. And that will enable us to exercise the rights of citizens.

Colored Citizens of Frankfort, Kentucky, to the U.S. Senate, petition of May 25, 1871, in the Congressional Globe *(1872).*

On the night of the 5th of last May, after I had heard a great deal of what they had done in that neighborhood, they came. It was between 12 and 1 o'clock at night when I was awakened and heard the dogs barking, and something walking, very much like horses. As I had often laid awake listening for such persons, for they had been all through the neighborhood, and disturbed all men and many women, I supposed that it was them. They came in a very rapid manner, and I could hardly tell whether it was the sound of horses or men. At last they came to my brother's door, which is in the same yard, and broke open the door and attacked his wife, and I heard her screaming and mourning. I could not understand what they said, for they were talking in an outlandish and unnatural tone, which I had heard they used at a negro's house. I heard them knocking around in her house. I was lying in my little cabin in the yard. At last I heard them have her in the yard. She was crying and the Ku-Klux [Klan] were whipping her to make her tell where I lived.

Elias Hill, black preacher of York County, South Carolina, to Congress, testimony of 1871, on the Ku Klux Klan, in the U.S. Congress' Report of the Joint Select Committee to Inquire into the Condition of Affairs in the Late Insurrectionary States (1872).

Down I went again, and I stayed down until they got done whipping me. Says he, "Now, by Christ, you must promise you will vote the democratic ticket!" I says, "I don't know how I will vote, it looks hard when a body thinks this way and that way to take a beating" . . . "You must promise to vote the democratic ticket, or you go dead before we leave you," he says.

Anonymous black South Carolinian, to Congress, testimony of 1871, on the Ku Klux Klan, in the U.S. Congress' Report of the Joint Select Committee to Inquire into the Condition of Affairs in the Late Insurrectionary States (1872).

It is not enough to provide separate accommodations for colored citizens even if in all respects as good as those of other persons . . . The discrimination is an insult and a hinderance, and a bar, which not only destroys comforts and prevents equality, but weakens all other rights. The right to vote will have new security when your equal rights in public conveyances, hotels, and commons schools, is at last established; but here you must insist for yourselves by speech, by petition, and by vote.

Senator Charles Sumner (R, Mass.), to the National Convention of Colored Citizens at Columbia, South Carolina, letter of October 2, 1871, in The Works of Charles Sumner (1883).

I never can agree . . . that if there be a hotel for the entertainment of travellers, and two classes stop at it, and there is one dining room for one class and one for another, served alike in all respects, with the same accommodations, the same attention to the

guests, there is anything offensive, or anything that denies the civil rights of one more than the other.

Senator Joshua Hill (Republican, Georgia), speech of 1872, in Fleming's Documentary History of Reconstruction (1906–1907).

We look to mixed schools to teach that worth and ability are to be the criterion of manhood and not race and color.

Frederick Douglass, article of May 2, 1872, in the New National Era.

It is said by some well-meaning men that the colored man has now every right under the common law; in reply I wish to say that that kind of law commands very little respect when applied to the rights of colored men in my portion of the country; the only law that we have any regard for is uncommon law of the most positive character . . . if you will place upon your statute-books laws that will protect me in my rights, then public opinion will speedily follow.

Black congressman James T. Rapier (Republican, Alabama), to Congress, speech of 1873, for a civil rights bill, in the Congressional Record (1873).

The results of the war, as seen in reconstruction, have settled forever the political status of my race. The passage of this bill will determine the civil status, not only of the Negro, but of any other class of citizens who may feel themselves discriminated against. It will form the capstone of that temple of liberty, begun on this continent under discouraging circumstances . . . until at last it stands in all its beautiful symmetry and proportions, a building the grandest which the world has ever seen, realizing the most sanguine expectations and the highest hopes of those who, in the name of equal, impartial, and universal liberty, laid the foundation stones.

Black congressman Robert Brown Elliot (Republican, South Carolina), to Congress, speech of January 5, 1874, for a civil rights bill, in the Congressional Record (1874).

If the States . . . continue to deny to any person within their jurisdiction the equal protection of the laws, or as the Supreme Court has said, "deny equal justice in its courts," then Congress is here said to have power to enforce the constitutional guarantee against inequality and discrimination by appropriate legislation . . . Never was there a bill more completely within the constitutional power of Congress. Never was there a bill which appealed for support more strongly to that sense of justice and fairplay which has been said, and in the main with justice, to be a characteristic of the Anglo-Saxon race. The Constitution warrants it; the Supreme Court sanctions it; justice demands it.

Black congressman Robert Brown Elliot (Republican, South Carolina), to Congress, speech of 1874, supporting the enactment of a civil rights bill, in the Congressional Record *(1874).*

. . . if this unjust discrimination is to be longer tolerated by the American people, which I do not, cannot, and will not believe until I am forced to do so, then I can only say with sorrow and regret that our boasted civilization is a fraud; our republican institutions a failure; our social system a disgrace; and our religion a complete hypocrisy . . . This country is where I intend to live, where I expect to die. To preserve the honor of the national flag and to maintain perpetually the Union of the States hundreds, and I may say thousands, of noble, brave, and true-hearted colored men have fought, bled, and died . . . I ask, can it be possible that that flag under which they fought is to be a shield and a protection to all races and classes of persons except the colored races? God forbid!

Black congressman John Roy Lynch (Republican, Mississippi), to Congress, speech of 1875, supporting the enactment of a civil rights bill in the Congressional Record *(1875).*

What is the President's Southern policy? In point of physical or external fact, it consists in withdrawing the military forces of the United States from the points in South Carolina and Louisiana where they have been previously stationed for the protection and support of the lawful Government of those States . . .

In point of actual results, it consists in the abandonment of Southern Republicans, and especially the colored race, to the control and rule not only of the Democratic party, but of that class at the South which regarded slavery as a Divine Institution, which waged four years of destructive war for its perpetuation, which steadily opposed citizenship and suffrage for the negro—in a word, a class whose traditions, principles, and history are opposed to every step and feature of what Republicans call our national progress since 1860.

Daniel H. Chamberlain, former governor of South Carolina, [carpetbagger from Massachusetts], speech of April 1877, in Allen's Governor Chamberlain's Administration in South Carolina *(1888).*

It is a great thing to have the supreme law of the land on the side of justice and liberty. It is the line up to which the nation is destined to march—the law to which the nation's life must ultimately conform. It is a great principle, up to which we may educate the people, and to this extent its values exceed all speech.

But today, in most of the Southern States, the fourteenth and fifteenth amendments are virtually nullified.

The rights which they were intended to guarantee are denied and held in contempt. The citizenship granted in the fourteenth amendment is practically a mockery, and the right to vote, provided for in the fifteenth amendment, is literally stamped out in face of government. The old master class is today triumphant, and the newly-enfranchised class is in a condition but little above that in which they were found before the rebellion.

Frederick Douglass, to blacks in Elmira, New York, speech of August 1, 1880, in The Life and Times of Frederick Douglass *(1895).*

There has been a universal discrimination here in Alabama, and, indeed, all over the South, in the treatment of the colored people as to cars they are permitted to ride in. The white people have always labored under the impression that whenever a colored man attempted to go into a ladies' car, he did it simply because it was a car for white people. Now if the white people looked at it as we look at it, taking a commonsense view of it, they would see that that idea is erroneous and false. We go into those cars simply because there are better accommodations there . . . But in the cars allotted to the colored people a white man comes in and smokes cigars, and chews tobacco, and curses and swears, and all that kind of thing, and the conductors on the various roads don't exercise their powers for the protection of the colored passengers.

J. A. Scott, black lawyer, to the U.S. Senate, testimony of 1883, on the Jim Crow railroad cars, in Fleming's Documentary History of Reconstruction *(1906–07).*

Though we have had war, reconstruction, and abolition as a nation, we still linger in the shadow and blight of an extinct institution. Though the colored man is no longer subject to be bought and sold, he is still surrounded by an adverse sentiment which fetters all his movements. In his downward movement he meets with no resistance, but his course upward is resented and resisted at every step of his progress.

Frederick Douglass, speech of September 24, 1883, in Three Addresses on the Relations Between the White and Colored People of the United States *(1886).*

Now where rests the responsibility for the lynch law prevalent in the South? It is evident that it is not entirely with the ignorant mob. The mob who breaks open jails and with bloody hands destroys human life are not alone responsible. These are not the men who make public sentiment. They are simply the hangmen, not the court, judge, or jury. They simply obey the public sentiment of the South—the sentiment created by wealth and respectability, by the press and pulpit. A change in public sentiment can be easily effected by these forces whenever they shall elect to make the effort. Let the press and pulpit of the South unite their power against the cruelty, disgrace and shame that is settling like a mantle of fire upon these lynch-law States, and lynch law itself will soon cease to exist.

Frederick Douglass, article of August 11, 1892, on lynching, in the Christian Reader.

It is important and right that all privileges of the law be ours, but it is vastly more important that we be prepared for the exercises of these privileges. The opportunity to earn a dollar in a factory just now is worth infinitely more than the opportunity to spend a dollar in an opera house.

Booker T. Washington, speech of September 18, 1895, which became known as the "Atlanta Compromise," at the Atlanta Exposition, in Up From Slavery: An Autobiography *(1901).*

If we are not striving for equality, in heaven's name for what are we living? I regard it as cowardly and dishonest for any of our colored men to tell white people or colored people that we are not struggling for equality . . .

Yes, my friends, I want equality. Nothing less . . . Now catch your breath, for I am going to use an adjective: I am going to say we demand social equality . . . I am no wild beast, nor am I an unclean thing.

Rise, Brothers! Come let us possess this land . . . Be discontented. Be dissatisfied . . . Be as restless as the tempestuous billows on the boundless sea. Let your discontent break mountain-high against the wall of prejudice, and swamp it to the very foundation.

John Hope, professor at Roger Williams University, Nashville, Tennessee, speech of January 22, 1896, to the black debating society of Nashville, responding to Booker T. Washington's "Atlanta Compromise," in Torrence's The Story of John Hope *(1948).*

The object of the [14th] amendment was undoubtedly to enforce the absolute equality of the two races before the law, but in the nature of things it could not have been intended to abolish distinctions based upon color, or to enforce social, as distinguished from political equality, or a commingling of the two races upon terms unsatisfactory to either.

Supreme Court Justice Henry Billings Brown, Court's majority opinion of May 6, 1896, in Plessy v. Ferguson, *163 U.S. 537 (1896).*

Our Constitution is color-blind, and neither knows nor tolerates classes among citizens. In respect of civil rights, all citizens are equal before the law. The humblest is the peer of the most powerful. The law regards man as man, and takes no account of his surroundings or of his color when his civil rights as guaranteed by the supreme law of the land are involved. It is, therefore, to be regretted that this high tribunal, the final expositor of the fundamental law of the land, has reached the conclusion that it is competent for a State to regulate the enjoyment by citizens of their civil rights solely upon the basis of race.

Supreme Court Justice John Marshall Harlan, dissenting opinion of May 6, 1896, in Plessy v. Ferguson, *163 U.S. 537 (1896).*

For nearly twenty years lynching crimes, which stand side by side with Armenian and Cuban outrages, have been committed and permitted by this Christian nation. Nowhere in the civilized world save the United States of America do men, possessing all civil and political power, go out in a band of 50 to 5,000 to hunt down, shoot, hang or burn to death a single individual unarmed and absolutely powerless . . . We refuse to believe that a country, so powerful

Ida B. Wells-Barnett, journalist, orator and advocate of women's rights. She was best known for her crusade against lynching. Courtesy of the Library of Congress.

to defend its citizens abroad, is unable to protect its citizens at home . . . Italy and China have been indemnified by this government for the lynching of their citizens. We ask that the government do as much for its own.

Ida B. Wells-Barnett, journalist, article of April 9, 1898, on lynching, in the Cleveland Gazette.

This, Mr. Chairman, is the Negroes' temporary farewell to the American Congress. He will rise up some day and come again. These parting words are in behalf of an outraged, heart-broken, bruised and bleeding, but God-fearing people, faithful, industrious, loyal people—rising people, full of potential force . . . I am pleading for the life, liberty, the future happiness, and manhood suffrage of one-eighth of the entire population of the United States.

Black congressman George H. White (Republican, North Carolina), to Congress, farewell speech of 1901, in the Congressional Record *(1901).*

The problem of the twentieth century is the problem of the color line.

W. E. B. Du Bois, 1903, in The Souls of Black Folk *(1903).*

Lynching took the lives of 3,224 persons between 1889 and 1918. Most of the victims were black. Justification for this mob violence usually included vague claims of sex crimes committed against white women. But less than 30% of the victims of lynch mobs were ever formally accused of a crime, much less proven guilty. Courtesy of the Library of Congress.

Mr. [Booker T.] Washington apologizes for injustice, North or South, does not rightly value the privilege and duty of voting, belittles the emasculating effects of caste distinctions, and opposes the higher training and ambition of our brighter minds . . . By every civilized and peaceful method we must strive for the rights which the world accords to men, clinging unwaveringly to those great words which the sons of the [Founding] Fathers would fain forget: "We hold these truths to be self-evident: That all men are created equal; that they are endowed by their Creator with certain unalienable rights; that among these are life, liberty, and the pursuit of happiness."

W. E. B. Du Bois, 1903, in The Souls of Black Folks *(1903).*

We will not be satisfied to take one jot or tittle less than our full manhood rights. We claim for ourselves every single right that belongs to a freeborn American . . . We want full manhood suffrage and we want it now . . . We want discrimination in public accommodation to cease . . . We want the Constitution of the country enforced . . . We are men! We will be treated as men. And We shall win!

W. E. B. Du Bois, speech of 1906, at Harpers Ferry, on the goals of the Niagara Movement, in Dusk of Dawn *(1940).*

The Celebration of the Centennial of the birth of Abraham Lincoln, widespread and grateful as it may be, will fail to justify itself if it takes no note of and makes no recognition of the colored men and women for whom the Great Emancipator labored to assure freedom . . . If Mr. Lincoln could revisit this country in the flesh, he would be disheartened and discouraged . . .

In many States Lincoln would see the black men and women, for whose freedom a hundred thousand soldier gave their lives, set apart in trains, in which they pay first-class fares for third-class service . . . he would observe that State after State declines to do its elementary duty in preparing the Negro through education for the best exercise of citizenship . . .

Added to this, the spread of lawless attacks upon the Negro, North, South, and West—even in the Springfield made famous by Lincoln . . . could but shock the author of the sentiment that "government of the people, by the people, should not perish from the earth."

Silence under these conditions means tacit approval.

Participants in the founding meeting of the Niagara Movement, ca. 1905. Courtesy of the Library of Congress.

Oswald Garrison Villard, editor of the New York Post, *open letter of February 12, 1909, on calling for a conference that ultimately resulted in the formation of the NAACP, in* Hughes' Fight for Freedom, the Story of the NAACP *(1962).*

We regard with grave concern the attempt manifest South and North to deny black men the right to work and to enforce this demand by violence and bloodshed . . .

As first and immediate step toward remedying these national wrongs, so full of peril for the whites as well as the blacks of all sections, we demand of Congress and the Executive:

(1) That the Constitution be strictly enforced and the civil rights guaranteed under the Fourteenth Amendment be secured impartially to all.

(2) That there be equal educational opportunities for all and in all the States, and that public school

expenditures be the same for the Negro and white child.

(3) That in accordance with the Fifteenth Amendment the right of the Negro to the ballot on the same terms as other citizens be recognized in every party of the country.

National Negro Committee, platform of 1909, in the NAACP papers.

The object of the National Association [NAACP] is to create an organization which will endeavor to smooth the path of the Negro race upward, and create a public opinion which will frown upon discrimination against their property rights, which will endeavor to see that they get in the courts the same justice that is given to their white neighbors, and that they are not discriminated against as they are now all over the country. We want to make race prejudice as unfashionable as it is now fashionable.

Moorfield Storey, first president of the NAACP, speech of 1910, in Howe's Portrait of an Independent: Moorfield Storey, 1845– 1929 (1932).

Some good friends of the cause we represent fear agitation. They say, "Do not agitate—do not make a noise; work." They add, "Agitation is destructive or at best negative—what is wanted is positive constructive work." Such honest critics mistake the function of agitation. A toothache is agitation. Is a toothache a good thing? No. Is it therefore useless? No. It is supremely useful, for it tells the body of decay and death. Without it the body would suffer unknowingly. It would think: all is well, when lo! Danger lurks.

W. E. B. Du Bois, article of 1910, in the Crisis.

This government cannot exist half-slave and half-free any better today than it could in 1861.

Mary White Ovington, executive secretary of the NAACP, article of August 1914, in the Crisis.

Try to imagine, if you can, the feelings of a Negro army officer, who clothed in the full panoply of his profession and wearing the decorations for valor of three governments, is forced to the indignity of a jim-crow car and who is refused a seat in a theatre and a bed in a hotel . . .

Think of the feelings in the hearts of boys and girls of my race who are clean, intelligent and industrious who apply for positions only to meet with the polite reply that, "We don't hire niggers."

Anonymous, black World War I veteran, to Victor F. Lawson, editor of the Chicago Daily News, letter of 1919, in Tuttle's Views of a Negro during "the Red Summer" of 1919 (1966).

We return from the slavery of uniform which the world's madness demanded we don to the freedom of civil garb. We stand again to look America squarely in the face and call a spade a spade. We sing: This country of ours, despite all its better souls have done and dreamed, is yet a shameful land.

It lynches. It disfranchises its own citizens. It encourages ignorance. It steals from us. It insults us. We return. We return from fighting. We return fighting.

Make way for Democracy! We saved it in France, and by the Great Jehovah, we shall save it in the United States of America, or know the reason why.

W. E. B. Du Bois, editorial of May 1919, on black World War I soldiers returning home, in the Crisis.

The Negro must have a country, and a nation of his own. If you laugh at the idea, then you are selfish and wicked, for you and your children do not intend that the Negro shall discommode you in yours. If you do not want him to have a country and a nation of his own; if you do not intend to give him equal opportunities in yours; then it is plain to see that you mean that he must die, even as the Indian to make room for your generations.

Why should the Negro die? Has he not served America and the world? Has he not borne the burden of civilization in this Western world for three hundred years? Has he not contributed his best to America? Surely all this stands to his credit, but there will not be enough room and the one answer is "find a place." We have found a place, it is Africa.

Marcus Garvey, leader of the Universal Negro Improvement Association, article of 1923, in An Appeal to the Soul of White America (1923).

There is no such thing as a fair and just Jim Crow system with "equal accommodations," and in every human nature there will never be. The inspiration of Jim Crow is a feeling of caste and a desire to "keep in its place," that is, to degrade, the weaker group. For there is no more reason for a Jim Crow car in public travel than there would be for a Jim Crow path in the public streets.

William Pickens, NAACP field secretary, article of August 15, 1923, on traveling by rail in a Jim Crow car across Texas, in the Nation.

Unless disfranchisement, arbitrary residential segregation, lynching, unequal apportionment of school funds, injustice in the courts, Jim Crowism, and the other evils which are foisted upon Negroes in parts of the United States can be ended, then democracy itself fails in the United States.

Walter White, NAACP assistant secretary, to a NAACP convention in Springfield, Massachusetts, speech of July 1930, in the New York Amsterdam News *(July 21, 1930).*

Under the laws of the country, which do not mean much, the Negro is entitled to every equality . . . The time has come when, if there is anything to be done for the Negro, he must do it himself . . . I am not telling you how to vote . . . but your ballot is your most powerful weapon.

Clarence Darrow, defense attorney, to the 22nd annual convention of the NAACP, Pittsburgh, Pennsylvania, speech of July 1931, in the Pittsburgh Courier *(July 11, 1931).*

Though thirteen million Negroes have more often than not been denied democracy, they are American citizens and will as in every war give unqualified support to the protection of their country. At the same time we shall not abate one iota our struggle for full citizenship rights here in the United States. We will fight but we demand the right to fight as equals in every branch of military, navy and aviation services.

NAACP, announcement of September 9, 1940, in Finch's The NAACP: Its Fight for Justice *(1981).*

A community is democratic only when the humblest and weakest person can enjoy the highest civil, economic, and social rights that the biggest and most powerful possess. To trample on these rights of both Negroes and poor whites is such a commonplace in the South that it takes readily to antisocial, antilabor, anti-Semitic, and anti-Catholic propaganda. It was because of laxness in enforcing the Weimar Constitution in republican Germany that Nazism made headway. Oppression of the Negroes in the United States, like suppression of the Jews in Germany, may open the way for a fascist dictatorship.

A. Philip Randolph, founder and president of the Brotherhood of Sleeping Car Porters. Courtesy of the Schomburg Center for Research in Black Culture.

By fighting for their rights now, American Negroes are helping to make America a moral and spiritual arsenal of democracy. Their fight against the poll tax, against lynch law, segregation, and Jim Crow, their fight for economic, political, and social equality, thus becomes part of the global war for freedom.

Asa Philip Randolph, president of the Brotherhood of Sleeping Car Porters, article of November 1942, in Survey Graphic.

We must not be delayed by people who say "the time is not ripe," nor should we proceed with caution for fear of destroying the "status quo." Persons who deny to us our civil rights should be brought to justice now. Many people believe the time is always "ripe" to discriminate against Negroes. All right then—the time is always "ripe" to bring them to justice. The responsibility for the enforcement of these statutes rests with every American citizen regardless of race or color. However, the real job has to be done by the Negro population with whatever friends of the other races are willing to join in.

Thurgood Marshall, NAACP special counsel, to the NAACP Wartime Conference, speech of July 13, 1944, in The Legal Attack to Secure Civil Rights.

We can no longer afford the luxury of a leisurely attack upon prejudice and discrimination. There is much that state and local governments can do in providing positive safeguards for civil rights. But we cannot, any longer, await the growth of a will to action in the slowest state or the most backward community. Our national government must show the way.

President Harry S Truman, to the NAACP's 38th annual convention, speech given in front of the Lincoln Memorial, June 29, 1947, in The Public Papers of the Presidents of the United States 1948 *(1949).*

Everybody knows that I recommended to the Congress the civil rights program. I did so because I believed it to be my duty under the Constitution. Some of the members of my own party disagreed with me violently on the matter, but they stand up and do it openly. People can tell where they stand.

President Harry S Truman, acceptance speech of July 14, 1948, at the Democratic convention in Philadelphia, Pennsylvania, in the Public Papers of the Presidents of the United States 1948 *(1949).*

The Democratic party commits itself to continuing the efforts to erradicate all racial, religious and economic discrimination.

We again state our belief that racial and religious minorities must have the right to live, the right to work, the right to vote, the full and equal protection of the laws, on a basis of equality with all citizens as guaranteed by the Constitution.

Democratic Party platform of 1948, in the New York Times *(July 15, 1948).*

We oppose and condemn the action of the Democratic convention in sponsoring a civil rights program

calling for the elimination of segregation, social equality by Federal fiat, regulation of private employment practices, voting and local law enforcement.

States' Rights ("Dixiecrats") Party platform of 1948, in the New York Times *(July 18, 1948).*

Harry Truman, Tom Dewey and Henry Wallace are birds of one feather. All three are kowtowing to minority blocs by advocating the so-called civil rights program. This time they cannot fool the people and especially the Democrats of the South.

Governor Strom Thurmond (South Carolina), presidential candidate of the States' Rights Party ("Dixiecrats"), speech of October 1948, in Time *(October 4, 1948).*

An alert, independent and aggressive Negro electorate in collaboration with organized labor and other progressive forces may be an important factor in determining the political complexion of Congress. The growing Negro vote in the South, allied with white progressives, can bring about changes of far-reaching importance in that region . . . This new electorate of both races threatens the continued domination of the courthouse gangs which have been the controlling factors in the Democratic party in the southern states. The success of such a coalition is limited only by the degree to which the white working class in the South can be liberated from the specious doctrine of "white supremacy" as preached by the Bilbos, the Rankins, and the Talmadges.

Henry Lee Moon, NAACP director of publicity, 1948, in Balance of Power: The Negro Vote *(1948).*

The right to vote is basic. At least one Negro was lynched last year solely on the ground that he was trying to exercise his right. Terror and the poll tax are but two of the methods used to keep Negroes from voting in the South. "Citizenship" without the privilege of voting is a mockery.

Supporters of the "separate but equal" dogma have adopted but a thin disguise for "keeping the Negro in his place." What is the Negro's place? The Negro cannot any longer accept the definition of his "place" that was formulated by slave owners.

Ira L. Mosley, black teacher at Lincoln High School, Venice, Illinois, article of March 20, 1949, in the St. Louis Dispatch.

2. School Desegregation and the *Brown v. Board of Education* Decision: 1949–1954

THE MARGOLD BIBLE

During the 1930s, the NAACP launched a concerted legal attack against school segregation and Jim Crow. Jim Crow was a term for officially sanctioned segregation that affected every aspect of American life, including schools, restaurants, trains and all forms of transportation, theaters, drinking fountains, and many public and private facilities. The name Jim Crow came from a comic black character that was portrayed by a white performer in an early 19th-century variety act.

In 1933 Nathan Ross Margold, a white Harvard-educated attorney, working for the NAACP, published a report that described a legal strategy for desegregating public schools. Known as the Margold Bible among NAACP insiders, it argued against a legal theory called the separate-but-equal doctrine, which was the very basis for institutionalized segregation in the United States.

The separate-but-equal doctrine was first established in 1896, when the U.S. Supreme Court ruled in *Plessy v. Ferguson* that the separation of races is constitutional as long as equal accommodations are made for each race. The Margold report pointed out that the justices writing the majority opinion had based their decision on cases and legal precedents that predated the Civil War and the 14th Amendment. Although the NAACP was prepared to legally campaign against segregation, it believed that the best strategy for eventually overturning *Plessy* would be one that gradually and indirectly challenged the decision. It also believed that the reform climate of the New Deal favored appeals for equal opportunity but not demands for integration.

CHARLES HOUSTON

The vice-dean of Howard University's law school, Charles Hamilton Houston, once said in 1935, "A lawyer's either a social engineer, or he's a parasite on society." Houston was the son of Mary Hamilton, a schoolteacher, and William Houston, a black attorney who had established a successful law practice that served black middle-class clients in segregated Washington, D.C. Charles Houston was born on September 3, 1895, eight months before the U.S. Supreme Court decided the case of *Plessy v. Ferguson*. A great part of his legal career would be spent in fighting to overturn this decision.

After serving as an army officer in World War I, Houston entered Harvard University Law School in 1919. He became the first black elected to the editorial board of the *Harvard Law Review*. Upon graduation from Harvard in 1924, Houston joined his father's firm but soon found that he was more interested in taking on cases that helped the oppressed rather than those that brought money into the firm. He believed that if the legal system was to change for black Americans, it would be because of a group of committed and well-trained black lawyers. Houston left his father's firm to join the law school faculty at Howard University in Washington, D.C., the largest all-black college

Charles Hamilton Houston in court. Courtesy of the Moorland-Spingarn Research Center, Howard University.

in the United States. At Howard he could train others in practicing law and also give them a thorough understanding of the Constitution. Only attorneys who had mastered constitutional law could successfully argue civil rights cases in federal courts. One of Houston's students was Thurgood Marshall, who would become the NAACP's special counsel and later the first black Supreme Court justice.

In 1935 Houston took a leave of absence from Howard University and became chief counsel for the NAACP. Drawing upon the Margold Bible, Houston mapped out a detailed, long-range strategy for fighting school segregation. The NAACP would first begin by attacking segregation in professional and graduate schools, then if they could achieve a series of victories and establish broad and clear precedents, they could challenge segregation in colleges, high schools and finally elementary schools.

Thurgood Marshall, who was now a practicing attorney in Baltimore, soon joined the NAACP's legal campaign. During 1936 Marshall and Houston traveled throughout the South meeting with NAACP regional officers and looking for cases that might challenge school segregation. That year, Lloyd Lionel Gaines, a 25-year-old black man, was seeking admission to the all-white law school at the University of Missouri. The state of Missouri said it would build a law school on the campus of the all-black Lincoln University if Gaines would agree to apply there. Although no funds were appropriated for such a law school and no building was planned, the state claimed that it would begin erecting one as soon as Gaines applied. Also, the state was prepared to pay his tuition in an out-of-state law school. Gaines sued the state for admission to the University of Missouri law school and lost his case before the Circuit Court of Boone County, as was expected. Houston appealed on his behalf to the U.S. Supreme Court.

Nearly two-and-a-half years later, on November 9, 1938, the U.S. Supreme Court finally heard the case of *Missouri v. Canada* (S. W. Canada was the registrar at the University of Missouri). At Howard University, Houston rehearsed his argument before legal scholars and law students. These rehearsals before a moot court at Howard would be the first of many rehearsals that would be argued over the next 14 years. Two students in the audience at the *Gaines* rehearsal, Robert Carter and Spottswood Robinson, would later represent the NAACP in *Brown v. Board of Education of Topeka* before the Supreme Court.

Houston argued before the Supreme Court that it was insufficient for the state of Missouri to simply set up a school and call it a law school. The separate-but-equal doctrine dictated that the black and white schools had to be truly equal. The Supreme Court ruled in Gaines' favor. He was entitled to attend the University of Missouri School of Law. The Court's opinion clearly stated that states had an obligation to provide equal education for all citizens, black and white. Moreover, states could not send black students out of the state instead of providing in-state facilities, and they also could not expect students to wait while school buildings were built within the state.

The *Gaines* decision had far-reaching implications for other segregated institutions, especially schools. If states were compelled to provide equal legal education for its black citizens, then did states also have to provide equal undergraduate colleges, high schools and elementary schools? Also possibly affected were parks, hospitals, libraries and many other public facilities.

After working as the NAACP's chief legal counsel for five years, Houston returned to his father's law firm, where he pursued a multitude of court cases dealing with segregation in the military and discrimination in transportation and labor unions. Thurgood Marshall, only 30 years of age, was named as Houston's successor at the NAACP. In 1946 Marshall set up the NAACP Legal Defense Fund, which was exclusively devoted to the association's legal campaigns.

On June 5, 1950, a few months after Charles Houston had died at the age of 54, the U.S. Supreme Court handed down its decisions in *Sweatt v. Painter* and *McLaurin v. Oklahoma State Regents*, two graduate school segregation cases. The Court ruled that black Americans have the right to attend state graduate schools and receive full educational benefits from such schools. Although the decision did not overturn *Plessy*, it said in effect that separate-but-equal education must be authentic, and if it wasn't, then the separation was unconstitutional.

Soon after the Supreme Court decision was issued in *Sweatt* and *McLaurin*, the NAACP Legal Defense Fund, led by Thurgood Marshall, convened a conference in New York City with 43 lawyers and 14 NAACP branch and state conference presidents. After much debate, the NAACP members decided that they would abandon the Margold Bible for a newer legal strategy: all-out opposition to *Plessy*. It was decided that in all of their future education cases, they would seek to attain schooling on a nonsegregated basis. Marshall argued that school segregation was inherently unconstitutional, for it stigmatized an entire race and therefore denied blacks "equal protection of the laws" as guaranteed by the 14th Amendment.

THE CASES OF BROWN V. BOARD OF EDUCATION

CLARENDON COUNTY, SOUTH CAROLINA

In order to establish the fact that separate schools could never be truly equal, the NAACP Legal Defense Fund had to prove that the consequences of segregation, including psychological, intellectual and

Thurgood Marshall, NAACP special counsel. Courtesy of the Library of Congress.

financial damages, prevented genuine equality from taking place. NAACP branches began gathering segregation cases from several states that challenged different aspects of the law. The Legal Defense Fund planned to launch a broad attack against school segregation and wanted to make it difficult for the Court to issue a decision limited to only a particular instance.

In 1950 there were over two million black children attending segregated elementary schools. NAACP Legal Defense Fund lawyers had found an appropriate test case for attacking school segregation in South Carolina's Clarendon County. In the Clarendon County school system, there were nearly three times as many black students as whites, but the white students received more than 60% of the educational appropriations. The per capita spending for black students was $43 per year, for whites, $179.

In March 1949, Thurgood Marshall and several top state and national NAACP officials met with a small group of Clarendon County black parents who were disturbed about the school board's unbalanced educational funding for black schools. The NAACP agreed to file a lawsuit against the school board if 20 Clarendon County plaintiffs could be assembled. It took nearly a year for the Reverend Joseph DeLaine, a courageous Clarendon County black schoolteacher, to gather the necessary signatures. For blacks to join in a lawsuit against the school board meant risking their jobs and losing their bank loans and their farms.

The first name on the lawsuit, filed in November 1950, was that of Harry Briggs, a 34-year-old gas station attendant and the father of five. In class-action suits, the name of the case bears the first name from the alphabetical list of plaintiffs and defendants, and so it became known as *Briggs v. Elliot*. The defendant was Clarendon County School District No. 22, and Roderick Elliot was one of the members of the school board.

For their new approach, the NAACP Legal Defense Fund knew it had to present scientific evidence that segregating black children caused irreparable psychological damage. Dr. Kenneth Clark was enlisted by Legal Defense Fund lawyers to study the black children in Clarendon County. Clark was a black psychologist who had received his doctorate from Columbia University and for several years had been studying the effects of segregation on children by using black and white dolls in his interviews with students.

Clark tested 16 children, ages six to nine, at Scott's Branch, a joint elementary and high school for black children. After Clark showed them the black and white dolls, 10 of the children responded that they liked the white dolls better; 11 of them said that the black dolls looked "bad"; and nine said the white doll looked "nice." Most disturbing was that seven of the 16 children picked the white doll as the one most like themselves. The results from these tests mirrored the results from tests that Clark had performed throughout the South. Years later Dr. Clark said, "These children saw themselves as inferior, and they accepted the inferiority as part of reality."

The psychological evidence was only one part of the NAACP's argument, the other was statistics that showed that within the separate-but-equal educational system, the Clarendon County black schools were grossly underfunded and understaffed. For example, in segregated schools, there was only one black teacher for every 47 black students, but in white schools, there was one teacher for every 28 students.

Despite this two-pronged argument against school segregation, the federal court for the Eastern District of South Carolina ruled in June 1951 that the separate-but-equal doctrine was not violated. In a 2–1 judicial decision, the court found that Clark's psychological evidence was unrelated to the case. However, the Court did request that Clarendon County correct the inequities in the facilities of the black schools.

The lone dissent came from Judge J. Waties Waring, who had opposed segregation for a long time. In his dissenting opinion, he wrote, "There is absolutely no reasonable explanation for racial prejudice . . . It is all caused by unreasoning emotional reactions and these are gained early in childhood . . . Segregation in education can never produce equality and . . . is an evil that must be eradicated."

The NAACP Legal Defense lawyers did not anticipate winning the case in South Carolina, but they believed the evidence presented showing the repercussions of segregation would later be valuable in making their appeal to the U.S. Supreme Court. Also, Waring's moving dissent gave them some optimism for continuing their campaign against school segregation. Although Marshall appealed the *Briggs* decision, it would be nearly two years until it was heard before the Supreme Court.

TOPEKA, KANSAS

Every school day Linda Brown, a seven-year-old black girl, had to cross a dangerous set of railroad tracks at a switching yard and then board a run-down bus to take her to a segregated school in Topeka, Kansas. Oliver Brown, Linda's father, had become fed up with this situation of having his daughter travel to a far-away school while there was a school much closer to home—a school for whites only. Aided by the NAACP, Oliver Brown sued the Board of Education of Topeka not for equal but separate facilities, but for the right of his daughter to attend the "white" school.

Brown v. Board of Education of Topeka would eventually be argued before the nation's highest court along with four other school segregation cases. The others cases consolidated under *Brown v. Board of Education* would include *Briggs v. Elliot*, Clarendon County, South Carolina; *Davis v. County School Board*, Prince Edward County, Virginia; *Gebhart v. Belton*, Wilmington, Delaware; and *Bolling v. Sharpe*, Washington, D.C.

Robert L. Carter, Thurgood Marshall's top assistant, and Jack Greenberg, a young white lawyer from Brooklyn, represented Oliver Brown in 1951 before the federal district court for Kansas. Greenberg called to the witness stand academic experts who testified on the damaging affects of segregation for black children. Hugh W. Speer, a white professor from the University of Kansas City, argued, "If colored children are denied the experience in school of association with white children, who represent ninety percent of our national society in which colored children must live, then the colored children's curriculum is being greatly curtailed. The Topeka school curriculum . . . cannot be equal under segregation." The defense attorney dismissed these arguments and pointed to how accomplished people like W. E. B. Du Bois attended segregated schools and appeared to bear no injury from the experience.

Although the court found that under the separate but equal doctrine the Topeka School Board had sufficiently maintained black schools and there was little imbalance in funding between the two school systems, it did say in an attachment to its opinion that "segregation of colored children in public schools has a detrimental effect upon the colored children—the impact is greater when it has the sanction of the law—for the policy of separating the races is usually interpreted as denoting the inferiority of the Negro group." This left the door open for making a strong appeal to the U.S. Supreme Court.

PRINCE EDWARD COUNTY, VIRGINIA

In the spring of 1951, Barbara Rose Johns, a 16-year-old Moton High School junior in Prince Edward County, was disgusted with how the local school board had continually ignored the demands by blacks parents for educational improvements in their children's schools. She convinced a few hundred students to go out on strike and to demonstrate for a better high school.

Spottswood Robinson, an NAACP Legal Defense Fund attorney, met with the striking students and was so impressed with their commitment that he told them if they could gather the support of their parents to attack segregation directly and not compromise for equalization, the NAACP would take on their case in the courts.

In May 1951, one month after the two-week Moton High School strike had begun, Robinson filed *Davis v. County School Board of Prince Edward County* in federal district court in Richmond, Virginia. The first name on the list of plaintiffs was Dorothy E. Davis, the 14-year-old daughter of a Prince Edward County farmer. The Legal Defense Fund, representing 117 Moton High School students, requested that the Virginia state law mandating segregated schools be abolished.

The following year, in May 1952, the three-judge federal district court panel unanimously upheld the separate-but-equal doctrine and ruled that separate schools in Prince Edward County was not a result of racism but rather the result of a long tradition of Southern attitudes and mores. The case, like the other school segregation cases, was appealed by the Legal Defense Fund to the U.S. Supreme Court.

THE ARGUMENTS BEFORE THE SUPREME COURT

By June 1952, the Supreme Court had agreed to hear both *Briggs v. Elliot* together with *Brown v. Board of Education of Topeka* in its coming fall term. Then, on October 8, only days before these cases were to be heard, the Court announced a postponement. A few weeks later, the Court announced that it would also hear three other school segregation cases—*Davis v. County School Board*, from Virginia; *Bolling v. Sharpe*, from Washington, D.C.; and *Gebhart v. Belton*, from the state of Delaware. The cases were consolidated under the name of the first case the Court had decided to hear—*Brown v. Board of Education of Topeka*.

At Thurgood Marshall's offices in New York City, Legal Defense Fund attorneys swiftly researched their briefs and wrote and rewrote them again and again. Constance Baker Motley, a Columbia Law School graduate who was a Legal Defense Fund member at the time, recalled, "There were weekly conferences to attend—and weekly commuting between Washington and New York. The conferences often involved as many as 50 people at one time and never less than 20. Sociologists, psychologists, historians, lawyers—all were involved. The writing of the brief, then, was a long arduous task. It took many months, and many more hours were spent just trying to agree on the approach the brief should take."

Marshall, who was the lead counsel for the NAACP, had already participated in 15 Supreme Court cases, more than any other Legal Defense Fund attorney, and had won 13 of them. But *Brown* would be the most important case he had ever argued before the Court. To prepare for the oral arguments to be presented before the nine Supreme Court Justices, Marshall and his colleagues participated in dry-runs at Howard Law School. Each attorney presented their oral arguments to mock judges and then answered the most difficult questions that would be asked of them. Their arguments were then critiqued by a group of law students, lawyers and faculty.

On December 9, 1952, every seat in the Supreme Court was filled by spectators, many of them black, and a few hundred more people lined the building's corridors seeking admission to witness the case of the century. No case ever to come before the nation's highest court affected more directly the minds, the hearts and the daily lives of so many Americans.

Robert Carter argued the first case, stressing the unconstitutionality of unequal education for blacks. He referred to the *Sweatt* and *McLaurin* cases as precedents for defining educational opportunities not only as physical facilities but also as intangible ones. Carter explained that segregated facilities might result in making students disadvantaged in the classroom. When arguing *Briggs*, Marshall took the same approach, but in his brief he included a written summary of Dr. Kenneth Clark's findings along with an amicus curiae brief assembled by a few of the most respected social scientists in the country.

John W. Davis, the 79-year-old noted constitutional attorney, was the chief counsel for the defense. Davis had argued more than 250 cases before the Supreme Court—more than any other attorney in the

20th century. He argued that the state of South Carolina had absolutely no reason to "reverse findings of 90 years." Davis also pointed to W. E. B. Du Bois' writings as evidence that only some blacks, not all, believed that school desegregation would improve their situation.

For several days, the hearings continued. The justices deliberated for several months without reaching any decision. Then, in June 1953, they decided that various questions needed to be answered by both sides. Oral rearguments in *Brown* were scheduled for the fall term.

In September 1953, Chief Justice Fred M. Vinson, who was leaning toward ruling against ending segregation, died unexpectedly of a heart attack at the age of 63. For one month, the Court was without a chief justice. On October 5, President Dwight Eisenhower appointed California governor Earl Warren as interim chief justice. Warren, a former California attorney general, espoused the philosophy of equality under the law and fair employment. However, his views on school desegration were unclear.

In December 1953, the Court heard the attorneys responses to the questions that the justices had asked after hearing the first oral arguments a year earlier. Although Warren, the new chief justice, commented very little during the arguments, he carefully observed and gathered information for making a decision. Some time after the hearing, it is not known exactly when, Warren made up his mind in favor of overturning the doctrine of "separate-but-equal." But it is widely known that Warren wanted to have the Court make a unanimous decision. A divided opinion on this controversial issue would make the decision even more difficult to implement. According to Richard Kluger's book, *Simple Justice* (1975), the definitive work on the *Brown* decision, Warren played an enormous role in having the Court issue a unanimous decision. However, in an interview years after he retired from the bench, Warren said that "the men who should have the most credit for a unanimous decision were those men [Justices Hugo Black, Stanley Reed and Tom Clark] who came out of the South."

"SEPARATE EDUCATIONAL FACILITIES ARE INHERENTLY UNEQUAL"

Shortly after noon on Monday, May 17, 1954, the Supreme Court delivered its opinion in *Brown v. Board of Education of Topeka*. Chief Justice Earl Warren read his first major opinion since he joined the Court. The heart of the decision was in two sentences: "We conclude, unanimously, that in the field of public education the doctrine of 'separate but equal' has no place. Separate educational facilities are inherently unequal."

Students and parents who initiated the Prince Edward County, Virginia school desegregation case, one of the cases that the U.S. Supreme Court considered with Brown v. Board of Education. *Courtesy of the Schomburg Center for Research in Black Culture.*

Immediately, radio and television broadcasts were interrupted with bulletins, and afternoon newspapers across the country began putting together extra editions about the landmark decision. The *Brown* decision marked the turning point in which the nation was finally willing to face the consequences of centuries of racial discrimination. While many Northerners praised the decision, especially several newspaper columnists, some white supremacists in the South were outraged, calling May 17, 1954, "Black Monday." Senator James O. Eastland of Mississippi declared, "The South will not abide by nor obey this legislative decision by a political court." There were also voices in the South that called for cooler heads to prevail and to accept the decision. Senator Russell B. Long of Louisiana announced, "My oath of office requires me to accept it as the law . . . I urge all Southern officials to avoid any sort of rash or hasty action."

On the night of May 17, 1954, there was a victory celebration among the NAACP lawyers in Washington, D.C. Thurgood Marshall, James Nabrit, Constance Baker Motley and several other Legal Defense Fund lawyers were present. The atmosphere was jubilant, and the attorneys were proud that they had won the most important civil rights case of the 20th century. But no one celebrating that night could have imagined that a civil rights movement—involving sit-ins, demonstrations and marches—would be required to implement the decision that was handed down that afternoon.

CHRONICLE OF EVENTS

1949

March: Thurgood Marshall, NAACP special counsel, and a delegation of top state and national NAACP officials meet with a small group of Clarendon County blacks in Columbia, South Carolina. It is agreed that the NAACP will file a test case against segregation in public schools if 20 Clarendon County plaintiffs are assembled.

November: Reverend Joseph DeLaine, a Clarendon County schoolteacher, enlists 20 plaintiffs for a class-action suit against the Clarendon County School Board. Heading the list in alphabetical order is Harry Briggs a 34-year-old gas station attendant and father of five. The case is known as *Briggs v. Elliot*, after Briggs and Roderick W. Elliot, chairman of School District No. 22 in Clarendon County.

1950

June 5: The U.S. Supreme Court issues decisions in the *Sweatt* and *McLaurin* cases. It upholds black Americans' rights to attend state graduate schools and receive full educational benefits from such schools.

June: Thurgood Marshall holds a meeting in New York City with legal scholars of the NAACP Legal Defense Fund. It is agreed that in all of their future education cases they will seek to obtain schooling on a nonsegregated basis.

August 25: Lucinda Todd, secretary of the Topeka, Kansas NAACP branch, writes to NAACP executive secretary Walter White that the segregated school situation in Topeka has grown "unbearable" and the branch is prepared to go to court to test the Kansas law.

1951

February 28: Brown v. Board of Education of Topeka is filed in the U.S. District Court of Kan-

sas. The lawsuit is named after Oliver Brown, the father of eight-year-old Linda Brown.

May: Dr. Kenneth Clark, a psychologist, performs black and white doll tests with 16 black school children between the ages of six and nine in Clarendon County, South Carolina. Eleven of them respond that the black dolls look "bad," and nine of them consider the white doll "nice." Seven of the 16 children pick the white doll as the one most like themselves. The NAACP uses this study as part of their argument for outlawing segregation in public schools.

May 23: NAACP attorney Spottswood Robinson files a lawsuit in federal court in Richmond, Virginia on behalf of 117 Moton High School students who ask that state law requiring segregated schools in Virginia be overturned. The case is titled *Davis v. County School Board of Prince Edward County.* The first name on the list of plaintiffs is Dorothy E. Davis, daughter of a Prince Edward County farmer.

May 28–29: Briggs v. Elliot trial is held in U.S. District Court for the Eastern District of South Carolina in Charleston, South Carolina.

June 21: Opinion is handed down in *Briggs v. Elliot.* Two of the three judges presiding over the case uphold segregation in public schools, based upon the separate but equal doctrine.

June 25: Brown v. Board of Education of Topeka trial opens in U.S. District Court of Kansas.

August: U.S. District Court of Kansas hands down a unanimous opinion in *Brown v. Board of Education.* It finds that "no willful, intentional or substantial discrimination" exists in the operation of Topeka public schools. But attached to the opinion is a "Finding of Fact" that states that "segregation of white and colored children in public schools has a detrimental effect upon colored children." This is used as a basis for appeal to the U.S. Supreme Court by the NAACP.

October: The house belonging to the Rev. Joseph DeLaine, who had led the case against the Clarendon County School Board of South Carolina, goes up in flames. Although no one is charged for arson, there is circumstantial evidence that the blaze was set in reprisal for the minister's civil rights activities.

October 21: Belton v. Gebhart and *Bulah v. Gebhart* trials open in U.S. district court in Wilmington, Delaware. Ethel Louise Belton and Shirley Barbara Bulah, black parents of elementary school-age children, are plaintiffs in a case against the Delaware State Board of Education. Francis B. Gebhart is one of the members of the Delaware State Board of Education.

1952

February 25: Davis v. County School Board of Prince Edward County trial opens in U.S. district court in Richmond, Virginia.

March: Opinion is issued in *Davis v. County School Board of Prince Edward County.* The court upholds the doctrine of "separate but equal."

April: Opinion is issued in *Belton v. Gebhart* and *Bulah v. Gebhart.* Collins Seitz, chancellor of Delaware, who presided over the trials, rules that the plaintiffs are entitled to immediate admission to the white schools in their communities.

June 9: The U.S. Supreme Court announces it will hear arguments in *Briggs* and *Brown* during the fall term, which begin in October.

July 12: NAACP Legal Defense Fund files an appeal in the Virginia case of *Davis v. County School Board of Prince Edward County* with the U.S. Supreme Court.

August: NAACP Legal Defense Fund attorneys at Thurgood Marshall's offices in New York City begin working around the clock in drafting briefs for the *Briggs* and *Brown* Supreme Court cases.

August 28: Supreme Court of Delaware upholds Chancellor Seitz's decision outlawing segregation in public schools in *Belton v. Gebhart* and *Bulah v. Gebhart.*

October 8: U.S. Supreme Court postpones oral arguments to be heard in *Briggs* and *Brown* until December 8. The Court will also hear *Davis v. Prince Edward County.*

November: U.S. Supreme Court will hear arguments in *Bolling v. Sharpe,* the District of Columbia school-segregation lawsuit, and also in *Belton v. Gebhart.* The school segregation cases will be known collectively as *Brown v. Board of Education of Topeka.*

November 4: The U.S. Supreme Court rules in favor of a lower court decision barring segregation in interstate railway travel.

December 9–11: Oral arguments in *Brown v. Board of Education* are heard before the U.S. Supreme Court. Thurgood Marshall is the chief counsel for the plaintiffs, and John W. Davis, representing the State of South Carolina, is the chief counsel for the defense.

1953

June 8: U.S. Supreme Court defers judgment in all five school-segregation cases, known as *Brown v. Board of Education of Topeka.* They are scheduled for oral reargument on October 12.

June: The NAACP Legal Defense Fund puts 100 lawyers, scholars and researchers to work in preparation for the reargument of *Brown v. Board of Education of Topeka.*

October 5: President Dwight D. Eisenhower appoints California governor Earl Warren as interim chief justice of the Supreme Court. He replaces Chief Justice Fred M. Vinson, who had died of a heart attack in September.

December 7–9: Oral rearguments in *Brown v. Board of Education of Topeka* are heard before the U.S. Supreme Court.

1954

March 1: The Senate unanimously confirms Earl Warren as chief justice of the Supreme Court.

May 17: In a landmark ruling, the U.S. Supreme Court rules unanimously, in *Brown v. Board of Education of Topeka,* that separate but equal educational facilities are "inherently unequal" and that segregation is therefore unconstitutional. The decision overturns the separate but equal doctrine that since 1896 *(Plessy v. Ferguson)* legitimized segregation.

Spectators in the lobby of the Supreme Court, December 7, 1953, awaiting the second round of arguments in Brown v. Board of Education. *Courtesy of the Library of Congress.*

May: There is widespread reaction to this ruling across the country. In the North the decision is applauded, but it outrages segregationists in the South.

July 11: The Citizens' Council, part of a collection of groups sometimes referred to as the White Citizens' Councils, is organized in Mississippi. Civil rights activists dub them the "white-collar Klan," after the Ku Klux Klan.

August 31: The Defense Department announces that all-black units no longer exist in the Armed Forces.

Fall: One hundred fifty formerly segregated school districts in eight states and the District of Columbia integrate. But a number of groups opposing integration emerge in the South.

October: The U.S. Supreme Court hears arguments in how *Brown v. Board of Education of Topeka* should be implemented.

November 15: In response to the U.S. Supreme Court's order for reargument on how the Court should implement *Brown*, the NAACP files its brief, stating that the Court should require desegregation by September 1955.

EYEWITNESS TESTIMONY

Is this the price that free men must pay in a free country for wanting their children trained as capable and respectable American citizens? . . . Shouldn't officials employ the dignity, foresight, and intelligence in at least the honest effort to correct outstanding evils?

. . . Is it a credit for Summerton [South Carolina] to wear the name of persecuting a segment of its citizens? Shall we suffer endless persecution just because we want our children reared in a wholesome atmosphere? What some of us have suffered is nothing short of Nazi persecution.

Reverend Joseph DeLaine, black schoolteacher, Clarendon County, South Carolina, open letter of 1950, in Kluger's Simple Justice *(1975).*

Separate schools shall be provided for children of white and colored races, and no child of either race shall ever be permitted to attend a school provided for children of the other race.

South Carolina State Constitution, 1950.

If one considers the purpose of public school education in a democracy, it is clear that here is the only place where a child encounters others from every economic level; here alone they come together to know one another; and one purpose of education is to develop respect for the historic concept of equality.

White children as well as Negroes are being short-changed where segregation is practiced. So far as Negroes are concerned, segregation itself implies a difference, a stigma, and relegates the segregated group more or less to the second class.

Harold J. McNally, associate professor of education at Columbia University, testimony of May 28, 1951, at the Briggs v. Elliot *school desegration trial, in the* Charleston [South Carolina] News and Courier *(May 29, 1955).*

The conclusion which I was forced to reach was that these children in Clarendon County, like other human beings who are subjected to an obviously inferior status in the society in which they live, have been definitely harmed in the development of their personalities; that the signs of instability in their personalities are clear, and I think that every psy-

chologist would accept and interpret these signs as such.

Dr. Kenneth Clark, assistant professor of psychology at the College of the City of New York, testimony of May 28, 1955, at the Briggs v. Elliot *school desegration trial, in Kluger's* Simple Justice *(1975).*

In a sense, not only the school system but the people of the South, and of many places outside the South are on trial. The decision may rank in importance with the Dred Scott decision of 1857.

The News and Courier, *Charleston, South Carolina, editorial of May 29, 1951, on the* Briggs v. Elliot *school desegration trial in U.S. District Court in Charleston, South Carolina.*

The Negro child is made to go to an inferior school; he is branded in his own mind inferior. This sets up a road block to his mind which prevents his ever feeling he is equal.

Thurgood Marshall, NAACP special counsel, closing argument of May 29, 1955, at the Briggs v. Elliot *school desegregation trial, in the* Charleston [South Carolina] News and Courier *(May 30, 1955).*

History confirms the judgment of U.S. judges who have since passed on this matter. I have assumed the doctrine to be well settled that states have the right to separate the races in public schools . . . It is a normal and not an abnormal procedure.

Robert Figg, Clarendon County School District defense attorney, closing argument of May 29, 1955, at the Briggs v. Elliot *school desegregation trial, in the* Charleston [South Carolina] News and Courier *(May 30, 1955).*

The more I think about this case, the more importance I think it will have in our main objective of securing legal support for our attack on segregation.

Our possibilities for winning here seem much better than they are in South Carolina.

Robert Carter, NAACP attorney, to Thurgood Marshall, memorandum of June 13, 1951, on Brown v. Board of Education of Topeka *case before the U.S. District Court for Kansas, in Kluger's* Simple Justice *(1975).*

Segregation of white and colored children in public schools has a detrimental effect upon the colored children. The impact is greater when it has the sanction of the law; for the policy of separating the races is usually interpreted as denoting the inferiority of

Thurgood Marshall (fourth from left) shown with other members of the NAACP Legal Defense Fund. Courtesy of the Library of Congress.

the Negro group. A sense of inferiority affects the motivation of a child to learn. Segregation with the sanction of law, therefore, has a tendency to retard the educational and mental development of Negro children and to deprive them of some of the benefits they would receive in a racially integrated school system.

U.S. District Court of Kansas, "Finding of Fact," attached to the opinion of August 1951, which unanimously ruled against the NAACP's lawsuit for integrating public schools in Brown v. Board of Education, *in Kluger's* Simple Justice *(1975). [This opened the door for an appeal by the NAACP to the U.S. Supreme Court].*

That is foremost in the minds of these people who want segregated schools: Let a Negro develop along certain lines. Athletics, that is all right. Music, fine—all Negroes are supposed to be able to sing. Rhythm—all Negroes are supposed to be able to dance. But we want an opportunity along with everybody else to develop in the technical fields. We want an opportunity to develop in the business and commerce of this nation. In other words, we want an opportunity to develop our talents, whatever they may be, in whatever fields of endeavor there are existing in this

country . . . I submit that in this segregated school system, you do not have that opportunity.

Oliver Hill, NAACP attorney, to the federal district court in Richmond, Virginia, oral argument of February 25, 1952, in Davis v. County School Board of Prince Edward County *(Virginia), in Kluger's* Simple Justice *(1975).*

We charge that we have been deprived of equal protection of the law where the state requires segregated schools. It denies them equal opportunities which the 14th Amendment adequately secures.

Segregation severely handicaps Negro children in the pursuit of knowledge and makes it difficult for them to pursue their education. It places them at a serious disadvantage.

Robert Carter, NAACP attorney, to the U.S. Supreme Court, oral argument of December 9, 1952, in Brown v. Board of Education of Topeka, *in Friedman's* Argument *(1969).*

Is it not of all the activities of government the one which most nearly approaches the hearts and minds of people the question of education of their young? Is it not the height of wisdom that the manner in which that shall be conducted should be left to those most immediately affected by it . . . I respectfully submit to the court that there is no reason assigned here why this court or any other should reverse the findings of 90 years.

John W. Davis, state of South Carolina defense attorney, to the U.S. Supreme Court, oral argument of December 9, 1952, in Brown v. Board of Education, *in Friedman's Argument (1969).*

The humiliation the children go through will affect their mind as long as they live . . . I believe that there is a body of law that holds that distinctions on the basis of race are odious and invidious.

Thurgood Marshall, NAACP special counsel, to the U.S. Supreme Court, oral argument of December 9, 1952, in Brown v. Board of Education of Topeka, *in Friedman's Argument (1969).*

Justice Felix Frankfurter: Do you really think it helps us not to recognize that behind this are certain facts of life, and the question is whether a legislature can address itself to those facts of life in despite of or within the Fourteenth Amendment, or whether, whatever the facts of life might be, where there is a vast congregation of Negro population as against the states where there is not, whether that is an irrelevant consideration? Can you escape facing those sociological facts, Mr. Marshall?

Thurgood Marshall: No, I cannot escape it. But if I did fail to escape it, I would have to throw completely aside the personal and present rights of those individuals.

Oral argument of December 9, 1952, before the U.S. Supreme Court, in Brown v. Board of Education of Topeka, *in Friedman's Argument (1969).*

It would appear to me that in 1952, the Negro should not be viewed as anybody's burden. He is a citizen. He is performing his duties in peace and in war, and today, on the bloody hills of Korea, he is serving in an unsegregated war.

All we ask of this Court is that it say that under the Constitution he is entitled to live and send his children to school . . . unsegregated, with the children of his war comrades. That is simple. The Constitution gives him that right.

The basic question here is one of liberty, and under liberty, under the due process clause, you cannot deal with it as you deal with equal protection laws,

because there you deal with it as a quantum of treatment, substantially equal.

You either have liberty or you do not . . .

We submit that in this case, in the heart of the nation's capital, in the capital of democracy, in the capital of the free world, there is no place for a segregated school system. This country cannot afford it, and the Constitution does not permit it, and the statutes of Congress do not authorize it.

James M. Nasbit Jr., NAACP defense lawyer, to the U.S. Supreme Court, oral argument of December 10, 1952, in Brown v. Board of Education of Topeka, *in Friedman's Argument (1969).*

United States Supreme Court today deferred judgment on five historic cases challenging racial segregation in elementary and high schools . . . Postponement comes after three years legal actions . . . costing $58,000 . . . work made possible only through contributions from citizens who understand significance to national life and impact upon world struggle. Funds entirely spent. Highest court now requests preparation of answers within three months to many broad questions requiring legal argument on historic constitutional factors, sociological data and authoritative opinion. No money available to meet emergency.

Opportunity for decent public education affecting nearly three million Negro American children depends upon resolution this dilemma. $15,000 needed immediately to forestall possibility these youngsters must wait decades before equal opportunity established. Please send your tax-deductible gift today to . . .

NAACP telegram of June 9, 1953, to hundreds of civil rights supporters, in Kluger's Simple Justice *(1975).*

We can now eat in Washington, but we must eat in Baltimore. We can now ride in Pullman cars, but we must ride in anything that rolls. We are voting in Atlanta, but we must vote in every county in Georgia. We have a democratic army in Korea, but we must have one in Fort Sill, Oklahoma, and Fort Leonard Wood in Missouri, and Fort Belvoir, Virginia . . .

As long as there is a color line, whether it be light or heavy, all of us are in this thing together, and if all will fight together we can win. In the meantime, none will be fully respected until all are respected; none will be wholly free until all are free.

Dr. Channing H. Tobias, NAACP board chair-
man, to the NAACP's 44th annual convention,
St. Louis, Missouri, speech of June 23, 1953,
in the Crisis *(August–September 1953).*

We lawyers can assure you of a carefully planned program of court cases. But this alone cannot suffice. We must have your support, both financial and moral, for that litigation. It is imperative that we have also an intensification of our community action by you so that in each community in the country we will have an active educational campaign among our church groups, fraternal groups, labor unions, and the general public, constantly emphasizing the disastrous impact of segregation. Like an eating cancer it destroys the morale of our citizens and disfigures our country throughout the world.

Thurgood Marshall, NAACP special counsel, to
the NAACP's 44th annual convention, speech
of June 25, 1953, in the Crisis *(August–Sep-*
tember 1953).

The staff of the Legal Defense and Educational Fund, consisting of six lawyers, six secretaries and two clerks, swung into action on June 9 . . .

By midsummer, some staff workers were going two and three days without sleep, taking time out only to eat. By the end of October, no one was getting more than three to four hours at a time . . .

Thurgood Marshall . . . has slept in his own bed at home eight times in the past four months and has only had dinner with his wife twice in the past three months. Six of the lawyers who came to New York to work on the brief have not seen their wives in three months. The secretaries and volunteers put in shifts of 15 to 20 hours a day, seven days a week, without requesting extra pay . . .

The staff has used 1,000,600 sheets of copy paper, 6,000,225 sheets of manifold, 2,700 stencils, more than 12 million sheets of mimeographing paper and 115,000 sheets of carbon paper.

NAACP press release of November 16, 1953,
on preparing the brief for Brown v. Board of
Education of Topeka, *in Slater's* Ebony *arti-*
cle of May 1974.

Children of that age are not the most considerate animals in the world, as we all know. Would the terrible psychological disaster being wrought, according to some of these witnesses, to the colored child be removed if he had three white children sitting somewhere in the same classroom?

Would white children be prevented from getting a distorted idea of racial relations if they sat with 27 Negro children? I have posed the question because it is the very one that cannot be denied.

You say that is racism. Well, it is not racism. Recognize that for sixty centuries and more, humanity has been discussing questions of race and race tension, not racism . . . [T]wenty-nine states have miscegenation in states now in force which they believe are of beneficial protection to both races. Disraeli said, "No man," said he, "will treat with indifference the principle of race. It is the key of history."

John W. Davis, state of South Carolina defense
attorney, to the U.S. Supreme Court, oral rear-
gument of December 7, 1953, in Brown v.
Board of Education of Topeka, *in Fried-*
man's Argument *(1969).*

I got the feeling on hearing the discussion yesterday that when you put a white child in a school with a whole lot of colored children, the child would fall apart or something. Everybody knows that is not true.

Those same kids in Virginia and South Carolina—and I have seen them do it—they play in the streets together, they play on their farms together, they go down the road together, they separate to go to school, they come out of school and play ball together. They have to be separated in school.

There is some magic to it. You can have them voting together, you can have them not restricted because of law in the houses they live in. You can have them going to the same state university and the same college, but if they go to elementary and high school, the world will fall apart.

Thurgood Marshall, NAACP special counsel, to
the U.S. Supreme Court, oral reargument of
December 8, 1953, in Brown v. Board of Education of Topeka, *in Friedman's* Argument
(1969).

As our lawyers argued for an integrated, democratic public school system, they had the practically solid support of Negroes in all sections of the country, as well as the endorsement of the most enlightened elements of all races and faiths in all parts of the country . . . Against them was arrayed the spokesman for the most benighted elements in the country, the professional hate-mongers, the timid souls who always fear change, the reactionaries who continue to look backward to the Nineteenth Century, the weak and insecure who dread the possibility of meeting other groups in free and open competition . . .

In fighting to eliminate segregation in public school education, the NAACP is fighting to strengthen American democracy.

Dr. Channing H. Tobias, NAACP board chairman, editorial of December 1953, on the Brown v. Board of Education of Topeka *case before the U.S. Supreme Court, in the* Crisis *(December 1953).*

Does segregation of children in public schools solely on the basis of race, even though the physical facilities and other tangible factors may be equal, deprive children of the minority group of equal educational opportunities? . . .

George E. Hayes (left), Thurgood Marshall (center) and James Nabrit Jr. (right), the NAACP attorneys who presented arguments in Brown v. Board of Education, *outside the Supreme Court after the Court announced its landmark decision. Courtesy of the Schomburg Center for Research in Black Culture.*

We believe it does . . . To separate them from others of similar age and qualifications solely because of their race generates a feeling of inferiority as to their status in the community that may affect their hearts and minds in a way very unlikely to ever be undone.

We conclude, unanimously, that in the field of public education the doctrine of "separate but equal" has no place. Separate educational facilities are inherently unequal.

Chief Justice Earl Warren, U.S. Supreme Court's unanimous opinion of May 17, 1954, in Brown v. Board of Education of Topeka *347 U.S. 483 (1954).*

The most gratifying thing in addition to the fact that it was in favor of our side is the unanimous decision and the language used—once and for all it's decided completely.

Once the decision is made public to the South as well as to the North, the people will get together for the first time and work this thing out . . .

Off-the-cuff I think it will take around five years for the entire country to have Jim Crow-free schools.

Thurgood Marshall, NAACP special counsel, statement of May 17, 1954, at a press conference, in the NAACP papers.

The South will not abide by nor obey this legislative decision by a political court.

Senator James O. Eastland (D, Miss.), statement of May 17, 1954, in the New York Times *(May 18, 1954).*

My oath of office requires me to accept it as the law. Every citizen is likewise bound by this oath of allegience to his country. I urge all Southern officials to avoid any sort of rash or hasty action.

Senator Russell B. Long (D, La.), statement of May 17, 1954, in the New York Times *(May 18, 1954).*

The United States Supreme Court by its decision has reduced the Constitution to a mere scrap of paper . . . The people of Georgia believe in, adhere to and will fight for their right under the United States and Georgia constitutions to manage their own affairs. They cannot and will not accept a bald political decree without basis in law or practicality which overturns their accepted pattern of life.

Georgia Governor Herman Talmadge, statement of May 17, 1954, in the Atlanta Constitution *(May 18, 1954).*

It demonstrates that the Supreme Court is becoming a political arm of the executive branch.
Senator Richard B. Russell, (D, Ga.), statement of May 17, 1954, in the Washington Post *(May 18, 1954).*

[It is] the most serious blow that has yet been struck against the rights of states in a matter vitally affecting their authority and welfare.
Senator Harry Byrd (D, Va.), statement of May 17, 1954, in the New York Times *(May 18, 1954).*

Desirable race relations is a matter of evolution and not of legislation. I am reminded at the moment of what Andrew Jackson told the chief justice of the Supreme Court, "You have handed down the decision. Now let's see you enforce it."
Congressman F. Edward Hébert (D, La.), statement of May 17, 1954, in the New Orleans Times-Picayune *(May 18, 1954).*

[The] long-litigated question has now been decided and is the law for all states of the nation, and Kansas education procedures will have to ultimately be adjusted to comply with it.
Kansas Governor Edward F. Arn, statement of May 17, 1954, in the New York Times *(May 18, 1954).*

The Supreme Court has finally reconciled the Constitution with the preamble of the Declaration of Independence.
Dr. Arthur M. Schlessinger Sr., Harvard University history professor, statement of May 17, 1954, in the New York Times *(May 18, 1954).*

The Supreme Court, in clear and simple language, has given an interpretation of the rather plain meaning of the "equal protection" clause [of the Constitution], carrying out the spirit which lies behind those words and which is really fundamental in our general conception of Americanism.
Dean Erwin N. Griswold, Harvard Law School, statement of May 17, 1954, in the New York Times *(May 18, 1954).*

I thank God I lived to see the day . . .
Mary Church Terrell, 90-year-old black civil rights leader, statement of May 17, 1954, in Bennett's Wade in the Water *(1979).*

You fools go ahead and have your fun, but we ain't begun to work yet.
Thurgood Marshall, comment of May 17, 1954, at the NAACP victory party in Washington, D.C., in Bennett's Wade in the Water *(1979).*

. . . The end of the world has not come for the South or for the nation. The Supreme Court's ruling is not itself a revolution. It is rather acceptance of a process that has been going on a long time. People everywhere could well match the court's moderation and caution.
Louisville *[Kentucky]* Courier, *editorial of May 18, 1954.*

. . . It [the Brown decision] does call for sober reappraisal of the manner in which we have lived up to our long-accepted obligation to provide adequate educational opportunity for all our children, regardless of race, creed or color. Where we have failed to provide equality, we must provide it—not alone because a new Court precedent places the dual system in jeopardy, but in justice to our own standards of fair and decent treatment.
The Arkansas Gazette, *editorial of May 18, 1954.*

As to the immediate future, the decision will do no service either to education or racial accommodation. In the states where most of the Negroes live, the public school systems face the prospect of considerable turmoil for some time to come.
The New Orleans Times-Picayune, *editorial of May 18, 1954.*

Human blood may stain southern soil in many places because of this decision, but the dark red stains of that blood will be on the marble of the United States Supreme Court Building.
The Jackson *[Mississippi]* Daily News, *editorial of May 18, 1954.*

It is hoped that this breaking down of custom and tradition can be bridged without too much friction . . .
Jacksonville *[North Carolina]* News, *editorial of May 18, 1954.*

It is no time for hasty or ill-considered actions. It is no time to indulge demagogues on either side nor to listen to those who always are ready to incite violence.

What is needed most in all the states affected is a calm, rational approach. Panic and the losing of tempers will cause more harm than good. Extremists and hotheads on either side neither can change the Supreme Court decision nor reach any practical solutions.

It is time for Georgia to think clearly.

The Atlanta Constitution, *editorial of May 18, 1954.*

. . . The South has a new problem. It may turn out to be the greatest problem of a region's history. But it calls for analysis and solution in a calm, orderly fashion.

Admittedly segregation has produced emotional reactions that have not always been good . . . But we are much concerned that the ending of segregation may produce feelings and problems far more difficult to deal with.

The Birmingham *[Alabama]* News, *editorial of May 18, 1954.*

Somehow, the South must keep the sweep of human history in proper perspective, must apply its intelligence coolly and dispassionately, and must find the resources for giving all its children equality of education. If the South as a region and North Carolina as a state, are able to do these things, they will find that the problem is far more manageable than it appears at the moment.

The Charlotte *[North Carolina]* News, *editorial of May 18, 1954.*

The court decision drove another nail into the coffin of states rights.

The Charleston *[South Carolina]* News & Courier, *editorial of May 18, 1954.*

The American people have faced many other issues, some much more vital on a national and local level than this one . . . And there is no reason to believe that we cannot approach this with calmness, reason and a genuine spirit of cooperation.

The main thing now is to face this thing squarely as an accomplished fact, and work out our destiny for the general good and good of the greater glory of our nation.

The Memphis *[Tennessee]* Commercial Appeal, *editorial of May 18, 1954.*

The South is and has been for years a land of change. Its people—of both races—have learned to

live with change. They can learn to live with this one. Given a reasonable amount of time and understanding they will.

The Nashville Tennessean, *editorial of May 18, 1954.*

In the end the new patterns will have to be hammered out across the table in thousands of scattered school districts, and they will have to be shaped to accommodate not only the needs but the prejudices of whites and Negroes to whom these problems are not abstractions but the essence of their daily lives.

The Arkansas Gazette, *editorial of May 18, 1954.*

It means racial strife of the bitterest sort. Mississippi cannot and will not try to abide by such a decision.

The Jackson *[Mississippi]* Daily News, *editorial of May 18, 1954.*

May 17, 1954, may be recorded by future historians as a black day of tragedy for the South, and for both races, but we can conduct ourselves in such fashion as to cause historians to record that we faced that tragedy and crisis with wisdom, courage, faith and determination.

The Jackson *[Mississippi]* Clarion-Ledger, *editorial of May 18, 1954.*

. . . The Supreme Court . . . squared the country's basic law with its conscience and deepest convictions . . . America has lived with change, and it will change now. With understanding among those in different regions of the country, with some patience and with zeal to make good on its tremendous promise, America will change for the better. In so doing it will renew the spirit of hope and idealism to which it was born.

The New York Herald Tribune, *editorial of May 18, 1954.*

The historic decision yesterday by the Supreme Court—declaring unconstitutional race segregation in the public schools—is one of the most important developments in the touchy problem of race relations since the emancipation of the slaves during the Civil War.

The Newark *[New Jersey]* Star-Ledger, *editorial of May 18, 1954.*

The United States Supreme Court has begun the erasure of one of American democracy's blackest marks with its ruling that racial segregation in public schools is unconstitutional.

The Des Moines *[Iowa]* Register, *editorial of May 18, 1954.*

Every fair-minded American will, we believe, applaud the Supreme Court's unanimous decision . . . The steadily changing social climate in this country since the ruling of 1896, and especially within the last few years has made an end of segregation in the public schools inevitable.

The Pittsburgh Post-Gazette, *editorial of May 18, 1954.*

The principle established by this decision is not that anybody has to give up any of his prejudices . . . the principle is a much simpler one that the state governments, North and South, must regard all men as created equal so far as opportunities at the disposal of the state are concerned.

The Chicago Tribune, *editorial of May 18, 1954.*

The Supreme Court of the United State has now said with unmistakable clarity and emphasis that racial segregation in the public schools must come to an end. With this pronouncement it has also struck a mighty blow at racial intolerance in every other phase of our national life as well.

The Minneapolis Tribune, *editorial of May 18, 1954.*

It will serve—and speedily—to close an ancient wound too long allowed to fester. It will bring to an end a painful disparity between American principles and American practices. It will help to refurbish American prestige in a world which looks to this land for moral inspiration and restore the faith of Americans themselves in their own great values and traditions.

The Washington Post, *editorial of May 18, 1954.*

The highest court in the land, the guardian of our national conscience, has reaffirmed its faith and the underlying American faith in the equality of all men and all children before the law.

The New York Times, *editorial of May 18, 1954.*

We may be sure that the present decision is not going to lead to civil war, but we may be almost as certain that it will provoke a social and political revolution.

The Los Angeles Times, *editorial of May 18, 1954.*

The conscience of America has spoken through its constitutional voice.

The Pittsburgh Courier, *black newspaper, editorial of May 18, 1954.*

There was fortunately no division [in the Supreme Court] along regional lines, and so the highest judicial body in the land presents to the world a united front for democratic freedom on behalf of all of us Americans, regardless of race, creed, color or national origin.

The Boston Chronicle, *black newspaper, editorial of May 18, 1954.*

. . . The decision serves as a boost to the spirit of democracy and it accelerates the faith of the intense devoutness in minorities who have long believed in and trusted the courts.

The Atlanta Daily World, *black newspaper, editorial of May 18, 1954.*

This means the beginning of the end of the dual society in American life and the system of segregation which supported it.

The Chicago Defender, *black newspaper, editorial of May 18, 1954.*

The Supreme Court decision is the greatest victory for the Negro people since the Emancipation Proclamation. It will alleviate racial troubles in many fields other than education.

The New York Amsterdam News, *black newspaper, editorial of May 22, 1954.*

We look upon this memorable decision not as a victory for Negroes alone, but for the whole American people and as a vindication of America's leadership of the free world.

Lest there be any misunderstanding of our position, we here rededicate ourselves to the removal of all racial segregation in public education and reiterate our determination to achieve this goal without compromise of principle.

"The Atlanta Declaration," May 22, 1954, announced at an NAACP conference in Atlanta, Georgia, in the Crisis *(June 1954).*

In 1954, the U.S. Supreme Court bans segregation in public schools. Courtesy of the Schomburg Center for Research in Black Culture.

We haven't solved the problem yet. We still have a good many odds and ends, but I want to say this, that one somewhat overconfident individual telephoned me right after the [Supreme] Court handed down its decision, and he said, "The NAACP is on its way out of business." I said, "I would be delighted to see the NAACP go out of existence because it was no longer necessary for such an organization to exist."

Walter White, NAACP executive secretary, statement of May 1954, in U.S. News & World Report (May 28, 1954).

3. The Emmett Till Case: 1955

"WITH ALL DELIBERATE SPEED"

When the U.S. Supreme Court handed down its decision in *Brown v. Board of Education of Topeka* in May of 1954, it did not set any deadline for an end to segregation in public schools. Instead, it asked the interested parties to provide suggestions on how the order could be enforced. "Because of the wide applicability of this decision, and because of the great variety of local conditions," wrote the court "the formulation of decrees in these cases presents problems of considerable complexity."

Although desegregation began in the fall of 1954 in Washington, D.C. and Baltimore, Maryland, the rest of the nation waited for the Court to issue specific instructions on how to end segregation in public schools. When the litigants in *Brown* came before the court again in 1954 to address the "problems of considerable complexity" cited by the court, the NAACP argued for desegregation by September 1955. On May 31, 1955, the court issued its guidelines. It simply instructed local school boards to implement desegregation plans "with all deliberate speed."

The ruling disappointed the NAACP and others who wanted decisive action. The ambiguous phrase meant that Southern school boards could comfortably delay desegregating their public schools.

In the South, the immediate effect of the Court's decision was the formation of the Citizens' Council (part of a collection of groups sometimes referred to as the White Citizens' Councils), which was organized in July 1954 in Indianola in the Mississippi Delta. The White Citizens' Councils were made up of business and professional people who were dubbed by their critics as "uptown Ku Klux Klans," since they did not indulge in wearing hoods and robes.

Lynchings, which had been on the decline, returned to the South. In the state of Mississippi, one of the most segregated states in the country at the time, more than 500 black people had been lynched since statistics were first compiled in 1882. It is likely that thousands of racially motivated murders were never officially reported.

In 1955 there were three widely reported such murders in Mississippi. The Reverend George W. Lee, an NAACP organizer, was lynched after he led a voter registration drive at the delta town of Belozi. Although he was killed by a shotgun blast to the face, local police ruled his death as a traffic accident. Lee had been the first black to register to vote in the county. Another NAACP organizer, Lamar Smith, was killed on the courthouse lawn in Brookhaven on a Saturday afternoon.

The most infamous case of that year and one that is often cited as the single incident that ignited the civil rights movement is the brutal murder of Emmett Louis Till, a 14-year-old boy from the South Side of Chicago who was visiting his relatives in Leflore County. The Till murder aroused the public, both black and white. It was reported on the front pages of virtually every black newspaper throughout the country. It prompted thousands of blacks to become directly involved in participating in civil rights demonstrations, marches and protests.

Chicago Boy

After the end of World War I, the black population of Chicago grew from 109,000 in 1920 to 234,000 in 1930 and to nearly a half a million by the 1950s. The overwhelming majority came from the South, and of them, about half came from Mississippi. They migrated to Chicago for jobs and for securing a better way of life. Emmett Till, nicknamed "Bo," was part of this emigrant community that had sprung up in the black working-class neighborhood in the South Side of Chicago. He was born near Chicago on July 25, 1941. His mother, Mamie Bradley Till, had moved to Chicago from Tallahatchie County, Mississippi, and his father, Louis Till, had been born in Missouri and had moved to Chicago, become a soldier and died in Europe in the summer of 1945.

Mamie Bradley Till, who was earning $3,900 a year as a voucher examiner in the Air Force Procurement Office in the summer of 1955, planned to take a vacation that August and send her son, Emmett, to visit his relatives in Leflore County, Mississippi. On August 20, 1955, Till and his cousin Curtis Jones boarded a train for their summer visit with their 64-year-old great-uncle Mose "Preacher" Wright, a sharecropper, and Wright's wife, Elizabeth.

Although Emmett Till attended an all-black elementary school and was familiar with segregation, he was unaware of the kind of discrimination he would find in Mississippi. His mother, who had left Mississippi when she was two years old, warned her son that in the South "if you have to get on your knees and bow when a white person goes past, do it willingly."

Emmett Till and his mother, Mamie Bradley Till. Courtesy of the Schomburg Center for Research in Black Culture.

WOLF WHISTLE

On the evening of August 24, after Emmett had been visiting for almost a week, he joined seven black boys and a girl—all teenagers, three of whom were visiting the Delta—in Mose Wright's 1946 Ford and drove to Bryant's Grocery and Meat Market, a country store in Money, a hamlet consisting of a few hundred residents located in Leflore County. The store was owned and operated by Ron Bryant, a 24-year-old former soldier, and his wife, Carolyn Bryant. She was 21-years-old and had won two beauty contests while in high school.

When the eight teenagers pulled up to Bryant's Grocery at about 7:30 P.M., Ron Bryant was hauling shrimp to Texas. He had left his wife alone with Juanita Milam, the wife of Bryant's brother-in-law, J.W. Milam. Outside the store, Emmett was showing off a photograph he carried in his wallet of a white girl who he claimed was his girlfriend in Chicago. A couple of the boys then began taunting Emmett, daring him to go inside the store and ask Carolyn Bryant for a date. His cousin, Curtis Jones, recalled that one of the local black boys told Till, "Hey, there's a [white] girl in that store there. I bet you won't go in there and talk to her."

Rather than duck away from the challenge that his boasting had provoked, Emmett entered Bryant's store alone. While the boys watched through the window from outside, Emmett bought two cents worth of bubble gum from Mrs. Bryant, and then, when he was leaving, he said, "Bye, baby," and reportedly wolf-whistled at her. Then Emmett's companions rushed in, pulled him away from the store and hustled him into the Ford and drove away.

A DEATH IN THE DELTA

The following day, the incident at Bryant's store had become just another good story to Emmett and his cousin. But through the grapevine, the story was getting around the town of Money. Emmett and Jones had decided to conceal the encounter from their great-uncle, Mose Wright, hoping it would soon be forgotten. However, it was far from forgotten by Carolyn Bryant's husband, Roy, who learned about it soon after he returned from Texas.

On August 28, after midnight, a car pulled up to Mose Wright's cabin, where Emmett and his cousin were staying. Roy Bryant and his brother-in-law J. W. Milam had come to get that "boy who done the talkin'." Mose pleaded with the two men that Emmett was only 14 and this was only his second visit to Mississippi. They ignored Mose's pleas and dragged Emmett into their car and drove away. As they were taking Emmett away, one of them reportedly said to Mose, "If you cause any trouble, you'll never live to be sixty-five."

Exactly what occurred next is unknown, and it has been subject to divergent accounts. According to William Bradford Huie, an Alabama journalist, who had paid $4,000 to Bryant and Milam to tell their story after they had been acquitted of murdering Till, the two men claimed they only intended to frighten Emmett, not to kill him. But Emmett refused to repent, they said, even after being pistol-whipped several times. Milam told Huie, "What else could we do. He was hopeless. I'm no bully; I've never hurt a nigger in my life. I like niggers in their place. I know how to work 'em. But I just decided it was time a few people got put on notice."

In Huie's account, he describes how Milam and Bryant drove Emmett to the Tallahatchie River and made the boy carry a 100-pound cotton-gin fan from the back of the truck to the river bank before ordering him to undress. Milam then fired one bullet at Till's head. Both men then tied the fan around the boy's neck and dumped his body into the Tallahatchie River.

The Milam and Bryant account of the incident has left some unanswered questions. For one, why would a 14-year-old boy refuse to repent if he was being beaten so viciously as the two Mississippians had described? It is known that Mose Wright complied with the kidnappers' orders that night. Mose Wright did not call the police, but Curtis Jones told the Leflore County sheriff that Emmett Till was missing.

A few hours after they had murdered Emmett Till, Bryant and Milam were charged with kidnapping and were jailed on suspicion of murder. Less than three days later, a white boy fishing in the Tallahatchie River found the decomposing body of a male human. A fan weighing about 100 pounds had been attached to the neck with barbed wire, and only the right side of the head was intact, suggesting terrible torture. One policeman said it was the worst beating he had observed in eight years of law enforcement. Above the right ear was a hole the size of a bullet, and on one finger was a ring inscribed with the initials "L.T." Emmett Till's body was discovered 12 miles north of Money, and only 15 miles from the birthplace of his mother, Mamie Bradley.

The body was so badly mangled and decomposed that Mose Wright could only identify it as Till's from the ring on the boy's finger, which bore the inscription "L.T. May 25, 1943." The ring had belonged to his father, Louis.

Upon learning of the death of her only child, 33-year-old Mamie Bradley Till demanded that the corpse be sent home immediately, despite the reluctance of the sheriff's office, which had the mortician order that the casket not be opened. That order was ignored when the casket reached the Illinois Central terminal in Chicago. Mrs. Bradley Till opened the casket to make sure it contained her son. After studying the hairline and the teeth, she declared that she wanted an open-casket funeral, and after crying, "Lord, take my soul," she collapsed. She later told reporters, "Have you ever sent a loved son on vacation and had him returned to you in a pine box, so horribly battered and water-logged that someone needs to tell you this sickening sight is your son—lynched?"

The condition of Emmett Till's body not only shocked and revolted the black residents of Chicago, but also the entire nation after *Jet* magazine published a harrowing photograph of the mutilated corpse.

Thousands lined the streets outside the Rainer Funeral Home on the first day that the pine casket was open for viewing. Mrs. Bradley Till wanted "the world [to] see what they did to my boy." After four days of open viewing, Emmett Till was finally buried on Saturday, September 6, as an estimated 2,000 mourners gathered outside the Roberts Temple Church of God on State Street.

The murder of Emmett Till aroused the black community to such an extent that contributions to the NAACP's "fight fund," the money used to help victims of racial attacks, reached record levels. The *Cleveland Call and Post*, a black newspaper, discovered through polling leading black radio preachers throughout the United States that five out of six were commenting on Till's murder and half were demanding that "something be done in Mississippi"—immediately.

THE TRIAL

Less than two weeks after Emmett Till was buried in Chicago, Milam and Bryant went on trial on September 19 for murder in a segregated courthouse in Sumner, Mississippi. Between 50 and 70 reporters, including many black reporters, descended on the sleepy town, whose population was barely ten times larger. The court proceedings triggered front-page coverage throughout the nation. Also, the trial received the unusual attention of radio and television coverage by local and national stations.

It was unknown whether any black witnesses would testify against the two white men. In 1955 for a black man to accuse a white man of murder in Mississippi meant risking his own life. Without any witnesses, the case against Milam and Bryant would collapse.

Though blacks accounted for 63% of the slightly more than 30,000 residents of Tallahatchie County, it was no surprise that none were selected to serve on the jury. Eligibility to serve on a jury depended upon suffrage, and no blacks were registered to vote in the county. Indeed, none of the residents could remember any blacks registered to vote there since the turn of the century. The result was an all-white jury that consisted of nine farmers, two carpenters and an insurance salesman.

On the third day of the trial, the prosecution's star witness, Mose Wright, took the witness stand. A packed courtroom with blacks and whites occupying segregated sections, watched intensely as the 64-year-old sharecropper singled out the defendants as the men who had come to his home and taken Emmett Till away. Wright pointed to J. W. Milam, declaring, "Thar he." He then identified Bryant as the second man.

Michigan congressman Charles Diggs, who attended the trial, said, "It was the first time in the history of Mississippi that a Negro had stood in court and pointed his finger at a white man as a killer of a Negro." It was not actually the first time, but it was definitely a very rare occurrence.

In addition to Mose Wright, two other black witnesses took the stand—Willis Reed, who had testified he had seen Emmett Till in the back of Milam's pickup truck and heard a beating in Milam's barn, and Reed's aunt, Amanda Bradley, who had heard the beating victim cry out, "Momma, Lord have mercy, Lord have mercy."

The trial took five long, hot days. The mood in the courtroom was informal. The judge was in shirt sleeves, smoking was permitted at all times, and bailiffs walked in and out carrying pitchers of ice water. Also, Bryant's infant children were allowed to play inside the court-room as the proceedings took place.

Bryant and Milam never took the stand. Their defense consisted of a half dozen character witnesses. In his closing argument, John C. Whit-ten, one of the five defense attorneys, said to the all-white jury, "I'm sure that every last Anglo-Saxon one of you has the courage to free these men in the face of that [outside] pressure." The special prosecu-tor, Robert B. Smith III, told the jury, "Once we get to the point where we deprive any of our people of their rights, we are all in dan-ger. Emmett Till down here in Mississippi was a citizen of the United States, he was entitled to his life and liberty."

BLACK FRIDAY

On Friday, September 23, 1955, after deliberating for one hour and seven minutes, the jury foreman, J. W. Shaw, read the verdict of "not guilty." Shaw later said that he believed that "'the state failed to prove the identity of the body." Another juror said, "If we hadn't stopped to drink pop, it wouldn't have taken that long." After hearing the ver-dict, Bryant and Milam embraced their wives, accepted the congratula-tions of well-wishers, lit up cigars and walked out of the courtroom.

Reaction throughout black communities across the nation was swift. Major rallies took place in Baltimore, Chicago, Cleveland, Detroit, New York and Los Angeles. The *Pittsburgh Courier*, a leading black newspaper, ran a half-inch black border around its front page, as well as a headline that proclaimed, "Sept. 23, 1955—BLACK FRIDAY!" Ma-jor white dailies around the nation also editorialized against the ver-dict. The New York *Post* declared, "There can be no rest for Till's murderers, or for those who have rationalized this brutal deed." The Southern papers responded defensively to these denunciations. The *Delta Democrat Times* of Greenville, Mississippi, editorialized that "to blame two million Mississippians for the irresponsible act of two is about as illogical as one can become."

The national press coverage of the Emmett Till case exposed the kind of injustice that could take place in the South at that time. How-ever, for black Americans, especially those living in the South, it was a sort of quiet victory. They saw for the first time black people take the witness stand in a court of law and testify against white people.

After testifying against Milam and Bryant on kidnapping charges before a second grand jury, Mose Wright left Mississippi for Chicago and never returned. In late November, the all-white grand jury dropped the kidnapping charges against Milam and Bryant.

Mose Wright is not known as a leader of the civil rights movement, but he did have a tremendous impact on a younger generation of activists, like Martin Luther King Jr. and Ralph Abernathy, who both gained national prominence by leading the boycott against the segregated bus system of Montgomery, Alabama.

CHRONICLE OF EVENTS

1955

May 31: The U.S. Supreme Court rules in reference to *Brown* that school desegregation will be under federal district court jurisdiction. Desegregation of public schools is not to be carried out by any specified time.

August 20: Emmett Louis Till, a 14-year-old black youth from the South Side of Chicago, and his cousin Curtis Jones, board an Illinois Central Railroad train to visit their relatives in the Mississippi Delta.

August 21: Emmett Till and Curtis Jones arrive in Mississippi.

August 24: Till joins a group of eight black teenagers for a drive to Money, Mississippi, where he buys two cents worth of bubble gum at Bryant's Grocery and Meat Market. He says, "Bye, baby" to Carolyn Bryant, a white woman, and reportedly whistles at her.

August 28: Roy Bryant, husband of Carolyn Bryant, and his brother-in-law J. W. Milam drag Emmett Till from Mose Wright's cabin in the late evening and later kill him for wolf-whistling at Carolyn Bryant.

August 29: Bryant and Milam are charged with kidnapping Emmett Till and are jailed on suspicion of murder.

August 31: The beaten and mutilated body of Emmett Till is discovered in the Tallahatchie River.

September 3–6: The body of Emmett Till lies in state in an open casket at the Roberts Temple Church of God on State Street in Chicago. Thousands line the streets outside the church for the open viewing. There is national revulsion over the murder, especially among black Americans.

September 6: Funeral services for Emmett Till are held; an estimated two thousand people attend. An all-white grand jury indicts Roy Bryant and J. W. Milam for murdering and kidnapping Emmett Till.

September 19: Bryant and Milam go on trial for murder in a segregated courthouse in Sumner, Mississippi. Reporters from across the country, including many from the black press, cover the trial.

September 21: Mose Wright, Emmett Till's great uncle, identifies Milam and Bryant as the men who dragged Emmett Till away.

September 23: After deliberating only a little more than one hour, the jury finds both Bryant and Milam not guilty of murder.

September & October: In response to the verdict in the Till case, blacks hold major rallies in Baltimore, Chicago, Cleveland, Detroit, Los Angeles and New York.

November 20: An all-white grand jury drops kidnapping charges against Bryant and Milam in the Emmett Till case.

November 25: The Interstate Commerce Commission bans segregation on trains and buses crossing state lines.

December: Milam and Bryant sell their story to Alabama journalist William Bradford Huie for $4,000. Both men admit killing Emmett Till. They claim they only intended to frighten the 14-year-old Chicago boy but were forced to kill him after he refused to repent.

Eyewitness Testimony

Before Emmett Till's murder, I had known the fear of hunger, hell and the Devil. But now there was a new fear known to me—the fear of being killed just because I was black. I knew once I got food, the fear of starving to death would leave. I also was told that if I were a good girl, I wouldn't have to fear the Devil or hell. But I didn't know what one had to do or not do as a Negro not to be killed. Probably just being a Negro period was enough, I thought.

Anne Moody, civil rights activist, recalling learning of Emmett Till's murder as a young girl in 1955, in Coming of Age in Mississippi *(1968).*

We knew they were out to mob the boy. They came and took the boy and killed him.

When I heard the men at the door, I ran to Emmett's room and tried to wake him and take him out of the back door into the cotton fields. But they were already in the front door before I could shake him awake.

Mrs. Mose Wright, great-aunt of Emmett Till, recalling the night of August 28, 1955, in the Cleveland Call and Post *(September 10, 1955).*

I guess Emmett was killed because of the "wolf" call he whistled at that pretty 21-year-old white lady in a store last Wednesday.

Wheeler Parker, friend of Emmett Till, statement of August 31, in the Associated Press (September 1, 1955).

It would appear that the state of Mississippi has decided to maintain white supremacy by murdering children.

Roy Wilkins, NAACP executive secretary, statement of August 31, 1955, in the Memphis Commercial Appeal *(September 1, 1955).*

Those who commit such dastardly acts are themselves enemies to our country, and those who do nothing toward bringing such criminals to justice are themselves parties to the crime.

William Henry Huff, NAACP Chicago branch attorney, to Governor Hugh White (Mississippi), telegram of August 31, 1955, in the Atlanta Daily World *(September 1, 1955).*

Parties charged with the murder are in jail. I have every reason to believe that the court will do their duty in prosecution. Mississippi does not condone such conduct.

Mississippi Governor Hugh White, to the NAACP, telegram of August 31, 1955, in the Greenwood [Mississippi] Commonwealth *(September 1, 1955).*

Negro Boy Was Killed
For "Wolf Whistle"

The New York Post, *headline of September 1, 1955.*

They told me I wouldn't live to be 65 if I remembered their faces and told anybody.

Mose Wright, 64-year-old great-uncle of Emmett Till, statement of September 1, 1955, in the Atlanta Daily World *(September 2, 1955).*

The people of Mississippi are no more responsible for this tragic murder and no more condone it than the people of New York, or any other state, are responsible for and condone murders committed there, but every decent and respectable citizen of this state will assume his or her responsibility for seeing that justice is administered through the courts of law and that the guilty parties shall pay for their crime.

The Greenwood Commonwealth, *Leflore County, Mississippi newspaper, editorial of September 2, 1955.*

. . . If convictions with maximum penalty of the law cannot be secured in this heinous crime, then Mississippi may as well as burn all its law books and close its courts, for we cannot then stand before the nation and world as a self-governing state capable of making and enforcing its own laws and punishing [those] who most grievously offend those laws.

The Clarksdale [Mississippi] Press-Register, *editorial of September 2, 1955.*

Intelligent Mississippians can only suppose it came about in the sick mind[s] of men who should be removed from society by due course of law.

The Jackson [Mississippi] Clarion-Ledger, *editorial of September 2, 1955.*

The brutal murder is grist for the mill of those who picture all the South as a region of violence. It assists the Communist propagandists. It delivers us into the hands of our enemies. Unless the officials of Mississippi vigorously follow up this murder and bring the guilty to justice, all of us will be smeared by it.

The Atlanta Constitution, *editorial of September 2, 1955.*

Oh, God, God. My only boy . . .

Darling you have not died in vain your life has been sacrificed for something.

Mamie Bradley Till, mother of Emmett Till, on meeting the casket of her son at the Chicago Illinois Central station, September 2, 1955, in the Chicago Defender *(September 10, 1955).*

Let the body be held; let the whole nation see what they done to my boy.

Mamie Bradley Till, mother of Emmett Till, statement of September 2, 1955, in the Cleveland Call and Post *(September 10, 1955).*

Mourners and curious filled the Roberts Temple Church of God, where the body of Emmett Louis Till was taken this morning from an undertaking chapel. Outside the church an estimated 1,000 persons stood in long lines waiting to view the body.

Associated Press, news dispatch of September 3, 1955, on open viewing of Emmett Till's body in Chicago.

50,000 View Body of 14-Year-Old Boy Found Slain in Mississippi.

Atlanta Daily World, *daily black newspaper, headline of September 4, 1955.*

Lynching Stirs Nation
Mississippi Slayers Indicted.

Cleveland Call and Post, *black newspaper, headline of September 10, 1955.*

Nation Shocked, Vow Action
In Lynching of Chicago Youth.

Chicago Defender, *weekly black newspaper, headline of September 10, 1955.*

This dastardly act on the part of these criminal-minded persons is so outrageous that it opens the door for condemnation of the United States. This occasion warrants that you speak out in no uncertain terms.

William Henry Huff, NAACP Chicago branch attorney, to President Dwight D. Eisenhower, message of September 1955, in the [Baltimore] Afro-American *(September 10, 1955).*

Northerners always think that we don't care what white folks do to the colored folks here, but that's not true. The people around here are decent, and they won't stand for this.

Supported by clergymen, Mamie Bradley Till sobs hysterically as the casket of her son Emmett Till arrives in Chicago from Greenwood, Mississippi. Courtesy of AP/Wide World Photos.

Deputy Sheriff John Cothran, Leflore County, Mississippi, statement of September 1955, in Newsweek *(September 12, 1955).*

Have you ever sent a loved son on a vacation and had him returned to you in a pine box, so horribly battered and water-logged that someone needs to tell you that this sickening sight is your son—lynched?

Mamie Bradley Till, statement of September 1955, in the Pittsburgh Courier *(September 17, 1955).*

Perhaps the purpose of this sorry and tragic error committed in my native Mississippi by two white adults on an afflicted Northern child is to prove to us whether or not we deserve to survive. Because if we in America have reached that point in our desperate culture when we must murder children, no matter for what reason or what color, we don't deserve to survive, and probably won't.

William Faulkner, statement of September 1955, in Peavy's Go Slow Now: Faulkner and the Race Question *(1971).*

Unless the administration acts at once to stop this wanton and ruthless taking of lives, the blood of "Bo" Till, Reverend George Lee, Lamar Smith and the long line of martyrs in the fight for first class citizenship for the Negro in America will be on its hands and "all the perfumes of Arabia will not wash it away."

Chicago Defender, editorial of September 10, 1955.

Two months ago I had a nice six-room apartment in Chicago. I had a good job. I had a son.

When something happened to Negroes in the South, I said "that's their business, not mine."

Now I know how wrong I was. The death of my son has shown me what happens to any of us, anywhere in the world, had better be the business of all of us.

Mamie Bradley Till, mother of Emmett Till, statement of September 1955, in the Cleveland Call and Post (September 24, 1955).

I went to the trial to see how it was going. It was just like a circus. The defendants were sitting up there eating ice-cream cones and playing with their children in court just like they were out at a picnic. Everybody was searched going into the courtroom to make sure that none of the Negroes carried any weapons. White folks were not searched.

Ruby Hurley, NAACP Birmingham office director, recalling the Emmett Till murder case in Raines' My Soul Is Rested (1977).

Witnesses were permitted to smoke while testifying in the witness chair; lawyers smoked while questioning the witnesses and speaking to the jury; Coca Colas were sold in the courtroom; and at no times were the defendants treated as if they were under arrest. Whenever they wished to, they could get up and walk around as if they were guests instead of prisoners.

James Hicks, New York Amsterdam News and National Negro Press Association journalist, article of October 10, 1955, on covering the trial of Milam and Bryant, in the [Baltimore] Afro-American.

Never in the history of our state has so much out-of-state interest been taken in a case involving white and Negro.

The Charleston Mississippi Sun, editorial of September 22, 1955.

Mose Wright, making a formation no white man in his county really believed he would dare to make, stood on his tiptoes to the full limit of his 64 years and his five feet three inches yesterday, pointed his black, workworn finger straight at the huge and stormy head of J. W. Milam and swore that was the man who dragged 14-year-old Emmett Louis Till out of his cottonfield cabin the night the boy was murdered.

"There he is," said Mose Wright.

Murray Kempton, journalist, covering the trial of Bryant and Milam in Sumner, Mississippi, article of September 22, 1955, in the New York Post.

There are people who want to destroy the way of Southern white people and Southern Negro people. They'll go to any odds to widen the gap between Southern people.

They would not be above putting a body in the river in the hopes it might be identified as Emmett Till.

Defense attorney John C. Whitten, representing Bryant and Milam, to the jury, closing argument of September 23, 1955, in the Atlanta Daily World (September 24, 1955).

Only so long as we can preserve the rights of everybody—white or black—we can keep our way of life. Once we get to the point where we deprive any of our people of their rights, we are all in danger. Emmett Till down here in Mississippi was a citizen of the United States, he was entitled to his life and liberty.

Special prosecutor Robert B. Smith III, to the jury, closing argument of September 23, 1955, in the New York Post (September 24, 1955).

I was expecting an acquittal . . . and I didn't want to be there when it happened.

Mamie Bradley Till, mother of Emmett Till, statement of September 23, 1955, on the jury's "not guilty" verdict in the Till murder case, in the Associated Press (September 23, 1955).

If we hadn't stopped to drink pop, it wouldn't have taken that long.

Anonymous juror, statement of September 1955, on the jury's deliberations, in Time (October 3, 1955).

By his death Emmett Louis Till took racism out of the textbooks and editorials and showed it to the world in its true dimensions. Now the ugliness is there for all the world to see. In the face of this, what can decent men do except redouble their efforts to cure ourselves of this evil thing? It is too late to help the Negro boy from Chicago who died so quickly in Mississippi, for others who die more slowly there is still time.

Commonweal, editorial of September 23, 1955.

Mississippi can handle its affairs without any outside meddling and its long history of proper court procedure can never be questioned by any group. The trial at Sumner added another chapter to this fact.

The Greenwood Commonwealth, *Leflore County, Mississippi, editorial of September 24, 1955.*

The trial is over, but the case is not closed. The year is 1955, and in America—as all over the world—the stereotypes of white supremacy are under fire. There can be no rest for Till's murderers, or for those who have rationalized this brutal deed. Like other great episodes in the battle for equality and justice in America, this trial has rocked the world, and nothing can ever be quite the same again—even in Mississippi.

The New York Post, *editorial of September 24, 1955.*

"What happened to 14-year-old Emmett Till?" will be asked time and time again and until it is answered, we of the South can only admit that Emmett Till is a damaging symbol—another skeleton in the South's closet.

The Chattanooga [Tennessee] Times, *editorial of September 24, 1955.*

It is best for all concerned that the Bryant-Milam case be forgotten as quickly as possible. It has received far more publicity than should have been given.

The Clarion-Jackson Ledger, *Jackson, Mississippi, editorial of September 25, 1955.*

If the United States can send the armed forces 6,000 miles across the sea to Korea to fight Korean Communists in the interest of world democracy, it would appear that the Federal Government should use its vast powers to stop the lynching of a colored

citizen by Mississippi racists in the interest of American democracy.

A. Philip Randolph, president of the Brotherhood of Sleeping Car Porters, to a rally in Harlem, New York, speech of September 25, 1955, in the [Baltimore] Afro-American *(October 1, 1955).*

Mississippi whines that she is misunderstood, that she is slandered, traduced, and maligned, that these are good people in the state who condemn the lynching-crime of Money. But where are they? Excepting the novelist William Faulkner, no responsible citizen has spoken out in rage and indignation.

The Crisis, *NAACP magazine, editorial of October 1955.*

Today the jungles of Mississippi are laughing at their mockery of justice—but the rest of the 47 states might well be crying for Mississippi.

James Hicks, New York Amsterdam News *and National Negro Press Association journalist, article of October 1, 1955, in the* Cleveland Call and Post.

The Emmett Till trial is over, but we, as Negroes, should never forget its meaning. The fact that Milam and Bryant were acquitted shows us how tremendous a job we face to bring complete democracy to our entire nation. Negroes and other clear-thinking Americans must combine their efforts to press for freedom and equality through both political and legal challenges.

Congressman Charles C. Diggs, black Michigan representative, article of October 8, 1955, in the Pittsburgh Courier.

It was the first time in the history of Mississippi that a Negro had stood in court and pointed his finger at a white man as the killer of a Negro.

Congressman Charles C. Diggs, black Michigan representative, speech of October 9, 1955, paying tribute to Mose Wright, great-uncle of Emmett Till, in the Cleveland Call and Post *(October 15, 1955).*

I feel that a giant glacier has been started by all this; it's moving onward and there's no stopping it.

You may chop at it, but you can't stop it.

Mamie Bradley Till, statement of October 1955, in the [Baltimore] Afro-American *(October 29, 1955).*

4. The Montgomery Bus Boycott: 1955–1957

THE CRADLE ROCKS

Montgomery, the capital of Alabama, is where the Confederate States were first organized in 1861 and where Jefferson Davis was inaugurated as the president of the Confederacy. This Southern city nestled in the middle of the cotton kingdom became known as the Cradle of the Confederacy. Almost 100 years later, racial segregation permeated everyday life in Montgomery as it did throughout most of the South. Not only were there separate schools for blacks and whites, but restaurants, movie theaters, public water fountains and even seating on the city's buses was segregated.

Black passengers were required to pay their fares at the front, then had to board the bus at the rear. By law and custom, the front rows of seats on the Montgomery City Bus Lines were reserved for white people. Blacks had to sit in the rear of the buses or in a sort of no man's land in the middle of the bus—provided that no white people desired those seats. Also, blacks had to give up their seats whenever a white passenger was left standing. There were no signs describing these rules, but everyone in Montgomery knew them.

Long before the Montgomery bus boycott of 1955 and 1956, there was some black protest to segregated transportation. Blacks had boycotted streetcar lines in more than 27 cities toward the end of the 19th century. For two years, from 1900 to 1902, Jim Crow lines in Montgomery were boycotted. Although their demands were met, blacks soon found that segregated seating was restored by city regulations. Section 10, Chapter 6 of the 1952 Montgomery City Code stated that "Every person operating a bus line shall provide equal accommodations . . . in such a manner as to separate the white people from the Negroes."

The actions taken by Rosa Parks, a 43-year-old seamstress and a former secretary of the Montgomery NAACP chapter, on December 1, 1955 gave birth to a form of protest that would become an integral part of the civil rights movement—nonviolent mass action.

All that day she worked hard at a Montgomery department store pinning up hems, raising waistlines and carrying dresses back and forth. When the closing time buzzer rang, she dashed out of the store and boarded a Cleveland Avenue bus, which was half empty, and sank into the first seat, on row 11, behind the "white" section. As the bus moved on from stop to stop, the white seats filled up and soon a white man was left standing. The bus driver, James Blake, who had once evicted Parks from a bus in 1943 for refusing to use the back door, ordered the blacks sitting in row 11 to move, since Montgomery's bus segregation law also forbade whites and blacks sitting in the same row. All of the blacks but Parks moved to the back of the bus. When she refused to budge, Blake called the police, and Parks was arrested for violating the municipal code segregating the races in Montgomery.

Although some versions of civil rights history depict Rosa Parks as a simple black woman whose feet were tired from working all day for the white folks, she was actually well aware of the larger concept of struggling for racial justice. In the late 1940s, she became the first secretary for the Alabama State Conference of NAACP Branches and organized an NAACP Youth Council chapter in Montgomery. In the

Rosa Parks, whose action sparked the Montgomery bus boycott, is fingerprinted after her arrest for violating a Montgomery municipal code segregating the races, December 1, 1955. Courtesy of AP/Wide World Photos.

summer prior to her arrest, she had attended an interracial workshop at Highlander Folk School in Monteagle, Tennessee, which was a well-known training center for labor organizing and antidiscrimination work.

News of Rosa Parks' arrest soon swept throughout the black community of Montgomery. E. D. Nixon, a pullman porter and a former president of the NAACP Alabama chapter, posted her bail bond. Nixon saw Parks' arrest as an ideal opportunity to attack the issue of segregation in Montgomery. "With your permission," Nixon told Rosa Parks, "we can break down segregation on the bus with your case." Despite the warnings from her family members that working with Nixon and the NAACP might get her lynched, Rosa Parks agreed to permit Nixon to use her arrest as a test case to break segregation in Montgomery.

THE BOYCOTT BEGINS

Nixon decided that the best way to mobilize the black community was by first enlisting the support of its most respected and important leaders, who for the most part were clergymen. On the day after Rosa Parks' arrest, a Friday, Nixon arranged a meeting for that evening with several black ministers, including the Reverend Ralph Abernathy, the 29-year-old minister of the First Baptist Church.

On the same day, Jo Ann Robinson, the president of the Women's Political Council, a black professional organization, began planning for a bus boycott in support of Parks, to start the following Monday. Robinson, who was an English professor at all-black Alabama State College, and her group had earlier asked the city of Montgomery for a revision of its bus seating policy. The city's commissioners were unresponsive. Consequently, the Women's Political Council had been discussing the possibility of taking direct economic action against the Montgomery City Bus Lines system.

When the ministers gathered Friday evening, word of the boycott was spreading throughout the black community. The Reverend L. Roy Bennett, president of the Interdenominational Ministers Alliance, chaired the meeting. He endorsed the boycott and called for the ministers to organize committees to implement the action. The clergymen agreed to announce the one-day boycott in their Sunday sermons and to meet again Monday evening to decide if the boycott should continue.

Robinson stayed up all night mimeographing 35,000 handbills that called for a bus boycott. The leaflet read, "This is for Monday, Dec. 5, 1955—Another Negro woman has been arrested and thrown into jail because she refused to get up out of her seat on the bus and give it to a white person . . . This has to be stopped . . . The woman's case will come up Monday. We are therefore asking every Negro to stay off the buses Monday in protest of the arrest and trial. Don't ride the buses to work, to town, to school, or anywhere on Monday . . ."

News of the boycott gained widespread circulation through an unexpected source. Nixon gave a copy of the boycott leaflet to Joe Azbell, a white reporter for the *Montgomery Advertiser*. He told Azbell, "If you promise you'll play it up strong in your Sunday paper, I'll give you a hot tip." On Sunday, December 4, the story of the impending boycott ran on the front page of the paper. Blacks who might have missed the fliers now knew of the bus boycott.

On Monday, December 5, over 90% of the blacks who regularly rode the buses stayed off them. Blacks walked, joined car pools, drove wagons and even rode mules. But they did not ride the buses. The historic Montgomery bus boycott had begun. It would last 381 days. From this boycott would emerge an effective strategy for social change, a determination to end Jim Crow and a new charismatic black civil rights leader.

"THERE COMES A TIME THAT PEOPLE GET TIRED"

On the same day that the bus boycott began, Rosa Parks was convicted and fined $10 plus $4 in court costs for violating Montgomery's segregation laws. That afternoon the ministers met to prepare for the evening's mass meeting. It was decided that an umbrella organization was needed to carry on the boycott. Abernathy came up with a name for the organization: the Montgomery Improvement Association (MIA). Twenty-six-year-old Reverend Martin Luther King Jr., who had come to Montgomery less than two years before, was nominated as its president. Since King was relatively new to Montgomery, he was unlikely to be the target of clerical infighting, and he could also move on to another job elsewhere in the event that the boycott failed and there was retribution from the white community.

Born in 1929 to the prestigious pastor of Atlanta's Ebenezer Baptist Church, King had deep roots in the black South. By the age of five, he was reciting stretches of biblical verse and had a vocabulary that one would expect from a child twice his age. He skipped two grades at Booker T. Washington High School and enrolled at Morehouse College as a freshman at the age of 15. He dreamed of becoming a lawyer or a teacher, but his father insisted that he become a minister. Following his graduation in 1948, he entered Crozer Theological Seminary in Pennsylvania for his Bachelor of Divinity degree.

Martin Luther King Jr. Courtesy of the Library of Congress.

Only one of six blacks in a student body of 100, King immersed himself in the world of philosophy, studying the ideas of Kant, Hegel, the religious existentialists and Walter Rauschenbusch. King was most impressed with Henry David Thoreau's 1849 essay, *Civil Disobedience*, which defended nonviolent resistance to oppression. He finished first in his graduating class, earning a fellowship to pursue a doctorate at Boston University's School of Theology.

While in Boston, King met Coretta Scott, a graduate of Antioch College who was studying voice at the New England Conservatory of Music. They were married in 1953, and although both wished to remain in the North, family ties and an attractive job offer brought them back to the South. "Finally we agreed," King wrote in *Stride Toward Freedom* (1958), "that, in spite of the disadvantages and inevitable sacrifices, our greatest service could be rendered in our native South. We came to the conclusion that we had something of a moral obligation to return—at least for a few years."

King arrived in Montgomery in September 1954 to serve as pastor of the Dexter Avenue Baptist Church, whose influential congregation comprised mainly black professionals and faculty members of Alabama State College. Poor black people in Montgomery referred to it as "the big people's church."

As the newly elected president of the Montgomery Improvement Association, King had about 20 minutes to prepare his speech for the evening rally at the Holt Street Baptist Church. He would later describe it as one of the most important speeches of his life. Long lines of men and women—maids, porters, teachers, students, laborers— were gathering before the doors of the church opened. By 7 P.M., the church was packed, and thousands more stood outside to listen to the proceedings through loudspeakers.

The meeting opened with the song "Onward, Christian Soldiers." Joe Azbell of the *Montgomery Advertiser* reported that there was a prayer that was interrupted "a hundred times" by "yeas" and "uh'uhs" and "that's right." The high point of the rally came when the virtually unknown leader of the new movement, the Reverend Dr. Martin Luther King Jr. began to speak.

"There comes a time," King said, "that people get tired. We are here this evening to say to those who have mistreated us so long that we are tired—tired of being segregated and humiliated; tired of being kicked around by the brutal feet of oppression. We have no alternative but to protest . . . If you will protest courageously, and yet with dignity and Christian love, when the history books are written in future generations, the historians will have to say, 'There lived a great people—a black people—who injected new meaning and dignity into the veins of civilization.' This is our challenge and our overwhelming responsibility." The crowd roared with approval, punctuating King's pauses with yeses and cheers. King had articulated their feelings and their vision.

Rosa Parks was then introduced from the rostrum, and she receiving a standing ovation. The group voted unanimously to boycott the buses until they gained their three demands: 1. courteous treatment of black passengers, 2. seating on a first-come, first-served basis, with blacks filling the bus from the rear and whites from the front and no reserved seats for whites or blacks and 3. hiring of black drivers on predominantly black routes.

"My Feet Is Tired, But My Soul Is Rested"

On Thursday, December 8, after only four days of almost total black boycott, leaders of the Montgomery Improvement Association (MIA), including King and attorney Fred Gray, met with Montgomery Mayor W. A. Gayle, his commissioners and representatives of the bus company. The MIA presented its three demands. Although King said that they were not seeking an end to segregation, only better treatment for black passengers, the whites refused to make any compromise. The city fathers drew the line. They also threatened legal action unless the black cab companies resumed charging the designated minimum fares for taxis.

At a mass meeting of bus boycotters that evening, it was decided that a complex organization of car pools would replace the black taxis that the boycotters had been using. More than 150 blacks volunteered their cars. Within seven days, the MIA had organized 48 dispatch and 42 pick-up zones. The boycott had overcome its first hurdle. Several thousand rode in the car pools; some hitchhiked or rode bicycles; and many simply walked. One elderly woman said, "My feet is tired, but my soul is rested." The days of the bus boycott went from days to weeks and then to months.

Montgomery's Get Tough Policy

By the end of January 1956, the white community was beginning to feel the impact of the boycott. Downtown storekeepers claimed they had lost a million dollars in sales due to the restricted travel of blacks. The bus company lost some 65% of its income and was forced to raise its fares and cut back on its schedules. Mayor Gayle announced a "get-tough" policy. In a television broadcast, he denounced the boycotters, "We have pussyfooted around on this boycott long enough . . . The white people are firm in their convictions that they do not care whether the Negroes ever ride a city bus again if it means that the social fabric of our community is to be destroyed so that Negroes will start riding the buses again."

An official policy of harassment against the boycotters began. On January 24, Mayor Gayle and his commissioners joined the White Citizens' Council. Blacks who were prominent figures in the boycott were fired from their jobs, while many others were threatened with the same. Many car-pool drivers were fined on trumped-up speeding charges.

Tensions in Montgomery escalated. The front porch of Martin Luther King Jr.'s home was bombed on January 30. King's wife, Coretta, escaped injury by running to a back room with her seven-week-old baby. A few days later, E. D. Nixon's home was bombed.

On February 21, 1956, a Montgomery grand jury indicted 89 blacks, including King and 24 other ministers, for violating a seldom-used 1921 law prohibiting boycotts. "In this state," the indictment read, "we are committed to segregation by custom and law; we intend to maintain it." The black leaders of Montgomery did not fear jail, instead they immediately surrendered. The first to surrender was E. D. Nixon, who told police, "You are looking for me? Here I am."

King voluntarily surrendered the next day, since on the day of the indictment he was visiting his parents in Atlanta. He was arrested for the first time in his life. The arrest of King and the other ministers turned the Montgomery bus boycott into a national news story.

On March 19, King, as the first defendant, went on trial. Newspaper, television and radio reporters from around the country descended on Montgomery to cover the story. For four days, 28 witnesses summoned by the defense gave their testimony of being mistreated by white bus drivers. One witness testified how she heard a black passenger threatened because he did not have the correct change. "The driver whipped out a pistol and drove the man off the bus."

Four days later, King was found guilty and ordered by the judge to pay a $500 fine and court costs or serve 386 days at hard labor. He was released on bond, and his conviction became headline news throughout the nation. As King left the courthouse that day, he was greeted by a crowd of boycotters that chanted, "Long live the King," and then they sang, "We ain't gonna ride the buses no more."

"GOD ALMIGHTY HAS SPOKEN FROM WASHINGTON"

On June 4, a three-judge federal district court handed down its decision in a case brought by four Montgomery black women to end bus segregation in the city. "We hold that the statutes requiring segregation of the white and colored races on a common carrier," the majority ruled, "violate the due process and equal protection clauses of the 14th Amendment." But Montgomery officials appealed the case to the United States Supreme Court. Now the High Court would decide the fundamental question as to whether or not bus segregation and, in effect, all segregation, was unconstitutional.

Meanwhile, the buses remained segregated and the boycott continued. White leaders continued their policy of harassment. The state of Alabama outlawed the NAACP as a foreign corporation that had failed to register and accused it of "causing irreparable injury to the property and civil rights of residents," referring to its role in the federal suit against Montgomery. The city of Montgomery obtained an indictment against the MIA on charges of operating a business—a car pool—without a license.

On November 13, 1956, while King was attending the proceedings on the legality of the MIA car pool, a reporter for the Associated Press handed him a note. It read: "The United States Supreme Court today affirmed the decision of a special three-judge U.S. district court in declaring Alabama's state and local laws requiring segregation on buses unconstitutional." King said the ruling was "a joyous daybreak to end the long night of enforced segregation in public transportation." Another black in the courtroom announced, "God Almighty has spoken from Washington, D.C.!"

The boycott, however, continued for another month until the actual Supreme Court order reached Montgomery. On December 21, 1956, at 5:55 A.M., Martin Luther King Jr., Glenn Smiley, E. D. Nixon and Ralph Abernathy boarded the first integrated bus in Montgomery's history. The 381-day struggle that began as a fight for simple courtesy ended as a major triumph for desegregation. King later wrote, "The skies did not fall when integrated buses finally traveled the streets of Montgomery."

All did not remain calm in the weeks after the buses were integrated in Montgomery. Buses were fired upon by white snipers; a black teenage girl was beaten by four or five whites as she got off the bus. Four black churches were bombed, the homes of Ralph Abernathy and Robert Graetz were dynamited on January 10, 1957 and someone fired a shotgun blast into the front door of King's home. However, on January 31, much to everyone's surprise, seven white men were arrested in connection with the bombings, and five were indicted. Although they had signed confessions of guilt, they were acquitted. But the bombings came to an end.

Out of the informal network of Southern churches that supported the Montgomery bus boycott emerged the Southern Christian Leadership Conference (SCLC). The new organization chose as its president Martin Luther King Jr. Ministers from 11 states all agreed on the necessity of a coordinating network for their various movements. The SCLC called upon blacks "to understand that nonviolence is not a symbol of weakness or cowardice, but as Jesus demonstrated, nonviolent resistance transforms weakness into strength and breeds courage in the face of danger."

The Montgomery bus boycott stirred the imaginations of blacks throughout the country. It sparked boycotts in Birmingham and Mobile in Alabama and also in Tallahassee, Florida. It also brought national fame to Martin Luther King Jr., whose advocacy of massive nonviolent resistance was attracting a growing number of followers who would eventually ignite a nationwide civil rights movement.

CHRONICLE OF EVENTS

1955

December 1: Mrs. Rosa L. Parks, a 43-year-old seamstress and a former Montgomery NAACP chapter secretary, is arrested for refusing to give up her seat to a white man on a segregated bus.

December 2: A meeting of local black leaders, chaired by Reverend L. Roy Bennett, decide to call a boycott of the Montgomery City Bus Lines system.

December 5: The Montgomery bus boycott begins, and 26-year-old Reverend Martin Luther King Jr. is elected president of the boycott committee of the Montgomery Improvement Association (MIA). Reverend Ralph Abernathy is put in charge of negotiating with city officials. Rosa Parks is fined $14 for violating Montgomery's bus segregation law.

December 8: The MIA, including King, meets with city commissioners and representatives of the bus company. The bus company rejects the MIA demands of implementing desegregated seating on a first-come, first-served basis, hiring black drivers for black neighborhoods and ordering drivers to be more courteous to black passengers. At a mass meeting of bus boycotters that evening, it is decided that the MIA will set up a complex carpooling system for the boycotters.

1956

January 21: A false settlement is announced by a Montgomery city commissioner and denied by leaders of the MIA.

January 24: Mayor W. A. Gayle of Montgomery and City Commissioner Frank Parks join the White Citizens' Council. Along with the police commissioner, all three city commissioners now belong to the segregationist organization.

January 26: Martin Luther King Jr. is arrested for driving at 30 MPH in a 25 MPH zone. The trumped-up speeding charge is part of an official Montgomery harrassment plan. Hundreds protest outside the Montgomery City jail, and King is released.

January 30: The home of Martin Luther King Jr. is bombed.

February 1: The home of Edgar Daniel (E. D.) Nixon, a former Montgomery NAACP chapter president, is bombed. Fred Gray, the black attorney representing Rosa Parks, files a lawsuit in United States District Court in Montgomery, Alabama challenging the constitutionality of bus segregation.

February 4: White students riot at the University of Alabama against the court-ordered admission of Autherin J. Lucy, the first black student in the school's history.

February 21: A grand-jury indicts 89 blacks, including King and four ministers, for violating a seldom-used 1921 law prohibiting boycotts.

February 22: Martin Luther King Jr. voluntarily surrenders to Montgomery police. He is booked, fingerprinted, photographed and then released.

February 28: The membership of the Montgomery White Citizens' Council grows to 12,000.

March 12: Southern senators and congressmen sign the "Declaration of Constitutional Principles," better known as the "Southern Manifesto." It takes issue with the Supreme Court's *Brown* decision on school desegregation.

March 19: Martin Luther King Jr. goes on trial for violating the boycott statute. He soon becomes a national figure, and the Montgomery bus boycott becomes a major nationwide news story.

March 22: King is found guilty and is sentenced to pay a fine of $500 or serve 386 days at hard labor. His conviction is appealed, and the other cases are held over pending a decision.

May 11: The MIA's federal court suit, *Browder v. Gayle*, begins in Montgomery.

May 27: Tallahassee, Florida bus boycott begins. It will continue until March 1958.

June 1: Alabama outlaws the NAACP.

June 5: A three-judge federal court in Montgomery rules 2–1 that bus segregation is unconstitutional. The city appeals the decision to the U.S. Supreme Court.

November 6: President Dwight D. Eisenhower is reelected, defeating Adlai Stevenson.

November 13: The United States Supreme Court invalidates a Montgomery, Alabama law that provides for segregation in intrastate bus travel.

November 14: Mass meeting of the MIA decides to discontinue boycott as soon as the Supreme Court decision is implemented.

December 20: The written order from the U.S. Supreme Court for ending segregation on buses arrives in Montgomery, Alabama.

December 21: Montgomery's buses are integrated, and the Montgomery Improvement Association calls off its boycott after 381 days.

The first integrated Montgomery bus is boarded by Reverend Martin Luther King Jr., Reverend Ralph Abernathy, Glenn Smiley and E. D. Nixon.

1957

January 10: The homes of the reverends Ralph Abernathy and Robert Graetz as well as four Montgomery black churches are bombed.

January 11: The Southern Christian Leadership Conference (SCLC) is founded, with the Reverend Martin Luther King Jr. as its president.

January 28: An unexploded bomb containing 12 sticks of dynamite is found on the porch of King's home.

January 31: Seven white men are arrested for the bombings.

May 30: The men arrested for the bombings are found not guilty by an all-white jury.

EYEWITNESS TESTIMONY

Every person operating a bus line shall provide equal accommodations . . . in such a manner as to separate the white people from the Negroes.
Section 10, Chapter 6, Code of the City of Montgomery, *1952.*

Well, in the first place, I had been working all day on the job. I was quite tired after spending a full day working. I handle and work on clothing that white people wear. That didn't come in my mind but this is what I wanted to know: when and how would we ever determine our rights as human beings? . . . It just happened that the driver made a demand and I just didn't feel like obeying his demand. He called a policeman and I was arrested and placed in jail.
Rosa Parks, seamstress and former Montgomery NAACP chapter secretary, on why she refused to give up her seat on a segregated bus on December 1, 1955, in Grant's Black Protest *(1968).*

There we was, all sitting around in Mrs. Parks' kitchen, and I said, "This is the case! We can boycott the bus lines with this and at the same time go to the Supreme Court."
E. D. Nixon, Montgomery bus boycott organizer, recalling meeting with Rosa Parks on December 1, 1955, in Selby's Odyssey: Journey Through Black America *(1971).*

Throughout the late morning and early afternoon we dropped off tens of thousands of leaflets. Leaflets were . . . dropped off at business places, storefronts, beauty parlors, beer halls, factories, barber shops, and every other available place. Workers would pass along notices to both other employees as well as to customers . . .

By 2 o'clock, thousands of the mimeographed handbills had changed hands many times. Practically every black man, woman, and child in Montgomery knew the plan and was passing the word along.
Jo Ann Robinson, Women's Political Council president and Alabama State College professor, recalling the beginning of the Montgomery bus boycott on December 5, 1955, in The Montgomery Bus Boycott and the Women Who Started It *(1987).*

Don't ride the bus to work, to town, to school, or any place Monday, December 5.

Rosa Parks. Courtesy of the Schomburg Center for Research in Black Culture.

Another Negro woman has been arrested and put in jail because she refused to give her bus seat.

Don't ride the buses to work, to town, to school, or anywhere on Monday. If you work, take a cab, or share a ride, or walk.

Come to a mass meeting, Monday at 7:00 P.M., at the Holt Street Baptist Church for further instruction.
Leaflet of December 3, 1955, in the verticle file, Schomburg Center for Research in Black Culture, the New York Public Library.

There was a knock on my door. This was about 11:30 Sunday night and I went to the door and there was a pamphlet sticking in the screen door handle. I got it and brought it in.

That Monday morning I went to school, the boycott was in progress. But a lot of blacks would've never known about it if the [Montgomery] *Advertiser* hadn't of said something about it in their Sunday edition. It went like wildfire all over town.

Rev. B. J. Simms, Montgomery Improvement
Association (MIA) transportation chairman, re-
calling the beginning of the Montgomery bus
boycott in early December 1955, in Garrow's
The Walking City: The Montgomery Bus
Boycott, 1955–1956 (1989).

People, don't ride the bus today. Don't ride it, for
freedom.

Sign at a Montgomery bus stop, December 5,
1955.

There comes a time when people get tired. We are
here this evening to say to those who have mistreated
us so long that we are tired—tired of being segregated and humiliated, tired of being kicked about by
the brutal feet of oppression. We have no alternative
but protest. For many years, we have shown amazing
patience. We have sometimes given our white brothers the feeling that we liked the way we were being
treated. But we come here tonight to be saved from
that patience that makes us patient with anything
less than freedom and justice.

Martin Luther King Jr., speech of December 5,
1955, to a mass meeting of bus boycotters at the
Holt Street Baptist Church, in Branch's Parting the Waters (1988).

Negroes were on almost every corner in the downtown area, silent, waiting for rides or moving about
to keep warm, but few got on the buses. Negro cabs
were packed tight and it seemed as if they stopped
to pick up more passengers at every corner. Some
appeared as if they would burst open if another
passenger got in. Scores of Negroes were walking,
their lunches in brown paper sacks under their arms.
None spoke to white people. They exchanged little
talk among themselves. It was an event almost solemn.

The Alabama Journal, article of December 6,
1955, on the first day of the Montgomery bus
boycott of December 5.

We are not asking an end to segregation. That's a
matter for the legislature and the courts. We feel that
we have a plan within the law . . . We don't like
the idea of Negroes having to stand when there are
vacant seats. We are demanding justice on that point.

Martin Luther King Jr., statement of December
7, 1955, at a news conference, in the Alabama
Journal (December 7, 1955).

Those drivers talk to us like we are dogs. Ordering
us to get up out of our seats and give them to white
passengers. Even other white passengers are not
above saying, "N——r" get up out of your seat.

Reverend J. R. King, MIA leader, statement of
December 1955, in the [Baltimore] Afro-American (December 17, 1955).

Not since the first battle of the Marne has the taxi
been put to as good a use as it has this last week in
Montgomery. However, the spirit animating our Negro citizens as they ride these taxis or walk from the
heart of Cloverdale to Mobile Road has been more
like that of Gandhi than of the "taxicab army" that
saved Paris.

Juliette Morgan, white librarian, letter to the
editor of December 12, 1955, in the Montgomery Advertiser.

Either fortuitously or with a purpose, Montgomery, the first Capital of the Confederacy, has been
made a guinea pig for the great sociological experiment.

The contributors to this experiment have been the
Supreme Court of the United States, the NAACP,
the ADA and a bunch of wild, well-financed political
radicals jealous of the South's peaceful and serene
way of life.

The Alabama Journal, editorial of December
18, 1955.

The situation in our city regarding the treatment
of Negroes on our city buses has caused us to bow
our heads in shame.

Why could not our city provide such laws for all
citizens as do some other Southern cities—Nashville,
Richmond, and we understand Mobile? These cities
have a first come, first served law. Thus all citizens
have equal opportunities for a ride. We hope this
problem will soon be solved and that the welfare of
all citizens will be a responsibility for all of us.

Mrs. Frances P. McLeod, to the Montgomery
Advertiser, letter of December 1955, in Robin-
son's The Montgomery Bus Boycott and the
Women Who Started It (1987).

Join The White Citizens' Council
Whites Only
Before it is too late
Help to preserve segregation in Alabama

Note of December 1955, in Robinson's The
Montgomery Boycott and the Women Who
Started It (1987).

Ain't gonna ride them buses no more,
Ain't gonna ride no more.
Why don't all the white folks know
That I ain't gonna ride no more.
Song sung by Montgomery boycotters, 1955.

My soul has been tired for a long time. Now my feet are tired, and my soul is resting.
Anonymous, Montgomery bus boycotter, statement of January 1956, in Time *(January 16, 1956).*

The Negroes are laughing at white people behind their backs . . . They think it's very funny and amusing that whites who are opposed to the Negro boycotters will act as chaffeur to Negroes who are boycotting the buses. When a white person gives a Negro a single penny for transportation or helps a Negro with transportation, even if it's a block ride, he is helping the Negro radicals who lead the boycott. The Negroes have made their own beds, and the whites should let them sleep in them.
Montgomery Mayor W. A. Gayle, statement of January 23, 1956, in the Montgomery Advertiser *(January 24, 1956).*

. . . Segregation is an institution of the South we don't intend to see scrapped.
Alabama state senator Sam Englehart, chairman of the Central Alabama Citizens Council, to a Montgomery rally denouncing racial integration, speech of February 10, 1956, in the New York Times *(February 11, 1956).*

We have walked for 11 weeks in the cold and rain. Now the weather is warming up. Therefore we will walk on until some better proposals are forthcoming from our city fathers.
Ralph Abernathy, statement of February 20, 1956, in the Montgomery Advertiser *(February 21, 1956).*

You've got this kind of situation: There is not a segregated department store in town, nor, so far as I know, a segregated elevator left in Montgomery. In other words, vertically we are desegregated, but riding horizontally, for some reason, it's quite different. Don't ask me why—I can't answer it. The thing is irrational, but that doesn't mean it's not powerful.
Grover C. Hall Jr., editor of the Montgomery Advertiser, *statement of February 1956, in an interview in* U.S. News & World Report *(February 24, 1956).*

Ralph Abernathy (left) and Martin Luther King Jr. (right) gained national prominence from leading the successful Montgomery bus boycott. Courtesy of the Schomburg Center for Research in Black Culture.

The Negroes are not on trial here, but Montgomery is on trial. The eyes of the world are focused here.
Anonymous, Montgomery bus boycotter and minister, statement of February 21, 1956, after his arrest for violating Alabama's antiboycott law, in Time *(March 5, 1956).*

As a clergyman and Congressman, I wish to state that from this moment on the White House is responsible for safeguarding the lives, physical security and civil liberties of 115 Negroes arrested for peaceably and non-violently trying to obtain what the Constitution promises and local, state and federal law enforcement officials refuse to give.
Congressman Adam Clayton Powell (D, N.Y.), to President Dwight D. Eisenhower, message of February 22, 1956, in the New York Post *(February 23, 1956).*

The whole world is looking to Alabama and expecting us to do something towards bringing about peace between the races. Certainly there is a place in Alabama where white and Negro citizens can have a meeting of the minds.

Alabama Governor James E. Folsom, statement of February 23, 1956, in the New York Post *(February 24, 1956).*

Montgomery whites claim not to be able to understand "their" Negroes. Well, I'll be glad to explain "their" Negroes are sick and tired of segregation, of the insults and mistreatment and daily humiliations. It's that simple. Their cups have run over.

Roy Wilkins, NAACP president, statement of February 23, 1956, in the Associated Press (February 24, 1956).

I feel sure we will win in the end. It might take plenty of sacrifice, but I don't think we'll ever again take such humiliating treatment as dished out by bus drivers in this city.

Rosa Parks, statement of February 1956, in the [Baltimore] Afro-American *(March 3, 1956).*

The Rosa Parks incident was completely spontaneous. You have to know the history of how people have been treated on the buses. Buses have been the sorest spot in Montgomery.

Fred D. Gray, black attorney representing Rosa Parks, statement of February 1956, in Newsweek *(March 5, 1956).*

Up until the indictment was handed down by the Montgomery County Grand Jury, there was a local problem growing out of the spontaneous resentment of the people. Now it has become our case and we intend to fight it.

Thurgood Marshall, NAACP special counsel, statement of February 1956, in the Chicago Defender *(February 23, 1956).*

There are those who would try to make of this a hate campaign. This is not a war between the white and the Negro but a conflict between justice and injustice. This is bigger than the Negro race revolting against white. We are seeking to improve not the Negro of Montgomery but the whole of Montgomery.

If we are arrested every day, if we are exploited every day, if we are trampled over every day, don't ever let anyone pull you so low as to hate them. We must use the weapon of love. We must have compassion and understanding for those who hate us.

We must realize so many people are taught to hate us that they are not totally responsible for their hate. But we stand in life at midnight, we are always on the threshold of a new dawn.

Martin Luther King Jr., to a mass meeting at the Dexter Avenue Baptist Church, speech of February 23, 1956, in Branch's Parting the Waters *(1988).*

They tell us here in the South, "go North, if you don't like it here." But we say we don't want to go North. This is our home, right here. We want to enjoy the fruit of our labor and our suffering. And they just don't understand.

Ralph Abernathy, statement of February 24, 1956, in the New York Herald Tribune *(February 25, 1956).*

I learned this morning from reliable sources that there is some indication that the bombing of the [Martin Luther] King [Jr.] and [E. D.] Nixon homes was not the work of irresponsible youth or cranks, but had the support of powerful vested interests in the community. There is some evidence that even the dynamite used passed through the hands of some people in the community who should be responsible for the maintenance of order.

Bayard Rustin, activist and writer, diary entry of February 27, 1956, in Liberation *(April 1956).*

The spontaneous mass revolt of Montgomery, Alabama Negroes at riding local jim-crow buses is further proof of the Negro's humiliating experience every time he rides a bus in the South. The experience shocks their bodies and shrivels their souls. It is irritating, demeaning, and often insufferable when bus drivers, as they frequently are in the Deep South, turn out to be vicious brutes. The very idea of separating citizens on public transportation by "race" in a democracy is repugnant in itself!

The Crisis, NAACP magazine, editorial of March 1956.

We are moving on to vict'ry
With hope and dignity.
We shall all stand together
Till every one is free.
We know love is the watchword
For peace and liberty
Black and white, all our brothers
To live in harmony.

Montgomery bus boycotters song, to the tune of the spiritual "Give Me That Old-Time Religion."

42,000 Walk.

The [Baltimore] Afro-American *headline of March 3, 1956, on the Montgomery bus boycott.*

They come and they sit in sparse barns like Bethel Baptist Church, with signs of their poverty and weakness all around them, and they sing the assurance of ultimate peace in victory. The most hostile white man who came to watch them had to confess that they are better led and surer of the end than he is. The deep South has come face to face with the cruel fact that one side possesses the privileges and the other all the saints.

Murray Kempton, journalist, article of March 6, 1956, in the New York Post.

They can threaten us. They can jail us. They can even kill us, but they'll never be able to pick us up and put us back on the buses.

Anonymous, Montgomery bus boycotter, statement of March 1956, in the Pittsburgh Courier *(March 31, 1956).*

We are all indebted to the Negroes of Montgomery. They say that they are confident of ultimate victory. In a sense, they have already won. They have given us a magnificent case study of the circumstances under which the philosophy of Thoreau and Gandhi can triumph. Moreover, the boycott movement has brought something new into the lives of the Negroes of Montgomery. They would loath to give it up. Whenever the boycott ends, it will be missed.

L. D. Reddick, Alabama State College history professor, article of March 15, 1956, in Dissent.

There are as many Yankee reporters dropping off planes and trains as there were carpetbaggers in the 1860s.

T. R. Waring, Charleston News & Courier *reporter, statement of March 1956, on the press coverage of the Montgomery bus boycott, in* Newsweek *(April 2, 1956).*

The amazing thing about our movement is that it is a protest of the people. It is not a one-man show. It's the people. The masses of this town who are tired of being trampled on are responsible.

Jo Ann Robinson, MIA leader and Alabama State University professor, statement of March 1956, in the [Baltimore] Afro-American *(March 10, 1956).*

If you don't get on them buses and pay them your fare and sit where we tell you, there may be violence, that is we might get mad and burn a cross somewhere or the first time we see a colored girl by herself, a gang of us will chase her and call her names and . . .

Anonymous, White Citizens' Council member, telephone conversation of March 1956, in the [Baltimore] Afro-American *(March 3, 1956).*

This will not mar or diminish in any way my interest in the protest. We will continue to protest in the same spirit of non-violence and passive resistance, using the weapon of love.

Martin Luther King Jr., statement of March 22, 1956, following his conviction for violating Alabama's antiboycott law, in the Greensboro [North Carolina] Daily News *(March 23, 1955).*

Behold the King! Long live the King!

Montgomery bus boycotters, chant of March 22, 1956, as Martin Luther King Jr. left the Montgomery County Courthouse after his conviction for violating the 1921 Alabama statute forbidding boycotts, in Newsweek *(April 2, 1956).*

Ralph Abernathy (left) shakes hands with Martin Luther King Jr. as a crowd of supporters cheer for King, who had just been found guilty of leading the Montgomery bus boycott, March 22, 1956. Coretta Scott King is center. Courtesy of AP/Wide World Photos.

There is now no rational basis upon which the separate but equal doctrine can be validly applied to public carrier transportation within the city of Montgomery and its police jurisdiction.

U.S. district court at Montgomery, Alabama, majority opinion of June 5, 1956.

U.S. Court Voids
Bus Segregation
In Montgomery.

The New York Times, headline of June 6, 1956.

There is no doubt that an end of segregation seating arrangements on public conveyances in the city of Montgomery will effect a dramatic change in the habits of the people . . . The commissioner is of the opinion that every step possible should be taken to prevent such a change.

Montgomery Mayor W. A. Gayle, statement of June 1956, in the [Baltimore] Afro-American (June 30, 1956).

Where segregation exists we must be willing to rise up en masse and protest courageously against it. I realize that this type of courage means suffering and sacrifice. It might mean going to jail. If such is the case we must honorably fill up the jailhouses of the South. It might even lead to physical death. But if such physical death is the price that we must pay to free our children from a life of permanent psychological death, then nothing could be more honorable. This is really the meaning of the method of passive resistance. It confronts physical force with an even stronger force, soul force.

Martin Luther King Jr., to the annual NAACP convention in San Francisco, speech of July 27, 1956, "The Montgomery Story," in U.S. News & World Report (August 3, 1956).

The United States Supreme today affirmed a decision of a special three-judge U.S. District Court in declaring Alabama's state and local laws requiring segregation on buses unconstitutional.

The Associated Press, news dispatch of November 13, 1956.

We have been going to the back of the bus for so long there is danger that we instinctively will go straight back there again and perpetuate segregation. Just sit down where a seat is convenient . . . I would be terribly disappointed if any of you go back to the bus bragging, "We, the Negroes, won a victory 'over the white people' " . . . I hope nobody will go back with undue arrogance. If you do, our struggle will be lost all over the South. Go back with humility and meekness.

Martin Luther King Jr., to a group of Montgomery bus boycotters, speech of November 13, 1956, following the U.S. Supreme Court's decision that invalidated Montgomery's bus segregation law, in Time (November 26, 1956).

> If cursed, do not curse back.
> If pushed, do not push back.
> If struck, do not strike back.
> Do not get up from your seat.

MIA leaflet distributed to bus boycotters following the U.S. Supreme Court's November 13, 1956 decision that invalidated Montgomery's bus segregation law.

Wherever the Klans may march, no matter what the White Citizens' Councils may want to do, we are not afraid because God is on our side.

Reverend S. S. Seay, Montgomery bus boycotter, statement of November 15, 1956, in the Alabama Journal (November 16, 1956).

Supreme Court Bans Jim-Crow Bus
Montgomery Boycott To End.

Cleveland Call and Post, black newspaper, headline of November 17, 1956.

Any attempt to enforce this decision will inevitably lead to bloodshed and riot. I don't think the white people of Montgomery will ever submit to this. As far as I'm concerned, they can move the Montgomery City Lines, lock, stock, and barrel, to Washington, D.C.

Luther Ingalls, Montgomery White Citizens' Council leader, statement of November 1956, in the Pittsburgh Courier (November 24, 1956).

This decision in the bus case has had a tremendous impact on the customs of our people here in Montgomery. It is not an easy thing to live under a law recognized as constitutional for these many years and then have it suddenly overturned on the basis of psychology . . .

The City Commission, and we know our people are with us in this determination, will not yield one inch, but will do all in its power to oppose integration of the Negro race with the white race in Montgomery, and will forever stand like a rock against social equality, intermarriage, and mixing of the races under God's creation and plan.

Montgomery city commissioners, statement of December 18, in the Montgomery Advertiser *(December 18, 1956).*

They'll find that all they've won in their year of praying and boycotting is the same lousy service I've been getting every day.

Anonymous, white Montgomery bus rider, statement of December 1956, in Time *(December 31, 1956).*

This is the time that we must evince calm dignity and wise restraint. Emotions must not run wild. Violence must not come from any of us, for if we become victimized with violent intents, we will have walked in vain, and our twelve months of glorious dignity will be transformed into an eve of gloomy catastrophe. As we go back to the buses let us be loving enough to turn an enemy into a friend. We must now move from protest to reconciliation. It is my firm conviction that God is working in Montgomery. Let all men of goodwill, both Negro and white, continue to work with Him. With this decision we will be able to emerge from the bleak and desolate midnight of man's inhumanity to man to the bright and glittering daybreak of freedom and justice.

Martin Luther King Jr., to a mass meeting at St. John A.M.E. Church, speech of December 20, 1956, in King's Stride Toward Freedom *(1958).*

For the first time in this "cradle of the Confederacy" all the Negroes entered buses through the front door. They sat in the first empty seats they saw, in the front of the buses and in the rear. They did not get up to give a white passenger a seat. And whites sat with Negroes.

George Barrett, journalist, article of December 22, 1956, on the first day of desegregated buses in Montgomery on December 21, 1956, in the New York Times.

We are glad to have you this morning.

Anonymous, Montgomery City Bus Lines driver, to Martin Luther King Jr., E. D. Nixon, Ralph Abernathy and Glenn Smiley, greeting of December 21, 1956, in King's Stride Toward Freedom *(1958).*

I figure if they stay in their place and leave me alone, I'll stay in my place and leave them alone.

Anonymous, white Montgomery bus passenger, statement of December 21, 1956, in the New York Post *(December 22, 1956).*

It is an historic occasion. I have hopes that it will grow into a greater peace and harmony between the races.

Martin Luther King Jr., statement of December 21, 1956, in the New York Amsterdam News *(December 29, 1956).*

Now this school mixing stuff, that'll be coming next, and I'm telling you . . . that's sure where we're gonna draw our line.

Anonymous, white Montgomery resident, statement of December 1956, in Barrett's New York Times Magazine *article of December 16, 1956.*

I went to bed many nights scared to death by threats against myself and my family. I could not sleep and I didn't know where to turn . . . There in my kitchen, almost out of nowhere, I heard a voice say, "Preach the gospel, stand up for the truth, stand up for righteousness." Since that morning I can stand up without fear. Tell Montgomery they can keep shooting and I am going to stand up to them. If I die tomorrow morning, I would die happy because I've seen the mountain top.

Martin Luther King Jr., to his congregation at the Dexter Avenue Baptist Church, sermon of January 28, 1957, in Walton's The Negro History Bulletin *article of April 20, 1957.*

5. The Crisis at Central High: 1957–1959

A Moderate Southern City

Little Rock, Arkansas was a city of the New South. By the mid-1950s, it had earned a reputation as a progressive community. It had a racially moderate mayor, congressman and newspaper, the *Arkansas Gazette*. The *Gazette*, one of the South's oldest and most respected newspapers, edited by Harry Ashmore, supported integration through its editorial policy. At the university level, Little Rock had begun to desegregate its schools as early as the late 1940s. About half of the student body at the city's University of Arkansas Graduate Center was black. By the early 1950s, its libraries, parks and public buses had all been integrated.

Despite these changes, Little Rock, like many Southern communities, was still fundamentally a socially and institutionally segregated town. But this city of a little over 105,000, of which 82,000 were white and 25,000 were black, was making progress in diminishing established racial patterns and attitudes.

Only five days after the Supreme Court had handed down its desegregation decision in *Brown v. Board of Education* in 1954, the Little Rock school board announced, "It is our responsibility to comply with federal constitutional requirements, and we intend to do so when the Supreme Court of the United States outlines the methods to be followed." It appeared unlikely that Little Rock would become the battleground for a fight over school integregation.

The Blossom Plan

During the interval between the two Supreme Court *Brown* decisions, Virgil T. Blossom, Little Rock's superintendent of schools, drafted a plan for implementing desegregation on a gradual basis. By the fall of 1954, his program, known as the Blossom Plan, was being explained in meetings with black and white teachers and administrators. Blossom proposed to begin with two new high schools that were scheduled to open in the fall of 1956. The next year the junior high schools would be integrated, and finally, the grade schools would be desegregated, at an unspecified date.

In May 1955, a few days before the Supreme Court handed down its *Brown* II decision, which ruled that desegregation need only be implemented "with all deliberate speed," the Little Rock school board adopted a plan that differed substantially from Blossom's original. This revised plan, known as the Little Rock Phase Program, provided for limited integration for only one high school, Little Rock Central, which was nationally recognized as one of the nation's best. It also delayed integrating Central until September 1957 and permitted only a handful of black students to join the student body of about 2,000 white students.

The location of the all-white Hall High School on the west side of town, where many of Little Rock's prominent and influential professional and business people resided, would be unaffected by the integration program for an unspecified time.

A second phase of the plan would open the junior high schools to a few blacks by 1960. No specific date for integrating the elementary schools was established, but the fall of 1963 was considered a real possibility. A final provision permitted students to transfer out of districts where their race was a minority, which virtually meant that integration would not take place at any of the all-black schools.

GOVERNOR ORVAL FAUBUS

Soon after the Supreme Court handed down the *Brown* II decision in May 1955, which set out the standards for guiding the lower federal courts in implementing school desegregation, white opposition to the Phase Program quickly surfaced. Arkansas segregationists called for a state constitutional amendment that would bypass the Court's directives. Robert Erving Brown, president of the segregationist Capital Citizens' Council, a small but vocal organization in Little Rock, told reporters, "The Negroes have ample and fine schools here, and there is no need for this problem except to satisfy the aims of a few white and Negro revolutionaries in the Urban League and the National Association for the Advancement of Colored People."

Although the governor of Arkansas, Orval Faubus, had never been an ardent segregationist and his election in 1954 was even considered a liberal victory, he came out in support of the segregationists. In January 1956, he announced that he could not "be a party to any attempt to force acceptance of change to which the people are so overwhelmingly opposed." Because the governor's term in Arkansas was for only two years, Faubus was forced to continually run for reelection. It is suspected that Faubus supported the hard-line segregationists because he believed he faced a difficult fight for reelection. No gubernatorial incumbent had won a third term in Arkansas in half a century. In response to the political climate, Faubus campaigned as the preeminent defender of white supremacy.

On September 2, 1957, the night before nine black students were to walk through the doors of Central High School, Governor Faubus went on statewide television and said that it would "not be possible to restore or to maintain order . . . if forcible integration is carried out tomorrow," despite the fact that absolutely no Little Rock school administrators anticipated any disturbances. Faubus announced that he was ordering National Guardsmen to surround Central High because of "evidence of disorder and threats of disorder." The guardsmen were to act "not as segregationists or integrationists but as soldiers."

The following day, the first day of school, 250 National Guardsmen stood on the sidewalk outside Central High. On the advice of the Little Rock school board, the black students did not attempt to gain admission. The board then went before a federal district judge, Ronald N. Davies, who was serving in Little Rock temporarily on assignment from North Dakota, and asked for his guidance. Judge Davies ordered the desegregation plan to go into effect "forthwith."

The next morning, Wednesday, September 4, when the nine black students sought to exercise their legal right to attend Central High, the Arkansas guardsmen blocked their entrance. The guardsmen had indeed acted as soldiers, but on the side of the segregationists. An angry mob of whites shouted: "Niggers. Niggers. They're coming. Here they come!" Fifteen-year-old Elizabeth Eckford, one of the "Little Rock nine," recalls, "I tried to see a friendly face somewhere in the mob . . . I looked into the face of an old woman, and it seemed a kind face, but when I looked at her again, she spat on me."

CRISIS AT LITTLE ROCK

The events outside Central High had directly challenged the authority of the federal government. The nation now turned its attention to President Dwight D. Eisenhower, who was constitutionally required to enforce the law of the land. Eisenhower, who did not support the *Brown* decision, was at first reluctant to intervene in Little Rock. At a press conference, he said, "You cannot change people's hearts merely by laws" and added a provocative remark about the white South's

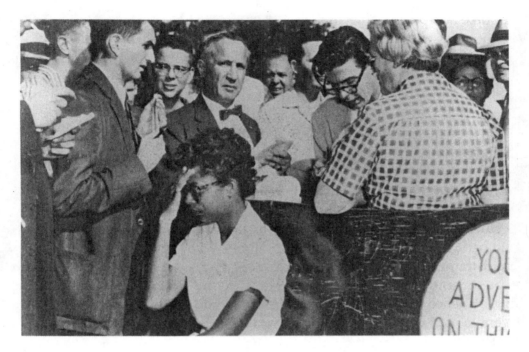

Elizabeth Eckford sits at a bus stop near Central High School, surrounded by a hostile mob. Courtesy of the Arkansas Democrat-Gazette.

concern for the "mongrelization of the races." The Republican president was looking ahead to the 1960 presidential election and did not wish to have the Democratic Party reestablish its grip on the majority of white Southern voters. But he could not simply ignore Faubus' defiance of a federal court. On September 14, to relieve the tension, but only briefly, Faubus met with Eisenhower at Eisenhower's summer home in Newport, Rhode Island.

Eisenhower informed the Arkansas governor that he had no objection to the presence of the National Guard at Central High, but the soldiers should be there to protect the nine black youngsters. Although Faubus appeared agreeable to Eisenhower's view, he suggested that the president defy the federal courts by ordering a one-year delay in the desegregation program. Eisenhower refused to budge, insisting that the federal courts must be obeyed. While it appeared that Faubus was willing to comply, he had an alternative plan in mind.

On September 20, Judge Davies ordered Governor Faubus to stop interfering with school desegregation at Little Rock and to remove the National Guard troops surrounding Central High. That evening, in a statewide television broadcast, Faubus announced his compliance but requested the black students to stay away from the school until he could work out a peaceful integration program. The following Monday, September 23, the Guard was withdrawn, and Governor Faubus already had left the state for a governor's conference in Georgia. But

Arkansas National Guard Colonel Marion Johnson, under Governor Faubus's orders, blocks entry of black students at Central High. Three of the students shown are Carlotta Walls, Gloria Ray and Ernest Green. Courtesy of the Arkansas Democrat-Gazette

by early morning, over a thousand angry white protesters had surrounded Central High.

Segregationists from across the South had flocked to Little Rock. White students sang, "Two, four, six, eight, we ain't gonna integrate," while the mob chanted, "Niggers, keep away from our school." At first unnoticed by the mob, the Little Rock Nine, accompanied by Daisy Bates, president of the Arkansas NAACP chapter, entered the school through a side entrance. Then someone shouted, "The niggers are inside! . . . The niggers are in our school." Local police could barely restrain the hysterical whites outside the school. The crowd began a new chant, "Come on out! Come on out!" Immediately, groups of white students exited from Central High to the crowd's approval. Little Rock's mayor, Woodrow Wilson Mann, fearful of violence, ordered the nine black students to be withdrawn. Daisy Bates told reporters that the black youngsters would not attempt to enter Central High again unless the president assured their protection.

THE 101ST AIRBORNE GOES TO SCHOOL

That evening President Eisenhower denounced the events outside Central High as a "disgraceful occurrence" and declared that a federal court's orders "cannot be flouted with impunity by an individual or mob of extremists." He issued a proclamation ordering those who had obstructed federal law "to cease and desist therefrom and to disperse forthwith." But an even larger mob of segregationists, outnumbering the Little Rock police, assembled outside Central High the next morning. Little Rock's mayor telephoned the U.S. Justice Department and formally requested the aid of the federal government.

On September 24, 1957, President Eisenhower acted. He ordered 1,000 troops from the 101st Airborne Division to Little Rock and federalized 10,000 members of the Arkansas National Guard. For the first time since Reconstruction, federal troops were dispatched to the South to protect the rights of black American citizens.

By 5:00 A.M., paratroopers had ringed the school, with bayonets fixed. The Little Rock Nine met at Daisy Bates' house that morning to be escorted to their classes by the federal troops. At first, the black students found it hard to believe that the soldiers with thick Southern accents were going to provide them with protection. But that is exactly what they did that morning and for the next two months. After the 101st Airborne was withdrawn from Little Rock in November, federalized Arkansas guardsmen continued to patrol Central High for the rest of the year.

INSIDE CENTRAL HIGH

The military presence at Central High did not prevent hard-line segregationists from harassing the Little Rock Nine. Throughout the school year, anonymous telephone callers to the parents of the black youngsters threatened to shoot their children with acid-filled water pistols. This never came to pass, but the nine did have to contend with verbal assaults every day. Ernest Green recalls that they were continuously called, "Nigger, nigger, nigger."

When Minniejean Brown was expelled in February 1958 for calling a white girl "white trash" after she was denounced as a "nigger bitch," segregationist students circulated a card that read "One Down, Eight to Go." Minniejean Brown moved to New York City, entered the private Lincoln School and graduated high in her class a year later.

On May 29, 1958, Ernest Green became the first black student to graduate from Central High. Although Little Rock police officers and federal troops stood guard as Green and 601 of his classmates received their diplomas, there were no disturbances. Ernest Green recalls that graduation day, "When they called my name, there was nothing, just the name, and then there was eerie silence. Nobody clapped. But I figured they didn't have to . . . because after I got that diploma, that was it. I had accomplished what I had come there for."

"Evasive Schemes" Are Unconstitutional

Eisenhower's decisive actions at Central High did not deter ardent segregationists, including Governor Faubus, from resisting integration in Little Rock's public schools. In response to these outside pressures, the Little Rock school board had earlier asked federal district Judge Harry J. Lemley of Arkansas to suspend the integration plan for two and one-half years because of the "unfavorable community attitude."

On June 27, 1958, Judge Lemley granted the request of the school board. He ruled that the tensions in Central High were "intolerable," and enforcing desegregation would have to be delayed. The NAACP immediately filed an appeal to the U.S. Supreme Court on behalf of the black children of Little Rock.

The Little Rock case, *Cooper v. Aaron* (William G. Cooper was a school board member; John Aaron was one of the black students), was argued before the Court in a special session on August 28, 1958. Although the Court did not decide the case that day, the questions by the justices indicated their leanings. Richard C. Butler, attorney for the Little Rock school board, argued that desegregation should be postponed until a clearer "national policy could be established."

Chief Justice Earl Warren asked Butler sharply, "Suppose every other school board in the South said the same thing: 'We'll postpone this thing until the law is clarified.' How would it ever be clarified? . . . Can we defer a program of this kind merely because there are elements in the community that will commit violence to prevent it from going into effect?"

On September 29, 1958, the Court filed its opinion unanimously, saying that ". . . the Constitutional rights of children not to be discriminated against in school admission on grounds of race or color declared by this court in the *Brown* case can neither be nullified openly and directly . . . nor nullified indirectly . . . through evasive schemes for segregation."

Two days before the Court's decision, Governor Faubus had ordered all public schools closed in Little Rock. He then aided a small group of hardline segregationists in setting up the Little Rock Private School Corporation, which attempted to lease the public schools on a segregated basis. Little Rock's public schools remained closed throughout the 1958–59 school term. White students enrolled in private schools, some attended school outside the city, and others did not attend any school. Most of the blacks enrolled in segregated county public schools just outside Little Rock.

On June 18, 1959, a three-judge federal court unanimously ruled that Faubus' scheme of leasing public schools to private corporations was unconstitutional. Two months later, on August 12, Elizabeth Eckford, who had courageously walked through the mob at Central High School two years earlier, enrolled without any incident. There was a mob present, but this time the Little Rock police strictly enforced the law and maintained order. Token desegregation of Little Rock's public schools was accomplished peacefully.

The crisis at Central High School focused the nation's attention on the question of civil rights and the enforcement of the 1954 *Brown* decision. Its effects would ripple across the nation and influence the growing civil rights movement.

CHRONICLE OF EVENTS

1957

August 27–30: A temporary injunction against integration is granted to the Mothers' League for Central High School, a segregationist organization in Little Rock, Arkansas. The school board is granted a stay of the injunction.

August 29: Congress passes the Civil Rights Act of 1957, the first federal civil rights legislation since 1875. It establishes a civil rights division at the Justice Department and a national Commission on Civil Rights. The act provides penalties for the violation of the voting rights of any United States citizen.

September 2: Arkansas Governor Orval Faubus announces that he intends to call out the state's National Guard to surround Central High School the next day.

September 3: Federal Judge Ronald N. Davies orders implementation of the desegregation plan "forthwith" for Central High School in Little Rock, Arkansas.

September 4: Arkansas National Guardsmen block the entrance of nine black students to Central High School.

September 9: Judge Davies directs the U.S. Justice Department to file an injunction against Governor Faubus to force immediate compliance with the desegration order.

September 10: The United States Justice Department files a petition for an injunction against Governor Faubus to force his immediate compliance with Judge Davies' desegregation order. Governor Faubus accepts summons for trial on September 20 but refuses to remove the National Guard from Central High School.

September 14: President Dwight D. Eisenhower meets with Governor Faubus in Newport, Rhode Island to discuss preventing further violence and to bring about desegregation of Arkansas public schools.

September 20: At the injuction hearing of Governor Faubus, Judge Davies orders Faubus to remove the Arkansas National Guard troops from Central High. Faubus announces his compliance in a televised speech but asks blacks to stay away from the high school until he can arrange for peaceful desegregation.

September 23: Black students are admitted to Central High School but are withdrawn after a few hours following riots by white students.

September 24: President Eisenhower announces in a nationwide televised address that he is sending U.S. Army troops from the 101st Airborne Division to Little Rock to enforce the federal order to desegregate Central High.

September 25: Federal troops escort nine black students to classes at Central High.

September 31: The 101st Airborne troops withdraw from Central High to Camp Robinson, 12 miles away, leaving the federalized Arkansas National Guard to ensure order.

November 27: Last of the U.S. Army 101st Airborne troops withdraw from Little Rock.

December 17: Minniejean Brown, one of the nine black Central High students, drops a bowl of chili on a white boy in the school cafeteria after he blocks her path. She is suspended for three days.

1958

February 17: Minniejean Brown, one of the nine black Central High students, is expelled by the Little Rock School Board for calling a white girl "white trash." Three white students are suspended for exhibiting printed cards that read "One Down, Eight to Go."

February 20: Little Rock School Board files in federal district court a request for permission to postpone integration for the next two and one-half years.

May 29: Ernest Green becomes the first black to graduate from Little Rock Central High School.

June 27: Federal Judge Harry Lemley grants a postponement of integration at Little Rock for two and one-half years.

August 18: U.S. Court of Appeals for the Eighth Circuit overrules Judge Lemley's inte-

The Little Rock Nine are escorted into Central High by U.S. troops sent to protect them, September 27, 1957. Courtesy of the National Archives.

gration postponement for Little Rock's public schools.

September 27: Little Rock votes against integration: 19,470 against, 7,561 for. Public schools are closed.

September 29: U.S. Supreme Court, in *Cooper v. Aaron,* denies Faubus' claim that "state officials have no duty to obey [the] federal court." It rules that "evasive schemes" cannot be used to circumvent integration.

October 25: Ten thousand students, led by Jackie Robinson, Harry Belafonte and A. Philip Randolph, hold a Youth March for Integrated Schools rally in Washington, D.C.

November 12: Little Rock school board resigns, and schools remain closed.

1959

January: Courts overrule closing of Virginia schools. Virginia Governor J. Lindsay Almond Jr. reopens schools. Prince Edward County, Virginia board of supervisors abandons school system; it stays closed until 1963.

June 18: A three-judge federal court unanimously rules that Arkansas laws permitting the leasing of public schools to private corporations is unconstitutional.

August 12: Little Rock public high schools reopen and are integrated in accordance with federal requirements. Four black students attend Central High.

September 7: Segregationists bomb the Little Rock school board office. There are no injuries.

Eyewitness Testimony

I was covered with shattered glass . . . I reached for the rock lying in the middle of the floor. A note was tied to it. I broke the string and unfolded a soiled piece of paper. Scrawled in bold print were the words: "Stone this time. Dynamite next."

Daisy Bates, president of NAACP Arkansas chapter, recalling the atmosphere in Little Rock in August 1957, two weeks before school integration was to begin, in The Long Shadow of Little Rock *(1962).*

The integration program will work. Our people will be reasonable.

Dr. Virgil Blossom, superintendant of Little Rock public schools, statement of August 31, 1957, in the New York Times *(September 1, 1957).*

This is a time for testing for all of us. Few of us are entirely happy over the necessary developments in the wake of the changes in the law. But certainly we must recognize that the School Board is simply carrying out its clear duty—and is doing so in the ultimate best interests of all the school children of Little Rock, white and colored alike. We are confident that the citizens of Little Rock will demonstrate on Tuesday for the world to see that we are a law-abiding people.

The Arkansas Gazette, *editorial of September 1, 1957.*

The mission of the State Militia is to maintain or restore order and to protect the lives and property of citizens. They will act not as segregationists or integrationists, but as soldiers called to active duty to carry out their assigned tasks.

But I must state here in all sincerity, that it is my opinion—yes, even a conviction—that it will not be possible to restore or to maintain order and protect the lives and property of the citizens if forcible integration is carried out tomorrow in the schools of this community. The inevitable conclusion, therefore, must be that the schools in Pulaski County, for the time being, must be operated on the same basis as they have been operated in the past . . .

Governor Orval Faubus, to the people of Arkansas, television address of September 2, 1957, in Southern School News *(October 1957).*

If the Supreme Court is to be defied this way we are getting back to Civil War conditions.

Wiley Braton, NAACP attorney, statement of September 3, 1957, in the New York Times *(September 4, 1957).*

If it were not for my own respect for due process of law, I would be tempted to issue an executive order interposing the city of Little Rock between Governor Faubus and the Little Rock school board.

The people of Little Rock recently had a school board election and elected by an overwhelming vote the school board members who advocated a projected court-approved Little Rock plan [of gradual integration].

The governor has called out the National Guard to put down trouble when none existed. He did so without a request from those of us who are directly responsible for preservation of peace and order. The only effect of his action is to create tension where none existed.

Little Rock Mayor Woodrow W. Mann, statement of September 3, 1957, in Southern School News *(October 1957).*

You are being watched! Today the world is watching you, the students of Central High. They want to know what your reactions, behavior and impulses will be concerning a matter now before us. After all, as we see it, it settles now to a matter of interpretation of law and order.

Will you be stubborn, obstinate, or refuse to listen to both sides of the question? Will your knowledge of science help you determine your action or will you let customs, superstition or tradition determine the decision for you?

This is the chance that the youth of America has been waiting for. Through an open mind, broad outlook, wise thinking and a careful choice you can prove that America's youth has not "gone to the dogs," that their moral, spiritual and educational standards are not being lowered. This is the opportunity for you as citizens of Arkansas and students of Little Rock Central High to show the world that Arkansas is a progressive, thriving state of wide-awake alert people.

Jane Emery, coeditor of the Tiger, Central High School student newspaper, article of September 1957, in Blossom's *It Has Happened Here (1959).*

Two, four, six, eight,
We ain't gonna integrate!

*Chant by a few groups of white students outside
Central High School in Little Rock, Arkansas,
September 3, 1957.*

Now, time and again a number of people—I, among them—have argued that you cannot change people's hearts merely by laws. Laws presumably express the conscience of a nation and its determination or will to do something. But the laws here are to be executed gradually, according to the dictum of the Supreme Court, and I understand that the plan worked out by the school board of Little Rock was approved by the district judge.

Now there seems to have been a road block thrown in the way of that plan, and the next decision will have to be by the lawyers and jurists.

*President Dwight D. Eisenhower, to the press,
statement of September 3, 1957, in* The Public
Papers of the Presidents of the United
States *(1958).*

Little Rock arose yesterday to gaze upon the incredible spectacle of an empty high school surrounded by National Guard troops called out by Governor Faubus to protect life and property against a mob that never materialized.

Mr. Faubus says he based this extraordinary action on reports of impending violence. Dozens of local reporters and national correspondents worked through the day yesterday without verifying the few facts the governor offered to explain why his appraisal is so different from that of local officials—who have asked for no such action . . .

Federal Judge Ronald N. Davies last night accepted the governor's statement at face value, and ordered the School Board to proceed on the assumption that the National Guard would protect the right of the nine enrolled Negro children to enter high school without interference.

Now it remains for Mr. Faubus to decide whether he intends to pose what could be the most serious constitutional questions to face the national government since the Civil War . . .

*Harry S. Ashmore, executive editor of the Ar-
kansas Gazette, editorial of September 4,
1957.*

The first Negro applicant to try to enroll at Little Rock Central High School yesterday, Elizabeth Eckford, 15, was twice blocked from entering the grounds,

walked calmly down two blocks, then sat out 35 minutes of vocal abuse while waiting for a bus to go home . . .

When she approached the Guardsmen at the corner, they drew together and blocked her entrance to the sidewalk. She crossed the street and started walking south on Capitol Avenue across the street from the front of the school. Before she had taken 25 steps she cut into the street and walked back to the line of Guardsmen. It was then that a crowd of 200 saw her and rushed into the scene.

The girl, silent and looking straight ahead, walked at a brisk pace down the line of troops. The crowd walked along with her and began a stream of cat-calling.

The Arkansas Gazette, *on the events at Central High School on September 4, 1957, in an
article of September 5, 1957.*

I have reason to believe that the telephone lines to the Arkansas executive mansion have been tapped—I suspect the federal agents. The situation in Little Rock and Arkansas grows more explosive by the hour. This is caused for the most part by the misunderstanding of our problems by a federal judge who decreed "immediate integration of the public schools of Little Rock" without hearing any evidence whatsoever as to the conditions now existing in this community . . . If these actions continue, or if my executive authority as governor to maintain the peace is breached, then I can no longer be responsible for the results. The injury to persons and property that would be caused—the blood that may be shed will be on the hands of the federal government and its agents . . . As governor of Arkansas I appeal to you to use your good offices to modify the extreme stand and stop the unwarranted interference of federal agents . . .

*Governor Orval Faubus, to President Eisen-
hower, telegram of September 4, 1957, in*
Southern School News *(October 1957).*

There is no basis of fact to the statements you make in your telegram that Federal authorities have been considering taking you into custody or that telephone lines to your Executive Mansion have been tapped by any agency of the Federal Government.

At the request of Judge Davies, the Department of Justice is presently collecting facts as to interference with or failure to comply with the District Court's

Elizabeth Eckford being turned away from Central High on September 4, 1957. Courtesy of the Arkansas Democrat-Gazette.

order. You and other state officials—as well as the National Guard which, of course, is uniformed, armed and partially sustained by the Government—will, I am sure, give full cooperation to the United States District Court.

President Eisenhower, to Governor Faubus, telegram of September 5, 1957, in The Public Papers of the Presidents of the United States *(1958).*

It is time for the Negro mass to do its own thinking and stop being misled by professional exploiters. The day of vote selling has passed.

What the Negro needs to do now is to busy himself, and qualify as many Negroes as possible during the next few weeks. And then when time arrives for officers to be selected to head the affairs of our state, we will be in position to weed out the undesirables.

The Arkansas State Press, *black weekly newspaper, editorial of September 6, 1957.*

Q: How long do you think this tension is going to last?
A: It's up to Governor Faubus.
Q: If you had your say, speaking personally, the Negro students could come to the school tomorrow?
A: Sir, it's the law. We are going to have to face it sometime.
Q: Do you think the day is going to come when your school is going to be integrated?
A: Yes.
Q: Are you opposed to integration yourself?
A: If it's a court order we have to follow it and abide by the law.
Q: Would you mind sitting next to a Negro in school?
A: No . . .

From a Mike Wallace television interview with Ralph Brodie, president of Little Rock's Central High School student body, in the Arkansas Gazette *(September 10, 1957).*

I am sure it is the desire of the Governor not only to observe the supreme law of the land but to use the influence of his office in orderly progress of the plans which are already the subject of the Court.

President Eisenhower, statement of September 14, 1957, in The Public Papers of the Presidents of the United States *(1958).*

I have assured the President of my desire to co-operate with him in carrying out the duties resting upon both of us under the Federal Constitution. In addition, I must harmonize my actions under the Constitution of Arkansas with the requirements of the Constitution of the United States.

Governor Orval Faubus, statement of September 14, 1957, in The Public Papers of the Presidents of the United States *(1938).*

In the last few hours three events of major importance have occurred in the City of Little Rock.

1. The Governor of Arkansas has withdrawn the contingent of Arkansas National Guard at Central High School.

2. The Little Rock School Board has announced its intention to proceed to carry into effect its plans for school admissions.

3. The local law enforcement agencies have announced that they are prepared to maintain law and order.

The sincere and conscientious efforts of the citizens of Little Rock prior to September second show that they are persons of good will and feel a responsibility to preserve and respect the law—whether or not they personally agree with it. I am confident that they will vigorously oppose any violence by extremists.

All parents must have a sympathetic understanding of the ordeal to which the nine Negro children who have been prevented from attending Central High School have been subjected. They and their parents have conducted themselves with dignity and with restraint. As I said this morning, I am confident that the citizens of the City of Little Rock and the State of Arkansas will welcome this opportunity to demonstrate that in their city and in their state proper orders of a United States Court will be executed promptly and without disorder.

President Eisenhower, statement of September 21, 1957, in The Public Papers of the Presidents of the United States *(1958).*

The big mob at the corner of the school ground caught sight of us approaching and someone said, "Here comes the niggers." They rushed at us. We stopped, and a man told us, "Go back. You're not coming in here. This is our school, and we're not letting any niggers in."

I told him we were not trying to get into school, that we were newsmen. One man said, "They're niggers. Let's kill 'em."

James Hicks, managing editor of the New York Amsterdam News, *dispatch of September 23, 1957, in the Associated Press.*

On the car radio I could hear that there was a mob. I knew what a mob meant and I knew that the sounds that came from the crowd were very angry. So we entered the side of the building, very, very fast. Even as we entered there were people running after us, people tripping other people. Once we got into the school, it was very dark; it was like a deep, dark castle. And my eyesight had to adjust to the fact that there were people all around me. We were met by school officials and very quickly dispersed our separate ways. There has never been in my life any stark terror or any fear akin to that.

Melba Pattillo [Beals], one of nine black students who integrated Central High, recalling September 23, 1957, in Hampton and Fayer's Voices of Freedom *(1990).*

"Look, they're going into the school."

At that instant, the eight Negroes—the three boys and five girls—were crossing the schoolyard toward a side door at the south end of the school. The girls were in bobby sox, and the boys were dressed in shirts open at the neck.

They were not running, not even walking fast. They simply strolled toward the steps, went up and were inside before all but a few of the 200 people at the end of the street knew it . . .

"They've gone in," a man roared. "Oh, God, the niggers are in the school." . . .

"Oh, my God," the woman screamed. She burst into tears and tore at her hair. Hysteria swept the crowd.

Relman Morin, Associated Press correspondent, on the events outside Central High, in a dispatch of September 23, 1957.

My first day inside Central High was very smooth—smoother than I expected. Outside was the main cause. If it wasn't for the people outside, we would have finished the day.

But I don't intend to quit. We'll try again. It's still my school, and I'm entitled to it.

Ernest Green, one of the nine black Central High students, in a New York Post article of September 24, 1959.

If there was trouble at Central High yesterday, it was all on the outside. We didn't have anything at all going on inside.

I got integrated yesterday. It was in my first English class. There was only 15 minutes to go, and a Negro boy came into class.

That was the first time I'd ever gone to school with a Negro, and it didn't hurt a bit.

Robin Woods, Little Rock junior and a member of the Central High Student Council, in a New York Post article of September 24, 1957.

The violence in Little Rock today was inspired and encouraged by one man—Governor Orval E. Faubus. This shameful spectacle stems from his repeated insistance, in public statements and in radio and television pronouncements, that violence was inevitable. He disrupted the groundwork for peaceful integration carefully laid down by the Little Rock Board of Education.

Roy Wilkins, NAACP executive secretary, statement of September 23, 1957, in the NAACP papers.

To make this talk I have come to the President's office in the White House. I could have spoken from Rhode Island, where I have been staying recently, but I felt that, in speaking from the house of Lincoln, of Jackson, and of Wilson, my words would better convey both the sadness I feel in the action I was compelled today to take and the firmness with which I intend to pursue this course until the orders at Little Rock can be executed without unlawful interference. In that city, under the leadership of demagogic extremists, disorderly mobs have deliberately prevented the carrying out of proper orders from a federal court . . . This morning the mob again gathered in front of the Central High School of Little Rock, obviously for the purpose of again preventing the carrying out of the court's order relating to the admission of the Negro children to that school. Whenever normal agencies prove inadequate to the task . . . the president's responsibility is inescapable . . . I have today issued an executive order directing the use of troops under federal authority to aid in the execution of federal law at Little Rock . . . Our personal opinions about the decision have no bearing on the matter of enforcement . . . Mob rule cannot be allowed to override the decisions of our courts . . . [Most southerners] do not sympathize with mob rule. They, like the rest of our nation, have proved in two great wars their readiness to sacrifice for America. And the foundation of the American way of life is our national respect for the law.

President Eisenhower, to the American people, radio and television address of September 24, 1957, in The Public Papers of the Presidents of the United States *(1958).*

I hereby order all persons, who are obstructing the enforcement of the orders of United States District Court for the Eastern District of Arkansas with respect to enrollment and attendance at the public schools of Little Rock, Arkansas, particularly Central High School, to cease and desist from such obstruction forthwith and to disperse and to retire ably to their abodes. I have ordered the troops under my command to take all steps necessary to enforce compliance with this order.

Major General Edwin A. Walker, U.S. Army, 101st Airborne Division, commander of the federal forces, proclamation of September 24, 1957, in the New York Times *(September 25, 1957).*

This is a tragic day in the history of the Republic—and Little Rock, Ark., is the scene of the tragedy.

In one sense we rolled back our history to the Reconstruction Era when Federal troops moved into position at Central High School to uphold the law and preserve the peace. Yet there is no denying the case President Eisenhower made in solemn words on television last night.

Law and order has broken down here . . .

Governor Faubus has refused to enforce the law, and instead had used them to defy the order of a Federal court—and in doing so had made this last painful step inevitable.

The Arkansas Gazette, *editorial of September 25, 1957.*

Sacrificed, ignored, trampled—the rights of a sovereign state! The big steamroller of totalitarian central government—heretofore considered something foreign to America—is now, an established fact in our land.

The Mobile [Alabama] Press, *editorial of September 25, 1957.*

We shall not attempt to argue here the legal authority of the President. That is for lawyers. There is no doubt that he has the military power. So has Soviet Russia the power to put down rebellion in the Ukraine . . .

The President could wipe out the State of Arkansas off the map. But he cannot solve the problem of race with either bombs or bayonets.

If the South again becomes occupied territory as it was for 10 years after the Civil War, the United States Government will have its hands full . . .

The Charleston [South Carolina] News and Courier, editorial of September 25, 1957.

Tremendous power seems to have been concentrated in Washington which overrides without hesitation the safeguards which were thought to be in effect through the sovereign character of the states. It would seem that when the federal government can take over the instrumentalities of the state, such as the National Guard, and use them contrary to the wishes of the state and its people, a blueprint for dictatorship has been established.

The New Orleans Times-Picayune, editorial of September 25, 1957.

A far-reaching and perhaps catastrophic step has been taken by President Eisenhower. Even the small minority [of Southerners] who believe in integration may well stop and ponder whether the President isn't sowing seeds of bitterness that will poison race relations in the South for many years.

The Richmond [Virginia] Times Dispatch, editorial of September 25, 1957.

The President has been patient in his handling of this pocket rebellion by the Governor of Arkansas, with its accompaniment of mob hysteria. But the Federal Constitution and the Law that flows from it are not a mass of empty words. They represent the will of the union, and behind them, rarely resorted to, is the force of the union. A challenge persisted in must be met with force by a Chief Executive loyal to his oath. And that, essentially, is what President Eisenhower said.

The Baltimore Sun, editorial of September 25, 1957.

The events in Little Rock are a sobering spectacle. But the fact that the crisis has been joined is a heartening reminder that the country is moving ahead in pursuit of its ideals of law and justice. We may hope that other nations will keep the situation in perspective even as we ourselves remember that the mobs in the streets do not present a fair picture of the state as a whole or even of the city of Little Rock.

The Washington Post, editorial of September 25, 1957.

No one with the good of our country at heart—and least of all the President—wants to see federal troops in action in this crisis. The wounds resulting from a prolongation of federal military force would add to those already suffered as a result of the shrieking hatreds of the extremists, the incredible folly of Governor Faubus, and the disappointing slowness of the President himself to assume the strong attitude of leadership that he has finally shown in the nick of time.

The New York Times, editorial of September 25, 1957.

The tragedy of Little Rock—and its tragedy is America's—has not been ended by the presence of U.S. troops. The troops have brought back temporarily the law and order that was destroyed by the rashness of a demagogic government and the quiescence of an ineffectual President. But force alone cannot restore the moral foundations of peace on which permanent law and order must be based. These have been battered beyond immediate repair and it may be a long time before this country recovers from the damage.

The New York Post, editorial of September 26, 1957.

It was 9:22 a.m.—40 minutes after the final bell had rung to start the day's classes at Central High.

Racing along Park Street came an olive-drab car—big enough to hold the nine Negro students the U.S. Army was taking to school. Jeeps filled with paratroopers escorted the car.

The cavalcade braked to a stop at the long walk leading up the concrete steps to the main entrance of the school. Three-hundred-fifty soldiers who surrounded the school came to attention.

Paratroopers in full battle dress formed a tight guard around the staff car. The Negro students filed out of the car and started up the walk.

Across the street a group of white students chanted: "Two, four, six, eight—we ain't gonna integrate."

Members of the 101st Airborne Division escort the Little Rock Nine to Central High School, September 27, 1957. Courtesy of the National Archives.

At 9:24 a.m. the Negroes crossed the threshold of the school. With military precision, it had taken the 101st Airborne Division two minutes to integrate Central High.

Anonymous U.S. News & World Report *correspondent, on September 25, 1957, in an article of October 4, 1957.*

The nine Negro pupils marched solemnly through the doors of Central High School, surrounded by 22 [Airborne troops] soldiers. An Army helicopter circled overhead. Around the massive brick schoolhouse 350 paratroopers stood grimly at attention. Scores of reporters, photographers, and tv cameramen made a mad dash for telephones, typewriters, and tv studios, and within minutes a world that had been holding its breath learned that the nine pupils, protected by the might of the U.S. military, had finally entered the "never-never-land."

Daisy Bates, president of NAACP Arkansas chapter, on September 25, 1957, in The Long Shadow of Little Rock *(1962).*

My heart ached Monday after having been taken from Central High School. I wondered just how does this system of law we have work.

Previous to Monday I thought that a few people could not decide against something, against an issue, and thus make a law ineffective. But to my astonishment it had happened. Not calmly or quietly, but with all the thunder of a falling mountain.

But that great thunder came to an end this morning. For I, Melba Patillo, a Negro, had the pride, pleasure and honor of seeing this great America with democracy in action. Just seeing the paratroopers and being escorted into Central High School gave me a feeling which I never experienced before. I shall never experience it again.

Melba Patillo [Beals], one of the nine black Central High students, statement in the New York Post *(September 26, 1957).*

What does all this mean to you students? You have often heard it said, no doubt, that the United States is a nation under law, and not under men. This means we are governed by laws . . . and not by the decrees of one man or one class of men . . . I believe that you are well-intentioned, law-abiding citizens who understand the necessity of obeying the law . . . You have nothing to fear from my soldiers and no one will interfere with your coming, going, or your peaceful pursuit of your studies.

Major General Edwin A. Walker, U.S. Army, 101st Airborne Division, to the student body of Central High School, speech of September 25, 1957, in the San Francisco Chronicle *(September 26, 1957).*

When I got to my English class one boy jumped up to his feet and began to talk. He told the others to walk out with him because a "nigger" was in their class. He kept talking and talking, but no one listened. The teacher told him to leave the room.

The boy started for the door and shouted: "Whose going with me?" No one did. So, he said in disgust, "chicken!" and left.

I had a real nice day.

Melba Pattillo [Beals], one of the nine black Central High School students, statement of September 25, 1957, in the New York Times *(September 26, 1957).*

Things would be better if only the grown-ups wouldn't mix in. The kids have nothing against us. They hear bad things about us from parents.

Ernest Green, one of the nine black Central High School students, statement of September 25, 1957, in the New York Times *(September 26, 1957).*

I went to lunch in school and there was a colored boy sitting alone by himself. That's not right. A white girl and a boy finally asked him to eat with them. That is right.

But they don't want to let you think for yourself. It's the parents who cause all this trouble. It's a problem. We don't know if we like integration. Let us try it. Make the parents go home.

Anonymous Central High student, statement of September 25, 1957, in the New York Post *(September 26, 1957).*

If the parents would just go home and leave us be we'd work this thing out for ourselves.

Anonymous white Central High School student, statement of September 25, 1957, in the New York Times *(September 26, 1957).*

101st Airborne on hand, performing with efficiency . . . Atmosphere more relaxed. Fewer guards accompanied blacks in. No demonstrations by students . . . Lipstick writing, "Nigger go home," on restroom walls. "Central High Mothers" evidently putting on a telephone campaign to scare women from sending their children . . . Some positive items reported, too. Colored and white at one table in the cafeteria at first lunch.

Elizabeth Huckaby, Central High assistant principal, journal entry of September 26, 1957, in Crisis at Central High *(1980).*

We are now an occupied territory. Evidence of the naked force of the Federal Government is here apparent, in these unsheathed bayonets in the backs of schoolgirls . . .

Governor Orval Faubus, to the people of Arkansas, television and radio address of September 26, 1957, in the New York Times *(September 27, 1957).*

Mr. Eisenhower and the Supreme Court have ruled on this segregation issue and in the final analysis, I don't think it can be anything but integration. They don't like it but the responsible people in this town are accepting integration reluctantly. It's only the outside agitators who are causing trouble.

I myself think it has come too fast, but I called my kids together the other day. I've got three of them in school and I said, "Treat those Negro kids nice, like you've always done."

Anonymous white Little Rock businessman, statement of September 1957, in U.S. News & World Report *(October 4, 1957).*

They're not going to get no place trying to shove something down people's throats. Even if they leave the troops at the school, what's to stop someone from sticking his foot out and tripping a nigger down the stairs?

Anonymous Little Rock factory worker, statement of September 1957, in U.S. News & World Report *(October 4, 1957).*

A minority of 300 has wrecked the tranquility of 120,000 people of Little Rock.

Virgil Blossom, superintendant of Little Rock public schools, statement of September 1957, in Newsweek *(October 7, 1957).*

The tragedy of Little Rock demonstrates the folly and danger of politically dictated federal power from Washington attempting to mold the lives and social order of the people of every section of our land into a uniform pattern agreeable to the views of those in control of the national government.

Senator Richard B. Russell (D, Ga.), statement
of September 1957, in U.S. News & World
Report (October 4, 1957).

We still mourn the destruction of the sovereignty
of Hungary by Russian tanks and troops in the streets
of Budapest. We are now threatened with the spectacle of the President of the United States using tanks
and troops in the streets of Little Rock to destroy the
sovereignty of the State of Arkansas.

Senator Herman F. Talmadge (D, Ga.), statement of September 1957, in U.S. News &
World Report (October 4, 1957).

It is time for the South to face up to the fact that
it belongs to the union and comply with the Constitution of the United States.

Senator Wayne Morse (D, Ore.), statement of
September 1957, in U.S. News & World Report (October 4, 1957).

In some states—where people wanted to integrate
but were afraid of trouble—they may go ahead now

The Little Rock Nine. Courtesy of the Schomburg Center for
Research in Black Culture.

that they see they really have the backing of the
federal government . . . In the Deep South, it'll
toughen resistance immeasurably.

Thurgood Marshall, NAACP special counsel,
statement of September 1957, in Newsweek
(October 7, 1957).

We, the parents of the nine colored children who
have enrolled at Little Rock Central High School want
you to know that your actions in safeguarding their
rights have strengthened our faith in democracy.

Parents of the nine black Little Rock children, to
President Dwight D. Eisenhower, telegram of
September 30, 1957, in the [Baltimore] Afro-
American (October 19, 1957).

I believe that America's heart goes out to you and
your children in your present ordeal. In the course
of our country's progress toward equality of opportunity, you have shown dignity and courage in circumstances which would daunt citizens of lesser
faith.

President Eisenhower, to the parents of the nine
black Little Rock students at Central High, personal message of October 4, 1957, in the Baltimore Afro-American (October 19, 1957).

It is not too difficult for a man to stand up and
fight for a cause with which he himself believes to
be right.

But it is quite another thing for a man to stand up
and fight for a cause with which he himself does not
agree but which he feels it is his duty to uphold.

President Eisenhower is a battle scarred veteran of
many a campaign who has been hailed from one end
of the world to the other.

But we submit that his victory over himself at Little
Rock was indeed his finest hour.

The New York Amsterdam News, editorial
of October 5, 1957.

At Money, Mississippi, Negroes stopped grinning.
At Montgomery, Alabama, they stopped running
and learned to walk. Little Rock's wanton attack
upon their young transformed God's long-suffering
child into angry, determined men.

Ebony, editorial of December 1957.

An outsider strolling through the quiet corridors,
finds it difficult to understand why troops are still
needed. But when you talk to students and their
parents, to school authorities and military officials,

you learn that Central High is not as peaceful as it looks.

A relentless campaign is being conducted inside the school to make life so miserable for the Negroes that they will abandon the attempt at integration and "voluntarily" return to Little Rock's all-Negro high school.

Louis Cassel, journalist, article of December 28, 1957, in the World Telegram & Sun.

I just can't take everything they throw at me without fighting back.

I don't think people realize what goes on at Central. You just wouldn't believe it.

They throw rocks, they spill ink on your clothes, they call you "nigger," they just keep bothering you every five minutes.

The white students hate me. Why do they hate me so much? I didn't realize how deep [white trash] affects white people.

Minniejean Brown, one of the nine black Central High students, statement of February 1958, on her expulsion for calling a white girl "white trash," in Southern School News *(March 1958).*

Federal troops continue to occupy Central High— in defiance of the Constitution, law, and precedent— while the Congress of the United States sits out the sessions and does nothing.

Never before in the history of America has any area of our so-called Free Republic been so shamefully treated.

The Arkansas Democrat, *editorial of March 10, 1958.*

How many of us would have had the fortitude to do what these youngsters have done? How often have we failed to take advantage of victories won for us? It is therefore the more remarkable that these young Negroes, living in the Deep South, fearlessly implemented the Court's action by their daily presence at Central High School.

Though their lot was not a happy one even inside the high school building, though they were pushed around, insulted, and beaten by some of the white students, the Negro pupils held their ground. The Supreme Court's integration ruling would have been meaningless had these Negro boys and girls failed to follow the course mapped out for them by the law. They should be applauded by all of us.

The Chicago Defender, *editorial of May 28, 1958.*

Little Rock Central High School peacefully graduated 602 seniors on May 27—one of them a Negro— after eight months and six days of integration protected by federal troops. Local police and the troops gave heavy protection at the graduation ceremonies but only one minor incident occurred . . .

Southern School News, article of June 8, 1958.

The plan of integration . . . has broken down under the pressure of public opposition . . . as a result the educational program at Central High School has been seriously impaired, that there will be no change in conditions between now and the time that school opens again in September, 1958, and if the prayer for relief is not granted the situation with the Board will be confronted in September and will be as bad as, if not worse than the one under which it has labored during the past school year, and that it is in the public interest that the requested delay be granted.

Judge Harry J. Lemley, U.S. District Court at Montgomery, Alabama, opinion of June 20, 1958, granting a two and one-half year postponement of integration at Little Rock public schools, in Race Relations Law Reporter *(August 1958).*

An impossible situation could well develop if the district court's order were affirmed. Every school district in which integration is publicly opposed by overt acts would have "justifiable excuse" to petition the courts for delay and suspension in integration programs. An affirmance of "temporary delay" in Little Rock would amount to an open invitation to elements in other districts to overtly act out public opposition through violent and unlawful means . . . This issue plainly comes down to the question of whether overt public resistance, including mob protest, constitutes sufficient cause to nullify an order of the federal court directing the board to proceed with its integration plan. We say the time has not yet come in these United States when an order of a federal court must be whittled away, watered down, or shamefully withdrawn in the face of violent and unlawful acts of individuals in opposition thereto . . .

Accordingly, the order of the district court is reversed . . .

U.S. Court of Appeals for the Eighth Circuit, opinion of August 18, 1958, reversing Judge Lemley's integration postponement, in Race Relations Law Reporter *(August 1958).*

We are living in a world that can come to an end in less than one hour. The people of this community could conceivably be saved from destruction by colored officers flying our latest inter-continental bombers. While you of Little Rock are showing your hate for the children of a minority group, the same group is ready to lay down their lives for you!

Anonymous white U.S. Air Force captain, Little Rock Air Force base, letter of September 14, 1958, in the Arkansas Gazette.

The Constitutional rights of children not to be discriminated against in school admission on grounds of race or color declared by this court in the Brown case can neither be nullified openly and directly by state legislators or state executives or judicial officers, nor nullified indirectly by them through evasive schemes for segregation whether attempted "ingeniously or ingenuously."

U.S. Supreme Court, unanimous opinion of September 29, 1958, in Cooper v. Aaron, *the Little Rock school desegregation decision.*

The white South is fond of saying, "Don't go too fast," "Don't push," "Don't flood us," "Give us time." Last year at Central High proved they don't mean what they say. If they can't be sincere with nine out of 2,000 they don't intend to be sincere. Some of the great powerful, secure and superior white people of Little Rock and Arkansas apparently are afraid these youngsters and others like them may upset the doctrine of innate Negro inferiority . . .

Gov. Faubus is a valuable enemy. He has aided in many ways in clarifying the issue of segregation. . . .

We must resist the temptation to backslide. Victory is near at hand, nearer than some of us think. The opposition is flopping about, but it knows that it doesn't have a leg to stand on . . . Common sense will take over and Arkansas will rejoin the union.

Roy Wilkins, NAACP executive secretary, to the annual meeting of the Arkansas State Conference of Branches of the NAACP, speech of November 2, 1958, in Southern School News *(December 1958).*

They treated me at Hall like they would any new student. I think I'll like it.

Estella Thompson, one of the second group of black students who integrated Little Rock public high schools, statement of August 12, 1959, in the New York Times *(August 13, 1959).*

6. The Sit-ins and Freedom Rides: 1960–1961

THE SIT-INS

On February 1, 1960, at 4:30 P.M., four black freshmen from North Carolina Agricultural and Technical (A & T) College walked into the local Woolworth's five-and-dime store, purchased toothpaste and some school supplies and then sat down at the lunch counter and demanded equal service with white persons. "I'm sorry," the waitress told them, "we don't serve coloreds in here." "I beg to disagree with you," Ezell Blair Jr. politely replied. "We've in fact already been served; you've already served us at a [store] counter only two feet from here." The waitress then dashed off and ignored the four young men. But instead of leaving, Ezell Blair Jr., Franklin McCain, Joseph McNeil and David Richmond remained seated until the store closed at 5:30 P.M. The following day they returned to the lunch counter, reinforced this time by some 20 fellow students, including four black women from Bennett College. Their sit-in, a form of nonviolent direct action, set in motion the student phase of the civil rights movement.

On the third day of the sit-in, they were joined by three white students from the Women's College of the University of North Carolina campus in Greensboro and scores of supporters from A & T and Bennett. The students occupied 63 of the 66 seats at the lunch counter. Soon they overflowed Woolworth's and began to sit-in at the lunch counter in the S. H. Kress store down the street. The Greensboro sit-in became national news and inspired student sit-ins throughout the South.

Within two weeks, sit-ins were taking place in Virginia and South Carolina, and within two months, the student sit-in movement had spread to 54 cities in nine states. Students in Northern cities also participated in the protest against segregated public facilities. For example, in New York, Woolworth stores were picketed by sympathetic white Columbia University students.

Tension increased in some Southern cities as more and more sit-ins took place. In mid-February, a group of black students from Fisk Uni-

Leaders of the student sit-in at a Woolworth's lunch counter in Greensboro, North Carolina. From left to right: Joseph McNeil, Franklin McCain, Billy Smith and Clarence Henderson. Courtesy of the News & Record, Greensboro, N.C. and John G. Moebes, photographer. Reprinted with permission of the News & Record. This reprint does not constitute or imply any endorsement or sponsorship of any product, service, company or organization.

versity and American Baptist Theological Seminary, supported by some white students from Vanderbilt University, staged a sit-in at a Woolworth's lunch counter in downtown Nashville. James Lawson, a theology student at Vanderbilt, initially led the demonstrators. For the past few years, he had been conducting nonviolent workshops, and he had drawn up these rules: "Do show yourself friendly on the counter at all times. Do sit straight and always face the counter. Don't strike back, or curse back if attacked. Don't laugh out. Don't hold conversations. Don't block entrances." Lawson reminded each student to "remember the teachings of Jesus, Gandhi, Martin Luther King."

As the number of students participating in the sit-in at the Woolworth's in Nashville grew, so did the number of white hecklers. Some taunted the white sympathizers with shouts of "nigger lovers." Others threw french-fried potatoes and gum at the demonstrators. Then on February 27, the situation escalated when a group of white Nashville teenagers attacked the sit-in students and pulled them off their lunch counter seats. None of the students fought back. When the Nashville police arrived, they did not arrest the white teens but arrested the 81 protesters and charged them with "disorderly conduct."

As thousands of students participated in the sit-in movement, such incidents were repeated elsewhere. Some demonstrators were subject to tear gas and billy clubs and were attacked by police dogs. By April, 2,000 people had been arrested, and thousands had marched on state capitols and downtown areas in Alabama, South Carolina, Georgia and Louisiana.

One of the most ambitious demonstrations took place in Atlanta, Georgia. On March 9, a full-page advertisement entitled *An Appeal for Human Rights* appeared in the *Atlanta Constitution*. The advertisement, sponsored by Morris Brown, Clark, Morehouse and Spelman college students, read in part, "Today's youth will not sit by submissively, while being denied all the rights, privileges and joys of life. We want to state clearly and unequivocally that we cannot tolerate, in a nation professing democracy and among people professing Christianity, the discriminatory conditions under which the Negro is living today in Atlanta, Georgia . . . We do not intend to wait placidly for those rights which are already legally and morally ours to be meted out to us one at a time." They demanded an end to segregation in restaurants, movie theaters, concert halls and other public facilities. The students also called for equality in education, housing and healthcare.

On March 15, at precisely 11:00 A.M., some 200 students staged a

Whites pour sugar, ketchup and mustard over the heads of sit-in demonstrators in Jackson, Mississippi. Photograph by Fred Blackwell. Courtesy of AP/Wide World Photos.

well-planned sit-in at the lunch counters and restaurants in the city hall, the state capitol building, the Fulton County Courthouse, two office buildings and the city's bus and train stations. The police arrested 77 of the demonstrators after they demanded service at these facilities. Although numerous meetings took place between the student leaders and the Atlanta business community, no resolution was reached.

THE FORMATION OF THE STUDENT NONVIOLENT COORDINATING COMMITTEE (SNCC)

On Easter weekend, a three-day convention attended by student representatives from Southern black colleges was held at Shaw University in Raleigh, North Carolina. They came to discuss their experiences in the sit-ins and coordinate future activities. The guiding force behind this conference was 55-year-old Ella Baker, the executive director of the Southern Christian Leadership Conference (SCLC).

Baker's opening address, "More Than a Hamburger," concentrated on the need for the students to change the entire social structure, to not only integrate lunch counters. She declared, "The younger generation is challenging you and me, they are asking us to forget our laziness and doubt and fear, and follow our dedication to the truth to the bitter end." Reverend Martin Luther King Jr. was also in attendance, and he echoed Baker's remarks. The sit-in movement, he said, is a "revolt against the apathy and complacency of adults in the Negro community."

The most applause at the conference came after a workshop recommendation advised that demonstrators choose jail over bail. One student declared, "The greatest progress of the American Negro in the future will not be made in Congress or in the Supreme Court; it will come in the jails." The meeting concluded with the formation of a student-run group that would organize the continuing sit-in effort—the Student Nonviolent Coordinating Committee, or SNCC, pronounced "snick."

JAIL OVER BAIL

Throughout the summer of 1960, students in Atlanta planned large-scale sit-ins at the major department stores and organized a boycott of downtown merchants. The fall campaign began on October 19 when Martin Luther King Jr. and 36 students were arrested for trespassing when they sat down at Rich's department store. The demonstrators, including King, declared they would "rather be jailed than bailed."

Atlanta Mayor William B. Harstfield intervened and arranged for a two-month truce. Charges were dropped against the students, and they were released. But King, however, was not granted his freedom. He had been arrested earlier for driving without a Georgia license, and the sit-in arrest was a violation of his probation. (On moving to Atlanta, King had neglected to obtain a Georgia driver's license within the prescribed time.) King was sentenced to four months of hard labor and sent to Reidsville State Prison.

When the news of King's arrest broke, the White House was inundated with demands for federal intervention on behalf of the imprisoned civil rights leader. It was a presidential election year, and King's arrest posed a moral and political challenge for both candidates, Senator John F. Kennedy of Massachusetts and Vice-President Richard M. Nixon. Although Nixon privately requested the Justice Department to determine if King's constitutional rights had been violated, he made no public statement on his arrest. With the election only a few days off and the states of Texas and South Carolina tipped in his favor, Nixon believed he could not afford to offend the white voters in those states.

The opposite reaction occurred within the Kennedy campaign. Harris Wofford Jr., a Notre Dame law professor who was advising Kennedy on minority affairs, suggested that Kennedy call Mrs. Coretta Scott King and express his sympathy. Sargent Shriver, a Kennedy brother-in-law and head of Kennedy's civil rights section, relayed the message to the Democratic candidate.

Mrs. King recalled the brief conversation with Kennedy in her autobiography. Senator Kennedy said, "I want to express to you my concern about your husband. I know this must be very hard for you. I understand you are expecting a baby, and I just wanted you to know that I was thinking about you and Dr. King. If there is anything I can do to help, please feel free to call me." The following morning, the senator's brother and campaign manager, Robert Kennedy, called the judge involved. His efforts persuaded the judge to release King on bail and drop the charges. Although King himself was personally grateful, he made no endorsement. However, King's father, Martin Luther King Sr., announced at his pulpit that Sunday, "Because this man was willing to wipe the tears from my daughter[in-law]'s eyes, I've got a suitcase of votes, and I'm going to take them to Mr. Kennedy and dump them in his lap."

The Kennedy campaign made sure black voters got the message by printing two million copies of a pamphlet detailing the phone calls. The pamphlets were delivered to black churches and schools. Its headline read, "NO COMMENT NIXON vs. A CANDIDATE WITH A HEART—SENATOR KENNEDY."

According to a postelection Gallup poll, Kennedy received 68% of the black vote. It was one of the closest elections in American history—Kennedy won by a margin of two-thirds of 1% of the popular vote.

Civil rights leaders and many student activists had high hopes for the Kennedy administration. In his inaugural address, the 43-year-old president declared that "the torch has been passed to a new generation of Americans." Although Kennedy did not introduce any new civil rights legislation or fulfill his campaign promise to eliminate housing discrimination in federally funded housing projects with an executive order, he did visibly change the federal policy of appointing blacks to government posts.

The courageous actions taken by students, white and black, men and women, would ultimately force the Kennedy administration to take a stand against segregation. By the end of 1960, some 70,000 supporters had participated in sit-ins, picketing, marches and rallies, with thousands more offering financial and moral support. The student sit-ins were a success. In less than six months, the lunch counter at the Woolworth's in Greensboro was open to all races, and on May 10, six Nashville lunch counters opened their doors to blacks. By the end of 1960, hundreds of other stores were no longer segregated.

Sitting down to have a cup of coffee or sitting anywhere in a movie theater may not seem like much today, but in 1960 it epitomized the humiliation of blacks caused by segregation. Demonstrators carried signs that read, "We do not picket just because we want to eat. We can eat at home or walking down the street. We picket to protest the lack of dignity and respect shown us as human beings." The sit-ins sparked a parallel movement against segregation in interstate transportation, the Freedom Rides.

The Freedom Rides

In March 1961, James Farmer, the new national director of the Congress of Racial Equality (CORE), issued a call for volunteers to participate in interracial "Freedom Rides" through the South to test racial discrimination in bus stations and terminals serving interstate travelers. Three months earlier, in December, the Supreme Court in *Boynton v. Virginia* had extended its 1946 (*Morgan v. Virginia*) prohibition against segregation to apply to not only buses and trains but to all terminals.

Civil rights leaders knew that the Supreme Court ruling would be meaningless without enforcement by the executive branch. A ruling from the Interstate Commerce Commission (ICC) would ensure compliance. "Our intention," James Farmer later stated, "was to provoke the southern authorities into arresting us and thereby prod the Justice Department into enforcing the law of the land."

CORE modeled its Freedom Rides of 1961 on those that it had organized in its 1947 "Journey of Reconciliation." Black and white CORE workers had traveled by bus throughout the upper South to test the rights they had won in the courts. Blacks sat at the front of the buses, and whites sat at the rear. With only a few arrests and hardly any violence, the Journey of Reconciliation received little or no attention by the press.

The 1961 Freedom Rides, like the rides in 1947, would also include an integrated group, but this time they would pass through the Deep South and challenge Jim Crow in terminal restaurants, waiting rooms and rest rooms, not only the seating aboard the buses. Also, when arrested, the Freedom Riders pledged to remain in jail rather than pay fines or be bailed out. Besides receiving national publicity from this tactic, Farmer believed that it would "make the maintenance of segregation so expensive for the state and the city that they would come to the conclusion that they could no longer afford it. Fill up the jails, as Gandhi did in India, fill them to bursting if we have to." Farmer envi-

James Farmer, founder of the Congress of Racial Equality (CORE). Courtesy of the Schomburg Center for Research in Black Culture.

sioned the Freedom Rides as a logical continuation of the sit-ins, "putting the movement on wheels, so to speak."

In April 1961, Farmer wrote to President Kennedy to advise him of the proposed CORE Freedom Ride. He included a map outlining the journey and requested that the law be enforced. CORE also informed the FBI, the Justice Department and the bus companies involved. CORE did not receive one reply. On May 4, after three days of training in nonviolent techniques, 13 volunteers—seven black and six whites—boarded two buses in Washington, D.C., bound for Alabama and then Louisiana. They planned to arrive in New Orleans on May 17, the anniversary of the 1954 *Brown* decision.

Among the 13, four were CORE staff members, including Farmer and James Peck, a white pacifist who had been on the Journey of Reconciliation. Most of the blacks had participated in the student sit-in movement. John Lewis, a 21-year-old black divinity student and leader of the Nashville sit-in movement, wrote in his application that he would "give up all if necessary for the Freedom Ride" because human dignity was "the most important thing in [his] life."

The Freedom Riders encountered only minor problems as they rolled through Virginia, North Carolina and Georgia. At the Greyhound terminal in Rock Hill, South Carolina, John Lewis and another rider were attacked by local thugs when they tried to enter the white rest room. Several more isolated incidents of violence or harassment occurred as the Freedom Ride wound its way south. Then on Mother's Day, May 14, the 13 Freedom Riders divided into two groups to travel from Atlanta to Birmingham. The riders braced for danger as their next stop was Anniston, Alabama.

When the Greyhound bus carrying the first group of Freedom Riders pulled into Anniston, it was surrounded by an angry mob of about 200 people who were armed with blackjacks, iron bars, clubs and tire chains. They smashed the Greyhound's windows and slashed its tires. Only the arrival of the police made it possible for the bus to depart, but with the mob in pursuit. About six miles outside of Anniston, the bus tires went flat, and it was forced into a gas station. The angry mob resumed its attack, smashing a window and tossing a firebomb through the rear door. The passengers, including the Freedom Riders, managed to escape before the bus burst into flames. The following day a photograph of the burning bus was on the front pages of almost every U.S. newspaper.

When the Trailways bus carrying the second group of Freedom Riders arrived in Birmingham, a mob of about 30 young men armed with baseball bats, lead pipes and bicycle chains were waiting for them. They beat some of the riders to the point where an FBI informant on the scene reported that he "couldn't see their faces through the blood." Jim Peck required 53 stitches for injuries to his head. Throughout the attack, there were no police within sight. Birmingham's Public Safety

Commissioner Theophilus Eugene ("Bull") Connor told reporters afterward that since it was Mother's Day, most of his men were off duty visiting their mothers. It was later learned from FBI notes that the bureau's informant had alerted his superiors earlier in the week that Connor had promised the Ku Klux Klan 15 minutes to attack the riders, whom he wanted beaten until "it looked like a bulldog got a hold of them." Connor had in fact arranged for Birmingham's police to stay away from the terminal.

Alabama Governor John Patterson made it clear at a press conference that he had no sympathy for the Freedom Riders. He told reporters, "When you go somewhere looking for trouble, you usually find it." He advised the CORE group to "get out of Alabama as quickly as possible." When the Freedom Riders attempted to resume their journey, the bus drivers refused to drive. Reluctantly, the group decided to fly to New Orleans. On May 17, the CORE-sponsored Freedom Ride disbanded. But a new phase of the Freedom Ride was about to emerge.

In Nashville and Atlanta, SNCC leaders quickly convened and agreed that the Freedom Ride should not be abandoned. Diane Nash, a Nashville student movement leader, said years later, "I strongly felt that the future of the movement was going to be cut short. The impression would have been that whenever a movement starts, all [you have to do] is attack it with massive violence and the blacks [will] stop."

Diane Nash and John Lewis organized a new group of about 20 black and white riders who headed for Birmingham from Nashville with the full knowledge of the brutal violence that had recently taken place. When they arrived in Birmingham, the Freedom Riders, along with five sympathizers, were arrested and taken into "protective custody."

Now alarmed by the possibility of further violence, U.S. Attorney General Robert Kennedy tried in vain to telephone Alabama Governor John Patterson. President Kennedy had previously called Patterson after the assault on the Freedom Riders at the Birmingham bus terminal, but Patterson would not take the president's calls. Frustrated at being unable to secure protection for the Freedom Riders, Robert Kennedy managed to reach the Greyhound bus dispatcher: "I think you should—had better be getting in touch with Mr. Greyhound or whoever Greyhound is and somebody better give us an answer to this question. I am—the government is—going to be very much upset if this group does not get to continue their trip. In fact I suggest that you make arrangements to get a driver immediately and get these people on the way to Montgomery . . ."

John Seigenthaler, a Justice Department aide, managed to find Governor Patterson and extract a promise of protection for the Freedom Riders. However, in a public statement, the governor declared, "We are going to do all we can to enforce the laws of the state on the highways and everywhere else, but we are not going to escort these agitators. We stand firm in that position." However, on May 20, 1961, a bus from Birmingham to Montgomery carrying the young Freedom Riders was accompanied by 16 Alabama highway patrol cars and one airplane.

Everything appeared calm until the bus reached the city limits of Montgomery. The police cars suddenly disappeared as the Greyhound pulled into the Montgomery bus terminal, and a surly mob greeted the riders. John Doar, second in command to Burke Marshall in the Civil Rights Division of the Justice Department, put through a call to Attorney General Robert Kennedy from his position across the street from the station. "The passengers are coming off," Doar reported, "A bunch of men led by a guy with a bleeding face are beating them. There are no cops. It's terrible. It's terrible. There's not a cop in sight. People are yelling, 'Get 'em, get 'em.' It's awful."

Several white thugs surrounded John Lewis and clubbed him to the ground. James Zwerg, a white exchange student from the University of Wisconsin attending Fisk University, was pummeled to the hot pavement. As several members of the mob took turns at hitting him, they chanted, "Kill the nigger-loving son of a bitch." The mob had grown to over a thousand, and not a single policeman had arrived.

When news of the vicious assault reached Washington, Robert Kennedy realized that Governor Patterson had reneged on his promise to protect the Freedom Riders. Beside the Freedom Riders being viciously beaten, so was John Seigenthaler, the president's representative. He had been knocked unconscious and was left lying in the street for nearly one-half hour. Now President Kennedy believed he had good reason to send federal marshals to Alabama, even if it would provoke a confrontation between the state of Alabama and the federal government.

The Justice Department secured an unprecedented court order enjoining the Ku Klux Klan, the National States' Rights Party and the Birmingham and Montgomery police from interfering with "peaceful interstate travel by bus." Deputy Attorney General (later Supreme Court Justice) Byron White led a contingent of U.S. marshals dispatched to Montgomery—400 arrived the evening of May 20 and 266 more the next morning. Governor Patterson protested, and Attorney General Kennedy was overheard on the telephone, saying, "John, John, what do you mean you're being invaded? Who's invading you, John? You know better than that."

While the federal marshals rushed to Alabama, Martin Luther King Jr. interrupted a speaking tour in Chicago and flew to Montgomery to address a mass rally for the Freedom Riders at Ralph Abernathy's First Baptist Church. As over 1,500 blacks and a handful of white sympathizers gathered at the church, a mob of several thousand angry whites surrounded the building. In his address, King declared, "The law may not be able to make a man love me, but it can keep him from lynching me." Meanwhile, the mob outside hurled bottles and stones and smashed windows. Finally the federal marshals arrived and lobbed tear gas into the hate-filled mob to disperse them. Inside the church, the Freedom Riders led the congregation in song, singing, "We shall overcome someday."

"Down Freedom's Main Line"

The White House put pressure on Governor Patterson to declare martial law. Reluctantly the Alabama governor agreed, and 800 National Guardsmen were ordered to Montgomery. While the Freedom Riders prepared to continue their journey on into Mississippi, Attorney General Kennedy secured a promise from Mississippi Senator James Eastland guaranteeing the physical safety of the riders into Mississippi. On the morning of May 24, heavily protected by National Guardsmen, the first busload of Freedom Riders left for Mississippi. They were escorted to the state line where Mississippi National Guardsmen and state policemen took over. The Freedom Riders kept up their morale by singing:

> Hallelujah, I'm traveling
> Hallelujah, ain't it fine,
> Hallelujah, I'm traveling
> Down Freedom's main
> line.

When they arrived in Jackson, all 12 on the first bus were arrested as they attempted to use "whites only" restrooms. They were given 60-day suspended sentences and $200 fines. Having decided to refuse payment, they were sent to Parchman Penitentiary.

Throughout the summer of 1961, more Freedom Riders arrived in Jackson and were arrested for trying to integrate the bus terminal. Robert Kennedy petitioned the Interstate Commerce Commission to ban segregation by regulation. The order was issued on September 22 and went into effect on November 1, 1961. It prohibited carriers of interstate passengers from having anything whatsoever to do with "any terminal facilities which are so operated, arranged, or maintained so as to involve any separation of any portion thereof, or in the use of thereof[,] on the basis of race, color, creed, or national origin." Interstate terminal segregation soon became a thing of the past.

The sacrifices made by the few hundred Freedom Riders had provoked the federal government into taking a clear stand against segregation. "Our philosophy was simple," James Farmer explained in *Freedom—When?* (1965), "We put on pressure and create a crisis and then they react. I am absolutely convinced that the ICC order wouldn't have been issued were it not for the Freedom Riders."

CHRONICLE OF EVENTS

1959

April–September: Congress of Racial Equality (CORE) sponsors sit-ins and interracial nonviolence workshops in Miami, Florida.

November–December: Nashville, Tennessee Christian Leadership Conference holds test sit-ins at department stores.

1960

February 1: Four black college students stage a sit-in at a Woolworth's lunch counter in Greensboro, North Carolina to protest a "whites only" serving policy. Within two weeks, the sit-ins spread to 11 cities in five Southern states.

February 27–29: Four hundred Nashville students protest segregated stores; 81 are charged with disorderly conduct. Black community raises $50,000 for bail, but students adopt a "jail, no bail" strategy.

March: CORE and NAACP call for a nationwide boycott of Woolworth's. Nashville students boycott downtown merchants. Informal organizations to support Southern sit-ins are formed in 21 Northern schools, including Har-

Black and white student demonstrators boycott segregated lunch counters in Greensboro, North Carolina. News & Record, *Greensboro, N.C. and John G. Moebes, photographer. Reprinted with permission of the* News & Record. *This reprint does not constitute or imply any endorsement or sponsorship of any product, service, company or organization.*

Nashville's department stores desegregated their lunch counters in May 1960. Diane Nash, a Fisk University student (second from left) led the campaign to desegregate the lunch counters and later organized students for the Freedom Rides. Courtesy of the Tennessean.

vard, Yale, Princeton, City College of New York, University of Chicago and the University of California/Berkeley.

March 2: Sixty-three students are charged with "conspiracy to obstruct trade and commerce" at two bus stations in Nashville.

March 16: Four blacks are served at Nashville's newly integrated Greyhound bus terminal but are badly beaten up; two bombs are found the following day at the terminal. San Antonio, Texas is the first large Southern city to integrate lunch counters.

April 15: The Student Nonviolent Coordinating Committee (SNCC) is founded at Shaw University in Raleigh, North Carolina.

May 10: Six Nashville stores desegregate lunch counters.

June 23: Hot Shoppes, Arlington, Virginia becomes the first national chain to desegregate.

July 25: Greensboro, North Carolina lunch counters are desegregated.

August 27: Race riots erupt in Jacksonville, Florida after 10 days of sit-ins; 50 are reported injured.

October 17: Four national chain stores report that lunch counters in 112 towns have been integrated.

October 22–25: Mass sit-in is held in Atlanta, Georgia; Martin Luther King Jr. is one of 80 people arrested and is subsequently transferred to a maximum security prison.

October 26: Democratic presidential nominee, Massachusetts Senator John F. Kennedy, telephones Mrs. King to express his concern; Robert Kennedy calls judge in King case to protest. In response to renewed requests by King's attorney, King is released and the charges are dropped.

November 8: John F. Kennedy is elected president by a slim margin of a little more than 100,000 votes.

December 5: U.S. Supreme Court rules that segregated bus terminals are unconstitutional.

1961

January 1: James Meredith, a young air force veteran, seeks to enter the University of Mississippi. After learning that Meredith is black, the school refuses his application; Meredith files a lawsuit against the school.

January–April: CORE leaders develop the idea of Freedom Rides.

May 1–13: Freedom Ride workshops begin in Washington, D.C. with seven blacks and six whites.

May 4: CORE Freedom Riders leave Washington, D.C. by bus.

May 8–10: Freedom Riders are arrested and assaulted in North and South Carolina.

May 13: Freedom Riders arrive in Atlanta, Georgia.

May 14: A white mob burns a Freedom Rider bus outside Anniston, Alabama. Riders aboard a second bus are beaten by Klansman in Birmingham.

May 17: Ten Freedom Riders from Nashville, Tennessee (eight black, two white) continue the ride via Greyhound bus accompanied by state police.

May 20: Freedom Riders are beaten at the Montgomery terminal. U.S. Attorney General Robert Kennedy sends 400 federal marshals to Montgomery. (Two hundred sixty-six more marshals arrive the next morning.)

May 23: SNCC, SCLC and CORE leaders decide to continue Freedom Rides despite violence and federal pressure for a "cooling off" period.

May 24: A group of 27 Freedom Riders leave Montgomery for Jackson, Mississippi accompanied by Alabama National Guard and news reporters.

May 25: When Freedom Riders arrive at the Jackson Greyhound bus terminal, they are arrested.

May 26: Twenty-seven Freedom Riders are convicted in Jackson and are sent to Parchman State Penitentiary.

June 16: Civil rights organization leaders meet with Robert Kennedy. Kennedy asks them to stop demonstrations such as the Freedom Rides and concentrate instead on voter registration.

August: An SNCC national conference targets Albany, Georgia and surrounding communities for a voter registration drive.

August 14: Freedom Riders trial begins in Jackson, Mississippi. Courts levy stiff fines; NAACP provides lawyers. Trials are held through 1962. (Convictions are overturned in 1965.)

November 1: Interstate Commerce Commission (ICC) implements ban on segregated travel facilities.

Eyewitness Testimony

There is more power in socially organized masses on the march than there is in guns in the hands of a few desperate men. Our enemies would prefer to deal with a small group rather than with a huge, unarmed but resolute mass of people. However, it is necessary that the mass-action method be persistent and unyielding. Gandhi said the Indian people must "never let them rest," referring to the British. He urged them to keep protesting daily and weekly, in a variety of ways. This method inspired and organized the Indian masses and disorganized and demobilized the British. It educates its myriad participants, socially and morally. All history teaches us that like a turbulent ocean beating great cliffs into fragments of rock, the determined movement of people incessantly demanding their rights always disintegrates the old order.

Martin Luther King Jr., in a Liberation *article of October 1959.*

I was from North Carolina but I had lived in New York and when I went back down there to school I realized the transition, the difference in public accommodations . . . It seemed to me that people in Alabama, where they had the Montgomery bus boycott, were at least trying to do something about it. The people in Little Rock, with the trouble at Central High School, were trying to do something. And we weren't.

I had heard people talk about demanding service but no one had ever done it. You either ate in Negro areas or you took a sandwich out. So I decided to see if we could do it.

Joseph McNeil, sit-in leader and North Carolina Agricultural and Technical College student, recalling the beginning of the 1960 lunch counter sit-in at Woolworth's in Greensboro, in Gove's Tuesday *magazine article of February 1966.*

We asked for service and the assistant manager came over and said it was a store policy not to serve Negroes. We told him we already had been served at Counter Nine, the toiletries counter, and showed him our receipts. He said he meant he didn't serve Negroes at the lunch counter, that it was primarily local custom, and we said we thought it was a bad custom and something should be done about it.

Franklin McCain, sit-in leader and North Carolina Agricultural and Technical College student, recalling the first day (February 1, 1960) of the boycott at the Woolworth's lunch counter in Greensboro, in Gove's Tuesday *magazine article of February 1966.*

We had the confidence . . . of a Mack truck . . . I probably felt better that day than I've ever felt in my life. I felt as though I had gained my manhood . . . and not only gained it, but . . . developed quite a lot of respect for it.

Franklin McCain, sit-in leader and North Carolina Agricultural and Technical College student, recalling the first day (February 1, 1960) of the sit-in at the Woolworth's lunch counter in Greensboro, in Chafe's Civilities and Civil Rights *(1980).*

We the undersigned are students at the Negro college in the city of Greensboro. Time and time again we have gone into Woolworth stores of Greensboro. We have bought thousands of items at hundreds of the counters in your stores. Our money being accepted without rancor or discrimination and with politeness toward us. When at a long counter just three feet away our money is not acceptable because of the color of our skins. This letter is not being written with resentment toward your company, but with a hope of understanding . . .

We are asking that your company take a firm stand to eliminate discrimination. We firmly believe that God will give courage and guidance in the solving of this problem.

Ezell Blair Jr., David Price, Joseph McNeil, David Richmond and Franklin McCain (sit-in leaders), to the president of F. W. Woolworth & Co., letter of February 1, 1960, in Wolff's Lunch at the Five and Ten *(1970).*

Some Negroes say we're moving, but not fast enough. I say that if it takes two or maybe three months to gain equal service with the white people in a chain store that has a hundred years of history behind it, we've done something pretty big.

Ezell Blair Jr., sit-in leader and North Carolina Agricultural and Technical College student, statement of February 1960, in Chafe's Civilities and Civil Rights *(1980).*

A group of twenty Negro students from A&T College occupied luncheon counter seats, without being served at the downtown F. W. Woolworth Co. store

The first Greensboro sit-in demonstrators. From left to right: David Richmond, Franklin McCain, Ezell Blair Jr. and Joseph McNeil. News & Record, Greensboro, N.C. and John G. Moebes, photographer. Reprinted with permission of the News & Record. This reprint does not constitute or imply any endorsement or sponsorship of any product, service, company or organization.

late this morning—starting what they declared would be a growing movement.

Today's twenty-man action followed the appearance at 4:30 p.m. yesterday of four freshman from Scott Hall at A&T who sat down and stayed, without service, until the store closed at 5:30 p.m.

Student spokesmen said they are seeking luncheon counter service, and will increase their numbers daily until they get it.

Today's group came in at 10:30 a.m. Each made a small purchase one counter over from the luncheon counter, then sat in groups of three or four as spaces became vacant.

There was not disturbance and there appeared to be no conversation except among the groups. Some students pulled out books and appeared to be studying.

The Greensboro [North Carolina] Record, *article of February 2, 1960.*

After attending a mass meeting in Harrison Auditorium, I was . . . inspired to go down to Woolworth's and just sit, hoping to be served . . . By luck I was able to get a ride down to the parking lot and there left the car, after which we walked to Woolworth's, read a passage from the Bible, and waited for the doors to open. The doors opened and in we went. I almost ran, because I was determined to get a seat and I was very much interested in being the first to sit down. I sat down and there was a waitress standing directly in front of me, so I asked her if I might have a cup of black coffee and two donuts please. She looked at me and moved to another area of the counter.

Anonymous North Carolina Agricultural and Technical College student, in a Register *(student) newspaper article of February 4, 1960, in Wolff's* Lunch at the Five and Ten *(1970).*

Negro patrons occupying seats at the lunch counter have a position which demands consideration. In downtown Greensboro, there are few, if any, restaurants or cafes where they can be served. Resentment against this dearth of facilities is not without justification.

But the way to remedy such a situation is through petition and negotiation, rather than through a sitdown strike.

The Greensboro Daily News, *editorial of February 5, 1960.*

We would like to make it clear that this mass movement was not begun to bring economic suffering to the state but to bring to the realization of the citizens of North Carolina that Negroes, who are also citizens of North Carolina, can no longer remain quiet and complacent and continue to accept such gross injustices from those who desire no change in old customs and traditions solely for the purpose of personal gain or because of the warped ideas which have been instilled in the minds of many responsible citizens.

Open letter from students of North Carolina Agricultural & Technical College at Greensboro, to North Carolina Attorney General Malcolm Seawall, letter of February 15, 1960, in NAACP's The Day They Changed Their Minds *(1960).*

What is fresh, what is new in your fight is the fact that it was initiated, led, and sustained by students. What is new is that American students have come of age. You now take your honored places in the worldwide struggle for freedom.

Martin Luther King Jr., to a rally in North Carolina, speech of February 16, 1960, in Branch's Parting the Waters *(1988).*

Many a Virginian must have felt a tinge of wry regret at the state of things in reading of Saturday's sitdowns. Here were the colored students, in coats, white shirts, ties, and one of them was reading

Goethe and one was taking notes from a biology text. And here, on the sidewalk outside, was a gang of white boys come to heckle, a ragtail rabble, slack-jawed, black-jacketed, grinning fit to kill. Eheu! It gives one pause.

James Kilpatrick, newspaper editor, editorial of February 22, 1960, in the Richmond, Virginia News Leader.

Negro citizens no longer intend to be treated like messenger boys at the food counter, asked to take their food standing up or eat it outside . . . As long as those who seek a change in Southern civilities seek it in a peaceful manner, their power (and their haunting image on the white man's conscience) will not diminish.

The Greensboro Daily News, *editorial of February 27, 1960.*

Currently the students at said school [A & T] are waging a sitdown strike to obtain eating privileges at F. W. Woolworth Store in Greensboro. Their efforts have gained more than a little attention in the state and region. They have even been joined by some white college students from some of the female colleges in the area. They must stick to their guns publicly. Closing the gap between the races will take time, and peaceful perseverance such as the A & T students are showing is just part of the process. We hope they win. We hope they win BIG and we hope they will SOON.

The Daily Tar Heel, *University of North Carolina at Chapel Hill newspaper, editorial of February 1960, in Wolff's* Lunch at the Five and Ten *(1970).*

There was a rope around the stools, showing that the counter was closed. We climbed over the rope. A policeman stood there and said quite clearly, "Do not sit down," and we sat down . . . I became suddenly aware of the crowd of people standing behind us . . . Young kids threw french fried potatoes at us, and gum, and cigarette butts. I looked down the counter at Barbara Crosby in a straight pink skirt and nice white blouse, and at Stephen in a dark suit, with a calculus book . . . The policemen simply lined up behind us and peeled us two by two off the stools . . . The crowd in the store . . . shouted out approval. They said about Barbara and me . . . Oh, white . . . WHITE, WHITE, WHITE! Three paddy wagons were blinking at us from the street. Once

Two white employees of a downtown cafe in Nashville, Tennessee prevent sit-in demonstrators from entering. Courtesy of AP/Wide World Photos.

more we had to walk through those crowds. Some one spit right in front of me . . . The TV cameras took lots of pictures and we drove off to the Nashville city jail.

Candie Anderson, Fisk University student, on participating in a sit-in at McClellan's variety store in Nashville, Tennessee, in February 1960, in Zinn's SNCC: The New Abolitionists *(1964).*

We, the students of the six affiliated institutions forming the Atlanta University Center—Clark, Morehouse, Morris Brown, and Spelman colleges, Atlanta University and the Interdenominational Theological Center—have joined our hearts, minds and bodies in the cause of gaining those rights which are inherently ours as members of the human race and as citizens of the United States . . .

We do not intend to wait placidly for those rights which are already legally and morally ours . . . To-

day's youth will not sit by submissively, while being denied all rights, privileges, and joys of life.

"An Appeal for Human Rights," full-page advertisement of March 1960, in the Atlanta Constitution, *in Lincoln's* Reporter *article of February 5, 1961.*

The North is no longer willing to accept segregation in any area of life, whether it is in public eating places; whether it's in public transportation; whether it's in public schools. There is a strong revolt against the whole system of segregation on the part of the Negro people all over the South and all over the nation.

It is natural and possible that the movement will go beyond eating places . . . ultimately, the movement will dramatize the problem of segregation in every area and any other areas with which we are confronted.

Martin Luther King Jr., statement of March
1960, in U.S. News & World Report *(April*
21, 1960).

We say we want freedom and equality and we mean to have it. The white southerner doesn't believe us and won't until we hit him and hit him hard in the pocketbook with sit-downs, picket lines and going to jail.

The [Baltimore] Afro-American, *editorial of*
March 19, 1960.

Do show yourself friendly on the counter at all times. Do sit straight and always face the counter. Don't strike back, or curse back if attacked. Don't laugh out. Don't hold conversations. Don't block entrances.

SNCC instructions for sit-in demonstrators in
Nashville, Tennessee, 1960, in Zinn's SNCC:
The New Abolitionists *(1964).*

You may choose to face physical assault without protecting yourself, hands at the sides, unclenched; or you may choose to protect yourself, making plain you do not intend to hit back. If you choose to protect yourself, you practice positions such as these:

To protect the skull, fold the hands over the head.

To prevent disfigurement of the face, bring the elbows together in front of the eyes.

For girls, to prevent internal injury from kicks, lie on the side and bring the knees upward to the chin; for boys, kneel down and arch over, with skull and face protected.

CORE instructions for nonviolent direct action,
1960, in Zinn's SNCC: The New Abolitionists *(1964).*

Is Our Money Separate?
Boycott placard, 1960.

Memo to: Woolworth's
Serving All Serves America.
Boycott Placard, 1960.

Don't Buy Where You Can't Eat.
Boycott placard, 1960.

We are not afraid of expulsion from school. We do not fear Nashville's jails. As long as we are half-slaves, we are prisoners as much as we were when were locked behind those jail bars.

Curtis Murphy, sit-in demonstrator and Ten-
nessee A&T State University student, state-
ment of March 1960, in the Chicago
Defender *(March 26, 1960).*

We are in what is called a "bull-tank" with four cells. Each cell has a commode and a small sink. There is running water in only two of the cells. One has cold water and the other, both cold and warm. We are in a cell with neither.

Breakfast—if you can call it that—is at 6:30 a.m. Another meal is served at 12:30 and I am still trying to get up enough courage to eat it. In the evening, we are served "sweet" bread and watery coffee.

But we all feel happy that we are doing all this to help our city, state and nation. This is something that has to be done over and over again and we are willing to do it as often as necessary.

We strongly believe that Martin Luther King was right when he said: "We've got to fill the jails in order to win equal rights."

Patricia Stephens, sit-in demonstrator, to James
R. Robinson, CORE executive secretary, letter
of March 1960, on serving a prison sentence at
the Tallahassee [Florida] County Jail, in a
CORE-lator *article of April 1960.*

You have taken up the deep groans of the century. The students have taken the passionate longings of the ages and filtered them in their souls and fashioned a creative protest. It is one of the glowing epics of the time . . .

Martin Luther King Jr., to a Founder's Day
audience at Spelman College, speech of April
10, 1960, in the Spelman Messenger *(May*
10, 1960).

In the first instance, we who are demonstrators are trying to raise what we call the "moral issue." That is, we are pointing to the viciousness of racial segregation and prejudice and calling it evil or sin. The matter is not legal, sociological or racial, it is moral and spiritual. Until America (South and North) honestly accepts the sinful nature of racism, this cancerous disease will continue to rape all of us.

James M. Lawson Jr., sit-in leader, to a SNCC
conference at Raleigh, North Carolina, speech of
April 1960, in Broderick and Meier's Negro
Protest Thought in the Twentieth Century
(1965).

Segregation is on its death bed now, and the only uncertain thing about it is when it will be buried.

Congressman Adam Clayton Powell Jr. Courtesy of the Schomburg Center for Research in Black Culture.

Martin Luther King Jr., to students at Fisk University, speech of April 27, 1960, in the Chicago Defender *(April 30, 1960).*

Every night before we go to sleep we thank God that in this small way we are able to help those who are denied equal rights. We do not consider going to jail a sacrifice but a privilege.

Sixty days is not long to spend in jail. We will do it again for a cause as great as this one.

Barbara Joan Broxton, jailed sit-in demonstrator and Florida A & M University student, statement of May 1960, in Baker's Southern Patriot *article of May 1960.*

We want the world to know that we no longer accept the inferior position of second-class citizenship. We are willing to go to jail, be ridiculed, spat upon and even suffer physical violence to obtain First Class Citizenship.

Statement, in a SNCC 1960 newsletter at Barber-Scotia College, Concord, North Carolina, in Baker's Southern Patriot *article of June 1960.*

I do not understand . . . It's no heaven on earth I left . . . Depends on what you mean by heaven. If you mean a place where everyone has so much money they have no sensitivity—no love, no sympathy, and no hopes beyond their own narrow little worlds . . . But to me the conceited, loud, self-centered, All-American free white and twenty-one college boy stinks . . . If I did not have my friends, I would be very much alone. And I don't want to eat in anyone's restaurant alone, to go to nobody's movie alone, to swim in nobody's pool alone. You dig?

Anonymous white SNCC worker, to his girlfriend, letter of 1960, in Zinn's SNCC: The New Abolitionists *(1964).*

By and large, the feeling that they have a destined date with freedom, was not limited to a drive for personal freedom, or even freedom for the Negroes in the South. Repeatedly it was emphasized that the movement was concerned with the moral implications of racial discrimination for the "whole world" and the "Human Race."

Ella J. Baker, SNCC founder, on the student sit-in demonstrators, in a Southern Patriot *article of June 1960.*

I too, hear America singing
But from where I stand

Ella Baker, a key adviser to the Student Nonviolent Coordinating Committee (SNCC). Courtesy of the Library of Congress.

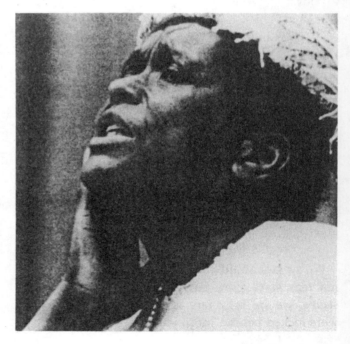

I can only hear Little Richard
and Fats Domino
But sometimes,
I hear Ray Charles
Drowning in his own tears
or Bird
Relaxing at Camarillo
or Horace Silver doodling
Then I don't mind standing
    a little longer.

Julian Bond, one of the founder's of SNCC, in
the Student Voice *(June 1960).*

Try to understand that what I'm doing is right. It isn't like going to jail for a crime like stealing and killing, but we are going for the betterment of all Negroes.

Clarence Graham, jailed sit-in demonstrator, to
his mother and father, letter of 1961, in Peck's
Cracking the Color Line *(1962).*

The *Freedom Ride* will differ from its predecessor in three important respects. First, it will penetrate . . . into the Deep South. Second, it will challenge segregation not only aboard buses but in terminal eating facilities, waiting rooms, rest stops, etc. Third, participants who are arrested will remain in jail rather than accept . . . bail or payment of fines . . .

The main purpose of the *Freedom Ride,* like the Journey 14 years ago, is to make bus desegregation a reality instead of merely an approved legal doctrine. By demonstrating that a group *can* ride buses in a desegregated manner even in the Deep South, CORE hopes to encourage other people to do likewise.

CORE statement of March 1961, in Lau's Di-
rect Action and Desegregation *(1989).*

It seems to us that the civil rights movement will not get anywhere by merely being patient.

We believe that there must be an element of patience, but the Negro community in the South is not willing to wait until next year for the rights which they should have had 10 or 20 years ago, and, unless this fight is pushed through non-violence, we fear that the forces of violence will really take over.

Gordon R. Carey, CORE field director, state-
ment of April 1961, in U.S. News & World
Report *(April 5, 1961).*

If there is arrest, we will accept that arrest . . . and if there is violence, we are willing to receive that violence without responding in kind.

James Farmer, CORE national director and
Freedom Rider leader, to the press, statement of
May 4, 1961, in the Associated Press (May 4,
1961).

When the Greyhound bus pulled into Anniston, it was immediately surrounded by an angry mob armed with iron bars. They set upon the vehicle, denting the sides, breaking windows, and slashing tires. Finally, police arrived, and the bus managed to depart. But the mob pursued it in cars. One car got ahead of the bus and prevented it from gathering speed. About six miles out, one of the tires went flat, and the bus was forced to pull over to a gas station.

Within minutes, the pursuing mob was again hitting the bus with iron bars. The rear window was broken and a bomb was hurled inside. Suddenly the vehicle became filled with thick smoke. The passengers, including the freedom riders, ducked toward the floor in order to breathe. A few climbed out of a window. Some tried to get out the door, but it was being held shut from the outside.

James Peck, white CORE member and Freedom
Rider, on arriving in Anniston, Alabama on
May 14, 1961, in Freedom Ride *(1962).*

I don't think I was scared . . . I felt my idea was more powerful than the mob's. Theirs was white supremacy; mine was equality under law for all men . . .

I was hit over the head with a club. Even now my chest hurts and I almost conk out every time I climb a few steps. But I'm ready to volunteer for another ride. Sure. Any time.

Henry Thomas, Freedom Rider and Howard
University student, statement of May 1961, on
the attack by a white mob outside of Anniston,
Alabama, in Eckman's New York Post *article*
of May 18, 1961.

When the bus arrived the toughs grabbed the passengers into alleys and corridors, pounding them with pipes, with key rings and with fists.

One passenger was knocked down at my feet by 12 of the hoodlums and his face was beaten and kicked until it was a bloody pulp.

Howard K. Smith, CBS News correspondent,
dispatch of May 14, 1961, on the attack on
Freedom Riders at the Birmingham bus termi-
nal, in the New York Times *(May 15, 1961).*

They dragged me out of the car. They tried to blackjack me.

Freedom Riders rest on the ground beside their bombed and charred bus, May 14, 1961. Courtesy of the Schomburg Center for Research in Black Culture.

And to keep the public from knowing what was happening, they tore the microphone out of my two-way radio unit. They tried to keep me from telling what was happening—in broad daylight, just three blocks from Birmingham's City Hall.

Clancy Lake, Birmingham radio reporter, on the attack on Freedom Riders in Birmingham on May 14, 1961, in a Birmingham News *article of May 15, 1961.*

I regret very much this incident had to happen in Birmingham.

I have said for the last 20 years that these out-of-town meddlers were going to cause bloodshed if they kept meddling in the South's business.

Birmingham Police Commissioner Eugene "Bull" Connor, to the press, statement of May 14, 1961, in the Birmingham News *(May 15, 1961).*

It is difficult for any Southerner who understands the problem confronting our people to sympathize with this radical extremist group which has invaded our state. They got just what they asked for.

Alabama Congressman George Huddleston, to Congress, speech of May 15, 1961, in the Congressional Record *(1961).*

In view of the tenseness of the situation, it is impossible to guarantee the safety of these agitators. Our advice to them is to get out of Alabama as quickly as possible. We will escort them to the nearest state line: however, we will not escort them to any other cities in Alabama to continue their rabble-rousing.

Alabama Governor John Patterson, public statement of May 15, 1961, in the Birmingham News *(May 16, 1961).*

We must demonstrate first to ourselves, our own people, that thuggery will not go unpunished.

In so proving to ourselves that, we the people, and not a bunch of thugs are rulers of our city, we will also be showing the nation and the world that, even though matters got out of hand we were properly very swift in bringing about order.

The Birmingham News, *editorial of May 16, 1961.*

There were police cars all around the bus, and helicopters flying overhead. But when we got inside the Montgomery city limits, it all disappeared. It was around noon when we got to the terminal and got off the bus. Paul Brooks went to call cabs for us. People were meantime gathering nearby, and a CBS cameraman was taking pictures. Suddenly a large man with a cigar hit the cameraman. He kept dragging him all over the street, beating him. The cameraman was small. There was not one policeman around.

Ruby Doris Smith, Spelman College student and Freedom Rider, on arriving in Montgomery, Alabama on May 20, 1961, in Zinn's SNCC: The New Abolitionists *(1964).*

. . . I would say about forty miles or less from the city of Montgomery, all sign of protection disappeared. There was no plane, no patrol car, and when we arrived at the bus station, it was eerie. Just a strange feeling. It was so quiet, so peaceful, nothing. And the moment we started down the steps of that bus, there was an angry mob. People came out of nowhere—men, women, children, with baseball bats, clubs, chains—and there was no police official around. They just started beating people. We tried to get all of the women on the ride into a taxicab. There was one cab there, and this driver said he couldn't take the group because it was interracial . . .

They beat up all of the reporters, then they turned on the black male members and white male members of the group. I was beaten—I think I was hit with a sort of crate thing that holds soda bottles—and left lying unconscious there, in the streets of Montgomery.

John Lewis, SNCC leader and Freedom Rider, on arriving at Montgomery, Alabama on May 20, 1961, in Hampton and Fayer's Voices of Freedom *(1990).*

The mob turned from Zwerg to us. Someone yelled: "They're about to get away!" Then they started beating everyone. I saw John Lewis beaten, blood coming out of his mouth. People were running from all over.

Every one of the fellows was hit. Some of them tried to take refuge in the post office, but they were turned out . . . We saw some of the fellows on the ground, John Lewis lying there, blood streaming from his head.

Ruby Doris Smith, on a mob attacking the Freedom Riders at the Montgomery bus terminal on May 20, 1961, in Zinn's SNCC: The New Abolitionists *(1964).*

I trailed the bus from Birmingham to Montgomery in a car and was on the bus platform in the middle of the violence but escaped injury.

The small group of men and women was attacked by a mob of 100 at first. But the mob rapidly grew into the thousands.

"Get those niggers," one darkhaired woman, primly clad in a yellow dress, shouted . . .

Using metal pipes, baseball bats, sticks and fists, the mob surged on the small group of Freedom Riders, clubbing, punching, chasing and beating both whites and Negroes. When some of the bus riders began to run, the mob went after them, caught them and threw them to the ground. The attackers stomped on at least two of them . . .

In two hours it was over, after the police used tear gas.

Stuart H. Lorry, journalist, in a New York Herald Tribune *article of May 21, 1961.*

I am asking the U.S. court in Montgomery to enjoin the Ku Klux Klan, the National States Right Party, certain individuals and all persons acting in concert with them, from interfering with peaceful interstate travel by buses . . . I am also arranging for U.S. officers to begin to assist state and local authorities in the protection of persons and property and vehicles in Alabama.

U.S. Attorney General Robert Kennedy, to Alabama Governor John Patterson, telegram of May 20, 1961, in the New York Times *(May 21, 1961).*

While we will do our utmost to keep the public highways clear and to guard against all disorder, we cannot escort bus loads or car loads of rabble rousers about our state from city to city for the avowed purpose of disobeying our laws, flaunting our customs and traditions and creating racial incidents.

Alabama Governor John Patterson, public statement of May 20, 1961, in the Associated Press (May 20, 1961).

The situation which has developed in Alabama is a source of the deepest concern to me as it must be to the vast majority of the citizens of Alabama and other Americans. I have instructed the Justice Department to take all necessary steps based on their investigations and information. I call upon the Governor and other responsible State officials in Alabama as well as the Mayors of Birmingham and Montgomery to exercise their lawful authority to prevent any further outbreaks of violence. I would also hope that any persons, whether a citizen of Alabama or a visitor there, would refrain from any action which would in any way tend to provoke further outbreaks. I hope that state and local officials in Alabama will meet their responsibilities. The United States Government intends to meet its.

President John Kennedy, public statement of May 20, 1961, on the interference with the Freedom Riders in Alabama, in The Public Papers of the Presidents of the United States *(1962–1964).*

These beatings cannot deter us from our purpose. We are not martyrs or publicity-seekers. We want only equality and justice, and will get it.

We will continue our journey one way or another. From here we go to Jackson, Mississippi, and then on to New Orleans. They may try to attack us and maybe bomb us, but we're ready for anything now.

James Zwerg, white Freedom Rider (attacked by a white mob at the Montgomery bus terminal on May 20, 1961), statement of May 20, 1961, in United Press International *(May 21, 1961).*

We aren't going to stop now. Why, those people in Alabama think they can ignore the President of the United States, and they think they can still win by threatening us Negroes over the head . . . They beat us and we're stronger than ever.

Diane Nash, SNCC leader, statement of May 22, 1961, in the New York Times *(May 23, 1961).*

Whatever one's views of the Freedom Rides, they have the right as citizens to ride a bus wherever it goes. Carrying out their passive techniques they have offered no provocation.

Alabama's shame, which is shared by the South, is also a serious blow to the security and prestige of the nation.

The Atlanta Constitution, *editorial of May 22, 1961.*

The gleaming petal of hope one can grasp out of the blood and dirt of the Alabama road is the fact that these youngsters overcame their fear and refused to hate. Even more it was the fact that there were white youngsters among the Negroes, and that one of the men who risked his life, lying unconscious on the roadway, was an aide of Attorney General Kennedy.

What was begun by the Freedom Riders on the Alabama road can be finished only in the minds of the vast majority of Americans, white and black alike. Without their act of mind and will even the best efforts of the Kennedy Administration will be futile.

Max Lerner, columnist, New York Post *editorial of May 22, 1961.*

The right of peaceful assembly has its limitations, just as the right of freedom of speech . . . The News believes the deliberate rushing to Montgomery by Martin Luther King and his retinue could be construed as nothing but further agitation of an already tense community . . .

The people of Alabama, Mr. [Robert] Kennedy, would feel more secure in the efforts to guarantee the rights of all citizens if you found a way to stop those who came here and foment trouble by their actions in the midst of already highly charged situations.

The Birmingham News, *editorial of May 22, 1961.*

I feel that the ride must continue in order to accomplish a goal—to fulfill and uphold the Supreme Court decision that people can travel from one part of the United States to another without being discriminated against.

John Lewis, Freedom Rider leader, statement of May 23, 1961, in the New York Herald Tribune *(May 24, 1961).*

A cooling-off period is needed. It would be wise for those traveling through these two states to delay their trips until the present state of confusion and danger has passed and an atmosphere of reason and normalcy has been restored.

U.S. Attorney General Robert Kennedy, to the press, statement of May 24, 1961, in the New York Times *(May 25, 1961).*

The agent provocateurs who have descended upon the Southern states, in the name of "peace riders" were sent for the sole purpose of stirring up discord, strife and violence. "Peace riders" is a revered Communist term, an old Communist technique. The movement was masterminded and directed by an organization known as the Congress on Racial Equality, called CORE.

Senator James Eastland (D, Miss.), to the Senate, speech of May 25, 1961.

I'm taking a ride on the Greyhound bus line.
I'm riding the front seat to Jackson this time.
Hallelujah, I'm traveling;
Hallelujah, ain't it fine?
Hallelujah, I'm traveling
Down Freedom's main line.

Song sung by Freedom Riders as they rode from Montgomery, Alabama to Jackson, Mississippi, May 24–26, 1961.

I took a trip down Alabama way.
Freedom's coming and it won't be long.
I met much trouble on Mother's Day.
Freedom's coming and it won't be long.

Song sung to the tune of "The Banana Boat Song" by Freedom Riders riding from Montgomery, Alabama to Jackson, Mississippi, May 24–26, 1961.

If you can't find me in the backa the bus;
You can't find me nowhere,
Oh-h, come on up to the fronta the bus,
I'll be ridin' up there.
I'll be ridin' up there—up there,
I'll be ridin' up there.
Oh-h come on up to the fronta the bus;
I'll be ridin' up there.

Freedom Riders' song, 1961.

Yes, we are the Freedom Riders
And we ride a long Greyhound;
White or black, we know no difference,
Lord, for we are Glory bound.

Southern collegiate folk song of the early 1960s.

With two rifle-carrying Guardsmen in the front seat and jeeps leading and following the bus we sped to the border. Waiting rooms at all stops along the way were closed. At the state line the commanding officer of the Guard boarded the bus and in a pleasant voice wished us luck, saying we could expect a long stay in Mississippi . . .

As we rolled toward Jackson, every blocked-off street, every back road taken, every change in speed

caused our hearts to leap. Our arrival and speedy arrest in the white bus station in Jackson, when we refused to obey a policeman's order to move on, was a relief. A paddy wagon rushed us down the street to the police station.

William Mahoney, Freedom Rider and Howard University student, on a May 26–27, 1961 ride from Alabama to Mississippi, in a Liberation *article of September 1961.*

Just as our Constitution is colorblind, and neither knows nor tolerates classes among citizens, so too is the Interstate Commerce Act.

U.S. Attorney General Robert Kennedy, to the press, statement of May 29, 1961, in the New York Times *(May 30, 1961).*

The time has come for this [Interstate Commerce] commission to declare unequivocally by regulation that a Negro passenger is free to travel the length of this country in the same manner as any other passenger.

U.S. Attorney General Robert Kennedy, to the Interstate Commerce Commission, petition of May 29, 1961, in the New York Times *(May 30, 1961).*

If the tragic events incident to the Freedom Riders have proved nothing else, they have shown that the Federal Government no longer can afford the luxury of permitting defiant state officials to disobey the law of the land.

Too, it clearly illustrates the moral shame that ill becomes the world's leading democracy at the very moment we are trying to convince millions of persons to close their ears to the siren song of the Communists and follow us.

The [Baltimore] Afro-American, *editorial of June 10, 1961.*

Though nary a bus terminal in the Deep South drops its racial barriers (but most of them will, and soon) as a result of the Freedom Rides, they are already a success. They have taught us that the lesson of Lot and his wife and the destruction of Sodom has meaning today: A nation can be saved by the few who are willing to lay down their lives for what they believe.

Len Holt, civil rights attorney and adviser to the Freedom Riders, in a Southern Patriot *article of June 1961.*

I am not a martyr. I want to live for my beliefs, not die for them. However, if I have to die, I will, for I know that what I believe in will not die but will live on forever. This is not just our fight, or America's fight, it is mankind's fight.

By our actions we tried to put a capital "D" in the word "democracy."

Why did I go? Because I had to.

Susan Herman, Freedom Rider and Fisk University student, in a Southern Patriot *article of June 1961.*

By joining the Freedom Riders we hoped to dramatize the fact that this is not just a student movement. We felt that our being university educators might help encourage the sea of silent moderates in the South to raise their voices. Without doubt the moderates have been derelict. I've heard it said that 60% of white Southerners take a neutral attitude on race. As always, it has been the listless, not the lawless, who are the deciding factor.

Reverend William Sloan Coffin Jr., Yale University chaplain, in a Life *article of June 2, 1961.*

The sit-in movement has proved itself a success. The Freedom Riders now add an exclamation point to that statement. Our next movement towards full equality will be an exclamation point to the success of the Freedom Rides. And a success they will be.

Jimmy McDonald, Freedom Rider and passenger on the bus that was bombed and burned in Anniston, Alabama on May 14, 1961, in a Freedomways *article of Summer 1961.*

In my judgment, there's no question of the legal rights of the freedom travelers—Freedom Riders, to move in interstate commerce. And those rights, whether we agree with those who travel, whether we agree with the purpose for which they travel, those rights stand, providing they are exercised in a peaceful way. We may not like what people print in the paper, but there's no question of their constitutional right to print it. So that follows, in my opinion, for those who move in interstate commerce.

So the basic question is not the Freedom Riders. The basic question is that anyone who moves in interstate commerce should be able to do so freely. That's a more substantive question, not the question merely of the Freedom Riders.

President John F. Kennedy, to the press, statement of July 19, 1961, in The Public Papers of the Presidents of the United States *(1962–1964).*

We stayed in the hot box two nights. It's a cell about six foot square, which they call the hot box. Long as they don't turn the heat on—with three in there—you can make it. There's no openings for light or air; there was a little crack under the door, but you couldn't see your hand before your face less you get down on your knees. When they got ready to feed you they hand the tray through a little door which they close—and then you can't eat unless you get down on your knees by the light comin' in the door—then you can see how to eat. And they had a little round hole in the floor which was a commode.

Willie Rogers, Freedom Rider, on his two-month sentence at Parchman State Penitentiary in Mississippi in 1961, in Zinn's SNCC: The New Abolitionists *(1964).*

One night at the county jail, a voice called up from the cell block beneath us, where other Negro prisoners were housed. "Upstairs!" the anonymous prisoner shouted. We replied, "downstairs!" "Upstairs," replied the voice; "Sing your freedom song." The Freedom Riders then sang. We sang old folk songs and gospel songs to which new words had been written, telling of the Freedom Ride and its purpose. We sang new words to old labor songs, too. One stanza rang out: "They say in Hinds County no neutrals have they met. You either follow Freedom Ride or you 'tom' for Ross Barnett." After the impromptu concert, the downstairs prisoners, whom the jailors had said were our enemies, shouted back: "That sounds good, Freedom Riders; you are our friends." They then sang for us. The girl Freedom Riders, in another wing of the jail, joined in the Freedom Ride songs, and for the first time in history, the Hinds County jail rocked with unrestrained singing of songs about Freedom and Brotherhood.

James Farmer, CORE national director and Freedom Rider, on his time (40 days) at Mississippi's Hinds County Jail, in a CORE-lator *article of August 1961.*

It was a nice set-up. When the windows were open we could talk to the fellows. We sang. We wrote Freedom Songs. A Negro minister from Chicago sang: "Woke Up In The Mornin' With My Mind Set On Freedom" so everyone began singing it. It started there . . . Other songs were composed—"I Know We'll Meet Again" was written by a fellow I knew from Nashville and Rock Hill. We would do ballet lessons in the morning to keep ourselves fit. There were different people from different areas. Somebody was giving Spanish lessons. But then, after about two weeks, we were awakened at 4:00 A.M. to find out that we were all going to Parchman State Penitentiary . . . It was a long ride in the night. We sang Freedom Songs.

Ruby Doris Smith, Freedom Rider, on her two-month sentence at Hinds County (Mississippi) Jail in 1961, in Zinn's SNCC: The New Abolitionists *(1964).*

I'll never forget this Sheriff Tyson—he used to wear those big boots. He'd say, "You goddam smart nigger, why you always trying to be so uppity for? I'm going to see to it that you don't ever get out of this place." They decided to take our mattresses because we were singing . . . So they dragged Hank Thomas out and he hung on to his mattress and they took him and it and dropped him with a loud klunk on his back . . . And then they put the wristbreakers on Freddy Leonard, which makes you twist around and around in a snake-like motion, and Tyson said, "Oh you want to hit me, don't you," and Freddy just looked up at him meekly and said, "No, I just want you to break my arm." And Sheriff Tyson was shaken visibly, and he told the trusty, "Put him back." I hung on to the mattress and said, "I think we have a right to them and I think you're unjust," and he said, "I don't want to hear all that shit nigger," and started to put on the wristbreakers. I wouldn't move and I started to sing "I'm Gonna Tell God How You Treat Me," and everybody started to sing it and by this time Tyson was really to pieces. He called to the trusties, "Get him in there!" and he went out the door and slammed it, and left everybody else with their mattresses.

Stokely Carmichael, SNCC leader and Freedom Rider, on his jail time at Mississippi's Parchman State Penitentiary in 1961, in Zinn's The New Abolitionists *(1964).*

How long must we wait? It's been a century. How gradual can you get? Montgomery has shown how far it has advanced on its own; we've seen this from the mob to the governor. As for the legal position about the right to serve whom one pleases, I would say that this position does not alter the fact that segregation is wrong. Segregation on the bus lines, trains, and planes is wrong intrastate as well as interstate. The press has made much of the interstate passage. However, the Freedom Riders are just as concerned with intrastate travel, because we're concerned with the injustice of segregation.

The Negro is seeking to take advantage of the opportunities that society offers; the same opportunities that others take for granted, such as a cup of coffee at Woolworth's, a good job, an evening at the movies, and dignity. Persons favoring segregation often refer to the rights of man, but they never mention the rights of Negro men.

Diane Nash, SNCC leader, from "Inside the Sit-ins and Freedom Rides," quoted in Ahmann's The New Negro *(1961).*

Civil Rights is the name of Freedom in this country for both black and white, and for both student and worker . . . I think that whether the Freedom Rides continue, or whether the struggle to end segregation and discrimination once and for all takes a different form, the fight for freedom will not stop until we have torn up the old, from root to branch, and established truly new human relations based on new beginnings. I think the Freedom Rides, and whatever may come after them, are a form of just such new beginnings!

Louise Ingram, Freedom Rider, in Freedom Riders Speak for Themselves *(1961).*

These students are not struggling for themselves alone. They are seeking to save the soul of America. They are taking our whole nation back to those great wells of democracy which were dug deep by the Founding Fathers in the formulation of the Constitution and the Declaration of Independence. In sitting down at lunch counters, they are in reality standing up for the best in the American dream. They courageously go to the jails of the South in order to get America out of the dilemma in which she finds herself as a result of segregation. One day historians will record this student movement as one of the most significant epics of our heritage.

Martin Luther King Jr., in a New York Times Magazine *article of September 10, 1961.*

> We shall overcome,
>   we shall overcome,
> We shall overcome someday.
> Oh, deep in my heart, I do believe,
> We shall overcome someday.

"We Shall Overcome," popular spiritual sung by civil rights activists.

7. The Albany Movement and James Meredith at Ole Miss: 1961–1962

ALL-BENNY

In late 1961, the small, southwestern Georgia city of Albany became the next big battleground for the civil rights movement. Albany (pronounced All-benny by many Georgians) was a farming center of 56,000 people, 40% of them black. Like many Southern towns at the time, it was a thoroughly segregated community. Despite the *Brown* decision, blacks were not admitted to white schools. Although there were a great number of blacks in Albany, only a few had been permitted to register to vote.

Before the Civil War, Albany was a trading center for the surrounding slaveholding plantations. W. E. B. Du Bois, in *The Souls of Black Folk* (1903), described the area: "For a radius of a hundred miles about Albany stretched a great fertile land, luxuriant with forests of pine, oak, ash, hickory, and poplar, hot with the sun and damp with the rich black swampland; and here the cornerstone of the Cotton Kingdom was laid."

By the end of the 19th century, Albany was a sleepy little town where blacks outnumbered whites and segregation was clearly established. The abolition of slavery did not mean the abolition of plantations. The huge farms replaced their cotton crops with peanuts, pecans and corn. As always, the owners and employers tended to be white, and the laborers tended to be black. These farms offered so much work that blacks from Atlanta and as far away as Tallahassee, Florida were attracted to this area. Albany soon became a financial center and in the minds of the locals was considered a cosmopolitan town.

In August 1961, a national conference of the Student Nonviolent Co-ordinateng Committee (SNCC) decided to focus its voter registration drive on Albany and the surrounding southwest Georgia counties. Although many of these outlying communities had black majorities, whites controlled their governments. After efforts by SNCC activists stalled in the nearby counties, SNCC decided to expand its goals to include desegregation of the community and to concentrate first on Albany. It would be one of SNCC's first attempts at mobilizing an entire black community, including people of all ages and classes.

Charles Sherrod, a 22-year-old SNCC field secretary, at first found many of Albany's blacks unreceptive to SNCC organizers despite their good intentions. He later wrote, "Sometimes we'd walk down the streets and the little kids would call us Freedom Riders and the people walking in the same direction on the same side of the street would go across the street from us, because . . . they didn't want to be connected with us in any way." Some of Albany's black ministers refused to allow SNCC activists to hold meetings in their churches for fear that the buildings might be bombed or stoned.

The SNCC organizers found their most responsive audience among high school students and at the all-black Albany College. On November 1, 1961, their efforts led to a sit-in at a bus station by nine students to test compliance with the Interstate Commerce Commission ruling barring segregation in interstate bus and train stations, which became effective that day. The Albany students were led by SNCC activists Sherrod and Cordell Reagon. They sat down in the whites-only waiting room and refused to leave. Even though the students left as planned when threatened with arrest by police, they made the point to Albany black residents that despite the law they did not have equal access to those facilities.

THE ALBANY MOVEMENT

A few weeks later, on November 17, 1961, after some squabbling between SNCC and various local civil rights groups, the Albany Movement was formed to coordinate efforts to protest against segregation. The umbrella organization included the Ministerial Alliance, the Federation of Women's Clubs, the Negro Voters League, the Criterion Club (a group of black professionals) and the NAACP and its Youth Council. Dr. William Anderson, an osteopath, whose business depended very little on whites, was chosen as the president of the Albany Movement.

Five black students were arrested on November 22 for their sit-in at the Trailways bus station lunch counter. Although SNCC notified the

Dr. William Anderson, president of the Albany Movement. Courtesy of the U.S. News & World Report Collection, Library of Congress.

Department of Justice of the arrests, the federal government failed to enforce the ICC ruling. In response, the Albany Movement held its first mass meeting three days later at Mount Zion Baptist Church. The people listened to speeches by the students who had been arrested and later sang freedom songs throughout the night, including "We Shall Overcome."

The movement was further galvanized when the five students went on trial on November 27. Movement members participated in a mass march, and 400 people signed a petition asking that the students, who had been expelled from Albany State for their arrests, be permitted to return to school. The next day the *Albany Herald*, the local paper, critized the march. The Albany Movement responded by organizing a boycott against *Herald* advertisers.

The most dramatic test of the federal government's willingness to act came on December 10 when several hundred black residents greeted an integrated group of Freedom Riders, five black and five white, at Albany's Central Railway Terminal. The blacks entered the white section, and the whites entered the black section. They were ordered out by Albany Police Chief Laurie Pritchett and were arrested for trespassing as they were leaving the terminal. A. C. Searles, editor of the black weekly *Southwest Georgian*, watched the scene and reported: "There was no traffic, no disturbance, no one moving. The students had made the trip to Albany [from Atlanta] desegregated without incident. Things had gone so smoothly I think it infuriated the chief." Again, the Department of Justice failed to act.

The Albany Movement went into full swing. During the next seven days, a series of mass meetings was held thoughout the black community. Hundreds of students marched downtown, protesting the arrest of the students. Most of them were arrested after they ignored police orders to end the march. Many of them remained in jail as they subscribed to the SNCC philosophy of refusing to be bailed out of jail. The following day, on December 13, over 200 protesters were arrested for marching on city hall without a permit. Police Chief Pritchett said, "We can't tolerate the NAACP, or the SNCC or any other nigger organization to take over the town with mass demonstrations."

KING COMES TO ALBANY

By December 15, over 500 people had been jailed. Dr. Anderson, president of the Albany Movement, decided to gain more publicity for the cause by inviting the revered national symbol of the fight against segregation, Martin Luther King Jr., to address a mass rally.

That Friday night, King told an audience of over 1,000 at Shiloh Baptist Church, "Don't stop now. Keep moving. Don't get weary. We will wear them down with our capacity to suffer." The next day King, along with Ralph Abernathy and Dr. Anderson, led 250 hymn-singing men, women and children in a mass march to city hall in Albany. All of the marchers, including its leaders, were arrested at city hall for parading without a permit.

King refused bail and announced, "If convicted, I will refuse to pay the fine. I expect to spend Christmas in jail. I hope thousands will join me." But Police Chief Laurie Pritchett had studied King's methods and said years later, "I found his method was nonviolence . . . to fill the jails, same as Gandhi in India. And once they filled the jails, we'd have no capacity to arrest and then we'd have to give in to his demands. I sat down and took out a map. How many jails were in a fifteen-mile radius, how many were in a thirty-mile radius? And contacted those authorities. They assured us that we could use their [jails]."

While King was in jail, there was some conflict between local black leaders and Wyatt Tee Walker, the executive secretary of the Southern

Christian Leadership Conference (SCLC). Walker had come to Albany with King from Atlanta. He pledged to use SCLC's resources and people for the cause. However, SNCC activists who derisively called Martin Luther King Jr. "De Lawd" were afraid that the SCLC would take over the Albany Movement. When the city commissioners learned about this division within the movement, they decided to play upon local blacks' desire to control their own movement. In return for the movement calling off further demonstrations, the city commissioners orally agreed to desegregate train and bus facilities, release on bond all demonstrators and listen to black complaints at a meeting before the city commissioners.

King, who had not been party to the negotiations, left Albany and returned to Atlanta. But a few weeks later, when the city failed to integrate the terminals or meet with blacks, it became apparent that the agreement between the city and the local Albany black leaders was a hoax.

Despite this setback, the Albany Movement in early 1962 launched a selective boycott against white businesses and the local bus system. The bus company was soon in financial trouble and was forced out of business.

On February 27, 1962, Martin Luther King Jr. and Ralph Abernathy returned to Albany to stand trial for their December arrests. They were found guilty of disorderly conduct and of parading without a permit. However, their sentencing was delayed until July because the judge requested a transcript of the trial.

On July 10, King and Abernathy were ordered to pay $78 in fines or serve 45 days in jail. They chose jail. The national press descended on Albany to cover the story. At a press conference, King told reporters that he would be sent to a prison work gang.

Alarmed by this situation, President Kennedy asked the Justice Department for a report on Albany. Burke Marshall, the assistant attorney general for civil rights, began discussions with Chief Pritchett and Albany's city commissioners. A few days after King and Abernathy were sentenced, they were unexpectedly released when an unidentified stranger mysteriously paid their fines. Chief Pritchett has since admitted that he arranged for the payment to be made, but to this day, he refuses to reveal the complete story. Abernathy told a mass meeting that evening, "I've been thrown out of a lot of places in my day, but never have I been thrown out of jail."

On July 17, 1962, King spoke to mass rallies at the Shiloh and Mount Zion Baptist churches. He announced, "[Our] protest will turn Albany upside down." Three days later, federal Judge Robert Elliott, a segregationist appointed by President Kennedy, issued a temporary restraining order against further demonstrations in Albany. King and a number of other leaders specifically were forbidden to march. King pledged to obey the federal court order, noting that the main support for minority rights was the federal court system.

"Ain't Gonna Let Nobody Turn Me 'Round"

At the Shiloh Baptist Church, Reverend Benjamin Welles preached to his Saturday audience, "I've heard about an injunction but I haven't seen one. I've heard a few names, but my name hasn't been called. But I do know where my name is being called. My name is being called on the road to freedom. I can hear the blood of Emmett Till as it calls from the ground . . . When shall we go? Not tomorrow! Not at high noon! Now!"

Singing "I Ain't Gonna Let Nobody Turn Me 'Round," 160 demonstrators, more than 100 of them under 18 years of age, marched with Welles from the Shiloh church toward Albany's city hall. The police intercepted the demonstrators, arrested the group and jailed them in the nearby town of Camilla. The next evening, Mrs. Slater King, wife of the Albany Movement's vice-president, drove to the Camilla jail to bring some food to the youngsters who were being held. Mrs. King was ordered to leave by the guards and when threatened by a deputy sheriff with arrest, she said, "If you want to arrest me, go ahead." The sherriff knocked her to the ground and kicked her until she lost consciousness. Mrs. King, who was six months pregnant, later suffered a miscarriage as a consequence of the brutal beating.

On July 24, after an appeals court judge set aside the injunction against demonstrations in Albany, nearly 2,000 black Albany residents marched through the streets in protest to what had happened to Mrs. King. The demonstrators, many of them teenagers, threw bricks, rocks and bottles at police. Pritchett commented to the press, "Did you see them nonviolent rocks?" King declared a Day of Penance and toured Albany's poolrooms, taverns and hang-outs, speaking out against violence and preaching nonviolence, "One thing about this movement is that it is nonviolent. As you know there was some violence last night. Nothing could hurt our movement more. It's exactly what our opposition likes to see . . . we don't need guns—just the power of souls."

Two days later, King led a prayer vigil in front of city hall. King, Abernathy and Dr. Anderson were arrested along with 10 others. A few hours later, another group of demonstrators came to city hall, and they too were arrested. While Chief Pritchett sought a permanent restraining order to stop further demonstrations, Albany Mayor Asa Kelly announced at a press conference that he and the city commissioners were "anxious to discuss problems with local Negroes" after King had left town.

On August 10, King was freed after two weeks in jail. He called off planned demonstrations and announced that he was returning to Atlanta for the weekend to give the city of Albany a chance to talk with local black leaders. The city commissioners refused to meet with the Albany Movement leaders. King returned to Albany on August 15 and managed to have the city commissioners hear black petitions. But the Albany officials announced that all such matters were now before the federal courts, so they would not act on them. Before returning to Atlanta, King told a mass rally that the commission held the black citizens of Albany in "utter contempt."

THE LESSONS OF ALBANY

By late 1962, the Albany Movement existed in little more than name. The Albany Movement was a staggering defeat for Martin Luther King Jr., who later admitted, "Our protest was so vague that we got nothing and the people were left depressed and in despair." It was, however, a moral victory for many of Albany's citizens. Dr. William Anderson, the Albany Movement's president, later said, "There was a change in attitude of the kids who saw their parents step into the forefront and lead the demonstrations. They were determined that they would never go through what their parents went through to get the recognition that they should have as full citizens."

Like all pioneering efforts, the Albany Movement provided many valuable lessons for future campaigns. It was the first time that the Student Nonviolent Coordinating Committee organized a large number of blacks for a sustained struggle. They would use these lessons in Mississippi during Freedom Summer.

The Southern Christian Leadership Conference realized that national attention did not necessarily mean the federal government would always step in to protect civil rights. King, as president of the SCLC, stressed to his lieutenants the importance of advance planning, training and choosing a specific target. King told his staff that he wanted the SCLC to be in "on the ground floor" and that he no longer wanted "to be a fireman." This strategy would later prove successful in Birmingham.

JAMES MEREDITH

James Howard Meredith was a native Mississippian, from Kosciusko in Attala County in the central part of the state. After serving nine years in the Air Force, he returned to his native state in the summer of 1960. The ex-Air Force sergeant had earned credits toward a college degree while in the service and enrolled at Jackson State College in

Mississippi. By January 1961, Meredith had decided that the educational opportunities at all-black Jackson were lacking. Inspired by John F. Kennedy's inaugural address and its emphasis on human rights, the 28-year-old Meredith decided to put Kennedy's words into action. That day, Meredith applied for a transfer from the all-black college to the all-white University of Mississippi, known as "Ole Miss," at Oxford.

Meredith's application to Ole Miss was rejected on the grounds that Jackson State was not a member of the Southern Association of Secondary Schools and that he did not have letters of recommendation from five alumni of the university. On May 31, 1961, he filed a lawsuit in the United States District Court of Southern Mississippi, claiming that he had been denied admission to the University of Mississippi on racial grounds. Federal District Judge Sidney C. Mize of Mississippi dismissed his suit on the grounds that racial discrimination could not be proved. Then in June 1962, the United States Court of Appeals for the Fifth Circuit found that Meredith had indeed been rejected "solely because he was a Negro." Judge Mize's decision was reversed, and Ole Miss was ordered to admit Meredith.

Throughout the summer of 1962, the state of Mississippi engaged in a series of legal maneuvers to prevent Meredith's admission. Finally, in September, the issue came before Justice Hugo L. Black of the Supreme Court, acting as circuit justice for the Fifth Circuit. He ordered the judgment of the circuit court into effect at once. A showdown between the state of Mississippi and the federal government was approaching.

GOVERNOR ROSS BARNETT

When Ross Barnett, an ardent segregationist, ran for governor of Mississippi in 1959, he successfully courted the white supremacist vote. One of his campaign buttons declared, "Never, Never." His first speech after becoming governor was to a White Citizens' Council group. The councils had been among Barnett's strongest supporters.

On September 13, 1962, after the federal district court had ordered the admission of Meredith to Ole Miss, Barnett told Mississippi residents in a televised speech, "There is no case in history where the Caucasian race has survived social integration . . . We must either submit to the unlawful dictate of the federal government or stand up like men and tell them, 'Never.' "

A week later, on September 20, the state board trustees for the University of Mississippi met and gave Barnett "the full power, authority, right, and discretion of this Board to act upon all matters pertaining to or concerned with" Meredith's registration, admission and attendance. In effect, Barnett was made registrar of Ole Miss. That same day, the Mississippi governor sped from Jackson to Oxford to personally deny Meredith's entrance to Ole Miss. Governor Barnett was in clear violation of court orders, but the Kennedy administration delayed action while state officials repeatedly barred Meredith, who was accompanied by federal marshals, from registering.

Meanwhile, behind the scenes, Attorney General Robert Kennedy and later, President John Kennedy, were engaging in a series of telephone calls with Governor Barnett and an intermediary, Tom Watkins, a Mississippi attorney and friend of the governor. The Kennedys sought assurances that the governor would cooperate "in maintaining law and order and preventing violence with federal enforcement of court orders." At one point, the governor proposed that he would withdraw Mississippi's state police if the federal authorities would stage a show of force. Robert Kennedy dismissed this plan as "a foolish and dangerous show."

Governor Barnett was found guilty of civil contempt on September 28 and given the weekend to Tuesday, October 2, to clear himself or face arrest and a fine of $10,000 a day. The next day, Barnett appeared at an Ole Miss football game in Jackson and told a cheering crowd waving Confederate flags, "I love Mississippi. I love her people, her customs! And I love and respect her heritage! Ask us what we say, it's to hell with Bobby K! Never shall our emblem go, from Colonel Reb to Old Black Joe." But on Sunday, September 30, 1962, Tom Watkins assured Attorney General Kennedy that Barnett would comply with the federal marshals to maintain peace and order. That morning, President John F. Kennedy read a proclamation that called on all persons engaged in the "obstruction of justice" to cease and "to disperse and retire peacefully forthwith."

MEREDITH ENTERS OLE MISS

On Sunday night, September 30, Meredith was flown to Oxford from Memphis, Tennessee by a federal plane. He was met at the university airport by U.S. Deputy Attorney General Nicholas Katzenbach and driven to the campus in a convoy of automobiles and military trucks. He was protected by a contingent of 300 federal marshals, carrying riot clubs and tear-gas cartridges, and a large group of Mississippi state troopers. As Meredith was escorted onto the Ole Miss campus, students gathered in front of the Lyceum Building heckling, "Two-four-one-three, we hate Kennedy," then with increasing violence shouting, "Kill the nigger-loving bastards." At dusk, bottles and bricks began to

Rioting erupts at the University of Mississippi after federal troops arrive to escort James Meredith onto the campus, September 30, 1962. Courtesy of the Library of Congress.

fly. The mob grew to over 2,500, most of them agitators from off the campus and out of town. (Of the 200 rioters later arrested, only 24 were students).

As the rioters repeatedly charged the federal marshals, President Kennedy made an address televised to the nation but aimed directly at the students and people of Mississippi, urging them to comply with the law. For the students of Ole Miss, he said these words, "The eyes of the nation and the world are upon you and upon all of us, and the honor of your university and the state are in the balance."

Meanwhile, the rioting on the campus was getting out of control. Gunshots were fired, and the federal marshals were nearly overwhelmed before being given the order to use tear gas. Paul Guihard, a correspondent from Agence France-Presse, was murdered; Roy Gunter, a young jukebox repairman, was killed by a stray .38-caliber bullet; and a marshal was shot in the throat. Hundreds were injured before federal troops joined the marshals around five o'clock in the morning and drove off the rioters.

On the morning of October 1, 1962, Chief United States Marshal James P. McShane escorted James H. Meredith to the office of the university registrar, and Meredith was enrolled at 8:30 A.M. That evening over 5,000 soldiers and federalized Mississippi National Guardsmen patrolled Oxford, a town of 6,500. These troops were soon withdrawn, and by the end of the month, only 500 remained to ensure Meredith's safety.

All of the troops were withdrawn on June 5, 1963, and Meredith graduated on August 18, 1963, with a bachelor of arts degree in political science. At the graduation ceremony, Meredith, a man to whom symbols had great significance, wore a Ross Barnett campaign button pinned to his graduation gown, the one that said, "Never, Never." He wore it upside down.

CHRONICLE OF EVENTS

1961

November: In Albany, Georgia, black leaders seek redress of their grievances with white officials but are rebuffed. SNCC activists test the ICC ruling banning segregated travel facilities; nine are ordered out of a white waiting room. SNCC notifies U.S. Justice Department but receives no reply.

November 17: A group of local black improvement organizations in Albany, Georgia form the Albany Movement.

November 22: Several students, including three from the NAACP Youth Council and two from SNCC, are arrested at an Albany Trailways bus station in separate demonstrations.

December 10: Eleven Freedom Riders are arrested in an Albany, Georgia railway station and charged with disorderly conduct.

December 11–14: The first phase of the Albany Movement begins with a series of mass meetings and marches involving hundreds of Albany blacks.

December 15: Martin Luther King Jr., Ralph Abernathy and Wyatt T. Walker arrive in Albany to speak at a rally.

December 16: King and Abernathy lead 250 people to Albany's city hall and are arrested for parading without a permit. King vows to remain in jail until the city desegregates.

December 18: Albany Movement leaders and city representatives reach an agreement to desegregate terminal facilities; King leaves jail. But in the following days, the city denies the agreement.

1962

February 26: U.S. Supreme Court rules that state-sponsored segregation in travel facilities is illegal.

February 27: Martin Luther King Jr. and Ralph Abernathy are convicted of leading Albany's December 16, 1961 march. Sentencing is delayed until July.

April: The Voter Education Project is begun. It is an outgrowth of Robert Kennedy's effort to get private tax-exempt support for voter registration in the South.

May 31: James H. Meredith files suit in U.S. district court claiming racial discrimination in his denied admission to the University of Mississippi.

July 10: Martin Luther King Jr. and Ralph Abernathy are sentenced. They choose to spend 45 days in jail instead of paying a fine.

July 11: The Albany Movement organizes a march and rally to show support for King and Abernathy; 32 people are arrested.

July 20: A federal district court enjoins King and other leaders from participating in further demonstrations.

July 24: A federal appeals court sets aside the injunction. That evening violent demonstrations occur in Albany.

July 25: King calls for a Day of Penance to atone for the violent behavior. He visits throughout the community and encourages people to be nonviolent.

August 10: King leaves Albany for Atlanta, Georgia.

August 15: The Albany City Commission refuses to meet any of the demands of the Albany Movement.

September 10: Justice Hugo L. Black of the Supreme Court, acting as circuit justice for the Fifth Circuit, upholds an earlier court of appeals decision that the University of Mississippi has to admit James H. Meredith, a black U.S. Air Force veteran.

September 13: Mississippi Governor Ross R. Barnett defies the federal government in a statewide broadcast, declaring he will "interpose" the authority of the state between the University of Mississippi and the federal judges who ordered the admission of Meredith.

September 20: Governor Barnett personally denies Meredith admission to the University of Mississippi.

September 24: U.S. Court of Appeals for the Fifth Circuit orders Board of Higher Education

James Meredith, protected by federal marshals, is escorted onto the University of Mississippi campus, October 1, 1962. Courtesy of the Library of Congress.

of Mississippi to admit Meredith or be held in contempt.

September 25: Governor Barnett defies court orders and again personally denies Meredith admission to the university.

September 26: Mississippi bars Meredith for the third time. Lt. Governor Paul Johnson and a contingent of state policemen turn back Meredith and federal marshals about 400 yards from the gates of the university.

September 28: Governor Barnett is found guilty of civil contempt of the federal court. U.S. Court of Appeals for the Fifth Circuit orders Barnett to clear himself of contempt or face arrest and a fine of $10,000 a day.

September 30: Mississippi state troopers and 300 federal marshals escort James H. Meredith to the campus of the University of Mississippi. President Kennedy federalizes the Mississippi National Guard and in a nationwide broadcast urges Mississippians to accept the orders. University of Mississippi students and adults from Oxford, Mississippi and other nearby communities riot on the university's campus. Two persons are killed and 100 more are wounded.

October 1: Some 5,000 federal soldiers restore order on the University of Mississippi campus. Meredith is escorted by federal marshals and registers on the campus.

November 20: President Kennedy issues an executive order barring racial discrimination in federally financed housing.

EYEWITNESS TESTIMONY

The [Mount Zion Baptist] church was packed before eight o'clock. People were everywhere, in the aisles, sitting and standing in the choir stands, hanging over the railing of the balcony, sitting in trees outside the windows . . . And when we rose to sing "We Shall Overcome," nobody could imagine what kept the church on four corners . . . I threw my head back and closed my eyes as I sang with my whole body. I remember walking dusty roads for weeks without food. I remember staying up all night for two and three nights in sucession writing and cutting stencils and mimeographing and wondering—How long?

Charles Sherrod, SNCC field secretary, recalling the beginning of the Albany Movement in November 1961, in Zinn's SNCC: The New Abolitionists *(1964).*

When I opened my mouth and began to sing, there was a force and power within myself I never heard before. Somehow this music . . . released a kind of power and required a level of concentrated energy I did not know I had.

Bernice Reagon, Albany Movement student activist, on the rally at Mount Zion Baptist Church in Albany, Georgia on November 25, 1961, in a Sing Out! *article of January/February 1976.*

Woke up this morning with my mind stayed on freedom,

Albany, Georgia demonstrators chanting "Freedom . . . Freedom" and waving papers they signed promising to go to jail if they are arrested for protesting segregation. Courtesy of AP/Wide World Photos.

Woke up this morning with my mind stayed on
  freedom,
Woke up this morning with my mind stayed on
  freedom,
  Hallelu, hallelu, hallelu, hallelujah.

Ain't no harm to keep your mind stayed on freedom,
  etc.

Walkin' and talkin' with my mind stayed on freedom,
  etc.

Singin' and prayin' with my mind stayed on freedom,
  etc.

Doin' the twist with my mind stayed on freedom,
  etc.

*"Woke Up This Morning with My Mind
Stayed on Freedom," popular song sung by Albany Movement activists.*

Although no one put a hand on me, I feel like I
been beaten. When you sleep on steel and concrete
you are automatically sore. I'm a trailer driver, on
the job a year, came back to work this morning,
found I got no job . . . they told me, "You a Freedom
Marcher" . . . my wife lost her job, too.
*Anonymous jailed Albany Movement demon-
strator, statement of December 1961, in Zinn's
Albany: A Study in National Responsibility
(1962).*

We are anything but through with the fight to be
full citizens right here in Albany . . . anybody who
thinks this town is going to settle back and be the
same as it was, has got to be deaf, blind, and dumb.
*Anonymous woman on the Albany Movement
executive committee, statement of December
1961, in Zinn's Albany: A Study in National
Responsibility (1962).*

We can't tolerate the NAACP or the SNCC or any
other nigger organization [taking] over this town
with mass demonstrations.
*Laurie Pritchett, Albany, Georgia police chief,
to the press, statement of December 13, 1961,
in Carson's In Struggle: SNCC and the
Black Awakening of the 1960s (1981).*

Martin King says freedom
Martin King says freedom
Martin King says free-dom
Free-dom Free-dom!

Let the white man say freedom
Let the white man say freedom

Let the white many say free-dom
Free-dom Free-dom!

I woke up this morning with my mind
Set on Freedom.
I woke up this morning with my mind
Set on Freedom.
*Spiritual sung to the tune of "Amen" by a
mass meeting at Shiloh Baptist Church in Al-
bany, Georgia, December 15, 1961, in Branch's
Parting the Waters (1988).*

Don't stop now. Keep moving. Don't get weary.
We will wear them down with our capacity to suffer.
*Martin Luther King Jr., to a rally at Shiloh
Baptist Church in Albany, Georgia, speech of
December 15, 1961, in Zinn's SNCC: The
New Abolitionists (1964).*

There are only two languages the white politicians
and the power structure understand. One is the
power of the almighty dollar bill. When those cash
registers are not ringing, they understand what you're
talking about.
*Ruby Hurley, Atlanta NAACP chapter presi-
dent, to an Albany Movement rally, speech of
December 15, 1961, in the Atlanta Constitution (December 16, 1961).*

Be here at 7 o'clock in the morning. Eat a good
breakfast. Wear warm clothes and wear your walking
shoes.
*Dr. W. G. Anderson, president of the Albany
Movement, to a rally at Shiloh Baptist Church,
speech of December 15, 1961, in the Atlanta
Constitution (December 16, 1961).*

Hundreds of our brothers and sisters, sons and
daughters are in jail. We will not rest until they are
released. I can't afford to stand idly by while hundreds
of Negroes are being falsely arrested simply because
they want to be free. We have a right to democracy.
It is deeply imbedded in the Constitution—the right
of assembly, freedom of speech.

You hear it said some of us are agitators. I am here
because there are twenty million Negroes in the
United States and I love every one of them. I am
concerned about every one of them. What happens
to any one of them concerns all directly.

I am here because I love the white man. Until the
Negro gets free, white men will not be free. I am
here because I love America. I'm going to live right
here in the United States and probably here in Geor-

gia the rest of my life. I am not an outsider. Anybody who lives in the United States is not an outsider in the United States.

Martin Luther King Jr., to a rally at Shiloh Baptist Church in Albany, Georgia, speech of December 16, 1961, in Watters' Down to Now: Reflections on the Southern Civil Rights Movement *(1971).*

I believe in segregation. I think it's the best way, but I am a realist enough to believe that we will have total integration one day.

It might not be in my lifetime or in my children's, but it will come. As the laws change to meet the times, I will support the law.

Laurie Pritchett, Albany, Georgia police chief, to the press, statement of December 17, 1961, in the New York Herald Tribune *(December 18, 1961).*

I will not accept bond. If convicted I will refuse to pay the fine. I expect to spend Christmas in jail. I hope thousands will join me.

This act of self-suffering and sacrifice is to arouse the conscience of the community and the nation against discrimination.

The guards in this jail call me "boy." I might add that I am the pastor of a church with 4,000 members.

Martin Luther King Jr., to the press, statement of December 17, 1961, in the New York Herald Tribune *(December 18, 1961).*

This is the first time in the history of the Negro non-violent movement that non-violence has been met with non-violence.

Laurie Pritchett, Albany, Georgia police chief, to the press, statement of December 18, 1961, in the New York Herald Tribune *(December 19, 1961).*

I'm sorry I was bailed out. I didn't understand at the time what was happening. We thought that the victory had been won. When we got out, we discovered it was all a hoax.

Martin Luther King Jr., statement of December 18, 1961, in Lewis' King: A Critical Biography *(1970).*

It is our belief that discrimination based on race, color or religion is fundamentally wrong and contrary to the letter and intent of the Constitution of the United States. It is our aim in the Albany Movement to seek means to ending discriminatory practices in public facilities, both in employment and in use. Further, it is our aim to encourage private businesses to offer equal opportunity for all persons in employment and in service . . .

It is our hope that through negotiations and arbitrations, through listening to each other, that we can achieve the purposes that will benefit the total community.

The problem of human rights belongs to us all, therefore, let us not falter in seizing the opportunity which almighty God has given to create a new order of freedom and human dignity. What is your pleasure, gentlemen, in proceeding with the negotiations?

Dr. W. G. Anderson, president of the Albany Movement, to the Albany City Commission, letter of January 23, 1962, in Levine's Eyes on the Prize: A Reader and Guide *(1987).*

The issue in Albany is much bigger than just the city buses; it involves the whole concept of human dignity. We will not be swayed from our campaign until we have some recognition of our basic right in civil liberties and freedom.

Dr. W. G. Anderson, president of the Albany Movement, statement of February 1962, in the [Baltimore] Afro-American *(February 17, 1962).*

All-benny Georgia lives in race
We're goin' to fight it from place to place
Keep your eyes
On the prize
Hold—on . . .

I know what I think is right
Freedom in the souls of black and white
Keep your eyes
On the prize
Hold—on . . .

Singing and shouting is very well
Get off your seat and go to jail
Keep your eyes
On the prize
Hold—on
Hold—on
Hold—on
Hold—on
Keep your eyes
On the prize
Hold—on
Hold—on

"Eyes on the Prize," sung by the Freedom Singers (SNCC group) in Albany, Georgia, 1962.

Ain't gonna let nobody turn me 'round,
  turn me 'round, turn me 'round,
Ain't gonna let nobody turn me 'round,
I'm gonna keep on walkin', keep on a-talkin',
Marching up to freedom land.

"Ain't Gonna Let Nobody Turn Me 'Round," popular song sung by Albany Movement activists and SNCC workers, 1962.

Request audience with your body to resolve grievances that have been pending for nearly a year. Terms relayed to us by Chief Pritchett are unsatisfactory. Long record of broken promises and bad faith agreements reveal conferences with Chief Pritchett are no avail. Respectfully request special meeting with City Commission . . .

Martin Luther King Jr., Dr. W. G. Anderson, Slater King and Ralph Abernathy, to the Albany City Commission and Mayor Asa Kelly Jr., telegram of July 15, 1962, in the Associated Press (July 16, 1962).

The City Commission is in receipt of a telegram from a purported Albany movement requesting a special meeting of the commission.

It is the decision of the commission not to deal with law violators.

Mayor Asa D. Kelly Jr., public statement of July 15, 1962, in the Associated Press (July 16, 1962).

We are in the midst of a great movement and we are soliciting the support of all the citizens of Albany. We had our demonstrations saying we will no longer accept segregation. One thing about the movement is that it is non-violent. As you know, there was some violence last night. Nothing could hurt our movement more. It's exactly what the opposition likes to see. In order that we can continue on a Christian basis with love and non-violence, I wanted to talk to you all and urge you to be non-violent, not to throw bottles. I know if you do this, we are destined to win.

Martin Luther King Jr., to a group of black Albany citizens, statement of July 25, 1962, in Watters' Down to Now (1971).

It took Gandhi 40 years to achieve independence. We can't expect miracles here in Albany.

Martin Luther King Jr., statement of July 1962, in Time (August 3, 1962).

Martin Luther King and 200 of his colleagues are in jail in Albany, Georgia, as a result of their protest against denial of the civil rights guaranteed them by the Constitution of the United States. Violation of the rights peaceably to assemble and to petition the government for redress of grievances, the bedrock of democratic institutions, is not only tragic but grossly repugnant to Americans everywhere. The National Urban League strongly deplores this disgraceful condition and urges the President of the United States to speak out against this situation which threatens the very fabric of our democracy.

Whitney M. Young Jr., National Urban League executive director, to President John Kennedy, telegram of August 1, 1962, in the vertical file (Albany Movement), Schomberg Center for Research in Black Culture, The New York Public Library.

I find it wholly inexplicable why the city council of Albany will not sit down with the citizens of Albany, who may be Negroes, and attempt to secure them, in a peaceful way, their rights. The U.S. government is involved in sitting down at Geneva with the Soviet Union. I can't understand why the government of Albany . . . cannot do the same for American citizens.

President John F. Kennedy, to the press, statement of August 1, 1962, in The Public Papers of the Presidents of the United States (1962–1964).

The non-violent resisters can summarize their message in the following terms: We will take direct action against injustice without waiting for other agencies to act. We will not obey unjust laws or submit to unjust practices. We will do this peacefully, openly, cheerfully—because our aim is to persuade. We adopt the means of non-violence because our end is a community at peace with itself. We will try to persuade with our words—but if our words fail we will try to persuade with our acts. We will always be willing to talk and seek fair compromise, but we are ready to suffer when necessary and even risk our lives to become witness to the truth as we see it.

Martin Luther King Jr., on the strategy of the Albany Movement, in a New York Times Magazine article of August 5, 1962.

Albany is as segregated as ever.

Laurie Pritchett, Albany, Georgia police chief,
statement of August 8, 1962, in the New York
Times *(August 9, 1962).*

The city commission of Albany has adjourned revealing to you, to the State of Georgia, to the United States and to the world, that it holds you in utter contempt . . .

It reveals it will not negotiate in good faith. This is tragic for the State of Georgia. Soon the city commission will have to realize that they are living in 1962 and not in 1853.

Martin Luther King Jr., to a mass rally in Al-
bany, Georgia, speech of August 15, 1962, in
the Atlanta Constitution *(August 16, 1962).*

If you did not have a movement like this, thousands of Negroes would be walking around with their heads buried. The victory of the Albany Movement has already been won. Thousands of Negroes have won a new sense of dignity and self-respect.

Martin Luther King Jr., to the press, statement
of August 16, 1962, in the New York Times
(August 17, 1962).

What did we win? We won our self-respect. It changed all my attitudes. This [Albany] movement made me demand a semblance of first-class citizenship.

Anonymous Albany, Georgia black citizen, re-
flecting on the Albany Movement, in Watters'
Down to Now *(1971).*

We could not have communicated with the masses of the people without music. They could not have communicated to us without music . . . through songs they expressed years of suppressed hope, suffering, even joy and love.

Charlie Jones, SNCC field secretary in Albany,
Georgia, statement of August 19, 1962, in
New York Times *(August 20, 1962).*

> Go down, Kennedy,
> Way down in Georgia land,
> Tell old Pritchett
> To let my people go.

"Old Pritchett," sung to the tune of the spiri-
tual "Moses," in Shelton's New York Times
article of August 20, 1962.

The importance of the Albany Movement is only now being realized. The eyes of the world have been on Albany, Georgia, since the mass demonstrations in December. Millions were shocked that "white people" would do such things to those "poor Negroes" in the South. Thousands were appalled at the brutality of the city officials here. Twelve hundred were arrested, many beaten . . . and on runs the blood into the streets of Albany where it is seen across the country, but there are only a few who really understand what we are doing, where we are going and what it all means . . .

Last Wednesday we met in a tent on ground which has been cleared off for the rebuilding of the church. We had about 50 people from Albany, six months ago, maybe four, maybe less or more, you couldn't have paid these people from Albany enough to come to Dawson, Sasser, or anywhere else in Terrell County. But something has happened in southwest Georgia which has a good chance of becoming a pattern for our grand strategy in the South. And we go about our way, feeling in the darkness . . . and the world listens and looks on, wondering.

Charles Sherrod, SNCC field secretary, field re-
port of September 1962, in Forman's The Making of Black Revolutionaries *(1972).*

No school will be integrated in Mississippi while I'm governor.

Mississippi Governor Ross Barnett, to the resi-
dents of Mississippi, broadcast address of Sep-
tember 13, 1962, in the New York Times
(September 14, 1962).

I respect the State of Mississippi whose citizens have made many contributions to the country, and the great University which you are privileged to serve. Historically, American citizens have freely and frequently disagreed with or disapproved of laws and court decisions but have obeyed them nevertheless. The federal courts have spoken unequivocally on this matter. All of us as citizens of the United States have a responsibility to obey the law and I as Attorney General have the responsibility to enforce the law. I am confident that you will act in such a way not only as to preserve order but to assist in meeting our responsibilities.

U.S. Attorney General Robert Kennedy, to the
board of trustees of the University of Missis-
sippi, telegram of September 19, 1962, in Bar-
rett's Integration at Ole Miss *(1965).*

Pursuant to the authority vested in me under the Constitution and the laws of the State of Mississippi, I, Ross R. Barnett, Governor of the State of Mississippi and for the protection of all citizens of the State of Mississippi, and all others who may be within the confines of the State of Mississippi . . .

Therefore you, James H. Meredith are hereby refused admission as a student to the University of Mississippi, and any other person or persons who, in my opinion, by such admission, would lead to a breach of the peace and be contrary to the administrative procedures and regulations of the University of Mississippi and the laws of the State of Mississippi.

Take due notice thereof and govern yourself accordingly.

Governor Ross R. Barnett, to James H. Meredith, proclamation of September 20, 1962, in Barrett's Integration at Ole Miss *(1965).*

The future of the United States of America, the future of the South, the future of Mississippi, and the future of the Negro rests on the decision of whether or not the Negro citizen is to be allowed to receive an education in his own state. If a state is permitted to arbitrarily deny any right that is so basic to the American way of life to any citizen, then democracy is a failure.

I dream of the day when Negroes in Mississippi can live in decency and respect and do so without fear of intimidation and bodily harm or of receiving personal embarrassment, and with an assurance of equal justice under the law.

The price of progress is indeed high, but the price of holding back is much higher.

James H. Meredith, handwritten statement ("last will and testament") of September 26, 1962, in Three Years in Mississippi *(1966).*

The situation is serious. The question of federal troops is the same as it has been. That is, we'll use whatever is necessary to do the job.

U.S. Attorney General Robert Kennedy, to the press, statement of September 26, 1962, in the New York Times *(September 27, 1962).*

Governor Barnett and all those who think like him must be shown that there definitely is an iron fist in that velvet glove the federal government has been soothing the segregationists with.

The Baltimore Afro-American, *editorial of September 29, 1962.*

The policemen are smiling. Newsmen—even those from the North—are received with open arms, and there's a feeling of relaxation in the crowd.

Difficult to believe that you are in the center of the most serious constitutional crisis ever experienced by the United States since the war of secession.

It is in these moments when you feel that there is the distance of a century between Washington and the irredentists of the South.

The Civil War has never ended.

Paul Guihard, Agence France-Presse reporter, dispatch of September 29, 1962 from Oxford, Mississippi, in the New York Times *(October 3, 1962). [This was the last report Guihard filed before he was killed during the rioting at the University of Mississippi on September 30, 1962).*

I don't give a damn whether they got U.S. marshals or not. That nigger ain't goin' to Mississippi University—period. It'll take federal troops to keep him alive.

Anonymous Mississippi law enforcement official, statement of September 1962, in Newsweek *(October 1, 1962).*

Americans are free, in short, to disagree with the law but not to disobey it. For in a government of laws and not of men, no man, however prominent or powerful, and no mob, however unruly or boisterous, is entitled to defy a court of law. If this country should ever reach the point where any man or group of men by force or threat of force could defy the commands of our court and our Constitution, then no law would stand free from doubt, no judge would be sure of his writ, and no citizen would be safe from his neighbors . . .

The eyes of the nation and all the world are upon you and upon all of us. And the honor of your university—and state—are in the balance.

I am certain the great majority of the students will uphold this honor.

There is, in short, no reason why the books on this case cannot now be quickly and quietly closed in the manner directed by the court.

Let us preserve both the law and the peace, and then healing those wounds that are within, we can turn to the greater crises that are without and stand united as one people in our pledge to man's freedom.

President John F. Kennedy, to the nation, broadcast speech of September 30, 1962, in The Public Papers of the Presidents of the United States *(1962–1964).*

As Governor of the State of Mississippi, I have just been informed by the Attorney General of the United

States that Meredith has today been placed on the campus of the University of Mississippi by means of government helicopters and is accompanied by federal officers.

I urge all Mississippians and instruct every state officer under my command to do everything in their power to preserve peace and to avoid violence in any form. Surrounded on all sides by the armed forces and oppressive power of the United States of America, my courage and my convictions do not waver. My heart still says, "Never," but my calm judgment abhors the bloodshed that would follow. I love Mississippi. I love her people. I love those ten thousand good Mississippians in the National Guard who have now been federalized and requested to oppose me and their own people. I know that we are completely surrounded by armed forces and that we are physically overpowered. I know that our principles remain true, but we must at all odds preserve the peace and avoid bloodshed.

To the officials of the federal government, I say: Gentlemen, you are tramping on the sovereignty of this great state and depriving it of a prestige of honor and respect as a member of the Union of states. You are destroying the Constitution of this great nation. May God have mercy on your souls. Mississippi will continue to fight the Meredith case and all similar cases through the courts to restore the sovereignty of the state and constitutional government.

Governor Ross Barnett, to the people of Mississippi, broadcast of September 30, 1962, in the Christian Science Monitor *(October 1, 1962).*

The madness grew. Lights shining from the Lyceum [Building] illuminated clouds of gas and silhouetted wave after wave of attackers running behind Confederate flags. The flare of burning cars would catch a student in a full Confederate uniform. It was not James Meredith who was the target that night— it was the Yankees, the federal government that had conquered the South and was about to inflict James Meredith on them. "Shoot the Yankees, shoot. Give me your gun if you won't shoot him," one boy implored three state patrolmen running before a gas barrage.

Robert Massie, journalist, on the riot at the University of Mississippi *on September 30, 1962, in a* Saturday Evening Post *article of November 10, 1962.*

By now, the mob was getting completely out of hand. You could hear the crunch of automobiles being wrecked.

Somebody commandeered an automobile and sent it, driverless, roaring full throttle toward the line of marshals. It swerved to the side and crashed into a tree.

Out of the night, a bulldozer came grinding across the campus toward the marshals. Somebody lobbed a tear-gas bomb onto the seat, and the driver jumped off. The bulldozer stalled short of its target.

A fire truck was seized by the rioters. Its hose was stripped away and used to shoot water at the marshals. Then some rioters drove the truck at the marshals, apparently intending to ram them. But the truck stalled.

Sterling Slappey, journalist, on the rioting at the University of Mississippi on September 30, 1962, in a U.S. News & World Report *article of October 15, 1962.*

Clouds of tear gas billowed around the Lyceum Building. The tree-dotted mall had the appearance of a battlefield as students and adults massed behind Confederate flags and charged repeatedly toward the marshals. Travel to and from the campus was extremely dangerous. Roving bands of students halted cars and questioned their occupants to determine if they were friend or foe. The troops were bombarded with bricks and sticks, and obscenities were shouted at the men.

Claude Sitton, journalist, on the rioting at the University of Mississippi on September 30, in a New York Times *article of October 1, 1962.*

If this stops me, then it's no different having been officially stopped. No one's said anything to me about leaving, and right at this point it's more for Americans than it's for me.

James Meredith, to the press, statement of October 1, 1962, in the New York Times *(October 2, 1962).*

Some newspapermen later asked me if I thought attending the university was worth all this death and destruction. The question really annoyed me. Of course, I was sorry! I hadn't wanted this to happen. I believe it could have been prevented by responsible political leadership in Mississippi. As for the federal government, the President and the Attorney General had all the intelligence facilities at their disposal, and

James Meredith, escorted by federal marshals, is jeered by white students as he leaves a building after attending classes at the University of Mississippi. Courtesy of the U.S. News & World Report Collection, Library of Congress.

I believe that they handled it to the best of their knowledge and ability. I think it would have been much worse if they had waited any longer. Social change is a painful thing, but the method by which it is achieved depends upon the people at the top. Here they were totally opposed—the state against the federal government. There was bound to be trouble, and there was.

James H. Meredith, on registering at the University of Mississippi on October 1, 1962, in Three Years in Mississippi *(1966).*

It is a tragic hour when the President of the United States sends federal troops and marshals into a peaceful community and causes violence, bloodshed and death . . . I urge our people to calmness and I call the President to put a stop to further violence by the immediate removal of Meredith and the withdrawal

of federal troops from Mississippi soil. When this is done, peace will prevail again in Mississippi.

Mississippi Governor Ross Barnett, to the nation, broadcast speech of October 1, 1962, in the Associated Press.

It is a fact that the Negro in America is treated something else than a first-class citizen in Mississippi. I am most concerned with the problem and I am intent on seeing that every citizen has an opportunity of being a first-class citizen. I am also intent on seeing that citizens have a right to be something if they work hard enough.

James Meredith, statement of October 2, 1962, in the New York Amsterdam News *(October 6, 1962).*

The flag of the Confederacy has become a rallying point for hoodlums and crackpots from whom men like Lee and Forrest would have turned away with cold contempt.

Inflamed by pious statements that invite violence while purporting to deplore it the mob has gathered to fight the good fight for anarchy.

That they will be turned back is scant relief for the shame and anger felt by reasonable people on both sides of the now-secondary issue of integration.

It will be a long time before any of us get the feel of slime off our hands.

Memphis Commercial Appeal, *editorial of October 2, 1962.*

People burdened with the thought of what has happened at Oxford may find some slight solace in evidence that some aspects of the South's position is being more widely understood . . . the law cannot dictate social practices, custom or convictions, and that it is a mistake for extremists and politicians on the mixing side to suppose that legal equality can be made an excuse for invading the right of free association.

The New Orleans Times-Picayunne, *editorial of October 2, 1962.*

No, this was not a Civil War battle. It was none the less a great crisis—a crisis of national identity, in which the nation had to discover whether it indeed was a nation with a law and a conscience and a leadership, or whether it was a headless wonder of 51 sovereignties. Despite the tragedy of the dead and the wounded, the American people surveyed the battlefield the next day with a sense of relief that they had come through the kind of crisis that tests a nation's very existence, and came through it stronger than when they went in.

Max Lerner, New York Post *columnist, editorial of October 2, 1962.*

Not only must Mississippi be brought into the national fabric as demanded by justice and law. It must be brought into the international 20th century— if, as a nation, we are to have our proper destiny in that century. It is no accident that the Administration insists so firmly on civil rights at home. The essence of our foreign policy is civil rights for all the earth.

C. L. Sulzberger, New York Times *columnist, editorial of October 3, 1962.*

I believe that the violence which arose is going to be a spark for other violence. The people who were

James Meredith, protected by U.S. marshals and troops, travels between dormitory and classrooms at the University of Mississippi. Courtesy of the U.S. News & World Report Collection, Library of Congress.

at Oxford came from a number of other areas as well as the university, and it seems likely to me that areas that are left now in the South are the hard-resistance areas.

Hodding Carter, editor of the Greenville Mississippi *Delta Democrat-Times, statement of October 1962, in* U.S. News & World Report *(October 15, 1962).*

I cannot see the end to Southern opposition to desegregation or integration . . . I can't see the end to it. I don't know when it will end. Not in my lifetime.

James J. Kilpatrick, editor of the Richmond, Virginia News Leader, *statement of October 1962, in* U.S. News & World Report *(October 15, 1962).*

It is thrilling to see one slight young man standing up to all of the forces of Mississippi . . . just as it has been thrilling to see thousands of other New Negroes challenging unjust laws and practices everywhere, inside and outside the South, in the past few years.

We salute James H. Meredith . . .

The Pittsburgh Courier, *editorial of October 6, 1962.*

As far as my relations with the students go, I make it a practice to be courteous. I don't force myself on them, but that's not my nature anyway. Many of them—most, I'd say—have been courteous, and the faculty members certainly have been. When I hear the jeers and the catcalls . . . I don't consider it personal. I get the idea people are just having a little fun. I think it's tragic that they have to have this kind of fun about me, but many of them are children of the men who lead Mississippi today, and I wouldn't expect them to act any other way . . .

It hasn't been all bad. Many students have spoken to me very pleasantly. They have stopped banging doors and throwing bottles into my dormitory now.

One fellow from my hometown sat down at my table in the cafeteria. "If you're here to get an education, I'm for you," he said. "If you're here to cause trouble, I'm against you." That seemed fair enough to me.

James Meredith, in a Saturday Evening Post *article of November 10, 1962.*

8. Birmingham and Tuscaloosa, Alabama: Spring 1963

BIRMINGHAM

In the spring of 1960, *New York Times* reporter Harrison Salisbury visited the South's largest industrial city, Birmingham, Alabama, to report on the booming steel town's race relations. "Whites and blacks still walk the same streets," Salisbury wrote, "But the streets, the water supply and the sewer system are about the only public facilities they share. Ball parks and taxicabs are segregated. So are libraries . . . Every channel of communication, every medium of mutual interest, every reasoned approach, every inch of middle ground has been fragmented by the emotional dynamite of racism, reinforced by the whip, the razor, the gun, the bomb, the torch, the club, the knife, the mob, the police and many branches of the state's apparatus."

By early 1963 the climate had changed little. Between 1957 and 1963, 18 unsolved bombings in black neighborhoods earned the city its nickname of "Bombingham." Birmingham was infamous for the Mother's Day mob attack on the Freedom Riders in 1961, when police purposely failed to intervene. Birmingham police chief, Eugene "Bull" Connor, directed his men to break up black political meetings, and since 1956 the NAACP had been kept out of Alabama. Connor, whose official title was commissioner of public safety, also punished whites who were deemed friendly to black rights. He twice had the manager of the city's bus terminal facilities arrested for flagrantly complying with federal orders to desegregate.

Martin Luther King Jr. called Birmingham the most segregated city in America. King, still smarting after his defeat in Albany, Georgia, wanted a victory to restore prestige to his Southern Christian Leadership Conference (SCLC). He also wanted to prove that nonviolence could still be effective, that "you can struggle without hating, you can fight without violence."

161

A decision to launch a campaign to end segregation in Birmingham was reached in a three-day strategy session conducted by the SCLC at its retreat in Dorchester, Georgia in January 1963. King, working with Ralph Abernathy, Wyatt Walker and Fred Shuttlesworth, president of the local civil rights organization—the Alabama Christian Movement for Human Rights (ACMHR), mapped out a careful plan of attack for fighting segregation in Birmingham. King believed that the debacle in Albany was caused by a nebulous protest strategy. This time the campaign would have a clear focus. They called their plan Project C—for confrontation.

PROJECT C

King and Shuttlesworth carefully selected boycott targets among downtown department stores, giving the protest economic leverage. Provisions were made for every possible contingency, including bail money for mass arrests. Extensive fund-raising by King and activist-entertainer Harry Belafonte raised several hundred thousand dollars.

To avoid wounding local sensibilities, King, Abernathy, Walker and Andrew Young repeatedly met with Birmingham's black leadership. A few hundred residents were recruited to teach the techniques of nonviolence in Birmingham's black churches. To further placate local black leaders, King postponed the direct action campaign until after the mayoral runoff election in April 1963 in order to aid the moderate candidate Albert Boutwell, an Alabama state senator, over the arch segregationist Bull Connor.

On April 2, 1963, the citizens of Birmingham chose Boutwell as their mayor. He had beaten Connor by 8,000 votes. The headline in the *Birmingham News* said, "A New Day Dawns for Birmingham." But King saw Boutwell as "just a dignified Bull Connor." Although Boutwell may have been a moderate segregationist compared to Connor, to the SCLC he was still a segregationist.

King and his SCLC colleagues arrived in Birmingham the day after the election. They promptly issued a manifesto spelling out the grievances of blacks in Birmingham. It called for an immediate end to racial restrictions in downtown lunch counters, rest rooms and stores, adoption of nonracial hiring practices, and the formation of a biracial committee to carry on continuing negotiations for further desegregation.

The first stage of Project C began on Wednesday, April 3, with a small group of protesters staging sit-ins at the segregated lunch counters in downtown department stores and drugstores. These efforts were quickly halted by Connor's police force, and by the end of the week, more than 150 demonstrators had been arrested.

A few days later, on April 6, the SCLC accelerated its demonstrations by having Shuttlesworth lead some 30 blacks in a march on city hall. The entire group was arrested and sent to jail. The next day, Palm Sunday, the Reverend A. D. King, Martin Luther King Jr.'s younger brother, led a prayer march through the downtown streets of Birmingham. In full glare of newspaper photographers and television cameras, demonstrators clashed with police who were using dogs and nightsticks.

King had anticipated that these kind of incidents would take place and hoped they would result in mobilizing large numbers of Birmingham blacks. Moreover, the demonstrations would focus national attention on the issue of civil rights. His calculations proved correct.

On April 10, city officials secured a state court injunction against further demonstrations. Alabama Circuit Court Judge W. A. Jenkins Jr. issued an order prohibiting 133 civil rights leaders, including King, Abernathy and Shuttlesworth, from participating or encouraging any sit-ins, picketing or other demonstrations. In Albany King had obeyed a similar order from a federal court. There he believed that he could not blatantly defy the very forces of national law that he was seeking as allies. But this time King announced that the law was designed to perpetuate a "raw tyranny under the guise of maintaining law and order." At a press conference, King announced his willingness to go to jail, and he would do so on Good Friday, April 12. "Here in Birmingham," King told reporters, "we have reached the point of no return."

Accompanied by Abernathy and Al Hibbler, the popular blues singer, King led about 50 hymn-singing marchers toward city hall, as they chanted "Freedom has come to Birmingham!" Nearly 1,000 blacks lined their route. Bull Connor, now infuriated, ordered his squad, who held snarling, snapping dogs, to arrest the demonstrators. Cameras from around the nation, even the world, captured the image of civil rights leaders Martin Luther King Jr., Ralph Abernathy and Fred Shuttlesworth being loaded into Bull Connor's windowless police van on Good Friday.

Letter from a Birmingham Jail

For King, this arrest marked his 13th in the South since his assumption as a leader in the anti-segregation effort. He was placed in solitary confinement in Birmingham's jail. He had no mattress or linen and slept on metal slats. One day after King's arrest, a full-page advertisement taken out by a local group of white moderate clergymen appeared in the *Birmingham News*. They attacked the demonstrations as "unwise and untimely" and concluded, "We do not believe that these days of new hope are days when extreme measures are justified in Birmingham."

From his prison cell, King replied to the ministers' letter by writing in the margins of the newspaper and on toilet paper. "I have yet to engage in a direct action campaign that was well-timed in the view of those who have not suffered from the disease of segregation," King wrote in what was later published as the essay *Letter from a Birmingham Jail.* "For years now, I have heard the word 'Wait.' It rings in the ears of every Negro with piercing familiarity. This 'Wait' has almost always meant 'Never.' We must come to see with one of our distinguished jurists that 'justice too long delayed is justice denied.' " The 6,500-word letter went on to explain to the clergy and to the world why the struggle against racism must not be deferred.

King's letter was first published as a pamphlet by the American Friends Service Committee, a Quaker group. It was reprinted in several national periodicals, and soon, with over a million copies in circulation, it became a classic of protest literature.

On April 20, 1963, King and Abernathy were freed on bail, but they emerged to find the demonstrations losing support. "We needed more troops," Wyatt Walker later recalled. "We had scraped the bottom of the barrel of adults who would go [to jail]." The civil rights leaders went directly to the Gaston Motel to plan the next phase of Project C.

THE CHILDREN'S CRUSADE

James Bevel, who had joined the SCLC in 1961 fresh from the Nashville sit-ins, had devised a strategy. He urged using Birmingham's black high school students as demonstrators. Bevel argued that while many adults might be reluctant to participate in marches and demonstrations, fearing that jail would cost them their jobs, children would be less fearful. King agreed with this strategy, and soon teenagers were crowding into the churches' nonviolent workshops. The children would march. King hoped this action would "subpoena the conscience of the nation to the judgment seat of morality."

On Thursday, May 2, the children began their demonstrations in Birmingham. Over 1,000 black children, ranging from six to eighteen years old, marched out of the Sixteenth Street Baptist Church to demonstrate and be arrested. Before reporters from around the nation, the young blacks sang freedom songs and chanted freedom slogans to hundreds of cheering adult spectators. Bull Connor brought in school buses to haul them away. By the end of the day, 959 children had been taken to Birmingham jails.

King was criticized for his "children's crusade" from every corner. From Washington, Attorney General Robert Kennedy called King to

Birmingham firemen used high-pressure hoses to disperse demonstrators, May 1963. Courtesy of the Schomburg Center for Research in Black Culture.

argue that the children could be seriously injured by Connor's police. "Real men," objected Black Muslim leader Malcolm X, "don't put their children on the firing line." King defended this strategy by responding that the children, by demonstrating, gained a "sense of their own stake in freedom and justice."

The next day, police barricaded the Sixteenth Street Baptist Church, where 1,000 black students had assembled. Connor had also ordered out the city's police dogs and firefighters. When some students tried to leave the church, the police struck. Using fire hoses at a pressure set to take off tree bark, they blasted the children, the jet streams ripping their clothes and leaving them bloodied on the ground. Several demonstrators were attacked indiscriminately by police swinging nightsticks, and attack dogs were set loose among the panicked crowd.

Across the nation, people watched television pictures of children being blasted with water hoses and attacked by police dogs. Newspapers and magazines, at home and abroad, featured the events in Birmingham on their front pages. The violent incidents had shocked the American public. They also had caught the attention of Washington. On May 4, the Justice Department sent Burke Marshall, assistant attorney general in charge of the department's civil rights division, to Birmingham to encourage negotiations between King and the city's business leaders.

For the next few days, the marches grew in size. By Monday, May 6, more than 2,000 demonstrators had been jailed. As the police repeatedly attempted to drive the marchers back into the black sections of the city, using hoses, dogs and clubs, some of them retaliated by jeering, taunting and throwing rocks. Fred Shuttlesworth was knocked against the side of a building by a high-pressure water jet of water, and was taken to the hospital badly bruised. Connor lamented that he had missed the scene and added, "I wish they'd carried him away in a hearse."

NEGOTIATION

By the time Burke Marshall arrived in Birmingham, many Birmingham merchants had become alarmed at the drop in sales and profits resulting from the boycotts and the turmoil that discouraged anyone from shopping in the downtown stores. Although at first they told Marshall that compromise was out of the question, Birmingham's merchants soon hastened their negotiations after they realized that continued disorder could ultimately result in damage to downtown stores.

"The city of Birmingham has reached an accord with its conscience," King, Shuttlesworth and Abernathy announced in a joint press conference on May 10, 1963. The four-point settlement provided: 1. desegregation of lunch counters, rest rooms, fitting rooms and drinking fountains in all downtown stores within 90 days; 2. placement of blacks in previously all-white clerical and sales positions in the stores, through upgrading or rehiring, within 60 days; 3. release of prisoners; and 4. establishment of permanent communication between white and black leaders. King viewed the agreement as "the most magnificent victory for justice we've seen in the Deep South." But, he cautioned, "We must move now from protest to reconciliation."

Like most compromises bridging bitter conflicts, this one elicited expressions of outrage from both sides. Some black critics charged King with bartering away their protest weapon for mere promises. Alabama Governor George Wallace disavowed any settlement, and Bull Connor urged a white boycott of stores that agreed to desegregate.

The night after the accord was announced, the Ku Klux Klan rallied outside Birmingham. Robert Shelton, grand dragon of the white supremacist group, said, "We would like to state at this time that any concessions that Martin Luther King or any other group of Negro leaders in Birmingham have received are not worth the paper they're written on or the bag that's holding the water. No business people in Birmingham or any other city have the authority to attempt any type of negotiations when it deals with governmental affairs or municipalities."

Following the Klan meeting, bombs exploded at the home of Martin Luther King Jr.'s brother and at the Gaston Motel, where King and his aides had been staying. Enraged blacks threw rocks at police. As rioting erupted, state troopers began beating blacks at random. Thirty-five blacks and five whites were injured, and seven stores were set ablaze.

President Kennedy warned that he would not permit extremists to undermine the agreement reached in Birmingham. On May 12, he ordered 3,000 federal troops to Fort McClellan, 30 miles outside of Birmingham. He hoped that the threat of federal intervention would motivate the state and local authorities to restore peace.

Exhausted, the city quieted down. Federal troops were not needed. Martin Luther King Jr., who had been in Atlanta visiting his family for the weekend, returned to counsel nonviolence and observance of the desegregation agreement. The conflict finally ended when the new mayor, Albert Boutwell and the new council honored the negotiated settlement.

TUSCALOOSA

On May 21, a federal district judge ordered the University of Alabama in Tuscaloosa to admit two black students to its summer session. Governor George Wallace immediately threatened to defy the court order and to bar the entrance of any black who attempted to desegregate the university. "I am the embodiment of the sovereignty of this state, and I will be present to bar the entrance of any Negro who attempts to enroll at the University of Alabama," announced Wallace.

Despite Wallace's pronouncements, he did not plan to have a replay of what took place at Ole Miss in 1962. On June 11, 1963, in a carefully scripted performance at the doorway of the campus building, Wallace first denied the demand by Deputy Attorney General Nicholas Katzenbach that the black students be admitted, then he stepped aside and let them enter.

Several hours after the first black students at the University at Alabama had registered, President Kennedy spoke to the nation on the issue of civil rights in a televised address. "The fires of frustration and discord are burning in every city," the president declared. "Where legal remedies are not at hand, redress is sought in the street, in demonstrations, parades and protests which create tensions and threaten violence—and threaten lives. We face, therefore, a moral crisis as a country and as a people . . . Next week, I shall ask Congress of the United States to act, to make a committment it has not fully made in this century to the proposition that race has no place in American life or law."

Kennedy delivered a new civil rights bill to Congress on June 19. The Southern Regional Council said the proposal for legislation, which covered public accommodations, schools, voting rights and equal employment, was "the strongest ever made by a president on Negro rights."

But Martin Luther King Jr., the SCLC, CORE, the NAACP, SNCC and other civil rights groups and activists knew by now that there could be no gain without some sort of massive action. They were not going to let this bill die in Congress. They would march on Washington to clearly demonstrate the degree of public demand for this legislation.

CHRONICLE OF EVENTS

1963

April 3: The first phase of the SCLC's Birmingham campaign begins with a series of sit-ins.

April 6: About 45 SCLC demonstrators march to Birmingham's city hall in silence and are arrested.

April 10: An Alabama state court enjoins Martin Luther King Jr. and other Birmingham leaders from leading demonstrations.

April 12: King leads a march of 50 demonstrators in Birmingham. King and Ralph Abernathy are arrested and placed in solitary confinement.

April 14: Coretta Scott King calls President John F. Kennedy to have him intercede in the release of her husband. U.S. Attorney General Robert Kennedy returns call for the president.

April 26: King and Abernathy are convicted on criminal contempt charges rather than charges of violating the April 10 injunction. They are fined because Birmingham officials do not want to have the two civil rights activists in jail.

May 2: Hundreds of school children join the SCLC demonstrations; 959 children are arrested.

May 3: Birmingham police chief Bull Connor uses police dogs and high-pressure water hoses on demonstrators. Rocks and bottles are thrown by black onlookers; the violent incident attracts nationwide media coverage.

May 4: U.S. Justice Department official Burke Marshall goes to Birmingham to encourage negotiations.

May 7: The SCLC agrees to a 24-hour truce; Bull Connor enlists Alabama Governor George Wallace's support, and 500 state troopers are sent to the Birmingham area.

May 10: The SCLC reaches an agreement with Birmingham city officials on instituting desegregation changes in return for an end to the demonstrations.

June 11: Guarded by federal troops, Vivian Malone and James Hood, enter the University of Alabama at Tuscaloosa after Governor George Wallace stands in the schoolhouse door. In a nationally televised speech, President Kennedy tells the nation that segregation is morally wrong and that it is time for action.

June 12: NAACP field secretary Medgar Evers is assassinated in front of his home in Jackson, Mississippi.

Eyewitness Testimony

I am prepared to go to jail and to stay as long as necessary.

Martin Luther King Jr., to the press, statement of April 11, 1963, in the New York Times *(April 12, 1963).*

Free-dom
Free-dom
Free-dom
Everybody want Free-dom
Free-dom
Free-dom

Spiritual sung by demonstrators in Birmingham, Alabama, April 1963.

On my way to freedomland.
On my way,
On my way to freedomland,
Oh, Lord,
Oh, Lord.

Spiritual sung by demonstrators in Birmingham, Alabama, April 1963.

Brutal use of police dogs against Negro citizens peacefully protesting segregated public facilities in Birmingham, Alabama shocks the conscience of America and reflects an ugly stain upon the United States throughout the entire world.

Harry Belafonte, actor and adviser to the SCLC, public statement of April 13, 1963, in the New York Times *(April 14, 1963).*

Both [King and Abernathy] were arrested, along with 50 other citizens, in violation of the constitutional guarantees of the first and 14th Amendments. Both are now in solitary confinement, allegedly "for their own safety."

We submit that these two distinguished Americans are political prisoners, and not criminals. We ask that you use the influence of your high office to persuade the city officials of Birmingham to afford at least a modicum of humane treatment. Neither of these men have mattresses or bed linens.

Wyatt Tee Walker, executive assistant to Dr. Martin Luther King Jr., to President Kennedy, telegram of April 14, 1963, in the New York Times *(April 15, 1963).*

We are confronted by a series of demonstrations by some of our Negro citizens, directed and led by outsiders. We recognize the natural impatience of people who feel that their hopes are slow in being realized. But we are convinced that these demonstrations are unwisely and untimely . . .

We . . . strongly urge our own Negro community to withdraw support from these demonstrations, and to unite locally in working peacefully for a better Birmingham. When rights are consistently denied, a cause should be pressed in the courts and in negotiations among local leaders, and not in the streets. We appeal to both our white and Negro citizenry to observe the principles of law and order and common sense.

Eight Alabama clergymen, to Dr. Martin Luther King Jr., public statement of April 13, 1963, in Liberation *(June 1963).*

Perhaps it is easy for those who have never felt the stinging darts of segregation to say, "Wait." But when you have seen vicious mobs lynch your mothers and fathers at will and drown your sisters and brothers at whim; when you have seen hate-filled policemen curse, kick and even kill your black brothers and sisters; when you see the vast majority of your twenty million Negro brothers smothering in an airtight cage of poverty in the midst of an affluent society; when you suddenly find your tongue twisted and your speech stammering as you seek to explain to your six-year-old daughter why she can't go to the public amusement park that has just been advertised on television, and see tears welling up in her eyes when she is told that Funtown is closed to colored children, and see ominous clouds of inferiority beginning to form in her little mental sky, and see her beginning to distort her personality by developing an unconscious bitterness toward white people; when you have to concoct an answer for a five-year-old son who is asking: "Daddy, why do white people treat colored people so mean?"; when you take a cross-country drive and find it necessary to sleep night after night in the uncomfortable corners of your automobile because no motel will accept you; when you are humiliated day in and day out by nagging signs reading "white" and "colored"; when your first name becomes "nigger," your middle name becomes "boy" (however old you are) and your last name becomes "John," and your wife and mother are never given the respected title "Mrs."; when you are harried by day and haunted by night by the fact that you are a Negro, living constantly at tiptoe stance, never quite knowing what to expect next, and are plagued with inner fears and outer resentments; when you are forever fighting a degenerating sense of "nobodiness"—then you will understand why we find it difficult to wait. There comes a time when the cup of endurance runs over, and men are no longer willing to be plunged into the abyss of despair. I hope, sirs, you can understand our legitimate and unavoidable impatience.

Martin Luther King Jr., to fellow clergymen, excerpt from "Letter from a Birmingham City Jail," April 16, 1963, in Why We Can't Wait *(1963).*

We may not get all of what we want all at once, but you can be rest assured the city of Birmingham will never be the same.

Ralph Abernathy, SCLC activist, to the press, statement of April 1963, in the New York Amsterdam News *(April 27, 1963).*

I'll stay in prison the rest of my days rather than make a butchery of my conscience. If I lived in Russia I could understand all this mess that's going on in Alabama . . .

We are determined. We will stop state court injunctions being used to stop peaceful protests. I'm tired of segregation. I'm tired of waiting.

The day is gone when they can stop a movement by jailing its leaders.

All our gains have come from nonviolent and legal struggle. Freedom must be demanded by the oppressed. It is never given up by the oppressors.

Now is the time to get up and move toward freedom land. They can't stop us now.

Martin Luther King Jr., statement of April 1963, in the [Baltimore] Afro-American *(May 4, 1963).*

I'm not afraid of an injunction. I've lived all my life under injunctions and restraining orders. We may have to go to jail, but I don't want you to worry about us. We'll have God by our side. They can't jail him. This movement must be kept going.

I can already bring you greetings from the Birmingham City Jail. I can tell you it's holy hell. For five days I was without a mattress, sleeping on steel. For nine days I was in solitary. For eight days they wouldn't even let me shave.

But I spent many hours with God and what joy and comfort He brought me.

Birmingham police turn dogs on demonstrators, May 1963. Courtesy of AP/Wide World Photos.

Ralph Abernathy, SCLC activist, to supporters, speech of April 1963, in the [Baltimore] Afro-American *(May 4, 1963).*

All you gotta do is tell them you're going to bring the dogs. Look at 'em run . . . I want to see them dogs work. Look at those niggers run.

Birmingham police chief Bull Connor, to the press, statement of May 3, 1963, in the Associated Press (May 4, 1963).

The dogs were terribly handled. They were deliberately unleashed into the crowds, biting women and children. The police made no effort to restrain them and the dogs were used to attack, not to contain the demonstrators. It was as though the police were trying to incite a riot.

Andrew Young, SCLC activist, statement of May 4, 1963, in the New York Post *(May 5, 1963).*

I am completely confident that local people, local white leadership in every area of the city's life, and responsible colored leadership in every area of their life, can establish understanding, communication and natural results. This is a trying hour, and the eyes of the world are fixed on us.

Birmingham Mayor-elect Albert Boutwell, public statement of May 4, 1963, in the New York Times *(May 5, 1963).*

The sad part of the picture is that as long as the trouble-makers disturb the peace and violate the laws of the community there can be little hope for progress toward improved race relations. But such progress is not what King and his group want. They thrive on trouble and the publicity it brings them. They give no thought to nor do they care what permanent damage they leave behind when the last possible dollar has been wrung from the Birmingham commotion and they move to greener pastures.

The Birmingham Post-Herald, *editorial of May 4, 1963.*

No American schooled in respect for human dignity can read without shame of the barbarities committed by Alabama police authorities against Negroes and white demonstrators for civil rights. The use of police dogs and high-pressure water hoses to subdue schoolchildren in Birmingham is a national disgrace. The herding of hundreds of teenagers and many not yet in their teens into jails and detention homes for demanding their birthright of freedom makes a mockery of legal process.

The New York Times, *editorial of May 5, 1963.*

If we can crack Birmingham, I am convinced we can crack the South. Birmingham is a symbol of segregation for the entire South.

Martin Luther King Jr., to a congregation at Ebenezer Baptist Church in Atlanta, Georgia, speech of May 5, 1963, in United Press International (May 5, 1963).

We're tired of waiting. We're telling Ol' Bull Connor right here tonight that we're on the march and we're not going to stop marching until we get our rights.

Fred L. Shuttlesworth, president of the Alabama Christian Movement for Human Rights, to a mass meeting in Birmingham, speech of May 1963, in the New York Times *(May 11, 1963).*

There are those who write history. There are those who make history. There are those who experience history. I don't know how many historians we have in Birmingham tonight. I don't how many of you would be able to write a history book. But you are certainly making history, and you are experiencing history. And you will make it possible for the historians of the future to write a marvelous chapter. Never in the history of this nation have so many people been arrested for a cause of freedom and human dignity!

Martin Luther King Jr., to a mass rally at St. Luke's Church in Birmingham, Alabama, speech of May 6, 1963, in Branch's Parting the Waters *(1988).*

Fight for freedom first, then go to school. Join the thousand in jail who are making their witness for freedom . . . It's up to you to free our teachers, our parents, yourself and the country.

Flier, Alabama Christian Movement for Human Rights, May 1963, in the New York Times *(May 7, 1963).*

You get an education in jail, too. In the schools you've been going to, they haven't taught you to be proud of yourselves . . . they haven't taught you the price of freedom . . . The white man has brainwashed us, tricked us; but Mr. Charlie's brainwashing is washing off now . . . And the most important thing in the struggle is to stay together . . . We've got to start learning to love one another enough to say: as long as one Negro kid is in jail, we all want to be in jail. If everybody in town would be arrested, everybody will be free, wouldn't they?

James Bevel, SCLC activist, to a group of Birmingham schoolchildren, speech of May 1963, in Baines' Birmingham, 1963: Confrontation Over Civil Rights *(1977).*

Don't think these smallest ones don't know what they want. They do.

They know they can't go to Kiddieland and ride the ponies like the white kids, and they know they can't appear on the afternoon TV shows like the white kids.

Ralph Abernathy, SCLC activist, statement of May 1963, in the [Baltimore] Afro-American *(May 18, 1963).*

I'll keep marching 'till I get freedom. I want to go to any school and any store downtown and sit in the movies and sit around in a cafeteria.

Anita Woods, 12-year-old Birmingham demonstrator, statement of May 1963, in the [Baltimore] Afro-American *(May 18, 1963).*

Birmingham police arrest a young demonstrator. Courtesy of the Schomburg Center for Research in Black Culture.

The mystery of the whole situation is how can these simple home folks be talked into going to jail by a bunch of rabble-rousers?

Birmingham police chief Bull Connor, to the press, statement of May 1963, in Garrow's Birmingham, Alabama, 1956–1963: The Black Struggle for Civil Rights (1989).

> Ain't gonna let Bull Connor
> Turn me round,
> Turn me round,
> Turn me round.

Chant, sung by school children at a march in Birmingham, Alabama in May 1963.

I saw 3,000 Negroes encircled in the Kelly-Ingram Park by policemen swinging clubs. The hoses were in action with the pressure wide open. On one side the students were confronted by clubs, on the other, by powerful streams of water. The firemen used the hoses to knock down the students. As the streams hit the trees, the bark was ripped off. Bricks were torn loose from the walls.

The hoses were directed at everyone with a black skin, demonstrators and non-demonstrators . . .

Meanwhile, over the public address system inside the church, I could hear a speaker admonishing the people to be non-violent . . . "We want to redeem the souls of people like Bull Connor."

Len Holt, civil rights attorney, on Birmingham police attacking demonstrators in Birmingham on May 6, 1963, in a National Guardian article of May 16, 1963.

Turn on your water, turn loose your dogs, we will stand here till we die.

Reverend Charles Phillips, Birmingham demonstration leader, public statement of May 5, 1963, in the New York Times (May 6, 1963).

All through the city the firemen drag their hoses, trying to douse this fire. But the demonstrators spring up first in one place and then in another—WE WANT FREEDOM!—then in another, then in another—WE WANT FREEDOM!—assembling, then spreading out from half a dozen churches across the town. Sometimes they picket, sometimes they march, sometimes they sit in. The water doesn't quench their truth, so the cops begin to try to put it away. They stuff the demonstrators into paddy wagons and rush them off to jail. The cars go rocketing through the streets of the city, from every direction—hands waving through the bars, the Negroes calling at the top of their voices: WE WANT FREEDOM! WE WANT FREEDOM! WE WANT FREEDOM! The city couldn't have provided them with a better public address system. The citizens of Birmingham stand on the sidewalks, eyes opening wide.

Barbara Demming, civil rights activist and journalist, on the events in Birmingham in early May 1963, in a Liberation article of summer 1963.

Before they went out to demonstrate they had to go in the church to write down their names and addresses so in case something happened we would know who they had in jail. And you'd put down "I'll stay there five days" or "I'll stay there 10 days." Sometimes you didn't stay there that long, but you'd say how long you were willing to stay before they came to get you.

And some, as soon as they got out of jail, they'd go right back in there—that's the way it was happening. Because when you get out you didn't want to stay home; you wanted to take part.

Notie B. Andrews, Birmingham demonstrator, recalling the nonviolent direct action campaign of May 1963, in the Alabama Christian Movement for Human Rights' Birmingham: People in Motion (1966).

At almost the precise moment merchants agreed to our demands, I heard one of the firemen across

President John Kennedy confers with his brother Robert (left), the attorney general, on how to resolve the situation in Birmingham. Courtesy of the National Archives.

the street from the 16th Street Church say, "Let's put some water on the reverend." I had moved freely among the firemen all day, helping to control the youngsters and was surprised by the statement. But as I looked toward the sound of the words, I caught sight of the powerful stream of water arching down upon me less than 50 feet away. Quickly I put my hands over my face and turned away as the water was knocked out of me, my chest ached, my head pounded, and my heart was trying to burst. Had I not thrown up my hands, my face probably would have been disfigured . . .
Fred L. Shuttlesworth, recalling the events in Birmingham on May 7, 1963, in an Ebony *article of August 1971.*

I waited a week to see Shuttlesworth get hit with a hose . . . I wish they'd carried him away in a hearse.
Birmingham Police Commissioner Bull Connor, to the press, statement of May 7, 1963, in the New York Times *(May 8, 1963).*

While much remains to be settled before the situation can be termed satisfactory, we can hope that tensions will ease, and that this case history, which has so far only narrowly avoided widespread violence and fatalities will remind every state, every community and every citizen how urgent it is that all bars to equal opportunity and treatment be removed as promptly as possible.
President John F. Kennedy, to the press, statement of May 8, 1963, in The Public Papers of the Presidents of the United States *(1962–1964).*

This President wants us to surrender this state to Martin Luther King and his group of pro-Communists who have instituted these demonstrations.
Alabama Governor George Wallace, public statement of May 8, 1963, in the New York Times *(May 9, 1963).*

Responsible leaders of both Negro and white communities of Birmingham, being desirous of promoting conditions which will ensure sound moral, economic and political growth of their city, in the interest of all citizens of Birmingham, after mutual considerations and discussion of the issues relating to the recent demonstrations in the city, have agreed to the following:

1. The desegregation of lunch counters, rest rooms, sitting rooms and drinking fountains . . .
2. The upgrading and hiring of Negroes on a non-discriminatory basis throughout the industrial community of Birmingham. This will include the hiring of Negroes as clerks and salesmen within the next 60 days, and the immediate appointment of a committee of business, industrial and professional leaders for the implementation of an area-wide program for acceleration of upgrading and the employment of Negroes in job categories previously denied to Negroes . . .
Fred L. Shuttlesworth, Martin Luther King Jr. and Ralph Abernathy, joint statement of May 10, 1963, in the New York Times *(May 11, 1963).*

Let every white person ask himself this question: What other way was there? To resist Negroes' demands unbendingly would have meant further demonstrations, further turmoil, further tragedy . . .

Birmingham had only one choice, distasteful as it was even to those who had to assume responsibility for making it in the name of the community. A time came when there was nothing left to do but make the choice. It now has been made, and sensible men and women will understand it.

The Birmingham News, editorial of May 10, 1963.

For a city like Birmingham with a history of difficult race relations, to reach a settlement like this after only a few hours of discussion in a most tense atmosphere is a tremendous step forward for Birmingham, for Alabama and for the South generally.

Burke Marshall, U.S. Department of Justice official, to the press, statement of May 10, 1963, in the New York Times (May 11, 1963).

All of us in all sections of the country have a great lesson to learn . . . the importance of getting a dialogue going between people in the North and South. We really have to start having great exchanges so that a Southern senator can talk to [Assistant U.S. Attorney General] Burke Marshall or the Attorney General to a Southern Governor and not lose votes for him, and a [Northern] politician can say something nice about some Southern leader and not feel that that is going to lose him the next election.

U.S. Attorney General Robert Kennedy, to the press, statement of May 10, 1963, in the New York Times (May 11, 1963).

We must not see the present development as a victory for the Negro; it is rather a victory for democracy and the whole citizenry of Birmingham—Negro and white. Our growth in nonviolence has been such that we cannot be satisfied with a "victory" over our white brothers. We must respond to every new development in civil rights with an understanding of those who have opposed us, and with an appreciation of the new adjustments that the new achievements pose for them.

Martin Luther King Jr., public statement of May 10, 1963, on the agreement reached with white Birmingham business and civil leaders, in the New York Times (May 11, 1963).

The lesson of Birmingham is that the Negroes have lost their fear of the white man's reprisals and will react today with violence if provoked. This could happen anywhere in the country today . . . the Negro masses will no longer stand by passively at the sight of police brutality.

Malcolm X, Black Muslim leader, to the press, statement of May 10, 1963, in the New York Times (May 11, 1963).

More shocking than the cruel police action itself has been the failure of "decent" Americans to raise a tremendous chorus of outrage over these practices . . .

Birmingham . . . has taught us the important lesson that we must be strong and resolute enough to relentlessly prosecute our fight for freedom alone . . .

As Dr. Martin Luther King, Jr. so aptly states it: "We are going on and on. We are not going to stop until the walls of segregation are crushed. We've gone too far to turn back now."

The [Baltimore] Afro-American editorial of May 18, 1963.

I have been invited often by the State Department to represent the United States at international student meetings abroad . . . but when I got back here with the team I couldn't ride in the same taxi with white runners . . . I say to President Kennedy: Don't invite me to go to Vietnam or Venezuela. Don't invite me to join the peace corps and go abroad to help other nations solve their problems. I say send me to Alabama or Mississippi.

Marvin Robinson, former track star and honor student in Birmingham, statement of May 1963, in the New York Post (May 20, 1963).

The fires of frustration and discord are burning in every city, North and South. Where legal remedies are not at hand, redress is sought in the streets in demonstrations, parades and protests, which create tensions and threaten violence—and threaten lives.

We face, therefore a moral crisis as a country and as a people . . .

I am therefore asking the Congress to enact legislation giving all Americans rights to be served in facilities which are open to the public—hotels, restaurants, theaters, retail stores and similar establishments. This seems to me to be an elementary right . . .

This is one country. It has become one country because all of us and all the people who came here had an equal chance to develop their talents.

We cannot say to 10 percent of the population that "you can't have that right. Your children can't have the chance to develop whatever talents they have, that the only way that they're going to get their rights is to go in the streets and demonstrate."

I think we owe them and we owe ourselves a better country than that.

President John F. Kennedy, to the American
people, television speech of June 11, 1963, in
The Public Papers of the Presidents of the
United States *(1962–1964).*

The Negro masses are no longer prepared to wait for anybody: not for elections, not to count votes, not to wait on the Kennedys or for legislation, nor, in fact, for Negro leaders themselves. They are going to move. Nothing can stop them from moving. And if that Negro leadership does not move rapidly enough and effectively enough they will take it into their own hands and move anyhow.

And out of this we can see a new phase for the civil rights movement. It is the phase of the use of mass action—nonviolent disobedience and nonviolent noncooperation.

Bayard Rustin, SCLC activist and author, mag-
azine Article of June 18, 1963, in Down the
Line: The Collected Writings of Bayard
Rustin *(1971).*

9. The March on Washington: 1963

A. PHILIP RANDOLPH

In July 1963, A. Philip Randolph, the architect of the March on Washington movement of 1941, once again mounted plans for a massive rally in the nation's capital. Randolph, 74, the founder and president of the Brotherhood of Sleeping Car Porters (BSCP), was the elder statesman of the civil rights movement. Founded in 1925, the BSCP was a union of black porters who worked on the nation's railroad cars. At that time, there were no railroad unions open to blacks. BSCP members traveled throughout the country and were involved in labor issues as well as civil rights matters. They were considered by many blacks as "civil rights missionaries on wheels."

In 1941, as the nation moved closer to entering World War II, Randolph planned a mass march on Washington to demand more jobs for blacks in the defense industries. At the time, 75% of the defense industry was barred to blacks. A day before the march, President Roosevelt met with Randolph and agreed to issue an executive order stating that "there shall be no discrimination in employment of workers in defense industries or government because of race, creed, color or national origin." Executive Order 8022 was the federal government's strongest civil rights directive since the Reconstruction period. Roosevelt also agreed to form the Fair Employment Practices Committee (FEPC). In return, Randolph called off the march on Washington.

With the rise of Martin Luther King Jr. in the mid-1950s, Randolph once again set forth plans for a national protest, aiming now to combine King's charismatic appeal with the NAACP's organizational strength. Although only 25,000 predominantly black marchers rallied in the capital on May 17, 1957, to commemorate the third anniversary of the NAACP's victory in the *Brown* case, the rally did establish a precedent, which was reinforced with youth marches in the two following years.

In January 1963, Randolph had suggested a march on Washington to dramatize the plight of unemployed blacks. Black unemployment was at 11%, but for whites, the figure was only 5%. A white family earned, on average, about $6,500 a year; a black family earned $3,500 a year. But Randolph's call was ignored. Then a few months later came the

A. Philip Randolph (right), who first planned a march on Washington in 1941, with Bayard Rustin, deputy director of the 1963 march. Courtesy of the A. Philip Randolph Institute.

violent attacks on demonstrators in Birmingham. Finally, Randolph's dream of a mass protest on the nation's capital for fair treatment and equal opportunity for blacks began to receive serious attention from various civil rights leaders, including Martin Luther King of the SCLC, James Farmer of CORE, Roy Wilkins of the NAACP, John Lewis of SNCC and Whitney Young of the National Urban League.

ORGANIZING THE MARCH ON WASHINGTON FOR JOBS AND FREEDOM

The coordination of Randolph's proposed march fell to his chief aide, Bayard Rustin, a veteran of the March on Washington movement of 1941 and one of the most skillful organizers in the civil rights movement. Fifty-one-year-old Rustin had worked with James Farmer of CORE on various protests and with King during the Montgomery bus boycott. It was Rustin who persuaded King to found a regional network of black ministers, which ultimately became the Southern Christian Leadership Conference (SCLC). He was involved in organizing all three of the March on Washington rallies of the 1950s.

In the spring of 1963, Randolph and Rustin met with labor and civil rights leaders to plan the August 28 march. In order to enlist a broader spectrum of supporters, they agreed to expand the goals of the march to include demands for passage of the Civil Rights Act, integration of schools and the enactment of a fair employment practices bill prohibiting job discrimination. To avoid any disastrous backlash against the march, the site of the rally was shifted, from the Capitol to the Lincoln Memorial.

At first, President Kennedy tried to persuade the civil rights leaders to call off the march, stressing that violence would likely occur. The president met with the civil rights leaders on June 22. Fearing civil disruption, he told them, "We want success in Congress, not just a big show at the Capitol. Some of these people are looking for an excuse to be against us. I don't want to give any of them a chance to say, 'Yes I'm for the [civil rights] bill, but I'm damned if I will vote for it at the point of a gun.' It seemed to me a great mistake to announce a march on Washington before the bill was even in committee. The only effect is to create an atmosphere of intimidation—and this may give some members of Congress an out."

However, since plans for the march were well under way by late June, the president could not expect the demonstration to be called

Bayard Rustin. Courtesy of the National Archives.

off. The president reluctantly endorsed the march. At a press conference on July 17, Kennedy told reporters that the March on Washington will be "in the great tradition of peaceful assembly for the redress of grievance."

The original organizers of the March—Randolph, Wilkins, Young, King, Farmer and Lewis—were joined by Mathew Ahmann, executive director of the National Catholic Conference for Interracial Justice; Reverend Eugene Carson Blake, chief executive of the United Presbyterian Church and vice-chairman of the Commission on Religion and Race of the National Council of Churches of Christ in America; Rabbi Joachim Prinz, president of the American Jewish Congress; and Walter P. Reuther, president of the United Auto Workers and chairman of the industrial union department of the AFL-CIO.

As deputy director of the March on Washington for Jobs and Freedom, it was Rustin's job to solve many unprecedented logistical problems, including moving thousands of people into Washington and out in one day, feeding them, working with nearly 1,500 organizations and making sure that the demonstration was a peaceful one. Years later Rustin recalled, "We wanted to get everybody from the whole country into Washington by nine o'clock in the morning and out of Washington by sundown. This required all kinds of things that you had to think through. You had to think how many toilets you needed, where they should be. Where is your line of march? We had to consult doctors on exactly what people should bring to eat so that they wouldn't get sick . . ."

The march was publicized by local civil rights and church groups throughout the country. From across the nation, "freedom buses" and "freedom trains" brought marchers to Washington—21 special trains and 16 regular trains carried march participants to Washington, and 1,514 special buses were pressed into service.

Some even walked to Washington. Fifteen members of CORE started out on foot from Brooklyn on August 15 and arrived on the evening before the march with five additional members who had joined the group in Philadelphia. Ledger Smith roller-skated 698 miles from Chicago, taking 10 days for the trip. "I'm tired," he told the crowd, "Let my legs speak for me."

August 28, 1963

One hundred years and 240 days after President Abraham Lincoln proclaimed, "All persons held as slaves within any state, or designated part of a state, the people whereof shall there be in rebellion against the United States, shall be . . . forever free," over 200,000

More than 250,000 demonstrators came to march on Washington. They represented a coalition of civil rights workers, church groups and labor leaders. Courtesy of the U.S. News & World Report Collection, Library of Congress.

Americans, the majority of them black but many of them white, descended on the nation's capital to declare that the time of patient waiting for long overdue equality was coming to an end.

By noon on August 28, 1963, a sea of placards was stretched out across the Lincoln Memorial: "We Demand Voting Rights Now!" . . . "We Demand Jobs for All Now!" . . . "We Demand Integrated Schools Now!" . . . "We Demand First-Class Citizenship Now!" Blacks and whites marched together from the Washington Monument to the Lincoln Memorial, and the next day in the *New York Times* it was reported as "the greatest assembly for a redress of grievances that this capital has ever seen."

As the throngs of demonstrators waited for the speeches to begin, Joan Baez led the crowd in singing "We Shall Overcome." Peter, Paul and Mary sang Bob Dylan's "Blowin' in the Wind": "How many times must a man look up before he can see the sky?"

The father of the march, A. Philip Randolph, began the program by placing the day's events into perspective: "Let the nation and the world know the meaning of our numbers. We are not a pressure group, we are not an organization or a group of organizations, we are not a mob. We are the advance guard of a massive revolution for jobs and freedom."

John Lewis, the 23-year-old SNCC leader, had planned to deliver a fiery speech that made many of his colleagues tremble. He intended to criticize the Kennedys and to denounce the civil rights bill as useless. After reading the text of Lewis' speech, the organizers of the march asked Lewis to tone down his address. King and Rustin were unable to persuade the young leader to compromise. But in deference to A. Philip Randolph, who told Lewis, "We've come this far, for the sake of unity, change it," Lewis reluctantly agreed to alter his text.

Although Lewis' remarks were modified only minutes before he delivered his address, he still managed to express his anger, but in a restrained sort of way: "To those who say 'be patient and wait,' we must say that we cannot be patient. We do not want our freedom gradually, but we want to be free now."

I HAVE A DREAM

The sweltering afternoon featured an array of speakers, each alloted 15 minutes. The prevailing memory of the rally, however, was the closing address by Martin Luther King Jr. At first, King's speech was a formal but powerful recitation of the struggle waged by black Americans for their freedom, then Mahalia Jackson called out from behind him, "Tell them about your dream!" Encouraged by the assembled marchers and sheer inspiration, King put aside his prepared text and began his exultant dream of freedom:

"I have a dream that one day this nation will rise up and live out the true meaning of its creed: 'We hold these truths to be self-evident; that all men are created equal.' I have a dream that one day on the red hills of Georgia the sons of former slaves and the sons of former slave owners will be able to sit down together at the table of brotherhood . . ."

King's magnificent speech symbolized the theme of the march. It was one of hope and racial harmony. Author James Baldwin later remarked, "That day, for a moment, it almost seemed that we stood on a height and could see our inheritance; perhaps we could make the kingdom real, perhaps the beloved community would not forever remain that dream one dreamed in agony."

A SENSE OF HOPE

At the end of the day's rally, President Kennedy publicly lauded "the deep fervor and the quiet dignity that characterizes the thousands who have gathered in the nation's capital from across the country to demonstrate their faith and confidence in our democratic form of government." He invited 10 of the main organizers, including John Lewis, to a reception in the White House. As the group met with Kennedy in the Cabinet Room, the president agreed that the march was indeed successful but cautioned them that "very strong bipartisan support" would be needed to get a civil rights bill through Congress. The votes, as yet, were not there, nor was there any indication that the march had changed the situation.

It is unclear whether the March on Washington accelerated the progress of the 1964 Civil Rights Act through Congress. For many months after the rally, legislators did not endorse the bill. However, the March on Washington did result in giving a sense of hope to thousands of Americans, both black and white, that the civil rights movement had firmly established itself.

For Bayard Rustin and the others who had planned the march, the day was only a brief vacation from their never-ending work of breaking down segregation. The field secretaries and organizers returned to the hard-core Deep South to continue their campaign for equality.

CHRONICLE OF EVENTS

1963

June 20: President John F. Kennedy meets with national civil rights leaders and reluctantly agrees to the March on Washington demonstration.

July 17: President Kennedy announces that the March on Washington will be "in the great tradition of peaceful assembly for the redress of grievance."

August 28: More than 200,000 people of all races and colors gather at the Lincoln Memorial in the March on Washington, the largest protest to date in the nation's history. March-ers demand legislation to end discrimination in education, housing, employment and courts; Martin Luther King Jr. delivers his "I Have a Dream" speech.

September 9: Tuskegee, Alabama schools open late, as Governor George Wallace tries to fight desegregation order.

September 10: President Kennedy federalizes the Alabama National Guard to enable black students to enter the school system.

September 15: Four black girls are killed in a bombing at the Sixteenth Street Baptist Church in Birmingham, Alabama.

November 22: President Kennedy is assassinated in Dallas, Texas; Lyndon B. Johnson becomes president.

An aerial view gives an idea of the huge throng that clustered around the Lincoln Memorial. Courtesy of the U.S. News & World Report Collection, Library of Congress.

EYEWITNESS TESTIMONY

We call upon you and upon all organizations—churches, fraternal societies, labor unions, civil groups, youth groups and professional associations—to accelerate the dynamic, non-violent thrust of the civil rights revolution by joining the March on Washington for Jobs and Freedom; to restore economic freedom to all this nation; to blot out once and for all the scourge of racial discrimination; the time is now.

Pamphlet, July 1963, in the March on Washington's To March on Washington (1963).

I think that the way the Washington march is now developed, which is a peaceful assembly calling for a redress of grievances, the cooperation with the police, every evidence that it is going to be peaceful, they are going to the Washington Monument, they are going to express their strong views. I look forward to being here . . . We want citizens to come to Washington if they feel that they are not having their rights expressed . . .

Some people, however, who keep talking about demonstrations never talk about the problem of redressing grievances . . . You just can't tell people, "Don't protest," but on the other hand, "We are not going to let you come into a store or restaurant." It seems to me it is a two-way street.

President John F. Kennedy, to the press, statement of July 17, 1963, in The Public Papers of the Presidents of the United States (1962–1964).

The Washington March of August 28 is more than just a demonstration.

It was conceived as an outpouring of the deep feeling of millions of white and colored American citizens that the time has come for the government of the United States of America, and particularly for the Congress of that government, to grant and guarantee complete equality in citizenship to the Negro minority of our population.

As such, the Washington March is a living petition—in the flesh—of the scores of thousands of citizens of both races who will be present from all parts of the country.

It will be orderly, but not subservient. It will be proud, but not arrogant. It will be nonviolent, but not timid. It will be unified in purpose and behavior, not splintered into groups and individual competitors. It will be outspoken but not raucous.

It will have the dignity befitting a demonstration in behalf of the human rights of twenty millions of people, with the eye and the judgment of the world focused upon Washington, D.C., on August 28, 1963.

Statement of August 27, 1963 by the leaders of the March on Washington for Jobs and Freedom, in the NAACP's Speeches by the Leaders: The March on Washington for Jobs and Freedom (n.d.)

The only weapon we have is protest. This ride isn't going to be a waste of time. I think this march will be remembered indefinitely.

Rev. Charles Billups, captain of a busload of black marchers from Alabama, statement of August 27, 1963, in the New York Times (August 28, 1963).

This week's March on Washington is not the culmination of the Negro's drive for civil equality but the beginning of a drive for economic preference and full employment. This may "annoy" whites, but the American Negro has obviously decided that he has to annoy the white man to wake him up.

James Reston, New York Times columnist, article of August 28, 1963.

We March for Effective Civil Rights Laws Now.

Placard, at the March on Washington, August 28, 1963.

We Demand Voting Rights Now.

Placard, at the March on Washington, August 28, 1963.

We Demand Integrated Schools Now.

Placard, at the March on Washington, August 28, 1963.

If You're Not Against Discrimination, You're Not for Freedom.

Placard, at the March on Washington, August 28, 1963.

Move on, move on, move on with the freedom fight, Move on, move on, we're fighting for equal rights.

Hymn sung by marchers at the March on Washington, August 28, 1963.

You are on the eve of a complete victory. You can't go wrong. The world is behind you.

Martin Luther King Jr. (second from left) is shown leading the crowd of marchers to the Lincoln Memorial, where they listened to him make his eloquent "I Have a Dream" speech. Courtesy of the U.S. News & World Report Collection, Library of Congress.

Josephine Baker, entertainer, to the rally at the Lincoln Memorial, August 28, 1963, in the New York Times *(August 29, 1963).*

We will kneel-in, we will sit-in, until we can eat in any counter in the United States. We will walk until we are free, until we can walk to any school and take our children to any school in the United States. And we will sit-in and we will kneel-in and we will lie-in if necessary until every Negro in America can vote. This we pledge you, the women of America.

Daisy Bates, Alabama NAACP regional director, to the rally at the Lincoln Memorial, address of August 28, 1963, in the New York Times *(August 29, 1963).*

Those who deplore our militancy, who exhort patience in the name of a false peace are in fact supporting segregation and exploitation. They would have social peace at the expense of social and racial justice. They are more concerned with easing racial tensions than enforcing racial democracy. The months and years ahead will bring new evidence of masses in motion for freedom. The March on Washington is not the climax of our struggle but a new beginning not only for the Negro but for all Americans who thirst for freedom and a better life.

A. Philip Randolph, president of the Brotherhood of Sleeping Car Porters, address at the Lincoln Memorial, August 28, 1963, in the

The shuffle of marching feet continued for hours as thousands upon thousands of demonstrators massed in the nation's capital. Courtesy of the U.S. News & World Report Collection, Library of Congress.

NAACP's Speeches by the Leaders: The March on Washington for Jobs and Freedom *(n.d.).*

We do not . . . come to this Lincoln Memorial in any arrogant spirit of moral or spiritual superiority to "set the nation straight" or to judge or to denounce the American people in whole or part.

Rather we come—late, late we come—in the reconciling and repentant spirit in which Abraham Lincoln of Illinois once replied to a delegation of morally arrogant churchmen. He said, "Never say God is on our side, rather pray that we may be found on God's side."

Eugene Carson Blake, vice-chairman of the Commission on Race Relations of the National Council of Churches, address at the Lincoln Memorial, August 28, 1963, in the NAACP's Speeches by the Leaders: The March on Washington for Jobs and Freedom *(n.d.)*

To those who say "be patient and wait," we must say that we cannot be patient. We do not want our freedom gradually, but we want to be free now. We are tired. We are tired of being beaten by policemen.

We are tired of seeing our people locked up in jail over and over again, and then you holler be patient. How long can we be patient? We want our freedom and we want it now. We do not want to go to jail but we will go to jail if this is the price we must pay for love, brotherhood and true peace.

John Lewis, chairman of the Student Nonviolent Coordinating Committee (SNCC), address at the Lincoln Memorial, August 28, 1963, in the NAACP's Speeches by the Leaders: The March on Washington for Jobs and Freedom *(n.d.)*

As an American, I stand for equal opportunity and full constitutional rights for all our people as a matter of morality, decency and simple justice. I am for civil rights and equal opportunity because freedom is an invincible value and so long as any person is denied his freedom, my freedom is in jeopardy. I am for civil rights and equal opportunity because American democracy cannot defend freedom in Berlin as long as we continue to deny freedom in Birminghan.

Walter P. Reuther, president of the United Auto Workers, AFL-CIO, address at the Lincoln Memorial, in the NAACP's Speeches by the Leaders: The March on Washington for Jobs and Freedom *(n.d.).*

I wanted with all my heart to be with you in Washington on this great day. My imprisoned brothers and sisters wanted to be there too! I cannot come out while they are still in, for their "crime" was the same as mine—demanding FREEDOM NOW! And most of them will not come out until the charges are dropped or their sentences served . . .

So we cannot be with you in body, but we are with you in spirit. By marching on Washington, your tramping feet have spoken the message of our struggle in Louisiana—you have given voice to the struggle of our people in Mississippi and Alabama, too and in California and Chicago and New York. You have come from all over the nation and in one mighty voice you have spoken to the nation.

James Farmer, CORE executive director, to the March on Washington, message of August 28, 1963, delivered to the rally at the Lincoln Memorial by Floyd B. McKissick, CORE national chairman, in the NAACP's Speeches by the Leaders: The March on Washington for Jobs and Freedom *(n.d.) [Farmer was in jail in Louisiana on charges stemming from civil rights demonstrations.]*

The hour is late. The gap is widening. The rumble of the drums of discontent, resounding throughout this land, are heard in all parts of the world. The missions which we send there, to "keep the world safe for democracy," are shallow symbols unless with them goes the living testament that this country practices at home the doctrine which it seems to promote abroad.

Whitney M. Young Jr., National Urban League executive director, address at the Lincoln Memorial, in the NAACP's Speeches by the Leaders: The March on Washington for Jobs and Freedom (n.d.)

Those of us gathered here before the Lincoln Memorial, and those of us gathered in witness around the nation, pledge ourselves that now is the time we respond to the demand of our conscience. Now is the time we grasp the ideal our faiths and our constitution hold before us. There is no turning back. In a decade or less we will have done our utmost to have secured a community of justice and fraternity and love among us, or we will have laid the seeds of our own destruction.

Mathew Ahmann, executive director of the National Catholic Conference on Interracial Justice, address at the Lincoln Memorial, August 28, 1963, in the NAACP's Speeches by the Leaders: The March on Washington for Jobs and Freedom (n.d.).

We are here today because we want the Congress of the United States to hear from us—in person—what many of us have told our public officials back home:

"We want freedom."

We came to petition our lawmakers to be as brave as our sit-ins and marchers, to be as daring as James Meredith, as unafraid as the nine children of Little Rock . . .

We have come asking the enactment of legislation that will affirm the right to "life, liberty and the pursuit of happiness," legislation that will place the resources and the honor of the government of all the people behind the pledge of equality in the Declaration of Independence.

Roy Wilkins, NAACP executive secretary, address at the Lincoln Memorial, August 28, 1963, in the NAACP's Speeches by the Leaders: The March on Washington for Jobs and Freedom (n.d.).

America must not become a nation of onlookers. It must not be silent. Not merely black America, but all of America. It must speak up and act, from the President down to the humblest of us, and not for the sake of the colored citizens but for the sake of America.

Joachim Prinz, president of the American Jewish Congress, address at the Lincoln Memorial, August 28, 1963, in the NAACP's Speeches by the Leaders: The March on Washington for Jobs and Freedom (n.d.).

I say to you today, my friends, so even though we face the difficulties of today and tomorrow, I still have a dream. It is a dream deeply rooted in the American meaning of its creed, "We hold these truths to be self-evident, that all men are created equal." I have a dream that one day on the red hills of Georgia, sons of former slaves and the sons of former slave owners will be able to sit down together at the table of brotherhood. I have a dream that one day even the state of Mississippi, a state sweltering with the heat of injustice, sweltering with the heat of oppression, will be transformed into an oasis of freedom and justice. I have a dream that my four little children will one day live in a nation where they will not be judged by the color of their skin, but the content of their character.

I have a dream today!

I have a dream that one day down in Alabama—with its vicious racists, with its governor having his

Martin Luther King Jr. delivered his memorable "I Have a Dream" speech from the steps of the Lincoln Memorial. Courtesy of the Schomburg Center for Research in Black Culture.

lips dripping with the words of interposition and nullification—one day right here in Alabama, little black boys and black girls will be able to join hands with little white boys and white girls as sisters and brothers.

I have a dream today . . .

So let freedom ring from the prodigious hilltops of New Hampshire; let freedom ring from the mighty mountains of New York; let freedom ring from the heightening Alleghenies of Pennsylvania; let freedom ring from the snow-capped Rockies of Colorado; let freedom ring from the curvaceous slopes of California. But not only that. Let freedom ring from Stone Mountain of Georgia; let freedom ring; let freedom ring from Lookout Mountain of Tennessee; let freedom ring from every hill and molehill of Mississippi. From every mountainside, let freedom ring.

And when this happens and when we allow freedom to ring, when we let it ring from every village and every hamlet, from every state and every city, we will be able to speed up that day when all God's children, black men and white men, Jews and gentiles, will be able to join hands and sing in the words of the old Negro spiritual: "Free at last, Free at last. Thank God Almighty, we are free at last!"

Martin Luther King Jr., president of the Southern Christian Leadership Conference (SCLC), address at the Lincoln Memorial, August 28, 1963, in the NAACP's Speeches by the Leaders: The March on Washington for Jobs and Freedom *(n.d.)*

The people were the real story here . . . not the speakers.

Roy Wilkins, NAACP executive secretary, statement of August 28, 1963, in the [Baltimore] Afro-American, *September 7, 1963.*

Up until this point, I don't think the country has realized how we feel. After this day they will.

Jean Boudwin, New York City post office worker and marcher, statement of August 28, 1963, in the New York Times *(August 29, 1963).*

I simply came here because I'm for freedom.

Tommy Greenwood, black marcher from Knoxville, Tennessee, statement of August 28, 1963. in the Washington Post *(August 29, 1963).*

If I ever had any doubts before, they're gone now. I've followed it this far. When I get back there tomorrow I'm going to do whatever needs to be done—I don't care if its picketing or marching or sitting-in or what, I'm ready to do it.

Hazel Mangie Rivers, marcher from Alabama, statement of August 28, 1963, in the New York Times *(August 29, 1963).*

We are not here as celebrities. We are Negroes and we have a stake in this.

Sammy Davis Jr., entertainer, statement of August 28, 1963, in the Washington Post *(August 29, 1963).*

It's so good to see our whole country sticking together in one strong body. People were afraid before, but there's nothing to fear now. I have high hopes that everything is going to come out all right.

Mahalia Jackson, gospel singer, statement of August 28, 1963, in the Washington Post *(August 29, 1963).*

The heart of the American Negro was revealed today. This was an unforgettable demonstration. It was dignified, extraordinarily disciplined and intensely patriotic.

Senator Jacob Javits (R, N.Y.), statement of August 28, 1963, in the Baltimore Sun *(August 29, 1963).*

I think it's uncalled for and unnecessary.

Senator Strom Thurmond (D, S.C.), statement of August 28, 1963, in the Baltimore Sun *(August 29, 1963).*

It was a great day for the civil rights movement, but we've got to have more of this type of thing before we are free.

Congressman Adam Clayton Powell Jr. (D, N.Y.), statement of August 28, 1963, in The [Baltimore] Afro-American, *September 7, 1963.*

Today over 100,000 Americans gathered in front of the Lincoln Memorial to "redress old grievances and help resolve an American crisis." It was a moving reminder that, 100 years after the Emancipation Proclamation, American citizens have not achieved the equality promised by Abraham Lincoln and guaranteed by the Constitution. The time truly has come to change rhetoric into reality.

The very fact that so many were willing to travel at their own expense, on their own time and from

People came from across the nation to attend the March on Washington for Jobs and Freedom. Courtesy of the U.S. News & World Report Collection, Library of Congress.

long distances to Washington to stand up and be counted underlines the urgency of the issue.

The more than 100,000 marchers represented many, many more who could not come in person to petition their government.

Congressman William Fitts Ryan (D, N.Y.), to Congress, speech of August 28, 1963, in the Congressional Record *(1963).*

At the demonstration I saw Americans who were dedicated to the principles of individual liberty, political freedom, and the Constitution of the United States. I saw there an integrated audience. It has been said that one picture is worth a thousand words. Today, millions of the American people saw, by television, people of various races, creeds, and nationalities standing together, singing together, speak-ing together, walking together, playing together, and working together in the nation's capital. Let no one tell me it is necessary to have segregation . . .

The participants were like actors in a mighty drama. Who was the audience, and where was the audience? Not here. The audience was back in every village, town, hamlet, city, and farm home in America—185 million people—because this great drama went out to the people this afternoon. I venture to say that there was more mass education on the issues of social justice and human rights in America than in all the history of our Republic.

Senator Hubert H. Humphrey (D, Minn.), to the Senate, speech of August 28, 1963, in the Congressional Record *(1963).*

There is much at stake in this historic battle. Time is wasting. We do not have much time. Speaker after speaker this afternoon did not hesitate to use the ugly word and say that a revolution is on in America—a peaceful revolution. But we never know the ultimate course of revolutions, if people who are revolting believe their rights are constantly faced with one setback after another.

I shall continue to pray that this revolution may be resolved quickly, to remove the danger of any threat to the Republic, and that it may be done within our constitutional process of government by law. But that is up to us, the politicians. We shall have much to answer if we start to water down, to duck and hedge, weave, and equivocate, in respect to the rightful demands of the colored people of America, expressed again in the shadows of Lincoln's shrine this afternoon, at the great historic meeting that was held there.

Senator Wayne Morse (D, Ore.), to the Senate, speech of August 28, 1963, in the Congressional Record *(1963).*

We have witnessed today in Washington tens of thousands of Americans—both Negro and white—exercising their right to assemble peaceably and direct the widest possible attention to a great national issue. Efforts to secure equal treatment and equal opportunity for all without regard to race, color, creed, or nationality are neither novel nor difficult to understand. What is different today is the intensified and widespread public awareness of the need to move forward in achieving these objectives—objectives which are older than this Nation.

President John Kennedy meets with the leaders of the March on Washington. From left to right: Whitney M. Young Jr., National Urban League; Martin Luther King Jr., Southern Christian Leadership Conference; John Lewis, Student Nonviolent Coordinating Committee (rear); Joachim Prinz, American Jewish Congress; Eugene Carson Blake, National Council of Churches; A. Philip Randolph, AFL-CIO vice-president; Kennedy; Walter Reuther, United Auto Workers; Vice-President Lyndon Johnson (rear); and Roy Wilkins, NAACP.

Although this summer has seen remarkable progress in translating civil rights from principles into practices, we have a very long way yet to travel. One cannot help but be impressed with the deep fervor and the quiet dignity that characterizes the thousands who have gathered in the Nation's Capitol from across the country to demonstrate their faith and confidence in our democratic form of government . . .

President John F. Kennedy, statement of August 28, 1963, in The Public Papers of the Presidents of the United States *(1962–1964).*

For the most part, they came silently during the night and early morning, occupied the great shaded boulevards along the Mall, and spread through the parklands between the Washington Monument and the Potomac. But instead of the emotional horde of angry militants that many had feared, what Washington saw was a vast army of quiet, middle-class Americans who had come in the spirit of the church

outing. And instead of the tensions that had been expected, they gave this city a day of sad music, strange silences and good feeling in the streets.

Russell Baker, journalist, article of August 29, 1963, in the New York Times.

There is a magnificent opportunity at hand to cut out once and for all a cancer in America demeaning and degrading to all Americans. Not colored persons alone, not white libertarians alone but Americans in general marched yesterday—and must march in unity and in brotherhood tomorrow and tomorrow.

The Washington Post, *editorial of August 29, 1963.*

The huge assemblage of Negro and white citizens in Washington yesterday to demand equality in all aspects of American life embodied, in concept and execution, the noblest tradition of our democracy. It reflected their conviction that, if enough of its people demonstrate that they care enough, no force in the

Marchers sang spirituals and folk songs. Courtesy of the U.S. News & World Report Collection, Library of Congress.

The New York Post, *editorial of August 29, 1963.*

All Americans have been asked by the Washington marchers: Does this country really stand for freedom, for justice, for equal opportunity? For fundamental fair play?

The Philadelphia Inquirer, *editorial of August 29, 1963.*

The atmosphere of yesterday's mass civil rights rally in Washington was one of orderliness, but it was an orderliness unafraid with fervor and with

Cool water of the Reflecting Pool along the Mall between the Washington Monument and the Lincoln Memorial was balm for aching feet of many after hours of standing. Courtesy of the U.S. News & World Report Collection, Library of Congress.

United States is more powerful than the appeal to conscience and basic morality.

The New York Times, *editorial of August 29, 1963.*

The demonstration in the nation's capital was in every way a credit to all of its leaders, and to all its participants. They did what they planned—to speak in a mighty voice for equal rights for all.

The New York Herald Tribune, *editorial of August 29, 1963.*

The passion for liberty burns bright in our country. To each legislator, the warning is sharp and distinct: Americans of every race and every creed are united in their demand for integration now. The voters are issuing their orders. The men they elect to office would be wise to listen—and obey.

determination. If anyone had previously doubted that the nation has come to the time when it has to live up to its moral, philosophical and political professions, the doubt can linger no more. Our Negro citizens will have their rights and their privileges as citizens, and will no longer wait through generation after generation. They will not wait through one more generation; and the country cannot ask them to wait.

The Baltimore Sun, *editorial of August 29, 1963.*

The demonstration in Washington sought dramatically to leave with all who would listen the impression that the South is still in a state of slavery. That is manifestly not true and to present it is not to further among realists his cause.

The Columbia [South Carolina] State, *editorial of August 29, 1963.*

"No Army can withstand the strength of an idea whose time has come," Victor Hugo wrote a century ago. An army embodying an idea whose time has come at long last marched in the streets of Washington yesterday.

The Virginian-Pilot, *editorial of August 29, 1963.*

The demonstration was huge and dramatic and designed to impress upon all America the existence of a problem that must and can be solved within the framework of our institutions by men of intelligence, understanding and goodwill.

The Atlanta Constitution, *editorial of August 29, 1963.*

It is too early for any clear evaluation to be made. Psychologically the effect was immediate and electric. To Negroes—and to America—this display of unity and togetherness, on the part of both leaders and followers was most significant. Participation of thousands upon thousands of dedicated white citizens who believe in the democratic concept, has made civil rights the nation's number one moral issue of the second half of the twentieth century.

The Pittsburgh Courier, black newspaper, *editorial of August 31, 1963.*

August 28, 1963 was the finest hour of the Negro's one-hundred-year march toward freedom. And since it was the finest hour for Negro Americans, it also becomes one of the finest hours in the history of America.

For the March on Washington by so many Negroes, side by side with so many whites, made it crystal clear to the world that the Negro, once looked upon as America's problem is definitely now a part of the solution.

This nation under God got a new birth of freedom August 28.

The New York Amsterdam News, black newspaper, *editorial of September 7, 1963.*

This was a historic day in which Americans spoke with one voice for freedom and jobs now.

Martin Luther King's warning was prophetic when he said in effect:

"The March is the beginning. Let no one think it represents a blowing off of steam and settle back to business as usual."

America, he said, has given us a promissory note for freedom and equality for all.

To date it has paid us with a bad check. The bank of justice declares it does not have sufficient funds. We are not morally bankrupt.

"We want it cashed now."

The [Baltimore] Afro-American, *editorial of September 7, 1963.*

Yes, it was a great day. But, as long as we have bigots in leadership like Stennis, Thurmond and Long, we will have a mighty task to accomplish. The attitude of these men makes it imperative that the great host of people in this country, who have come to see the meaning of this struggle, continue to pray together and to go to jail together, as Dr. King says, so that one day we may proudly say we are all free at last.

Jackie Robinson, former Brooklyn Dodger, in a New York Amsterdam News *article of September 7, 1963.*

Some came by bus, some came by train,
Some walked I think, some took a plane,
And hordes of people, swelled the scene,
To March on Washington.
Some go to school, some work each day.
Some live a thousand miles away,
The poor, the rich, the old and grey,
To March on Washington.
This is our task, this is our fight.
Our numbers show tremendous might.

Former Brooklyn Dodger Jackie Robinson and his son at the March on Washington. Courtesy of the U.S. News & World Report Collection, Library of Congress.

Paul D. McAllister, black poet, "March on Washington," in the [Baltimore] Afro-American, *September 7, 1963.*

When the day was done, everyone recognized that there had never been a day like it before and that all of those present had participated in the making of history.

The Crisis, *NAACP magazine, editorial of October 1963.*

Millions of white Americans, for the first time, had a clear, long look at Negroes engaged in a serious occupation. For the first time millions listened to the informed and thoughtful words of Negro spokesmen, from all walks of life. The stereotype of the Negro suffered a heavy blow. This was evident in some of the comment, which reflected surprise at the dignity, the organization and even the wearing apparel and friendly spirit of the participants . . . A great deal has been said about a dialogue between Negro and white. Genuinely to achieve it requires that all the media of communication open their channels wide as they did on that radiant August day.

Martin Luther King Jr., writing of the March on Washington, August 28, 1963, in Why We Can't Wait *(1964).*

10. Freedom Summer: 1964

"Let Us Continue"

Martin Luther King Jr. and his family sat by their television set on November 23, 1963, "hoping and praying that John Kennedy would not die." Corretta Scott King recalled their vigil in her memoir, *My Life with Martin Luther King, Jr.* (1969): "We felt that President Kennedy had been a friend of the Cause and that with him as President we could continue to move forward. We watched and prayed for him. Then it was announced that the President was dead. Martin had been very quiet during this period. Finally, he said, 'This is what is going to happen to me also.' "

Black Americans sharing the national trauma over the murder of the young president were a bit apprehensive about his successor, Lyndon Baines Johnson, a Southerner from Texas. In some parts of the Deep South, the news of Kennedy's death was met with cheers and applause because of his support for civil rights. It was now unclear whether Congress would pass Kennedy's sweeping civil rights bill.

The legislation, first proposed by Kennedy on June 19, 1963, included outlawing exclusion of blacks from hotels, restaurants, theaters and other places of public accommodation; permitting the Justice Department to bring suits to desegregate schools; prohibiting discrimination in any state program receiving federal aid; and outlawing racial barriers in employment and labor union membership.

Although Johnson had stood out in the 1930s as a federal administrator in Texas who had treated both blacks and whites equally, his record on civil rights legislation was uninspiring. In Congress he had voted against six civil rights bills. Even though he was credited with shepherding the passage of the Civil Rights Act of 1957 through Congress, critics noted that he had compromised away the few strong provisions for enforcement. Johnson later explained his weak civil rights record in his book, *The Vantage Point* (1971), "One heroic stand and I'd be back home, defeated, unable to do any good for anyone, much less the blacks and the underprivileged."

As vice-president, Johnson effectively chaired Kennedy's subcabinet on equal employment and strongly promoted the president's civil rights bill. Johnson came to recognize that the civil rights movement had altered the nation's political agenda. He also strongly believed that Kennedy's presidency, and his martyrdom, had made civil rights an issue that no successor could ignore.

On November 27, having barely settled into the Oval Office, President Johnson, in his first address to Congress and to the nation, called for passage of the civil rights bill to bring alive "the dream of equal rights for all Americans whatever their race or color . . . Let us continue," he said "the ideas and the ideals which [Kennedy] so nobly represented must and will be translated into effective action." Overnight, Lyndon Johnson's commitment made him the nation's most powerful champion of civil rights legislation.

Unlike his past reliance on consensus politics, Johnson insisted that the civil rights bill be passed without any compromises. Throughout the early months of 1964, the new president stressed his message of no compromise on civil rights in press conferences, cabinet meetings, Congress and other locations, including the New York World's Fair. He also held several private talks with Southern senators, many of whom had directed successful filibusters against other civil rights bills. Johnson decided that the bill would either pass with all of its provisions or die in yet another Southern filibuster. Johnson later wrote in *The Vantage Point* that he decided to consider the advice once given to him by a fellow Texan: "John Nance Gardner, a great legislative tactician, as well as a good poker player, once told me that there comes a time in every leader's career when he has to put in all his stack. I decided to shove in all my stack on this vital measure."

When the House passed the bill on February 10, 1964, by an overwhelming 290–130 vote, Johnson did not take time to celebrate but immediately phoned lobbyists Clarence Mitchell of the NAACP and Joseph Rauh of Americans for Democratic Action and, after offering brief congratulations, said, "All right, you fellows. Get over to the Senate. Get busy. We've won in the House, but there is a big job across the way."

The Johnson administration directed its campaign at the one senator who could secure the necessary votes for the bill's passage, Senate Minority Leader Everett Dirksen. Although Dirksen had previously opposed all civil rights legislation, like Johnson, he recognized that the civil rights movement, especially black activism, was beginning to change the political landscape. Senator Hubert Humphrey, floor manager for the bill, recalled, "I courted Dirksen almost as persistently as I did [my wife] Muriel." On June 10, Humphrey's persistence had clearly paid off. Dirksen announced in the Senate that the country was changing and that "on the civil rights issue we must rise with the occasion." He then declared his support for the civil rights bill and called for the debate to end. The Senate invoked cloture for the first time in its history in a civil rights debate; the vote was 73–27.

The Civil Rights Act of 1964 passed the Senate with every provision intact on June 19. This was exactly a year from the day President Kennedy had proposed the legislation, saying it should be enacted "not merely for reasons of economic efficency, world diplomacy and domestic tranquility—but above all because it is right."

President Johnson signed the bill into law on July 2, 1964. While some Southern senators decried the bill's passage, it was Senator Richard Russell of Georgia who set the tone for Southern reaction. In a statement to his constituents that echoed the finality and dignity of Robert E. Lee's call for the South to accept the verdict of history, he declared, "It is the law of the Senate and we must abide by it." He urged his fellow Georgians "to refrain from violence in dealing with this act."

THE VOTER EDUCATION PROJECT (VEP)

In late 1961, as SNCC operations in Mississippi came under continued violent harassment, the Kennedy administration offered civil rights groups monetary aid through liberal philanthropies if they would turn their efforts to voter registration. By April 1962, SNCC and other civil rights groups formally founded the Voter Education Project (VEP). Local NAACP chapters, CORE groups, SCLC and SNCC field staffs drew funds from the VEP for voter registration drives in their respective communities. Of the more than five million blacks of voting age in the South's 11 states, only 1,386,654 were registered at the start of the VEP. Over one-half million more were registered by April 1964, or 38.6 percent of those eligible.

Breakthroughs were achieved in every state but one—Mississippi. The early voter registration drives were quite discouraging—3,871 new black names had been added to voter rolls after two years of effort and left some 394,000 black adults unregistered. In a 1962 report to VEP, SNCC leader Robert Moses wrote, "We are powerless to register people in significant numbers anywhere in the state and will remain so until the power of the Citizens' Councils over state politics is broken, the Department of Justice secures for Negroes across the board the right to register, or immediate registration to vote. Very likely, all three will be necessary before a breakthrough can be obtained."

The civil rights groups in Mississippi—the NAACP, CORE, the SCLC and other local organizations—banded together in 1962 to form the Council of Federated Organizations (COFO). Aaron Henry, head of Mississippi's NAACP, was named president, and 31-year-old Harlem-born, Harvard-educated Robert Moses became COFO's director.

come let us build a new world together
STUDENT NONVIOLENT COORDINATING COMMITTEE 8½ RAYMOND STREET, N.W. ATLANTA 14, GEORGIA

SNCC poster. John Lewis, chairman of the SNCC (left). Courtesy of the Schomburg Center for Research in Black Culture.

During the fall of 1963, COFO launched its first major campaign, dubbed the Freedom Vote. The project was designed to demonstrate to Mississippi whites and to the federal government that blacks were interested indeed in voting and to provide blacks with practice in casting ballots. In 1963 COFO ran a mock election to parallel the gubernatorial race. Aaron Henry ran for governor with Ed King, a white chaplain at Tougaloo College as his running mate for lieutenant governor. Nearly a quarter of the eligible black voters and nearly three times the actual number on the voting rolls (27,791) turned out to cast 90,000 ballots. It clearly demonstrated that black Mississippians were interested in participating in the political process. Out of these efforts grew the Mississippi Freedom Democratic Party (MFDP) and the famed Freedom Summer of 1964.

INTIMIDATION AND FEAR

In the fall of 1963, COFO launched an ambitious voting rights project for the following summer. Known as the Mississippi Freedom Summer project, it would involve hundreds of student volunteers from the across the nation who would move into black neighborhoods in Mississippi to encourage registration and to support Freedom Party candidates.

A call went out for volunteers, and the National Council of Churches set up a spring training center at the Western College for Women at Oxford, Ohio. College students—some 700—came from Bryn Mawr, Cornell, Harvard, Mount Holyoke, Stanford, Yale and a number of other prestigious schools. They had to be at least 18 years of age, able to pay their own way and willing to live with black families and share dangers the families faced. The volunteers were mostly white, Northern and upper middle class, but the staff people—mainly SNCC, some CORE and a few SCLC—were mostly black, Southern and with lower-class parents.

Mississippi reacted to the Freedom Summer project as though it were an invasion. Crosses were burned on the night of April 24, 1964, in 64 of the state's 82 counties. Jackson, Mississippi Mayor Allen Thompson expanded the city's police force from 200 to more than 300 officers. He purchased 250 shotguns and a 13,000 pound armored personnel carrier called "Thompson's tank," an armored vehicle that had 12-gauge steel walls, bulletproof windows and a submachine gun mounted on the turret. The state enacted a "bill to restrain movements of individuals under certain circumstances," in effect, declaring martial law.

Students at orientation sessions heard a series of speakers tell them that where they were going their rights would not be respected. R. Jess Brown, one of four lawyers in the state of Mississippi who had civil rights workers as clients, gave them his best legal counsel, "If you're riding down somewhere and a cop stops you and starts to put you under arrest even though you haven't committed any crime—go on to jail." He added, "Mississippi is not the place to start conducting Constitutional law classes for policemen, many of whom don't have a fifth-grade education." Jim Foreman, SNCC executive secretary, stated the situation quite simply, "I may be killed and you may be killed."

On Saturday, June 20, the first contingent of volunteers—200 of them—departed for Mississippi from Oxford, Ohio. The following day, three civil rights workers, including one of the summer volunteers, were reported missing. The volunteer was Andrew Goodman, 21-years-old, son of a New York building contractor and a junior at Queens College. Goodman had arrived in the town of Meridian with CORE worker James Chaney, a 21-year-old black Mississippian, and 24-year-old Michael Schwerner, a former New York social worker, who with his wife Rita had set up the Meridian CORE office in January.

On Sunday, June 21, the three young men were returning to Meridian after inspecting a burned-out church 55 miles to the northwest of Neshoba County. Passing through Neshoba's county seat, Philadelphia (population 5,500), they were arrested for "speeding." Released

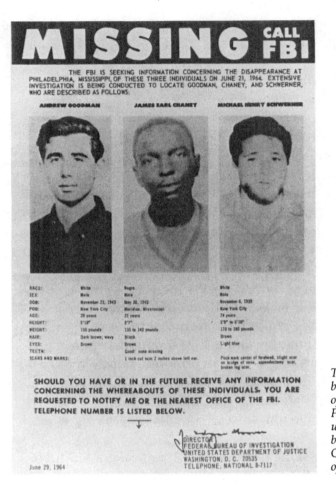

The FBI searched for months before finally finding the bodies of the three young Mississippi Freedom Summer Project volunteers, who had apparently been murdered by a racist mob. Courtesy of the Federal Bureau of Investigation.

late in the evening, about 10:30 P.M. after Chaney had paid a $20 fine, they drove off and were never seen alive again—except by their murderers, the Philadelphia Ku Klux Klan.

According to William Bradford Huie, an investigative reporter who learned the details of the murders from a paid informant, details that were later confirmed by testimony at the federal court trials of the killers, Philadelphia Deputy Sheriff Cecil Price escorted the civil rights workers to a deserted dirt road where three cars filled with Klansman awaited them. One of them said to the three young men, "So you wanted to come to Mississippi? Well, now we're gonna let you stay here. We're not even gonna run you out. We're gonna let you stay here with us." All three were pulled from their car and then shot at close range in the head. Their bodies were buried by a bulldozer and their car burned. The next day, Sheriff Lawrence Rainey told reporters he saw no cause for alarm, "If they're missing, they just hid somewhere, trying to get a lot of publicity."

As the national press focused on the events in Mississippi, the White House ordered an investigation. A large contingent of FBI agents were dispatched to hunt for the missing young men. Former

CIA Director Allen Dulles was also enlisted to look into the state of law enforcement in Mississippi.

It was not until early August that the bodies of Chaney, Goodman and Schwerner were found buried in an earthen dam on a farm a few miles outside of Philadelphia. On December 4, 1964, 21 men, including Sheriff Lawrence Rainey and Deputy Sheriff Cecil Price, were charged in connection with the murders of the three civil rights workers. Charges against the men were subsequently dropped in state court, but Price and six of the accused were later found guilty in 1967 of violating federal civil rights laws.

Although the disappearance of the three civil rights workers cast a sense of fear and gloom over Freedom Summer, only a few students decided to leave the project. The Mississippi Freedom Summer Project persisted and adopted the spirit of the SNCC philosophy: When beaten down, get right up again; when intimidated, carry on in the face of fear. The project succeeded in establishing nearly 50 Freedom Schools where young blacks were provided with remedial instruction and classes in black history. At community centers, adults were instructed on how to go about registering to vote.

THE MISSISSIPPI FREEDOM DEMOCRATIC PARTY

The outstanding achievement of Freedom Summer was the establishment of the Mississippi Freedom Democratic Party (MFDP), an alternative to the Mississippi "Jim Crow" Democratic party. COFO set up this new party and was able to enroll nearly 60,000 disfranchised blacks. Following the rules prescribed by the Democratic National Committee, the MFDP selected 68 delegates, 64 of them black, to attend the 1964 Democratic National Convention in Atlantic City, New Jersey. The aim of the MFDP was to challenge the seating of the all-white regular Mississippi delegation at the Democratic convention. The MFDP planned to contest the seats traditionally held by white Mississippians on the grounds that the MFDP delegates belonged to the only freely chosen party in the state, since blacks had been systematically denied access to selecting delegates in the Mississippi Democratic Party.

The MFDP initially looked upon its challenge to the white Mississippi delegation as a way to dramatize the illegal exclusion of blacks from the political process. But unexpectedly, the MFDP gained widespread sympathetic support from such quarters as the California Democratic Council (a liberal faction within the state party), several Northern delegations and Joseph L. Rauh, labor attorney, counsel for the Americans for Democratic Action (ADA) and member of the credentials committee of the Democratic Party. Rauh agreed to prepare the MFDP's case against the seating of Mississippi regulars. Rauh promised, "If there's anybody at the Democratic convention challenging the seating of the outlaw Mississippi Democrats, I'll make sure that the challengers are seated." Liberal support had raised the hopes of the MFDP.

The Freedom Party delegates arrived at the August convention in Atlantic City by bus, train, dilapidated cars and even hitchhiking. They represented a cross-section of rural and urban blacks in Mississippi. The delegation also included four white activists, among them the Reverend Edwin King, a native Mississippian who had risked his safety to help found the Freedom Party in 1963.

On the first day of the convention, August 22, the MFDP presented its case to the national Democratic Party's credentials committee. The MFDP did not expect to get a majority vote of the credentials committee to seat the MFDP delegates, but they did hope that their sympathizers on the committee would force a minority committee report to the convention floor, where open debate and a vote could take place.

"I have only an hour," began Joseph Rauh to the nationally televised hearings of the credentials committee, "to tell you a story of moral agony that could take years." He pointed out how the constitutional rights of Mississippi blacks had been violated and how violence and intimidation had been used to prevent blacks from registering. "Are you going to throw out of here people who want to work for Lyndon Johnson, who are willing to be beaten and shot and thrown in jail to work for Lyndon Johnson?" Rauh asked. "Are we for the oppressor or the oppressed?" Rauh then summoned a series of witnesses to Mississippi's brutality: Rita Schwerner, James Farmer, Roy Wilkins, Aaron Henry and the Reverend Edwin King, who testified, "I have been imprisoned, I have been beaten, I have been close to death. The Freedom party is an open party. They"—pointing to the spokesmen for the Mississippi Democratic regulars—"are a closed party of a closed society."

Fannie Lou Hamer of Ruleville, Mississippi and an MFDP delegate, delivered the most moving account of all. She told how she was fired from a plantation, where she had worked for 18 years, the day she registered to vote. Hamer described the violence she had suffered in retaliation for attending a civil rights meeting. She closed by asking, "Is this America, the land of the free and the home of the brave, where we are threatened daily because we want to live as decent human beings?" Hamer then broke down and wept before network television cameras that were providing live national coverage of the testimony.

President Johnson, who was watching the proceedings on television, believed that the live coverage of the hearings threatened his vision of a smooth convention where he would be triumphantly nominated. He ordered his White House aides to call the television networks and announce that a press conference would be held immediately. Although Johnson's press conference preempted the live coverage of the hearings in Atlantic City, evening news programs presented film footage of Hamer's emotional appeal to the credentials committee. Soon the committee was inundated with telephone calls and telegrams from Americans favoring the MFDP.

Johnson now wanted to prevent any divisive floor debate over the MFDP. He insisted on a compromise solution acceptable to a majority of the Southern delegates. He figured that he already had the black vote, for where else could they go? Certainly not to the Republican party, who had nominated Barry Goldwater in a clear turn to the far right. The president was particularly concerned about heading off a mass defection by the South to the Republican Party. This meant averting a Dixie walkout of the convention over the MFDP issue.

Johnson first proposed that the MFDP delegates could attend the convention and could speak out, but they would not be permitted to vote. The MFDP rejected this plan. Then Johnson, through Senator Hubert Humphrey, who was about to be offered the vice-presidency, conveyed his willingness to grant MFDP's top leaders, Aaron Henry and Ed King, two seats at-large (not as representatives of Mississippi), while the remaining delegates would be reclassified as "guests" of the convention. In addition, at the next convention, in 1968, the party would refuse to seat any state delegation that practiced discrimination.

Although the convention gladly accepted the compromise, MFDP delegates hotly debated the issue. National black spokesmen Roy Wilkins and Martin Luther King Jr. both favored it as a symbolic victory, but SNCC and CORE staff members were against its acceptance. Fannie Lou Hamer described the proposal as a "token of rights on the back row that we get in Mississippi. We didn't come all this way for that mess again." Most of the Freedom Democrat delegates agreed with Hamer. This attitude stunned the established civil rights and liberal leadership.

On August 26, the MFDP delegates decisively rejected the compromise. The MFDP announced, "We must stop playing the game of accepting token recognition for real change and of allowing the opposition to choose a few leaders to represent the people at large."

The MFDP had made the country take notice, and it had, in political terms, forced a serious confrontation. Mississippi's closed society had been exposed in the network coverage of the credentials committee testimony before a national audience. The MFDP firmly established itself as a political party of Mississippi blacks.

The MFDP delegation returned to Mississippi disillusioned with their liberal allies but with a deeper understanding of the workings of politics. Fannie Lou Hamer and the other MFDP members continued

From left to right: John Lewis, Aaron Henry, Roy Wilkins and James Farmer at the 1964 Democratic National Convention in Atlantic City, New Jersey. Courtesy of the Library of Congress.

their political work in the Delta, and in 1968 the Democratic Party honored the pledge it had made in 1964, seating the Mississippi Freedom Democratic Party at its national convention in Chicago. Appearing before the Democratic National Convention as a delegate, Hamer received a standing ovation.

By 1968 a black man, Robert Clark, sat in the Mississippi state legislature. Aaron Henry was also elected to that body in 1979. Overall, the Mississippi Freedom Democratic Party set in motion a significant increase in the number of black persons registered in the South. It also paved the way for opening up the Democratic Party to other minorities and women.

CHRONICLE OF EVENTS

1964

January 8: President Lyndon B. Johnson's State of the Union address calls the passage of a civil rights act essential to "increased opportunity for all."

April 26: SNCC members organize the Mississippi Freedom Democratic Party (MFDP).

June 21: Three young civil rights workers—two white and one black—Michael Schwerner, Andrew Goodman and James Chaney, are abducted and murdered in Neshoba County, Mississippi.

June 22: U.S. Attorney General Robert Kennedy orders the FBI to search for the missing men.

June 23: The charred remains of the three civil rights workers' station wagon is found by the FBI in a swamp 15 miles northeast of Philadelphia, Mississippi.

June 25: President Johnson authorizes the use of 200 Navy men for the search of the three missing civil rights workers.

June: Mississippi Freedom Summer Project (MFSP) launches voter registration campaigns; four MFDP congressional candidates qualify for the Democratic Party primary.

July 2: President Johnson signs the Civil Rights Act of 1964 outlawing discrimination in voting and public accommodations and requiring fair employment practices.

August 4: The bodies of Goodman, Schwerner and Chaney are found buried in a recently built earthen dam near Philadelphia, Mississippi.

August 6–12: The MFDP state convention is attended by some 2,500 supporters; 68 delegates are selected for the Democratic National Convention.

August 22–26: The MFDP asks to be seated at the Democratic National Convention in Atlantic City, New Jersey. The MFDP challenges the seating of the "regular" Mississippi delegation. Party leadership, including President Johnson, rejects the challenge and proposes instead a compromise, which the MFDP refuses.

September 8: Prince Edward County, Virginia public schools reopen after five years and enroll seven whites and 1,400 blacks.

November 3: President Johnson is reelected in a landslide. The black vote is estimated at 85–97% Democratic, with 75% percent of registered blacks voting.

December 4: Johnson issues an executive order barring discrimination in federal aid programs. The FBI charges 21 men, most of them members of the Ku Klux Klan, including a local sheriff and his deputy, with conspiring to abduct and kill Schwerner, Chaney and Goodman. [In 1967, seven are convicted of violating the federal civil rights laws.]

December 10: Martin Luther King Jr. is awarded the Nobel Peace Prize.

EYEWITNESS TESTIMONY

No memorial or eulogy could more eloquently honor President Kennedy's memory than the earliest possible passage of the civil rights bill for which he fought so long. We have talked long enough in this country about equal rights. We have talked for one hundred years or more. It is time now to write the next chapter, and to write it in the book of law.

President Lyndon Johnson, to a joint session of Congress, speech of November 27, 1963, in The Public Papers of the Presidents of the United States *(1964–1969).*

Let me make one principle of this administration abundantly clear: All of these increased opportunities—in employment, in education, in housing, and in every field—must be open to Americans of every color. As far as the writ of federal law will run, we must abolish not some, but all racial discrimination. For this is not merely an economic issue, or a social, political, or international issue. It is a moral issue, and it must be met by the passage this session of the [civil rights] bill now pending in the House.

President Lyndon Johnson, State of the Union address of January 8, 1964, in The Public Papers of the Presidents of the United States *(1964–1969).*

After three years of struggling, accompanied by extreme harassment in Mississippi, COFO has decided that only by confrontation within the state of the civil rights movement and the forces maintaining the status quo can significant change in the social and legal structure be effected.

Council of Federated Organizations (COFO), press release of April 1964, in McCord's Mississippi: The Long Hot Summer *(1965).*

Outsiders who come in here and try to stir up trouble should be dealt with in a manner they won't forget.

The Neshoba *[Mississippi]* Democrat, *editorial of April 9, 1964.*

You can cut years off the fight throughout the South by concentrating on Mississippi and showing how there can be progress even in the toughest state.

Michael Schwerner, statement of April 1964, to Richard Woodley, journalist, in Woodley's Reporter article of July 16, 1964. [Schwerner was

one of the three civil rights workers murdered on June 21, 1964, in Mississippi.]

"Mama, I believe I done found an organization that I can be in and do something for myself and somebody else, too."

"Ain't you afraid of this?"

"Naw, mama, that's what's the matter now—everybody's scared."

James Chaney, Mississippi Freedom Summer Project volunteer, conversation of spring 1964 with his mother, in Newsweek *(July 6, 1964). [Chaney was one of the three civil rights workers murdered on June 21, 1964, in Mississippi.]*

> How dismal the day
> Screams out and blasts the night.
> What disaster you will say,
> To start another fight.
>
> See how heaven shows dismay
> As her stars are scared away;
> As the sun ascends with might
> With this hot and awful light.
>
> He shows us babies crying
> We see the black boy dying
> We close our eyes and choke our sights
> And look into the dreadful skies.
>
> Then peacefully the night
> Puts out the reddened day
> And the jaws that used to bite
> Are sterile where we lay.

Andrew Goodman, Mississippi Freedom Summer volunteer, poem of spring 1964, "Corollary to a Poem by A. E. Housman," for his creative writing course at Queens College, in The Massachusetts Review *(Autumn–Winter 1964–1965). [Goodman was one of the three civil rights workers murdered in Mississippi in June 1964.]*

Mississippi is the last stronghold of the old Confederacy and feelings are bitter, but those who are going there have made their decisions rationally.

We know there is a chance of being hurt, of being jailed, or being killed, but we still believe in the cause so strongly that we must go.

Anonymous Mississippi Freedom Summer Project volunteer, statement of May 1964, in the New York Times *(May 17, 1964).*

Two COFO [Council of Federated Organizations] centers are already in operation. In Meridian [Mississippi], Mike and Rita Schwerner, a young married couple from New York City, have transformed a dingy second floor doctor's office into a pleasant five-room center with a 10,000 book library, a Ping-Pong table, a sewing machine, several typewriters, a phonograph, a movie projector, and drawing materials for children. The program appears to be running smoothly . . . They report no unusual harassment from city officials and are now busy setting up a system of block captains for canvassing Negro neighborhoods for voter registration.

Richard Woodley, journalist, in a Reporter *article of May 21, 1964. [Michael Schwerner was one of three civil rights workers killed in Neshoba County, Mississippi on June 21, 1964.]*

We're tired of all this beatin', we're tired of takin' this. It's been a hundred years and we're still bein' beaten and shot at, crosses are still being burned because we want to vote. But I'm goin' to stay in Mississippi and if they shoot me down, I'll be buried here.

Fannie Lou Hamer, Mississippi Democratic Freedom Party (MDFP) vice-chairman, statement of May 1964, in DeMuth's Nation *article of June 1, 1964.*

For two days lectures and workshops had been mounting an unrelenting assault on the volunteers. I wondered uneasily if this perhaps was not the real screening process. We were being frightened, and I sensed that this was a calculated process; a sharp, scalpeled insertion of reality intended to kill or cure. The terror and violence of Mississippi was detailed and dissected. The extents of police brutality were catalogued, and the unreal world of the barbarous newsreel and the tabloid spread was suddenly becoming our world. The volunteers listened to the incredible stories of beatings and murder and knew surely and profoundly that this incredible world was credible.

Tracy Sugarman, journalist and activist, on a training session at the Western College for Women in Oxford, Ohio, in the spring of 1964, in Stranger at the Gates *(1966).*

No administration in this country is going to commit political suicide over the rights of Negroes . . . This is part of what we're doing . . . getting the country involved through yourselves. That is, to open up the country . . . and get pressure—public pressure, continual, mounting, steady public pressure—

on all of the agencies of the federal government and on all of the informal processes of this country. That's the only way we'll get any kind of creative solution to what's going on down there.

Don't come to Mississippi this summer to save the Mississippi Negro . . . Only come if you understand, really understand, that his freedom and yours are one . . . Maybe we're not going to get very many people registered this summer. Maybe, even, we're not going to get very many people into freedom schools. Maybe all we're going to do is live through this summer. In Mississippi, that will be so much.

Bob Moses, Mississippi Freedom Summer Project director, to student volunteers at Western College for Women in Oxford, Ohio, training session speech of June 14, 1964, in Cagin and Dray's We Are Not Afraid *(1988).*

We will neither welcome them with open arms nor toss them out of town. We will have to see how they act. I suppose it's a summer skylark to them, like joining the Peace Corps. But I don't mind saying I wish they'd stay at home.

Canton, Mississippi Mayor Stanley Matthews, to the press, statement of June 14, 1964, in the New York Times *(June 15, 1964).*

All race-mixers will some day be brought to justice for their crimes against humanity and all future generations, and, since race-mixing is morally more criminal than murder, it would give me great satisfaction if I were selected to sit on such a jury.

You are right about one thing—this is going to be a long, hot summer—but the "heat" will be applied to the race-mixing TRASH by the DECENT people . . . When your communist-oriented GOONS get to Mississippi, I hope they get their just dues . . .

Charles J. Benner, States' Right Party National representative, to James Forman, SNCC chairman, letter of June 16, 1964, in McCord's Mississippi: The Long Hot Summer *(1965).*

I may be killed and you may be killed. If you recognize that, the question of whether we're put in jail will become very, very minute.

James Forman, SNCC executive secretary, to Mississippi Freedom Summer Project student volunteers at Western College for Women in Oxford, Ohio, speech of June 16, 1964, in the New York Times *(June 17, 1964).*

Mississippi is going to be hell this summer. Monday Jim Forman, executive secretary of SNCC, stood up during one of the general sessions and calmly told the staff (who already knew) and the volunteers that they could all expect to be arrested, jailed, and beaten this summer, and, in many cases, shot at . . . It is impossible for you to imagine what we are going in to, as it is for me now, but I'm beginning to see . . .

Xtoph, Mississippi Freedom Summer Project volunteer, to home, letter of June 17, 1964, in Sutherland's Letters from Mississippi *(1965).*

Many say Mississippi is a bad place to live. Well it is, if you hate going to the back of a street car, if you hate using the back door to a restaurant, and hate to hear a white call your parents girl and boy . . . if you hate all these things and many others, I join you in saying Mississippi is the worst state to live in.

Anonymous black fifteen-year-old Freedom School student, essay of June 1964, in Mc-Cord's Mississippi: The Long Hot Summer *(1965).*

Although you may be as white as a sheet, you will become as black as tar . . . You're going to be classified into two groups in Mississippi: niggers and nigger-lovers. And they're tougher on nigger-lovers.

R. Jess Brown, Jackson, Mississippi black attorney, to Freedom Summer Project volunteer students at Western College for Women in Oxford, Ohio, speech of June 18, 1964, in the New York Times *(June 19, 1964).*

The passage of the civil rights bill may well be the single most important act of our Congress in several decades. It gives hope to Negroes that the American people and Government mean to redeem the promise of the Declaration of Independence and the Emancipation Proclamation.

James Farmer, CORE executive director, to the press, statement of June 19, 1964, on the Senate's passage of the Civil Rights Act of 1964, in the New York Times *(June 20, 1964).*

There is no evidence Mississippi officials are going to comply. One may as well get ready for massive defiance.

James Forman, SNCC executive secretary, to the press, statement of June 19, 1964, in the New York Times *(June 20, 1964).*

You can't legislate good will and therefore the only thing that will eliminate discrimination and segregation is education, not legislation.

Malcolm X, Black Muslim leader, to the press, statement of June 19, 1964, in the New York Times *(June 20, 1964).*

It is ironical that this event occurs as we approach the celebration of Independence Day. On that day we won our freedom. On this day we have largely lost it.

Alabama Governor George Wallace, to the press, statement of June 19, 1964, on the Senate's passage of the Civil Rights Act of 1964, in the New York Times *(June 20, 1964).*

Most of us are at a point now where we feel it'll be only a miracle if any of them are found alive.

Anonymous Freedom Summer Project volunteer, Jackson, Mississippi, statement of June 22, 1964, on the disappearance of three civil rights workers, in the New York Post *(June 23, 1964).*

Since the Mississippi invasion was first announced many weeks ago, I have repeatedly and consistently called on those planning the project to abandon it. I have pointed out repeatedly that their drive could only succeed if they could provoke incidents, strife, and violence to get the federal government to intervene—that this was the real purpose of those organizations sponsoring this summer project. It was also clear, as I pointed out, that Mississippi had been selected by them as the whipping boy . . .

The real purpose of those in charge of this drive on my State is to provoke incidents and violence.

I am also deeply concerned about the safety and welfare of the people of Mississippi.

I pray that the missing men will be found safe and sound.

Senator John Stennis (D, Miss.), to the Senate, speech of June 24, 1964, in the Congressional Record *(1964).*

The tragedy which may have happened to the young boys in Mississippi can neither be ignored nor begged.

The right of a U.S. citizen to travel anywhere in this country, and to help citizens register to vote in that place, if he wishes to, cannot be denied. The residents of Mississippi can travel constitutionally and legally into and around New York. And the residents of New York can travel constitutionally and legally into and around Mississippi. That is why we are a nation, and not a collection of States . . .

There is no room for interposition, secession or the idea that New Yorkers or citizens of any other State are foreigners in Mississippi. If this be the confrontation, the Nation must face it unflinchingly and it dare not fail in its responsibility.

Senator Jacob Javits (R, N.Y.), to the Senate, speech of June 24, 1964, in the Congressional Record *(1964).*

I suspect that if Mr. James Chaney, a native Negro of Mississippi had been alone at the time of the disappearance, this case, like many before it, would have gone unnoticed.

Rita Schwerner, wife of Michael Schwerner, statement of June 1964, in the National Guardian *(July 4, 1964).*

Surely there are parents in Mississippi who like myself have experienced the softness, the warmth, and the beauty of a child whom they cherish and love and want to protect . . . I want to beg them to cooperate in every way possible in the search for these three boys . . .

Carolyn Goodman, mother of Andrew Goodman, to the press, statement of June 25, 1964, in the New York Times *(June 26, 1964).*

I want to say something about James Chaney. He was a Negro, a friend, and a brother to my boy Mickey. Mickey knew this was a bright, bright boy, and he opened a world of hope for [him]. They would go out in the field together . . . working together to help the people. Mickey and Rita [Schwerner] ate in the Chaney home, and when there was no food for anyone else, Mrs. Chaney somehow found some for them.

I've never met Mrs. Chaney, but . . . I wish . . . I could take her in my arms.

Anne Schwerner, mother of Michael Schwerner, to the press, statement of June 25, 1964, in the New York Times *(June 26, 1964).*

America, if Jim Chaney had gone to Neshoba alone and disappeared somewhere out there, it would not have made very much difference. Because, America, Jim Chaney is black. Black men have disappeared for three hundred years across the length and width of this nation. You did not care. If you had cared, you would have done something about it . . .

You have noticed Mississippi now, because two white men are missing along with Jim Chaney. Andy Goodman and Mickey Schwerner had to come down here before you heard of Jim Chaney, or Meridian, or Neshoba County. Negroes died out there before and died down in Natchez; they died at night in the Delta. Andy Goodman and Jim Chaney and Mickey Schwerner are missing. America, we have paid a high price for your attention.

Jane Stembridge, white SNCC activist, Greenwood, Mississippi, to Mary King, SNCC activist, Atlanta, Georgia, "Open letter to America" of June 30, 1964, in King's Freedom Song *(1987).*

They say that freedom is a constant struggle,
They say that freedom is a constant struggle,
They say that freedom is a constant struggle,
O Lord, we've struggled so long,
We must be free, we must be free.

They say that freedom is a constant crying,
They say that freedom is a constant crying,
They say that freedom is a constant crying,
O Lord, we've cried so long,
We must be free, we must be free.

They say that freedom is a constant sorrow,
They say that freedom is a constant sorrow,
They say that freedom is a constant sorrow,
O Lord, we've sorrowed so long,
We must be free, we must be free.

They say that freedom is a constant moaning,
They say that freedom is a constant moaning,
They say that freedom is a constant moaning,
O Lord, we've moaned so long,
We must be free, we must be free.

They say that freedom is a constant dying,
They say that freedom is a constant dying,
They say that freedom is a constant dying,
O Lord, we've died so long,
We must be free, we must be free.

Song of the Freedom Singers, first used at an Oxford, Ohio Mississippi Freedom Summer Project training session after it was learned that three civil rights workers were missing, June 1964.

The choice before Americans this summer seems very clear. They can either accept at face value the statements of the Attorney General that the federal government does not have sufficient power to protect the citizens of the country within its own borders— in which case the consequences will fall on those of us who live and work in Mississippi—or they can use the influence and power they have over their own government to ensure that the events in Philadelphia are not repeated within the coming hours and days in Mississippi.

Council of Federated Organizations (COFO), to parents of Freedom Summer Project volunteers, letter of June 1964, in the National Guardian *(July 4, 1964).*

Now it is one o'clock and our bus, inconsequential to whoever observes it, is traveling down a Tennessee road, far into the country. I have always thought that between the hours of one and three a.m. America comes closest to her real promise. There is a true unity between all her travelers sharing, for the particular night, a lonely vigil, a personal responsibility for the land.

But it was at this hour six days ago that Mickey, James and Andy disappeared on the frontier of Mississippi and it was Americans who apparently captured them, men who speak the same language, sing the same anthem, fight the same wars as those of us on this bus. We all inhabit the same night in the same land, but somehow that is not enough.

Paul Cowan, Freedom Summer Project student volunteer, to his sister Holly, letter of June 1964, in an Esquire *article of September 1964.*

I'm afraid that every hour that passes reduces the chances that our friends will be found alive.

James Farmer, CORE executive director, to the press, statement of July 1964, in the [Baltimore] Afro-American, *July 4, 1964.*

We must not approach the observance and enforcement of this law in a vengeful spirit. Its purpose is not to punish. Its purpose is not to divide, but to end divisions—divisions which have all lasted too long. Its purpose is national, not regional.

Its purpose is to promote a more abiding commitment to freedom, a more constant pursuit of justice, and a deeper respect for human dignity . . .

This Civil Rights Act is a challenge to all of us to go to work in our communities and our states, in our homes and in our hearts, to eliminate the last vestiges of injustice in our beloved country.

President Lyndon Johnson, to the American people, radio and television address of July 2, 1964, on signing the Civil Rights Act of 1964, in The Public Papers of the Presidents of the United States *(1964–1969).*

Many of the houses are shacks—rough wood, falling apart, dirty, flies, dark, your imagination can fill in the rest. The people are largely apathetic or afraid, and almost always ignorant—centuries of ignorance that often leaves me with the feeling of the impossibility of my task. But perhaps our work—the filling out of forms—is interpreted by enlightened men as what it should mean, since this ignorance has as its obvious cause the whole rotten system.

Joel Bernard, Mississippi Freedom Summer Project volunteer, to his parents, letter of July 9, 1964, in a New York Post *article of August 9, 1964.*

We are trying to get people to go down to the courthouse to register. In Mississippi there are no deputy registrars, the only people that can register are at the Courthouse at the County Seat. The county seat for Leflore County is Greenwood. This in itself restrains Negroes from voting because they don't like to go to the courthouse, which has bad connotations

A Mississippi Freedom Summer Project volunteer leads a Freedom School class. Courtesy of the Staughton Lynd Collection. State Historical Society of Wisconsin.

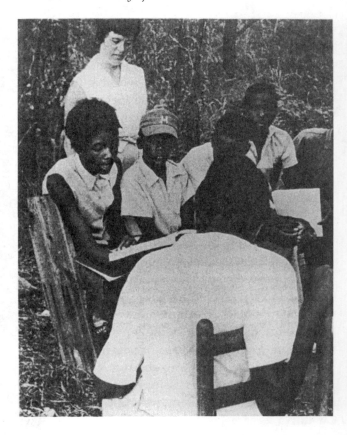

for them. Behind the courthouse is the Yazoo River. The river also has bad connotations; as Albert Darner said, it's "Dat river where dey floats them bodies in."

Bob, Mississippi Freedom Summer Project volunteer, to his mother, letter of July 15, 1964, in Sutherland's Letters from Mississippi *(1965).*

We are not afraid. My grandmother was afraid. My mother was afraid. But I'm not afraid and my children aren't afraid. They use terror to make us afraid, but one day they will have to stop because if we're not afraid, what will be the use of their terror?

Anonymous black Mississippi woman, at a Freedom Summer Project meeting, statement of July 1964, in Paul's National Guardian *article of July 25, 1964.*

The bodies of the three young men were found near Philadelphia. The press came back to ask volunteers "how you feel about it." Everyone had had to resolve how he felt about it long ago to be able to continue to work, and there was no new way to feel about it. Relief, perhaps, that the world would believe it now. After the news was exchanged, few people mentioned it—they just let it sink and add to the sediment of anger and pain that was growing under everything they did.

Sally Belfrage, Mississippi Freedom Summer Project volunteer, recalling the discovery of the three slain civil rights workers on August 4, 1964, in Freedom Summer *(1965).*

We know the horrors of this place . . . but still it was news that no one doubted and yet no one can quite accept. There is no training for death.

Anonymous Mississippi Freedom Summer Project volunteer, statement of August 4, 1964, in the New York Post *(August 5, 1964).*

Our grief, though personal, belongs to the nation. The values our son expressed in his simple action of going to Mississippi are still the bonds that bind this nation together—its Constitution, its law, its Bill of Rights. Throughout our history, countless Americans have died in the continuing struggle for equality. We shall continue to work for this goal and we fervently hope that Americans so engaged will be aided and protected in this noble mission.

Robert Goodman, father of Andrew Goodman, to the press, statement of August 5, 1964, in the New York Times *(August 6, 1964).*

It is my hope that the work that Mickey, Andy and James were engaged in will not only continue but that the efforts to liberate the Negroes of Mississippi in particular and the South in general from the consistent and brutal violation of their civil rights will be redoubled.

Rita Schwerner, wife of Michael Schwerner, to the press, statement of August 5, 1964, in the New York Times *(August 6, 1964).*

We won't be intimidated. As a matter of fact, the death of the three workers will incite us to increase our forces in Mississippi.

Mimi Hernandez, CORE representative, statement of August 5, 1964, in the New York Post *(August 6, 1964).*

We are waging a war against the closed society of Mississippi . . . Until the killing of black mothers' sons is as important as the killing of white mothers' sons we must keep on.

Ella Baker, SNCC adviser, to the Mississippi Freedom Democratic Party (MFDP) convention in Jackson, Mississippi, speech of August 6, 1964, in the National Guardian *(August 15, 1964).*

I am not here to memorialize James Chaney, I am not here to pay tribute—I am too sick and tired. Do you hear me, I am sick and tired. I have attended too many memorials, too many funerals. This has got to stop. Mack Peter, Medgar Evers, Herbert Lee, Lewis Allen, Emmett Till, four little girls in Birmingham, a 13-year-old boy in Birmingham, and the list goes on and on. I have attended these funerals and memorials and I am sick and tired. But the trouble is that you are not sick and tired and for that reason you, yes you, are to blame, everyone of your damn souls. And if you are going to let this continue now then you are to blame yes YOU . . . Yes, I am angry, I am. And it's high time that you got angry too, angry enough to go up to the courthouse Monday and register—everyone of you.

David Dennis, Mississippi Freedom Summer Project assistant director, to a memorial service for James Chaney in Meridian, Mississippi, address of August 7, 1964, in Sutherland's Letters from Mississippi *(1965).*

All Mississippi Negroes should now stand up for their rights. Since my son has been murdered, if we don't stand up for our civil rights now, his death will

Mothers of the three slain civil rights workers, Mrs. Fannie Lee Chaney, Mrs. Carolyn Goodman and Mrs. Anne Schwerner (left to right), link arms after the funeral service for Andrew Goodman in New York City. Courtesy of AP/Wide World Photos.

have been in vain, and the death of the other two boys.

Fannie L. Chaney, mother of James Chaney, to the press, statement of August 7, 1964, in the National Guardian *(August 15, 1964).*

The tragedy of Andy Goodman cannot be separated from the tragedy of mankind. Along with James Chaney and Michael Schwerner, he has become the eternal evocation of all the host of beautiful young men and women who are carrying forward the struggle for which they gave their lives.

Rabbi Arthur J. Leylveld, eulogy for Andrew Goodman, August 9, 1964, in the New York Times *(August 10, 1964).*

"We are not afraid. Oh Lord deep in my heart, I do believe. We Shall Overcome Someday" and then I think I began to truly understand what the words meant. Anyone who comes down here and is not afraid I think must be crazy as well as dangerous to this project where security is quite important. But the type of fear that they mean when they, when we, sing "we are not afraid" is the type that immobilizes . . . The songs help to dissipate the fear. Some of the words in the songs do not hold real meaning on their own, others become rather monotonous—but when they are sung in unison, or sung silently by oneself, they take on new meaning beyond words or rhythm . . . There is almost a religious quality about some of these songs, having little to do with the usual concept of god. It has to do with the miracle that youth has organized to fight hatred and ignorance.

Heather, Mississippi Freedom Summer Project volunteer, to her brother, letter of August 16, 1964, in Sutherland's Letters from Mississippi *(1965).*

America is burning its own cross on the graves of its children because it has not taken the responsibility for enforcing the democratic way of life.

John Lewis, SNCC chairman, to the press, statement of August 1964, in the [Baltimore] Afro-American *(August 15, 1964).*

One can't move onto a plantation cold; or canvas a plantation in the same manner as the Negro ghetto in town. It's far too dangerous. Many plantations—homes included—are posted, meaning that no trespassing is permitted, and the owner feels that he has the prerogative to shoot us on sight when we are in the house of one of *his* Negroes.

Joel, Mississippi Freedom Summer Project volunteer, to his parents, letter of August 18, 1964, in Sutherland's Letters from Mississippi *(1965).*

Are you going to throw out of here the people who want to work for Lyndon Johnson? Will the Democratic Party stand for the oppressors or the oppressed, for the loyalists or the disloyal regular [Mississippi] party?

Joseph L. Rauh Jr., attorney representing the Mississippi Freedom Democratic Party (MFDP), to the credentials committee at the Democratic National Convention in Atlantic City, New Jersey, testimony of August 22, 1964, in the Washington Post *(August 23, 1964).*

This is the Democratic Party's moment of truth. The moral issue is whether the Democratic Party will endorse racism or take the high road to equality.

Martin Luther King Jr., to the credentials committee at the Democratic National Convention in Atlantic City, New Jersey, testimony of August 22, 1964, in the National Guardian *(August 29, 1964).*

The first Negro began to beat [me], and I was beat until I was exhausted . . . After the first Negro . . . was exhausted, the State Highway Patrolman ordered the second Negro to take the blackjack. The second Negro began to beat . . . I began to scream, and one white man got up and began to beat me on my head and tell me to "hush."

One white man—my dress had worked up high— he walked over and pulled my dress down and he

Fannie Lou Hamer, a grass-roots Mississippi leader who played a prominent role in the Mississippi Freedom Democratic Party. Courtesy of the Lawrence Henry Collection, Schomburg Center for Research in Black Culture.

pulled my dress back, back up . . . All of this is on account we want to register, to become first-class citizens, and if the Freedom Democratic Party is not seated now, I question America.

Fannie Lou Hamer, Mississippi Freedom Democratic Party, vice-chairman, to the credentials committee at the Democratic National Convention in Atlantic City, New Jersey, testimony of August 22, 1964, on being beaten in jail by black prisoners on orders from Mississippi state highway patrolmen in 1963, in White's The Making of a President 1964 (1965).

It is time for the Democratic Party to clean itself of racism.

John Lewis, SNCC chairman, to the press, statement of August 23, 1964, in the Washington Post *(August 24, 1964).*

We did not come to Atlantic City to get the same kind of back in the bus treatment we have gotten in Mississippi.

Aaron Henry, MFDP leader, to the press, statement of August 23, 1964, in the Washington Post *(August 24, 1964).*

We didn't come all this way just for two votes. It is all we get in Mississippi—a token of our rights. We want equal votes.

Fannie Lou Hamer, MFDP vice-chairman, to the press, statement of August 1964, on the Democratic Party's compromise of granting two seats at-large to the Mississippi Freedom Democratic Party, in the National Guardian *(September 5, 1964).*

> Go tell it on the mountain,
> Over the hills and everywhere,
> Go tell it on the mountain
> To let my people go.
>
> Who's that yonder dressed in black?
> Let my people go.
> Must be the hypocrites turnin' back.
> Let my people go.

"Go Tell It on the Mountain," hymn sung by Fannie Lou Hamer and MFDP delegates at a rally on the Boardwalk in Atlantic City, New Jersey, August 24, 1964.

Here at home one of our greatest responsibilities is to assure fair play for all of our people.

Every American has the right to be treated as a person. He should be able to find a job. He should be able to educate his children, he should be able to vote in elections and he should be judged on his merits as a person.

Well, this is the fixed policy and the fixed determination of the Democratic Party and the United States of America.

President Lyndon Johnson, to the Democratic National Convention in Atlantic City, New Jersey, nomination acceptance speech of August 27, 1964, in The Public Papers of the Presidents of the United States *(1964–1969).*

When a reporter goes in Mississippi, the questions he asks can suddenly become personal. Why does a white official parry your inquires with defensive arrogance? Why does a Negro sharecropper welcome you with a glass of cold water, because he has nothing more to give?

And why must you ride through Mississippi after dark with a 12-gauge shotgun on your lap?

Chris Wren, journalist, in a Look *article of September 8, 1964.*

The sheriff, a deputy, and the constable with a police dog kept following us wherever we went. We would talk to people about registering and when we left the sheriff would call them over and tell them to ignore us—and back up his order with all kinds of threats. We kept calling on people and talking to them. But they wouldn't even look at us. They would just look right past us at those cops. Other times they'd see those police sitting there in their cars, and taking notes, and they'd slam the door right in our faces.

Dave Kendall, Freedom Summer Project volunteer, to Jerry DeMuth, journalist, in DeMuth's Nation *article of September 14, 1964.*

I am mindful that only yesterday in Birmingham, Alabama, our children, crying out for brotherhood, were answered with fire hoses, snarling dogs and even death. I am mindful that only yesterday in Philadelphia, Mississippi, young people seeking to secure the right to vote were brutalized and murdered . . . Therefore, I must ask why this prize is awarded to a movement which is beleaguered . . . which has not won the very peace and brotherhood which is the essence of the Nobel Prize.

After contemplation, I conclude that this award which I received on behalf of the movement is profound recognition that nonviolence is the answer to the crucial political and moral questions of our time—the need for man to overcome oppression and violence without resorting to violence and oppression.

Martin Luther King Jr., speech of December 10, 1964, in Oslo, Norway, accepting the Nobel Peace Prize, in the New York Times *(December 11, 1964).*

We here in the Organization of Afro-American Unity are with the struggle in Mississippi one thousand per cent. We're with the efforts to register our people in Mississippi to vote one thousand per cent. But we do not go along with anybody telling us to help nonviolently . . . You get freedom by letting your enemy know that you'll do anything to get your freedom; then you'll get it. It's the only way you'll get it.

Malcolm X, Black Muslim leader, to a group of McComb, Mississippi teenagers visiting New York City, speech of December 31, 1964, in Malcolm X Speaks *(1965).*

11. Selma and the Voting Rights Act: 1965

THE MOVEMENT COMES TO SELMA

Despite increases in the number of blacks registered to vote in the South between 1962 and 1964, it was apparent that registration was still proceeding at a hopelessly slow pace, especially in the rural black belt counties. Only two million of the South's five million voting-age blacks were registered in 1964. In Florida, Tennessee and Texas, the percentages of eligible blacks registered to vote were well over 50%—57.7%, 69.4% and 63.8% respectively. But for the entire region, only 40.8% of blacks eligible to vote were on the rolls. In Alabama, only 22.8% of the black voting-age population (about 500,000), or only 114,000, were registered at the end of 1964.

In Dallas County, Alabama, where blacks composed 57% of the total population and 15,115 were of voting age, only 320 blacks were registered to vote at the end of 1964, but 9,543 whites were on the voting rolls. Martin Luther King Jr. wrote in the *New York Times Magazine* of March 14, 1964, "Selma [in Dallas County] has succeeded in limiting Negro registration to the snail's pace of about 145 persons a year. At this rate, it would take 103 years to register the 15,000 eligible Negro voters of Dallas County."

Following the passage of the landmark Civil Rights Act of 1964, Martin Luther King Jr. and other civil rights leaders concluded that their next legislative goal should be for a strong federal voting rights law that would end barriers to registration. They had learned from the demonstrations in Birmingham that attacks upon peaceful civil rights protesters could prompt the administration and the Congress to act. The campaign for voting rights would center on Selma, Alabama, a city situated almost in the center of the black belt and where blacks comprised a majority of the 29,000 residents but only 3% of the voting rolls.

Situated above the murky Alabama River, Selma, the seat of Dallas County, is some 50 miles west of Montgomery, the capital of Alabama. Originally a cotton center and a slave market in the antebellum days,

215

Selma became an important arsenal and supply depot during the Civil War, second only to Richmond. It was where Birmingham Police Commissioner Bull Connor was born and raised and where Alabama's White Citizens' Council first met.

In early 1963, several SNCC workers spent several months canvassing black homes in Selma to discuss voting rights and how Dallas County officials prevented blacks from registering. They discovered that the voter registration board only met two days a month and rejected black applicants who failed to cross a "t" in registration forms and for other inconsequential items. If applicants were able to submit a perfect form, registrars asked them probing questions about Alabama state codes.

On October 7, 1963, the SNCC workers held a Selma Freedom Day to inauguarate a voter registration campaign. A group of about 200 blacks lined up at the Dallas County Courthouse to register. Sheriff James "Jim" Clark's men arrested the organizers, while FBI agents and two Justice Department lawyers watched and did nothing to intervene. The organizers, who had been holding signs that read "Register To Vote" and "Register Now for Freedom," were charged with "unlawful assembly." Sheriff Clark had a photographer snap pictures of every person in line and threatened to show the pictures to their employers.

The SNCC office in Selma was raided in January 1964, records and leaflets were seized, and nine workers were arrested. Voter registration efforts in Selma by the SNCC were overshadowed in 1964 by the Mississippi Freedom Summer Project. Also, an injunction in the state courts against all civil rights activists hampered further work until the injunction was set aside in late 1964.

"WE ARE NOT ASKING, WE ARE DEMANDING THE BALLOT"

A few weeks after accepting the Nobel Peace Prize, Martin Luther King Jr. announced in Selma on January 2, 1965, "We will dramatize the situation to arouse the federal government by marching by the thousands to the places of registration. We are not asking," he warned, "we are demanding the ballot."

As in Birmingham, the marches began gradually. King, in conjunction with several SNCC workers, first led dozens, then hundreds of blacks to attempt to get their names on the voter rolls. By the end of January, over 2,000 blacks had been arrested. The campaign attracted blacks of all ages and occupations; civil rights workers told one another, "Brother, we got a movement goin' on in Selma."

The national media converged on Selma. But Sheriff Jim Clark maintained restraint and managed to deny SCLC the confrontation it had wanted. On Monday, February 1, King decided to provoke Clark by having himself arrested along with Ralph Abernathy and several hundred other marchers, many of them schoolchildren. Two years earlier, King's "Letter from a Birmingham Jail" had aroused national attention, and he was hoping this tactic would result in the same indignation.

Indeed, King's incarceration made national headlines and brought more print and broadcast reporters swarming into Selma. The day after King's arrest, Clark's deputies arrested 550 more young black marchers. Defiantly they sang, "Ain't Gonna Let Clark Turn Me 'Round." The national television news covered the mass arrests and each evening showed children being sent off to jail. Clark did not recognize the symbolism of the arrests. Every arrest became an indictment of the Selma police, and every beating enlisted new civil rights supporters.

Two days after King's arrest, the militant Black Muslim minister Malcolm X arrived in Selma at the invitation of SNCC. While King was still in jail, Malcolm X told an overflowing crowd at Brown Chapel African Methodist Episcopal Church that "the white people should thank Dr. King for holding people in check, for there are other [black leaders] who do not believe in these [nonviolent] measures." Fearing that Malcolm X's message could derail the campaign, Andrew Young and other SCLC activists convinced a reluctant Coretta King to give a calming follow-up speech on the nonviolent ideals of the movement. After his speech, Malcolm X confided to Coretta King that he regretted not being able to visit her jailed husband and told her, "I didn't come to Selma to make his job difficult. I really did come thinking that I could make it easier. If the white people realize what the alternative is, perhaps they will be more willing to hear Dr. King." A few weeks later, Malcolm X was assassinated by former Black Muslim colleagues.

On the same day of Malcolm X's speech, President Lyndon Johnson held a press conference and issued a statement in support of voting rights. This was the first time the president directly responded to the events in Selma. "I should like to say that all Americans should be indignant when one American is denied the right to vote," said Johnson. "The loss of that right to a single citizen undermines the freedom of every citizen. That is why all of us should be concerned with the efforts of our fellow Americans to register to vote in Alabama . . . I intend to see that that right is secured for all citizens." Also on that day, a federal judge issued an order instructing the Dallas County registrars to meet "more often" than twice monthly.

BLOODY SUNDAY

By mid-February, the SCLC had decided to expand its efforts to the nearby small town of Marion, the seat of Perry County. On the eve-

Malcolm X, one of the most fiery and controversial civil rights leaders of the 20th century. Courtesy of the Schomburg Center for Research in Black Culture.

ning of Wednesday, February 18, a small civil rights march was attacked by law enforcement officers and one demonstrator, 26-year-old Jimmie Lee Jackson, was shot in the stomach by an Alabama state trooper. Jackson died a week later. His funeral drew 200 mourners, and King delivered an angry eulogy. King asked, who killed Jimmie Lee Jackson, and then declared that he was killed by every lawless sheriff, every racist politician from governors on down, every indifferent white minister and every passive Negro who "stands on the sidelines in the struggle for justice."

A few days after Jackson's funeral, King announced a mass march from Selma to Montgomery—some 50 miles—to protest against police brutality and the denial of voting rights. The SCLC's James Bevel, a young militant minister, had conceived of the idea for the march. "I can't promise you that it won't get you beaten," King told his followers, "but we must stand up for what is right."

Alabama Governor George Wallace immediately responded, "Such a march cannot and will not be tolerated," and he issued an order prohibiting the march, which was scheduled to begin on Sunday, March 7. The four-day march was to begin across the Edmund Pettus bridge in Selma and continue along Route 80 to the state capitol in Montgomery. The marchers would present a petition of grievances to Governor Wallace.

On the morning of Sunday, March 7, 1965, about 600 blacks, with knapsacks, satchels and bedrolls, stepped out of the Brown Chapel African Methodist Episcopal Church for the 50-mile trek to Montgomery. The marchers were led by the SCLC's Hosea Williams and SNCC's John Lewis (King and Abernathy were in Atlanta ministering to their congregations). State troopers' cars with Confederate insiginia lined the sides of Highway 80, and the troopers wore gas masks beneath their blue hard hats and stood with their billy clubs ready.

Scores of newsmen looked on, as the long column of freedom-singing marchers approached the Edmund Pettus Bridge, the gateway out of Selma. About 100 state troopers, commanded by Major John Cloud, barred the opposite end of the bridge. After crossing the Pettus bridge over the Alabama River, the marchers' path was blocked by the Alabama state troopers and Sheriff Clark's local lawmen. Hosea Williams tried to speak to Cloud twice, but the major responded, "There is no word to be had . . . You have two minutes to turn around and go back to your church." Within a minute, the command to attack was given.

The march across the Edmund Pettus Bridge begins on March 7, 1965, with Hosea Williams and John Lewis (in raincoat, far right) forming the front rank. Copyright, photo by the Birmingham News, *1999. All rights reserved. Reprinted with permission.*

In a sudden lurching movement, Alabama state troopers ram forward, knocking marchers about like tenpins. Copyright, photo by the Birmingham News, *1999. All rights reserved. Reprinted with permission.*

The marchers panicked and ran, trying to flee the tear gas, the charging horsemen, the flailing nightsticks and chains and electric cattle prods. Women and children, old and young marchers and even bystanders were savagely attacked by troopers and Clark's deputies. John Lewis had his skull fractured, 16 marchers ended up in the hospital, and another 50 received emergency treatment.

The brutality was brought into homes across the nation on television screens and in newspaper and magazine photographs. Television networks interrupted their regular programming with film footage of the police assault; ABC broke into its broadcast of the film *Judgment in Nuremberg.*

In the halls of Congress, leaders on both sides of the aisle reacted to the violence with anger. Republican Senator Jacob Javits called law enforcement in Selma an "exercise in terror." Over 50 congressional speeches denouncing the city were delivered within two days. President Johnson publicly deplored the brutality. Thousands of people in cities across the country marched in sympathy demonstrations over the next few days.

In Montgomery, Governor Wallace held his ground. "Those folks in Selma have made this a seven-day-a-week job, but we can't give one inch. We're going to enforce state law."

Soon scores of sympathizers from the North began arriving in Selma. King announced the march would resume on Tuesday, March

9, despite a temporary federal restraining order. Leroy Collins, former governor of Florida and head of the newly established federal Community Relations Service, flew into Selma to confer with both sides. He persuaded the Alabama authorities not to interfere with Tuesday's marchers if they would turn back at an agreed upon point. Concerned about future federal cooperation and the possibility of further violence, King agreed to limit the march.

On Tuesday, March 9, King led some 1,000 blacks and 450 white sympathizers over the Pettus Bridge and a quarter of a mile down the highway toward Montgomery. The marchers were halted by state troopers and were then granted permission to pray. Major Cloud ordered his men to break ranks and move to the shoulders of the highway, but King decided not to proceed and led the marchers who were singing "Ain't Gonna Let Nobody Turn Me 'Round" back to Brown Chapel.

AN AMERICAN TRAGEDY

Back at Brown Chapel, King declared the march a victory and promised that they would get to Montgomery one day. However, the SNCC people wanted to storm Montgomery that day; James Forman, SNCC executive secretary, argued that the restraint of the state troopers this time was indeed another example of white racism. He declared that no one was attacked because "they don't beat white people. It's Negroes they beat and kill."

That evening three white Unitarian ministers were assaulted by local whites as they left a black soul food restaurant in Selma. Among the victims was the Reverend James J. Reeb, a welfare worker in Boston's black slums. Two days after the attack he died from the blows. The death of the 38-year-old minister triggered a national outcry and demonstrations in several cities.

On Saturday, March 13, Governor Wallace flew to Washington, D.C. to meet with President Johnson. The president tried to convince Wallace to assist with the march. Justice Department official Burke Marshall, who was present at the meeting, recalled "President Johnson putting his arm around him [Wallace] and squeezing him and telling him it's a moment of history, and how do we want to be remembered in history? Do we want to be remembered as petty little men, or do we want to be remembered as great figures that faced up to our moments of crises?"

After Wallace left the White House, Johnson held a news conference and announced, "What happened in Selma was an American tragedy," and in a solemn voice said, "The blows that were received, the blood that was shed, the life of the good man that was lost, must strengthen the determination of each of us to bring full equality and equal justice to all of our people. This is not just the policy of your government or your president. It is the heart and the purpose and the meaning of America itself." The president backed up his words with action. He announced that on Monday, March 15, he would send a voting rights bill to Congress that would "strike down all restrictions used to deny the people the right to vote."

"WE SHALL OVERCOME!"

That Monday evening, President Johnson delivered a nationwide television address to a joint session of Congress to request the passage of a strict voting rights bill. It was the first time a president had personally given a special message on domestic legislation in 19 years. Seventy million people tuned in to watch the momentous occasion. Johnson began slowly, amid a hush so quiet that even the clicks of photographers' cameras could be clearly heard in the chamber. The president first reviewed the protest in Selma, then said in his slow Texas drawl, "It is wrong—deadly wrong—to deny any of your fellow Americans the right to vote." He asked Congress to approve the administration's new bill without delay and without any hesitation because "outside this chamber is the outraged conscience of a nation."

Johnson noted that the protest in Selma was a turning point in American history and compared it to the events at Concord, Lexington and Appomattox. "At times history and fate meet at a single time in a single place to shape a turning point in man's unending search for freedom . . . So it was last week in Selma, Alabama." Speaking not only to the politicians present but to his fellow Americans, Johnson eloquently pleaded, "Even if we pass this bill, the battle will not be over. What happened in Selma is part of a far larger movement which reaches into every section and every state of America. It is an effort of American Negroes to secure for themselves the full blessings of American life." Then, with his thumbs raised and his fists clenched, Johnson declared, "Their cause must be our cause too. It is not just Negroes, but all of us, who must overcome the crippling legacy of bigotry and injustice. And," the president concluded emphatically with the movement's slogan, "we *shall* overcome!"

Congress gave Johnson a standing ovation, the second of the night. Martin Luther King, Jr. who was the president's special invited guest, watched the address in absentia—as he remained in Selma to deliver a eulogy for James Reeb. King's colleagues and friends had never seen him cry before, but this time "tears actually came to Dr. King's eyes,"

In an address to a joint session of Congress on March 15, 1965, President Lyndon Johnson presented his proposal for a voting rights act. Courtesy of the Lyndon Baines Johnson Library.

John Lewis recalled, "when President Johnson said, 'We shall overcome.' "

James Foreman, SNCC's executive secretary, was less impressed. Speaking in a church in Montgomery a day after Johnson's speech, he said, "I want to know, did President Johnson mean what he said? See, that's what I want to know, because there's only one man in the country that can stop George Wallace and those posses . . . these problems will not be solved until [the man] in that shaggedy old place called the White House begins to shake and gets on the phone and says, 'Now listen, George, we're coming down there and throw you in jail if you don't stop that mess' . . . I said it today and I will say it again: If we can't sit at the table, let's knock the fuckin' legs off, excuse me."

The following day, Wednesday, March 17, a federal judge, Frank M. Johnson Jr., handed down a decision allowing the Selma–to–Montgomery march to take place. Although the ruling cleared the way for the march, Governor Wallace still did not agree to provide the marchers with police protection. President Johnson responded by federalizing the Alabama National Guard and ordering its nearly 2,000 members to oversee the march. He also dispatched 2,000 Army troops, 100 FBI agents and another 100 federal marshals. The Selma–to–Montgomery march would finally get underway on Sunday, March 21.

THE WALK OF HOPE

On Sunday morning, about 3,200 people, black and white, gathered at Brown's Chapel for the 54-mile march to Montgomery. King told the crowd, "Walk together, children; don't you get weary, and it will lead us to the Promised Land. And Alabama will be a new Alabama, and America will be a new America." Then the group composed of experienced marchers and those who had never marched before headed off for the Alabama capital. In the lead were King and Abernathy, flanked by Ralph Bunche of the United Nations, also a Nobel Peace Prize winner, and Rabbi Abraham Heschel of the Jewish Theological Seminary of America. Behind them came poor blacks and movie stars, housewives and clergymen, nuns and college students and civil rights workers from various organizations.

The procession moved out along Highway 80 with helicopters clattering overhead and armed troops standing at intervals along the road. Although a few hundred white bystanders carried Confederate flags and held up signs that read, "Nigger lover," "Martin Luther Coon" and "Nigger King go home," on the whole, the spectators watched in silence as King and his fellow marchers continued on their journey.

The trip to Montgomery took the marchers across flat farmlands, rough cotton patches and pine thickets. At night the marchers slept in tents they pitched along the road. Food and supplies were brought to them from the march headquarters in Selma. On the third day, rain drenched the marchers, but it failed to dampen their spirit. "Lift 'em up and lay 'em down, we are coming from Selma town!" a black man chanted out in the tradition of an old spiritual. The marchers pushed forward to the beat. Spectators along the roadside answered the call-and-response greetings from the marchers:

> What do you want?
> Freedom!
> When do you want it?
> Now!
> Where are we going?
> Montgomery!

By the fourth day of the march, Wednesday, some 25,000 people were moving toward Alabama's capital city. They were about four miles from Montgomery. "We have a new song to sing tomorrow," King told the marchers, "We *have* overcome."

Writers, artists and performers participated in the Selma–to–Montgomery march. James Baldwin and Joan Baez march with James Forman, executive secretary of the Student Nonviolent Coordinating Committee. Courtesy of the Lawrence Henry Collection, Schomburg Center for Research in Black Culture.

On Thursday, March 25, the Montgomery capitol came into view, the Alabama flag and the stars and bars of the Confederate banner waving above the dome. The marchers passed the Dexter Avenue Baptist Church, King's congregation during the Montgomery bus boycott. On the steps of the capitol—where Jefferson Davis took the oath as president of the Confederate States of America—Martin Luther King Jr. addressed the triumphant crowd as millions watched on television. "Last Sunday . . . [we] started on a mighty walk from Selma, Alabama. We have walked on meandering highways and rested our bodies on rocky byways." King called for more marches on segregated schools, on poverty and on ballot boxes "until race barriers disappear from the political arena."

Then, working up to a grand climax punctuated by "amens" and "yessuhs" from several blacks in the crowd, King assured the audience, "The battle is in our hands . . . I know some of you are asking today. 'How long will it take?' I come to say to you this afternoon, however difficult the moment, however frustrating the hour, it will not be long, because truth pressed to earth will rise again. How long? Not long, because no lie can live forever. How long? Not long, because you will reap what you sow. How long? Not long, because the arm of the moral universe is long but it bends toward justice."

That same evening an act of violence dampened the day's triumphant mood. Four Klansmen shot and killed a white Detroit housewife, Viola Luizzo, who was transporting a group of marchers from Montgomery back to Selma. Within hours, the crime was solved by the FBI because they discovered one of their informants was in the car with the Klansmen. The death of Mrs. Luizzo soon became as much a symbol of the voting rights campaign as the march she had assisted.

In a nationwide television address, President Johnson announced that the FBI had arrested the men responsible for Luizzo's murder and said, "My father fought them [the Klan] many long years ago in Texas, and I have fought them all my life, because I believe them to threaten the peace of every community where they exist."

Appearing on the television program the "Today" show, Governor Wallace defended the state of Alabama, "Of course I regret the incident, but I would like to point out that people are assaulted in every state of the union . . . With 25,000 marching in the streets and chanting and maligning and slandering and libeling the people of this state, as they did for several hours on this network and the other networks, I think the people of our state were greatly restrained."

THE DIGNITY OF MAN

Following the Selma–to–Montgomery march, attention shifted to the Voting Rights Act. The bill was sent to Congress on March 19, 1965, authorizing the attorney general to send federal examiners to supersede local registrars and regulations wherever discrimination occurred. It provided the Justice Department with a speedy alternative to fighting disfranchisement cases in the lengthy court system.

Johnson managed to gain bipartisan support for the bill in the Senate, partly by having his attorney general enlist Republican minority leader, Everett Dirksen, in drafting the legislation. This strategy resulted in having 66 Senate cosponsors of the bill, only one vote short of the two-thirds needed to end the anticipated Southern filibuster.

Although heated debate did take place, on May 21, the cloture vote finally came, and the Senate ended the filibuster by a vote of 70 to 30. Senator Harry Byrd of Virginia told an aide, "You know, you can't stop this bill. We can't deny the Negroes a basic constitutional right to vote." In the House, the bill underwent five weeks of debate before gaining approval. On August 3, 1965, the House of Representatives

Roy Wilkins meets with President Lyndon Johnson in the White House to review some of the strategies employed to secure passage of the Voting Rights Act of 1965. Courtesy of the Library of Congress.

passed the voting rights bill by 328 to 74, better than a four-to-one margin. The following day the Senate followed suit with nearly the same decisiveness, 79 to 18.

For the signing ceremonies of August 6, President Johnson invited the major civil rights leaders, including Martin Luther King Jr., Roy Wilkins and James Farmer, and two lesser known figures of the movement, Rosa Parks, who had triggered the Montgomery bus boycott, and Vivian Malone, who had enrolled at the University of Alabama in 1963 after federal marshals escorted her past Governor George Wallace.

The signing ceremony took place in the President's Room of the Capitol rotunda, where President Abraham Lincoln had signed the Emancipation Proclamation 104 years earlier. "The vote is the most powerful instrument ever devised by man for breaking down injustice and destroying the terrible walls which imprison men because they are different from other men . . ." said the President. "[The Voting Rights Act of 1965] is one of the most monumental laws in the entire history of American freedom."

FREE AT LAST?

Although the Voting Rights Act of 1965 was a significant victory for the civil rights movement, it was only one rung on the long ladder ahead for gaining equality, justice and dignity. Segregation remained unbroken in many sections of the country, North and South, unemployment for black Americans was disproportionately high, and violent racial incidents still took place.

The passage of the Voting Rights Act did permit black Americans to participate freely in local and national elections. Blacks were elected to such public offices as mayors and state and congressional representatives. One year after the bill was signed, 9,000 blacks had registered to vote in Dallas County, Alabama. Local segregationists lost their power as more and more black people registered to vote. But on the national level, segregationist senators, such as James Eastland of Mississippi and Strom Thurmond of South Carolina, continued to hold their positions.

The influence of black voters did affect federal appointments. President Johnson selected Thurgood Marshall as his solicitor general and two years later nominated him to serve as the nation's first black associate justice of the Supreme Court. President Jimmy Carter later appointed Andrew Young to the position of United Nations ambassador. Young eventually became mayor of Atlanta, Georgia, and by the mid-1980s, black mayors had been elected in over 250 cities.

The Selma–to–Montgomery march was the last major demonstration on a national level involving both blacks and whites. The movement for racial equality that first gained momentum in the mid-1950s with the Montgomery bus boycott and again in the early 1960s with the sit-ins and Freedom Rides did not come to an end in Selma, it only transformed itself into a new movement. The slogan of "black power" would soon replace the movement's anthem of "We Shall Overcome."

Although the civil rights movement changed directions after 1965, the movement that spanned over a period of 10 years did indeed achieve a remarkable number of accomplishments. More civil rights legislation was passed and more court decisions affecting equal rights were handed down between the years of the *Brown* decision of 1954 and the Voting Rights Act of 1965 than during any other decade in American history.

The civil rights movement dramatically changed the face of the nation and gave a sense of dignity and power to black Americans. Most of all, the millions of Americans who participated in the movement brought about changes that reinforced our nation's basic constitutional rights for all Americans—black and white, men and women, young and old.

CHRONICLE OF EVENTS

1965

January 4: The U.S. Justice Department files school desegregation suits in Louisiana and Tennessee, the first filed under the 1964 Civil Rights Act.

January 18–19: Martin Luther King Jr. leads a voter registration march to Selma, Alabama courthouse; 67 demonstrators are arrested.

February 1–2: Mass marches are held in Selma; more than 700 demonstrators are arrested; King and Abernathy are also arrested and refuse bond.

February 4: A federal judge bans the use of a complex voter registration test in Selma and orders the Selma registration board to process at least 100 voter applications per day.

February 7: Cabinet-level Council on Equal Opportunity is created to coordinate all federal civil rights activities.

February 8: A small group of protesters go to a Selma voter registration office and demand to be registered immediately; the group is arrested. Two hundred students march to the courthouse to protest the arrests.

February 11–18: Marches, protests and registration efforts continue in Selma.

February 18: In nearby Marion, Alabama, marcher Jimmie Lee Jackson is shot and killed while trying to protect his mother from a state trooper's attack.

February 21: Malcolm X is assassinated during a rally at the Organization of Afro-American Unity at the Audubon Ballroom in New York City.

March 7: Six-hundred marchers set out for Montgomery from Selma, led by SCLC's Hosea Williams and SNCC's John Lewis. "Bloody Sunday" results when state troopers attack the marchers with nightsticks and tear gas as they attempt to cross the Edmund Pettus Bridge; more than 50 are injured. Outrage is expressed around the nation. The SCLC petitions a federal judge, Frank M. Johnson Jr., for an order permitting a march to Montgomery without state interference.

March 9: Martin Luther King Jr. leads a group of marchers to the edge of a state trooper barricade on the outskirts of Selma. After a prayer, King leads the marchers back to Selma. Later, local whites attack three white Unitarian ministers who participated in the demonstration, seriously injuring the Reverend James J. Reeb.

March 11: Reeb dies from his injuries. His death triggers demonstrations in many Northern cities for federal intervention and voting rights legislation.

March 16: SNCC march in Montgomery is attacked by mounted police using cattle prods.

March 17: Judge Johnson issues a court order, allowing the Selma–to–Montgomery march to take place.

March 20: President Johnson federalizes the Alabama National Guard to protect the demonstrators.

March 21–25: Thousands of demonstrators, led by King, participate in and complete the five-day march. The march ends at the Alabama state capitol, where King addresses a rally of about 50,000 people. Following the rally, Viola Liuzzo, a white housewife and activist from Detroit, is shot to death as she is transporting participants between Selma and Montgomery. (Three Klansmen are later convicted for this crime.)

July 13: Thurgood Marshall is nominated as solicitor general of the United States, the first black to hold this office.

July 24–26: Martin Luther King Jr. and the Southern Christian Leadership Conference (SCLC) conduct civil rights demonstrations in Chicago.

August 3: The House of Representatives passes the Voting Rights Act, 328–74.

August 3: The Senate passes the Voting Rights Act.

August 6: President Johnson signs the Voting Rights Act of 1965, eliminating literacy and other voter examinations and allowing federal examiners to register black voters in many southern counties.

August 11–16: Rioting occurs in the predominantly black Watts section of Los Angeles; it is one of the worst race riots in U.S. history.

EYEWITNESS TESTIMONY

We will seek to arouse the federal government by marching by the thousands to the place of registration . . . We must be willing to go to jail by the thousands. We are not asking, we are demanding the ballot.

Martin Luther King Jr., to a church rally in Selma, Alabama, speech of January 18, 1965, in Oates' Let the Trumpet Sound (1982).

All Americans should be indignant when one American is denied the right to vote. The loss of that right to a single citizen undermines the freedom of every citizen. This is why all of us should be concerned with the efforts of our fellow Americans to register to vote in Alabama. The basic problem in Selma is the slow pace of voting registration for Negroes who are qualified to vote . . . I hope that all Americans will join with me in expressing their concern over the loss of any American's right to vote . . . I intend to see that that right is secured for all citizens.

President Lyndon Johnson, to the press, statement of February 4, 1965, in The Public Papers of the Presidents of the United States (1964–1969).

When the King of Norway participated in awarding the Nobel Prize to me he surely did not think that in less than sixty days I would be in jail. He, and almost all world opinion will be shocked because they are little aware of the unfinished business of the South.

By jailing hundreds of Negroes, the city of Selma, Alabama, has revealed the persisting ugliness of segregation to the nation and the world. When the Civil Rights Act of 1964 was passed many decent Americans were lulled into complacency because they thought the day of difficult struggle was over.

Why are we in jail? Have you ever been required to answer 100 questions on government, some abstruse even to a political scientist specialist, merely to vote? Have you ever stood in line with over a hundred others and after waiting an entire day seen less than ten given the qualifying test?

This is Selma, Alabama. There are more Negroes in jail with me than there are on the voting rolls . . .

This is the U.S.A. in 1965. We are in jail simply because we cannot tolerate these conditions for ourselves or our nation.

We need the help of all decent Americans.

Martin Luther King Jr., "A Letter from Martin Luther King from a Selma, Alabama Jail," an SCLC solicitation advertisement in the New York Times (February 5, 1965).

We are going to bring a voting bill into being in the streets of Selma, Alabama. President Johnson has a mandate from the American people. He must go out and get a voting bill this time that will end the necessity for any more voting bills.

Martin Luther King Jr., to a rally at the Brown Chapel African Methodist Episcopal Church in Selma, Alabama, speech of March 1, 1965, in the New York Times (March 2, 1965).

Jimmie Lee Jackson is speaking to us from the casket and he is saying to us that we must substitute courage for caution.

His death says to us that we must work passionately and unrelentingly to make the American dream a reality. His death must prove that unmeritted suffering does not go unredempted.

Martin Luther King Jr., eulogy of March 3, 1965, at Zion's Chapel Methodist Church in Marion, Alabama, for slain civil rights marcher Jimmie Lee Jackson, in the New York Times (March 4, 1965).

You gotta do what the spirit say do,
You gotta do what the spirit say do.

And what the spirit say do, I'm gonna do, oh Lord,
You gotta do what the spirit say do.

You gotta march when the spirit say march,
You gotta march when the spirit say march,

And when the spirit say march, you better march,
  oh Lord,
You gotta march when the spirit say march.

"Do What the Spirit Say Do," song sung by young marchers in Selma, Alabama, March 1965.

There were troopers—all in blue. And, there were all these guys on horses. We kept walking until we got within hearing distance, and this guy with the bullhorn, says, "I'm Major John Cloud, and I'll give you two minutes to disperse and go back to your

The marchers are met by gas-masked Alabama state troopers after crossing the Edmund Pettus Bridge, March 7, 1965. Copyright, photo by the Birmingham News, 1999. All rights reserved. Reprinted with permission.

church." About a minute-and-a-half later, he said, "Troops advance!"

John Lewis, SNCC chairman, recalling March 7, 1965 ("Bloody Sunday"), in Selma, Alabama, in Lyons' Ebony *article of March 1990.*

The troopers rushed forward, their blue uniforms and white helmets blurring into a flying wedge as they moved.

The wedge moved with such force that it seemed almost to pass over the waiting column instead of through it.

The first 10 or 20 Negroes were swept to the ground screaming, arms and legs flying, and packs and bags went skittering across the grassy divider strip and on to the pavement on both sides.

Those still on their feet retreated.

The troopers continued pushing, using both the force of their bodies and the prodding of their nightsticks.

A cheer went up from the white spectators lining the south side of the highway.

The mounted possemen spurred their horses and rode at a run into the retreating mass. The Negroes cried out as they crowded together for protection, and the whites on the sidelines whooped and cheered.

The Negroes paused in their retreat for perhaps a minute, and screaming and huddling together.

Suddenly there was a report like a gunshot and a grey cloud spewed over the troopers and the Negroes.

"Tear gas!" someone yelled.

Roy Reed, journalist, article of March 8, 1965, on Alabama state troopers attacking civil rights marchers as they attempted to cross the Edmund Pettus Bridge in Selma on March 7, 1965, in the New York Times.

Tear gas canisters erupted from the blue line of officers and fell among the faltering column of demonstrators.

A billow of white gas covered the scene with a weird haze as officers waded into the gas, swinging their clubs.

Instantly, the strange drama of order and precision dissolved into a welter of screams, shouts, coughing and the thud of wooden clubs on flesh.

Marchers broke and ran in all directions.

Possemen chased them across fields and lots.

Demonstrators climbed over parked cars in an effort to escape. Others crawled under the vehicles or sought better shelter . . .

Bedrolls and packs, carried by the demonstrators for their proposed long protest hike, were dropped or hurled to the ground.

"God, we're being killed," "Please, no," and other screams and pleas cut the air.

Tom Lankford, journalist, article of March 8, 1965, on March 7, 1965 ("Bloody Sunday"), in Selma, Alabama, in the Birmingham News.

I was knocked out for maybe five minutes. When I woke up I was in a cloud. I couldn't breathe and I couldn't see. I was coughing and I was sick. It was like the world had gone away. I laid there on the grass for a few minutes and then I felt around me, trying to see if anybody else was still there. I couldn't feel anybody. They were all gone. I was the only one left . . . They tried to get the horses to run over us. They came charging through where we were laying on the grass and tried to hit us with the horses, but the horses had more sense. One posseman tried to get his horse to rear up and land on top of a man near me, but the horse wouldn't do it. Horses have more sense.

Jim Benston, marcher, recalling March 7, 1965 ("Bloody Sunday"), in Selma, Alabama, in Hinckle and Welsh's Ramparts *magazine article of June 1965.*

I'll tell you, I forgot about praying, and I just turned and ran. And just as I was turning the tear gas got me; it burned my nose first and then got my eyes. I was blinded by the tears. So I began running and not seeing where I was going. I remember being scared that I might fall over the railing and into the water. I don't know if I was screaming or not, but everyone else was. People were running and falling and ducking and you could hear the horses' hooves on the pavement and you'd hear people scream and hear the whips swishing and you'd hear them striking the people. They'd cry out; some moaned. Women as well as men were getting hit. I never got hit, but one of the horses went right by me and I heard the swish sound as the whip went over my head and

cracked some man across the back. It seemed to take forever to get across the bridge. It seemed I was running uphill for an awfully long time. They kept rolling canisters of tear gas on the ground, so it would rise up quickly. It was making me sick. I heard more horses and I turned back and saw two of them and the riders were leaning over to one side. It was like a nightmare seeing it through the tears. I just knew then that I was going to die, that those horses were going to trample me. So I kind of knelt down and held my hands and arms up over my head, and I must have been screaming—I don't really remember.

Sheyann Webb, marcher [eight-years-old at the time], recalling March 7, 1965 ("Bloody Sunday"), in Selma, Alabama, in Nelson and Webb's Selma, Lord, Selma *(1980).*

I heard the horses' hooves and I turned and saw the riders hitting at the people and they were coming fast toward me. I stopped and I got up against the wall of one of the apartment buildings and pressed myself against it as hard as I could. Two horsemen went by and I knew if I didn't move I would be trapped there. I saw the people crying as they went by and holding their eyes and some had their arms up over their heads. I took off running.

Rachel West Nelson, marcher [9-years-old at the time], recalling March 7, 1965 ("Bloody Sunday"), in Selma, Alabama, in Nelson and Webb's Selma, Lord, Selma *(1980).*

They literally whipped folk all the way back to the church. They even came up in the yard of the church, hittin' on folk. Ladies, men, babies, children—they didn't give a damn who they were . . . That was one hell of a day.

Willie Bolden, SCLC activist, on March 7, 1965 ("Bloody Sunday"), in Selma, Alabama, in Raines' My Soul Is Rested *(1977).*

I am shocked at the terrible reign of terror that took place in Alabama today. Negro citizens engaged in a peaceful and orderly march to protest racial injustice were beaten, brutalized and harassed by state troopers, and Alabama revealed its law enforcement agents have not respect for democracy nor the rights of its Negro citizens.

Martin Luther King Jr., to the press, statement of March 7, 1965, in the New York Times *(March 8, 1965).*

We are no longer fighting for a seat at the lunch counter. We are fighting for seats in the legislature.

A marcher lies injured on the curb, while an Alabama state trooper runs to the rear and mounted possemen prepare to surge forward. Copyright, photo by the Birmingham News, *1999. All rights reserved. Reprinted with permission.*

James Bevel, SCLC activist, to the press, statement of March 7, 1965, in the National Guardian *(March 13, 1965).*

Those folks in Selma have made this a seven-day-a-week job but we can't give in one inch. We're going to enforce state laws.

Alabama Governor George Wallace, to the press, statement of March 7, 1965, in the New York Herald Tribune *(March 8, 1965).*

I don't know see how President Johnson can send troops to Vietnam—I don't see how he can send troops to the Congo—I don't see how he can send troops to Africa and can't send troops to Selma, Alabama.

Next time we march we may have to keep going when we get to Montgomery. We may have to go on to Washington.

John Lewis, SNCC chairman, to the press, statement of March 7, 1965, in the New York Times *(March 8, 1965). [Lewis was attacked by Alabama state troopers during the march across the Edmund Pettus Bridge in Selma on March 7.]*

If a man is 36, as I am, and refuses to stand up, he may go and live to be 80 but he is just as dead as he is at 80. A man dies when he refuses to stand up for what is right, for what is justice, for what is true.

Martin Luther King Jr., to a crowd of supporters at the Brown Chapel AME Church, speech

of March 8, 1965, in the Birmingham News
(March 9, 1965).

If federal troops are not made available to protect the rights of Negroes, then the American people are faced with terrible alternatives. Like the citizens of Nazi-occupied France, Holland, Belgium, Denmark and Norway, Negroes must either submit to the heels of the oppressors or they must organize, underground, to protect themselves from the oppression of Governor Wallace and his storm troopers.

Roy Wilkins, NAACP executive director, to
President Johnson, telegram of March 8, 1965,
in the New York Herald Tribune *(March 9,*
1965).

I abhor the violent and brutal attack upon Americans who attempt only to march peacefully . . . The Americans so brutally attacked yesterday sought only their constitutional rights to vote.

Senator Ralph Yarborough (D, Tex.), to the
Senate, speech of March 8, 1965, in the
Congressional Record *(1965).*

Sunday's outrage in Selma, Alabama, makes passage of the legislation to guarantee Southern Negroes the right to vote an absolute imperative for Congress this year.

Senator Walter Mondale (D, Minn.), to the
Senate, speech of March 8, 1965, in the
Congressional Record *(1965).*

These Americans, so brutally attacked in Selma, sought only their constitutional right to register and vote. They did not resist arrest. They were, however, gassed, clubbed, and beaten at random in their efforts to pursue equality. While I do not condone lawlessness or defiance of law and order, I am equally appalled at any violent or unmerciful attack upon Americans who attempt only to march peacefully in their quest for civil rights.

Congressman Carleton J. King (R, N.Y.), to
Congress, speech of March 9, 1965, in the
Congressional Record *(1965).*

It is a sad and morbid commentary that bleeding American citizens must still fill hospitals, while a governor permits them to be clubbed down in the name of "the law," when all they are asking, under the law, is the simplest, most basic American right—the vote.

The Atlanta Constitution, *editorial of March*
9, 1965.

The news from Selma, Alabama, where police beat and mauled and gassed unarmed, helpless and unoffending citizens will shock and alarm the whole nation. It is simply inconceivable that in this day and age, the police who have sworn to uphold the law and protect the citizenry could resort, instead, to violent attacks upon them . . .

The situation calls for more than mere reproach and anguish, but it is not easy to say what can be done to prevent the repetition of this scandalous misuse of police power. Congress, as a beginning must promptly pass legislation that will put into federal hands the registration of voters that the Alabama authorities will continue to obstruct as long as they have discretion. At least such legislation will put beyond contest the rights that the Negro citizens have been trying to gain by demonstration.

The Washington Post, *editorial of March 9,*
1965.

Ever since the events of Sunday afternoon in Selma, Alabama, the administration has been in close touch with the situation and has made every effort to prevent a repetition. I am certain Americans everywhere join in deploring the brutality with which a number of Negro citizens of Alabama were treated when they sought to dramatize their deep and sincere interest in attaining the precious right to vote.

President Lyndon Johnson, public statement of
March 9, 1965, in The Public Papers of the
Presidents of the United States *(1964–*
1969).

The men and women who were clubbed and beaten by the state police and other law enforcement officers are attempting only to exercise the most fundamental right of American citizens—the right to register and vote.

George Meany, AFL-CIO president, to Presi-
dent Johnson, telegram of March 10, 1965, in
the New York Herald Tribune *(March 11,*
1965).

Voter registration and voting rights are not the issues involved in these street demonstrations. The voting rights of every person in Alabama are now being considered by litigation pending in the federal courts. I have said many times before, and I say again, that any individual who is qualified to vote is entitled to vote.

Alabama Governor George Wallace, to President
Lyndon Johnson, telegram of March 12, 1965,
in the New York Times *(March 13, 1965).*

What happened in Selma was an American tragedy. The blows that were received, the blood that was shed, the life of the good man [Rev. James J. Reeb] that was lost, must strengthen the determination of each of us to bring full and equal and exact justice to all of our people.

This is not just the policy of your Government or your President. It is in the heart and the purpose and the meaning of America itself.

We all know how complex and how difficult it is to bring about basic social change in a democracy, but this complexity must not obscure the clear and simple moral issues.

It is wrong to do violence to peaceful citizens in the streets of their town. It is wrong to deny Americans the right to vote. It is wrong to deny any person full equality because of the color of his skin.

President Lyndon Johnson, to the press, state-
ment of March 13, 1965, in The Public Papers of the Presidents of the United States
(1964–1969).

For reasons, known only to themselves, outside racial agitators have chosen to make Selma what they call a "focal point," in their national drive to raise money, gain political power and to pressure the president of the United States and the Congress into enacting new and stronger civil rights laws. We refer specifically to Martin Luther King and his SCLC group, SNCC, CORE, the Communist Party and their various front groups and camp followers and other outside agitators by the hundreds.

Selma Mayor Joe T. Smitherman and Sheriff
James G. Clark, joint public statement of March
14, 1965, in the Selma-Times Journal *(March*
14, 1965).

In Selma, Alabama, thousands of Negroes are courageously providing dramatic witness to the evil forces that bar our way to the all-important ballot box. They are laying bare for all the nation to see, for all the world to know, the nature of segregationist resistance. The ugly pattern of denial flourishes with insignificant differences in thousands of Alabama, Louisiana, Mississippi, and other Southern communities. Once it is exposed, and challenged by the marching feet of Negro citizens, the nation will take

action to cure this cancerous sore. What is malignant to Selma must be removed by Congressional surgery so that all citizens may freely exercise their right to vote without delay, harassment, economic intimidation and police brutality. Selma is to 1965 what Birmingham was to 1963.

Martin Luther King Jr., article of March 14,
1965, in the New York Times Magazine.

We are for peaceful demonstrations, but we don't think that peaceful demonstrations should run eight long weeks.

I wonder how long the people of New York would put up with eight weeks of demonstrations in Times Square, in the Boston Common, in the city of Philadelphia.

Alabama Governor George Wallace, to the
press, statement of March 15, 1965, in the
New York Times *(March 16, 1965).*

At times history and fate meet at a single time in a single place to shape a turning point in man's unending search for freedom. So it was at Lexington and Concord. So it was a century ago at Appomattox. So it was last week in Selma, Alabama . . .

Wednesday I will send to Congress a law designed to eliminate illegal barriers to the right to vote . . .

This time, on this issue, there must be no delay, no hesitation and no compromise with our purpose . . .

We have already been waiting a hundred years and more, and the time for waiting is gone.

But even if we pass this bill, the battle will not be over. What happened in Selma is part of a far larger movement which reaches into every section and state of America. It is the effort of American Negroes to secure themselves the full blessings of American life.

Their cause must be our cause too. Because it is not just Negroes but really it is all of us, who must overcome the crippling legacy of bigotry and injustice.

And we shall overcome!

President Lyndon Johnson, to Congress, special
message of March 15, 1965, in The Public Papers of the Presidents of the United States
(1964–1969).

I can only pray that oratory becomes fact, that words become law. We will continue to interpose our bodies and our strength until Negroes of America are in fact, not just in rhetoric, truly free.

*James Farmer, CORE national director, to the
press, statement of March 16, 1965, in the
New York Times (March 17, 1965).*

The protest has reached its present state of crisis mainly because of the discriminatory practices of Alabama officials in denying Negroes the right to vote and because of the bullying tactics of the Alabama highway patrol and the Dallas County sheriff's deputies.

*Senator Robert Kennedy (D, N.Y.), to the
press, statement of March 18, 1965, in the
New York Herald Tribune (March 19, 1965).*

Every act of violence, every hand raised by one against another, every injury and every death that has occurred in those racial riots and demonstrations was provoked and intentionally caused by the great Peace Prize winner "King" Martin Luther, the man with the key to the White House, the man that can pull strings and see our national leaders dance . . . I am warning everyone that continued agitation can only lead to further violence. The patience of my people is exhausted.

*Congressman William J. Dickinson (R, Ala.),
to Congress, speech of March 18, 1965, in the
Congressional Record (1965).*

I say to you tonight that the street warfare and demonstrations that once plagued Czechoslovakia, that ripped Cuba apart, that destroyed Diem and Vietnam, that raked China, that has torn civilization and established institutions of the world into bloody shreds now courses through the streets of America—rips asunder the town of Selma and laps at the doorstep of every American, black and white.

Tonight I should like to ask you, the people of Alabama, for restraint. I am asking you to stay away from the points of tension. I do not ask you for cowardice. But I ask you for restraint in the same tradition that our outnumbered forefathers followed. I ask you to exercise that superior discipline that is yours.

Alabama Governor George Wallace, to the Alabama state legislature, speech of March 18, 1965, in the New York Times (March 19, 1965).

Over the next several days the eyes of the nation will be upon Alabama, and the eyes of the world will upon America. It is my prayer, a prayer in which I hope all Americans will join me earnestly today, that the march in Alabama may proceed in a manner honoring our heritage and honoring all for which America stands.

President Lyndon Johnson, to the press, statement of March 20, 1965, in The Public Papers of the Presidents of the United States (1964–1969).

You will be the people that will light a new chapter in the history books of our nation. Those of us who are Negroes don't have much. We have known the long night of poverty. Because of the system, we don't know how to make our nouns and verbs agree. But thank God we have our bodies, our feet and our souls.

Walk together, children, don't you get weary, and it will lead us to the promised land. And Alabama will be a new Alabama, and America will be a new America.

Martin Luther King Jr., to marchers at Brown Chapel AME Church in Selma, Alabama, speech of March 21, 1965, in the New York Times (March 22, 1965).

We entered Selma . . . and we stayed on dirt roads all the way to the Negro church district that was our destination. As we pulled to a stop, three slim young Negro women walked past our car. One of them leaned over to us and said with absolute simplicity: "Thank you for coming." . . .

The scene inside the church burst upon me. Every seat, every aisle was packed. They were shoulder to shoulder—the Princeton professor and the sharecropper's child, the Senator's wife and the elderly Negro mammy . . .

Outside, in hazy sunlight, the marchers formed . . . They moved in voiceless exaltation. I exchanged smiles with Jim Foreman who walked arm in arm with Dr. King in the front rank. And behind them were all those with whom I had traveled . . .

George B. Leonard, journalist and marcher, on March 21, 1965, the first day of the Selma-to-Montgomery march, in a Nation article of May 10, 1965.

When we get to Montgomery, we are going to go up to Governor Wallace's door and say, "George, it's all over now. We've got the ballot."

Ralph Abernathy, SCLC activist, to the press, statement of March 21, in the New York Times (March 22, 1965).

Leaders of the Selma–to–Montgomery march, (far left) Bayard Rustin, A. Philip Randolph, John Lewis and Ralph Abernathy, (right) Martin Luther King Jr. and Coretta Scott King. Courtesy of the Lawrence Henry Collection, Schomburg Center for Research in Black Culture.

We want the right to vote, and we want it now. You white brothers can join the ranks, too. Come, enter the ranks of humanity. Just fall in the rear. Come along with us. We're going to tell brother Wallace he'll have to go.

Bill Bradley, black marcher and CORE activist from San Francisco, statement of March 1965, in the Chicago Defender *(April 2, 1965).*

This is no holiday. It is tragic to think we have to walk like this, that such a demonstration must be carried out to dramatize the plight of these people. One must sacrifice himself to help others.

Sherill Smith, marcher from San Antonio, Texas, statement of March 1965, in Booker's Ebony *article of May 1965.*

I don't know whether it will do any good; only the man up above knows.

Cager Lee, marcher, 82-year-old grandfather of Jimmie Lee Jackson, who was fatally shot by Alabama state troopers in a demonstration on February 18, 1965, statement of March 21, 1965, in the Baltimore Sun *(March 22, 1965).*

[We advanced] past cheering Negro homes, then the business section of town with sunny-faced, camera-clad whites peering hostilely from windows and balconies. We marched six-abreast while helicopters buzzed over us. There was an amazing amount of restraint on both sides.

Kathy Lange, marcher, recalling the Selma–to–Montgomery march of March 21–25, 1965, in Peace News *(April 16, 1965).*

Like living lights, they seem intent on leading this land out of an iniquitous darkness, and into a promised time where all men might have an opportunity to stand in all their true height, when unfair laws will be swept aside by justice. Yes, indeed, they sense, feel and know "We Shall Overcome!"

Julius Higginbotham, journalist, on the Selma–to–Montgomery march of March 21–25, 1965, in a Pittsburgh Courier *article of March 27, 1965.*

2:46 p.m.: Road sign. Montgomery, 47 miles. From house rooftop, 10-year-old boy waves two Confederate flags. Marchers sing, ". . . and before I'll be a slave, I'll be buried in a grave and go home to my Lord and be free."

Peter J. Kumpa, journalist, notebook entry of March 21, 1965, in the Baltimore Sun *(March 22, 1965).*

I want my grandchildren to live in a world where they are not afraid of their fellow man.

Timothy Murphy, 59-year-old white marcher from New York City, statement of March 23, 1965, in the New York Times *(March 24, 1965).*

Ain't going to let no posse turn me 'round
Keep on walkin', keep on talkin',
Marching up to Freedom Land.

Hymn sung by Selma–to–Montgomery marchers, March 21–25, 1965.

10:30 a.m.: Raining Dixie. Visibility zero. Can't see two ranks ahead. Negroes wet. Whites wet. FBI wet. Regular army wet. United States marshals wet. TV men wet. Pressmen wet. Notes wet. All wet.

Peter J. Kumpa, journalist, notebook entry of March 23, 1965, in the Baltimore Sun *(March 24, 1965).*

12:15 p.m.: March resumes with some new words to "Yankee Doodle."
   Wallace said we couldn't march,
   Now we're marching to Montgomery,
   To make him eat baloney.

Peter J. Kumpa, journalist, notebook entry of March 24, 1965, in the Baltimore Sun *(March 25, 1965).*

What do you want?
Freedom!

Thousands of demonstrators, black and white, participated in the five-day, 54-mile march from Selma to Montgomery. Courtesy of the Lawrence Henry Collection, Schomburg Center for Research in Black Culture.

Marchers entering Montgomery, Alabama, where Martin Luther King Jr. addressed a rally of about 50,000 people in front of the state capitol. Courtesy of the Lawrence Henry Collection, Schomburg Center for Research in Black Culture.

When do you want it?
Now!
Where are we going?
Montgomery!

Chant, between marchers and roadside spectators during the Selma–to–Montgomery march, March 21–25, 1965.

Then the marchers came. There were the known people. King and old Phil Randolph, the stiffness of the years in his legs, and Roy Wilkins, and Whitney Young. But there were few that could be recognized. Civil rights when it comes out of the lecture halls and goes into the back roads of places like Selma, Alabama, does not attract many personalities. It attracts only people whose names are nothing and who have nothing that shows, and they take chances with their lives, and yesterday they walked through Montgomery, those nameless little people who changed the ways of the nation, and with them were people from everywhere, white people and black people, and they walked together in a parade the South has never seen. And they showed forever on this humid day that what they stand for cannot be stopped.

Jimmy Breslin, journalist, article of March 26, 1965, in the New York Herald Tribune.

Right now we're out here and Wallace is in there. But he'd better remember that pretty soon some of us will be in there and he may be out here, because 34 percent of those state legislature seats are ours.

*James Bevel, SCLC activist, statement of March
25, 1965, in the [Baltimore] Afro-American
April 3, 1965.*

They told us we wouldn't get here. And there
were those who said that we would get here only
over their dead bodies, but all the world knows that
we are here and that we are standing before the
forces of power in the state of Alabama saying, "We
ain't goin' let nobody turn us around."

There never was a moment in American history
more honorable and more inspiring than the pilgrimage of clergymen and laymen of every race and faith
pouring into Selma to face danger at the side of its
embattled Negroes . . .

Our whole campaign in Alabama has been cen-
tered around the right to vote . . .

We are on the move now. The burning of our
churches will not deter us . . . We are on the move
now . . . The beating and killing of our clergymen
and young people will not divert us. We are on the
move now . . .

Let us therefore continue our triumph and march
. . . Let us march on segregated housing . . . Let
us march on segregated schools . . . Let us march
on poverty . . . Let us march on ballot boxes until
the Wallaces of our nation tremble away in silence . . .

I know you are asking today, "How long will it
take?" I come to say to you this afternoon, however
difficult the moment, however frustrating the hour,
it will not be long, because truth pressed to earth
will rise again.

How long? Not long, because no lie can live forever.

How long? Not long, because you will reap what
you sow.

How long? Not long. Because the arm of the moral
universe . . . bends toward justice.

*Martin Luther King Jr., to a rally of about
50,000 people outside the Alabama state capitol
building in Montgomery, speech of March 25,
1965, in the New York Times, March 26,
1965.*

Mrs. Liuzzo went to Alabama to serve the struggle
for justice. She was murdered by the enemies of
justice, who for decades have used the rope and the
gun, the tar and the feathers to terrorize their neighbors.

They struck by night, as they generally do, for
their purposes cannot stand the light of day.

My father fought them in Texas. I have fought
them all my life, because I believe them to threaten
the peace of every community where they exist.

I shall continue to fight them because I know their
loyalty is not to the United States, but to a hooded
society of bigots.

Men and women have stood against the Klan at
times and places where to do so required a continuous act of courage. If Klansmen hear my voice today,
let it both be an appeal—and a warning—to get out
of the Klan now and return to a decent society—
before it is too late . . .

No nation can long endure, either in history's
judgment or in its own national conscience, if hoodlums or bigots can defy the law and get away with
it. Justice must be done, in the largest city as well as
the smallest village—on the dirt road as well as the
interstate highway.

*President Lyndon Johnson, to the nation, speech
of March 25, 1965, after four Ku Klux Klan
members were arrested for "conspiracy to violate the civil rights" of Mrs. Viola Gregg
Liuzzo, a murdered white marcher in Selma,
Alabama, in The Public Papers of the Presidents of the United States (1964–1969).*

Thirty-four days ago, I asked the Congress to keep
our nation's century-old promise to the American
Negro.

I called on Congress to enact the Voting Rights Act
of 1965 . . .

It is my devout hope that the Congress will now
continue its excellent display of deliberation with
speed and enact the voting rights bill without delay.

There can be no forgetting, however, that neither
a Voting Rights Act nor any other single act will solve
the civil rights problems of the nation or insure equal
justice and equal opportunity for our Negro citizens.
Those goals can be achieved only as the result of
individual understanding, of community responsibility, and of national good faith.

*President Lyndon Johnson, public statement of
April 20, 1965, on the eve of the Senate's con-
sideration of the Voting Rights Act, in The
Public Papers of the Presidents of the
United States (1964–1969).*

The central fact of American civilization—one so
hard for others to understand—is that freedom and

justice and the dignity of man are not just words to us. We believe in them. Under all the growth and the tumult and abundance, we believe. And so, as long as some among us are oppressed—and we are part of that oppression—it must blunt our faith and sap the strength of our high purpose.

Thus, this is a victory for the freedom of the American Negro. But it is also a victory for the freedom of the American nation. And every family across this great, entire, searching land will live stronger in liberty, will live more splendid in expectation, and will be prouder to be American because of the act that you have passed that I will sign today.

President Lyndon Johnson, remarks of August 6, 1965, on the signing of the Voting Rights Act of 1965, in The Public Papers of the Presidents of the United States *(1964–1969).*

12. The Legacy of the Civil Rights Movement

BLACK POWER!

The years between the passage of the Voting Rights Act of 1965 and the assassination of Martin Luther King Jr. in 1968 marked a turning point in the history of the civil rights movement. Although a significant amount of legislation had been passed to guarantee basic equal rights for black Americans, vast inequities still existed. In one of his most eloquent statements on the issue of inequality, President Lyndon Johnson conceded this fact in his commencement address at Howard University in June 1965, ". . . for the great majority of Negro Americans—the poor, the unemployed, the uprooted and the dispossessed . . . They still are another nation. Despite the court orders and laws, despite the legislative victories and the speeches, for them the walls are rising and the gulf is widening."

In the summer of 1966, James Meredith, who had integrated the University of Mississippi in 1962, set out to march 225 miles from Memphis, Tennessee to Jackson, Mississippi. He believed that this "march against fear" would demonstrate to his fellow black Mississippians that they indeed could bring about social change by exercising their right to vote. On the second day of his pilgrimage, Meredith was injured in an attempted assassination.

Many civil rights leaders who had initially tried to dissuade Meredith from undertaking the march rushed to his hospital room and discussed how they would resume the march, beginning at the location where he was attacked. Besides Martin Luther King Jr., Roy Wilkins and Whitney Young, two newcomers joined the group: Floyd McKissick of CORE and SNCC's newly elected chairman, Stokely Carmichael. These two leaders, along with other young members of SNCC and CORE, had already begun questioning the effectiveness of nonviolence. Some also objected to the participation of friendly whites in the march. One young activist announced, "This should be an all-black march. We don't need any more white phonies and liberals invading our movement. This is our march."

The roots of black power first surfaced in Lowndes County, Alabama in 1966. Courtesy of the Lawrence Henry Collection, Schomburg Center for Research in Black Culture.

King and other established civil rights leaders had hopes that the "Meredith march," like the Selma–to–Montgomery march, would secure passage of a civil rights act, which would afford federal protection for civil rights workers, but instead they came into conflict over the march's "manifesto." The manifesto, drafted by Stokely Carmichael, demanded that the pending legislation be thoroughly revised and condemned the Johnson administration for its lax enforcement of existing civil rights acts. In the interest of preserving unity within the movement, King reluctantly endorsed the manifesto, but Wilkins and Young wanted no part in such a march and they quickly left Memphis.

At every town along the march route, large and enthusiastic crowds greeted King, Carmichael and McKissick, who stood at the head of several hundred supporters. King's followers sang "We Shall Overcome," but they were drowned out by SNCC's new version, "We Shall Overrun." As they approached Greenwood, Mississippi, Willie Ricks, a SNCC field secretary, discovered that the cry of "Black Power!" could stir up an audience. Carmichael observed that local blacks would scream back with approval.

In Greenwood, Carmichael was briefly arrested along with numerous other marchers for erecting sleeping tents on the grounds of a black high school contrary to orders of state troopers. Following his release, he addressed a crowd of about 3,000 at a protest rally. Also present were several correspondents from the national media. Leaping onto a flatbed truck, the fiery young SNCC leader with a raised arm and a clenched fist salute told his supporters, "This is the twenty-seventh time I have been arrested—and I ain't going to jail no more!" Carmichael shouted to the cheering crowd, "The only way we're gonna stop them white men from whippin' us is to take over. We been saying freedom for six years—and we ain't got nothin'. What we gonna start now is 'Black Power!' " As the crowd roared back, "Black Power!" Carmichael rhythmically shouted, "What do you want?" "Black Power!" "What do you want?" "BLACK POWER!" "What do you want? Say it again!" "BLACK POWER! BLACK POWER! BLACK POWER! BLACK POWER!" The slogan made headlines across the nation the following day.

In the days following the Meredith March Against Fear, many civil rights leaders condemned the concept of black power. King, for example, said, "I happen to believe that a doctrine of Black Supremacy is as evil as White Supremacy. I don't think that anything can be more tragic than the attitude that the Black Man can solve his problems by himself." The Congress of Racial Equality (CORE) defined the slogan of black power differently. In a resolution adopted at one of its conventions, it defined black power in these terms: "Black Power is not hatred. It is a means to bring the Black Americans into the covenant of Brotherhood. Black Power is not Supremacy; it is a unified Black Voice reflecting racial pride in the tradition of our heterogeneous nation." At

Stokely Carmichael speaks to a group of students on the campus of Florida A & M University, April 1967. Courtesy of the Schomburg Center for Research in Black Culture.

the close of the Meredith March Against Fear, McKissick announced to a final rally, "Nineteen sixty-six shall be remembered as the year we left our imposed status as Negroes and became Black Men . . . 1966 is the year of the concept of Black Power."

Like many slogans, "black power" could be interpreted in a variety of ways. Liberals used it to demand reform; both separatists and integrationists adopted it as did proponents of nonviolence and violence. Politicians referred to it as a way to win over black votes, and businessmen employed it as a means to expand into black markets. Although black power was a term created to inspire both Northern and Southern blacks to organize politically, the net effect resulted in dividing blacks from whites and from each other. By the end of 1966, all whites were expelled from SNCC. The days of coalition politics had come to an end.

Black power did indeed bring about a significant cultural change in the black community. It made blacks proud to be black. Black became beautiful. James Brown sang, "Say it loud—I'm black and I'm proud." A generation of blacks threw away their hair straighteners and wore Afros; they began studying and writing about black history; and they wore their color, in Langston Hughes' words, "like a banner for the proud."

THE BLACK PANTHERS

A number of new black nationalist groups emerged during the mid-1960s that reflected the mood of militant urban blacks in the North. Although in the South, many blacks were seeking basic political rights, many Northern urban blacks remained poor and powerless despite having civil rights. Many were becoming more and more skeptical of civil rights leaders who preached the arrival of residential integration. Instead, urban blacks increasingly demanded community control over their neighborhoods.

In October 1966, Huey Newton and Bobby Seale, two college-educated young men from Oakland, California, who worked at a neighborhood antipoverty center, formed the Black Panther Party for Self-Defense. The Black Panther Party (BPP) was created to combat police brutality in the ghetto and to provide new programs for the city's poor black residents. In some ways, the Panthers were the Northern version of SNCC. Its membership consisted of young outspoken blacks who were willing to confront white authority. Newton and Seale had been inspired by Stokely Carmichael's call for "black power," and they had taken the name for their party from SNCC's successful campaign to build a Panther Party in Lowndes County, Alabama.

Although the Black Panther Party was only one of many new black nationalist groups, it soon received wide media coverage out of proportion to its actual numbers. Dressed in military attire, the Panthers monitored the police presence in black neighborhoods and defended themselves by carrying guns, which, under California law at the time, were legal if not concealed. The Panthers rarely fired their rifles, but they did keep their weapons prominently in view, in homage to Mao Tse-tung's slogan for revolutionaries, "Power flows from the barrel of a gun."

The Panthers' weekly newspaper raged against police brutality, racism and the justice system. In every issue, it printed its 10-point program, which demanded trial by a jury of one's peers, decent housing, full employment and control by black people over their own communities.

The Black Panthers espoused the philosophy of armed revolt as a political act in order to arouse the black community. Their militant attitude also aroused the white establishment, especially FBI Director J. Edgar Hoover, who later described the Panthers as "hoodlum-type revolutionaries." In August 1967, Hoover ordered the FBI's Counter-Intelligence Program (COINTELPRO) "to expose, disrupt, misdirect, discredit, or otherwise neutralize the activities of black nationalist, hate-type organizations and groupings, their leadership, spokesmen, membership and supporters, and to counter their propensity for violence and civil disorder." Soon thereafter, the FBI was engaging in forging correspondence, posters and leaflets and infiltrating the Panthers and other black protest groups with agents, some of whom even took part in planning and decision-making.

The Panthers' provocative display of firearms precipitated police raids on their offices that resulted in arrests and the shooting deaths of several of their members. Under this barrage of harassment, the Black Panthers were unable to cultivate a following or raise the funding needed to transform their revolutionary philosophy into a viable political black power movement.

Days of Rage

The great achievements of the civil rights movement in the early and mid-1960s left many Northern urban blacks virtually untouched. Many still lived in the midst of crime and poverty, their children still attended inadequate schools and dropped out early, and they still had little chance to get decent jobs. New civil rights laws could not change the fact that their own futures were dim. As they witnessed the heroic progress of the civil rights movement in the South, their own frustration mounted. Frustrated by a movement that appeared to be passing them by, many young blacks took their fury into the streets. Cities erupted in violence all across the United States during three consecutive summers.

A week after President Johnson signed the Voting Rights Act in August 1965, a devastating six-day riot took place in Watts, a black neighborhood of Los Angeles, leaving 34 dead and causing millions of dollars of property damage. A confrontation between white police and young blacks had ignited the mayhem in Watts, as it would in many of the subsequent racial disorders of the 1960s.

There were more riots or black rebellions during 1966, but the worst summer of violence occurred in 1967, when racial unrest hit over 100 cities across the country. The largest riots took place in Newark, New Jersey and Detroit, Michigan, with the violence in Detroit lasting a full week and resulting in 43 deaths, 2,000 wounded and over 7,000 arrests. Up until the 1992 Los Angeles riots, the five days of rioting in Detroit composed the worst civil disorder in 20th-century America.

That summer, President Johnson appointed a special commission to study the causes of urban rioting. On March 2, 1968, the National Advisory Commission on Civil Disorders, known as the Kerner Commission, released its report and warned that America "is moving toward two societies, one black and one white—separate and unequal."

THE DEATH OF MARTIN LUTHER KING JR.

Seeking a new direction for the civil rights movement and an alternative to violence, Martin Luther King Jr. planned a Poor People's March on Washington for April 28, 1968. King hoped to rejuvenate the movement by bringing together all people—black and white. He announced, "We will place the problems of the poor at the seat of the government of the wealthiest nation in the history of mankind. If that power refuses to acknowledge its debt to the poor, it will have failed to live up to its promise to insure life, liberty and the pursuit of happiness to its citizens."

In March 1968, King took a break from planning the Poor People's March to travel to Memphis, Tennessee, where striking black sanitation workers had asked for his support. The strike had begun as a simple workers' grievance and a race issue. On January 31, 1968, 22 employees in the sewer department were sent home when it began to rain. White employees, however, were not, and when the rain stopped, they returned to work and were paid the full day's wages. When the black workers complained, they were paid two hours "call-up" pay. The black sanitations workers formed a union and then asked the city for better wages and working conditions. Memphis Mayor Henry Loeb refused to negotiate with the union and threatened to fire the workers if they did not return to work. Black community leaders appealed to King to lead just one march and to address just one meeting.

On Thursday morning, March 28, King was in Memphis to lead a march to city hall. The protest march was quickly aborted when there was an outbreak of violence by a black youth gang that went on a looting and burning spree. The Memphis police responded with tear gas and bullets. The governor of Tennessee sent in 3,500 National Guard troops, but by the time the rioting had ended, over 150 stores had been burned and looted, 60 people were injured and a 16-year-old boy had been killed.

King was horrified that violence had broken out and that someone had been killed on a march he had led. Although distraught, King vowed to remain in Memphis to prove that it was still possible "to hold a nonviolent march."

On the night of April 3, King spoke to an enthusiastic rally of about 2,000 people at Mason Temple Church. There had been a bomb scare that morning and other threats against his life. King gave the crowd a sense of hope but also alluded to the acceptance of his own martyr-

On the balcony of the Lorraine Motel in Memphis, Tennessee, April 3, 1968, from left to right: Hosea Williams, Jesse Jackson, Martin Luther King Jr. and Ralph Abernathy. Courtesy of AP/Wide World Photos.

dom. He ended his speech, one of the greatest of his career, with a direct reference to his own death: "Well, I don't know what will happen now. We've got some difficult days ahead. But it really doesn't matter to me now. Because I've been to the mountaintop. I won't mind. Like anybody, I'd like to live a long life. Longevity has its place but I'm not concerned about that now. I just want to do God's will. And He's allowed me to go up to the mountain. And I've looked over and I've seen the Promised Land. So I'm happy tonight. I'm not worried about anything. I'm not fearing any man. 'Mine eyes have seen the glory of the coming of the Lord.' "

The next day, April 4, while the 39-year-old civil rights leader was talking with his colleagues on the balcony at the Lorraine Motel, a crack from a high-powered rifle rang out. A bullet tore into the right side of King's face, throwing him violently back against the motel room. One hour later, Martin Luther King Jr., who was called by Ralph Abernathy "the most peaceful warrior of the 20th century," was pronounced dead in the emergency room at St. Joseph Hospital.

Within hours after the announcement of King's death, a wave of violence ripped through nearly 130 cities. In Washington, D.C., over 700 fires ignited by arsonists illuminated the night as federal army troops in full combat gear took battle positions around the Capitol and on the grounds of the White House. By the end of the week, 21,000 federal troops and 34,000 National Guardsmen had been called out to subdue the rioting in scores of cities across the country. When it was all over, 46 persons were dead, more than 3,000 were injured, and some 27,000 were arrested.

On the day of King's assassination, Senator Robert F. Kennedy was campaigning for the Democratic presidential nomination in Indianapolis. He was warned by his advisers to stay clear of black neighborhoods, but Kennedy chose instead to address a scheduled rally in the Indianapolis ghetto. After informing the mostly black audience of King's death, Kennedy discarded his prepared speech and told the crowd, "In this difficult time for the United States, it is perhaps well to ask what kind of a nation we are and what direction we want to move in . . . Considering the evidence . . . that there were white people who were responsible, you can be filled with bitterness and with hatred and a desire for revenge. We can move in that direction as a country, in great polarization, black people amongst blacks and whites amongst whites, filled with hatred toward another. Or we can make an effort, as Martin Luther King did, to understand and to comprehend, and replace that violence, that stain of bloodshed that has spread across the land, with an effort to understand, compassion, and love."

Kennedy concluded his talk by quoting from his favorite poet, Aeschylus, "Even in our sleep pain which cannot forget falls drop by drop upon the heart until in our own despair, against our will, comes wisdom through the awful grace of God." Two months later, Robert Kennedy fell to an assassin's bullet in Los Angeles.

Also two months later, on June 8, a man identified as King's assassin—James Earl Ray—was captured at a London airport. Although Ray pleaded guilty to charges of killing King and was sentenced to 99 years in prison, there were reports that he was part of a larger conspiracy. The House Select Committee on Assassinations, chaired by Congressman Louis Stokes, investigated these allegations and concluded that "there is a likelihood" that Ray assassinated King "as a result of a conspiracy" with unindicted conspirators.

When King died, the dreams and the hopes of the civil rights movement also passed away. Martin Luther King Jr. symbolized the heroic campaign for racial harmony and equality by nonviolent means. He was able to inspire blacks to stand up to racism and also to enlist the support of whites in the struggle for racial equality. No other black leader could match King's ability to rally large numbers of people from both races to actively participate in the cause for civil rights.

King's dream of a movement rejuvenated by poor people was never realized. Although Ralph Abernathy led the Poor People's March on Washington in April 1968, the nation barely noticed the passing mule train or the erected shantytown called Resurrection City.

The militant factions of the movement had divided the traditional leadership of the civil rights movement and had antagonized many white liberals. By the late 1960s, the civil rights movement had fed into and affected a number of other protest movements, including the anti-Vietnam War and the women's rights movement.

A Time of Change

From Montgomery to Selma, the civil rights movement did indeed bring about important changes in American life. In towns and cities throughout the South, "whites only" signs that had stood for generations have come down from hotels, rest rooms, theaters and other facilities. Segregated lunch counters and riding in the back of the bus have become things of the distant past. Hate groups, such as the Ku Klux Klan, which once flourished without federal restraint, have for the most part been successfully curbed.

An improved black middle class has emerged because of increased access to government and corporate jobs. But the mass of black people remain disproportionately poor, badly educated and unable to take advantage of the opportunities that have gone to more prepared blacks.

In 1903, W. E. B. Du Bois wrote, "The problem of the twentieth century is the problem of the color line." As the end of the 20th century approaches, the United States remains a deeply divided and unequal society. Despite the *Brown* decision of 1954, public education is still far from integrated. Statistics show that blacks in America are still more likely than whites to die in infancy, live in poverty and drop out of school. Blacks earn less money than whites and work at lower skilled jobs. Most live in segregated neighborhoods despite court rulings and legislation outlawing racial discrimination.

Protection of voting rights represents the movement's most outstanding achievement. Fewer than one in four adult blacks in the South could register to vote in 1954; by 1970 over two-thirds were on the voting lists. When Congress passed the Voting Rights Act of 1965, only 100 black officials held elective office in the country; by 1993 there were nearly 8,000, including 38 congressmen and some 300 mayors. The most radical change occurred in Mississippi, where 74% of voting-age blacks are registered and where the greatest number of elected black officials hold office.

"Keep Hope Alive"

During the 1980s, black influence in electoral politics was symbolized by the emergence of the Reverend Jesse L. Jackson, then of Chicago. Jackson, who was an aide to Martin Luther King Jr. from 1966 to 1968, gained national attention in the 1970s for his call to ghetto youths to excel in school.

In his 1984 bid for the Democratic presidential nomination, Jackson was able not only to gain the support of blacks but also to attract a considerable amount of white support. Jackson spoke of a "rainbow coalition" that would transcend racial lines. This strategy enabled him to win primaries in South Carolina, Louisiana and Washington, D.C. and to finish third in delegates at the Democratic National Convention. In his address at the convention, Jackson summarized the theme of his campaign for unity: "Our flag is red, white and blue, but our nation is a rainbow—Red, Yellow, Brown, Black and White—we're all precious in God's sight . . . We have proven that we can survive without each other. But we have not proven that we can win and make progress without each other. We must come together."

In his second bid for the Democratic presidential nomination in 1988, the seasoned candidate emphasized broad appealing themes of economic opportunity for all Americans. In a landmark primary election in Michigan, Jackson won 54% of the vote. Only 20 years earlier, that state's Democratic presidential primary had gone to Alabama segregationist George Wallace. In a field of seven candidates, Jackson was one of the two who survived until convention time. He came in second behind the winner, Governor Michael Dukakis of Massachusetts.

More than any other black leader since Martin Luther King Jr., Jackson was able to inspire millions of Americans, black and white, with his vision of equality that was right around the corner. In a rousing, fervent, fiery speech at the Democratic National Convention, Jackson spoke more to those who were watching on television than those seated in the convention hall, "Wherever you are tonight, you can make it. Hold your head high. Stick your chest out. You can make it. It gets dark sometimes, but the morning comes. Don't you surrender. Suffering breeds character, character breeds faith, in the end faith will not disappoint. You must not surrender. You may or may not get there but just know that you're qualified and you hold on and hold out. We must never surrender. America will get better and better. Keep hope alive. Keep hope alive. Keep hope alive for tomorrow night and beyond. Keep hope alive!"

The victories of the civil rights movement for the most part were won by a largely anonymous group of citizens, black and white, many of them young, who dared to risk their lives for the cause of freedom. As long as there are men and women of every race and nationality who are willing to take a stand against inequalities and racial prejudice, the civil rights movement will indeed continue.

Civil and human rights victories extend far beyond the U.S. Supreme Court and the Capitol building. The end of apartheid in South Africa is a shining example. Nelson Mandela, who spent 27 years in jail for the cause of freedom, was profoundly influenced by Dr. King and his philosophy of nonviolent direct action.

In his inaugural address, in 1994, as the first black president of South Africa, Mandela emphatically declared, "We have triumphed in the effort to implant hope in the breasts of millions of our people. We enter into a covenant that we shall build the society in which all South Africans, both black and white, will be able to walk tall, without any fear in their hearts, assured of their inalienable right to human dignity—a rainbow nation at peace with itself and the world."

Today, America is fast becoming a global village. Cities and towns across the nation are composed of people from many different races and nationalities. As a growing number of people from all parts of the world continue to immigrate to the United States, the remarkable accomplishments that were achieved by the civil rights movement in the 1950s and 1960s will undoubtedly play an important role in shaping our national character throughout the 21st century. The sounds of marching footsteps and stirring freedom songs and chants will resonate for many years to come.

CHRONICLE OF EVENTS

1966

January 7: Martin Luther King Jr. begins an SCLC campaign in Chicago, Illinois in conjunction with local organizations to protest segregation in public schools and to seek improved housing and job opportunities for the city's black residents.

May 16: Stokely Carmichael is named chairman of SNCC, replacing John Lewis. The change is interpreted to mean that SNCC is following a more militant course.

June 1–2: Approximately 2,400 people attend the White House Conference on Civil Rights.

June 5: James Meredith sets out on a one-man "march against fear" from Memphis, Tennessee to Jackson, Mississippi.

June 6: Meredith is wounded by a sniper.

June 7–26: The "Meredith march" is continued by King, CORE director Floyd McKissick, Carmichael and other activists. During this march, the slogan "black power" is first used by Stokely Carmichael.

July 2–5: CORE national convention adopts a resolution supporting the black power concept.

July 4–9: NAACP national convention disassociates itself from the black power doctrine.

July 10: King launches a drive to make Chicago an "open city." He leads a march of mostly 30,000 blacks to Chicago's city hall, where he calls on city officials to end discriminatory real estate practices, end police brutality and increase black employment.

July 12–15: Three nights of rioting sweep Chicago's West Side black district in the wake of a police decision to shut off a fire hydrant that had been opened illegally to give black children relief from the stifling heat. Two blacks are killed, scores of police and civilians are wounded, and 372 persons are arrested.

August 5: King leads an integrated march to Chicago's Marquette Park area where he is met by a crowd of whites who jeer and throw bricks and bottles at the marchers.

August 30: Constance Baker Motley is confirmed as a U.S. district judge, becoming the first black woman on the federal bench.

October: The Black Panther Party (BPP) is founded in Oakland, California by Huey Newton and Bobby Seale.

November 8: Edward W. Brooke (R, Mass.) becomes the first black elected to the U.S. Senate since Reconstruction.

December: SNCC decides to exclude whites from membership but allows them to continue to be involved in projects.

1967

April 4: King speaks out against U.S. involvement in the Vietnam War during a speech at Riverside Church in New York City.

May 12: H. Rap Brown replaces Carmichael as SNCC chairman.

June 13: Thurgood Marshall is nominated to the Supreme Court by President Lyndon Johnson, becoming the first black Supreme Court associate justice.

July: Race riots occur in major cities throughout the nation, including Chicago, Illinois, Cleveland, Ohio, Detroit, Michigan, Memphis, Tennessee, Milwaukee, Wisconsin and Newark, New Jersey.

July 27: President Johnson appoints a National Advisory Commission on Civil Disorders to inquire into the causes of the urban rebellions. The report is published in 1968.

August 25: FBI Director J. Edgar Hoover orders the FBI's Counter-intelligence Program (COINTELPRO) to launch an effort to "expose, disrupt, misdirect, discredit, or otherwise neutralize the activities of black nationalist, hate-type organizations and groupings, their leadership, spokesmen, membership, and supporters, and to counter their propensity for violence and civil disorder."

November 7: Carl B. Stokes is elected mayor of Cleveland, Ohio, becoming the first black to serve as mayor of a major American city.

December 4: King announces plans to lead a contingent of poor whites, poor blacks and

A mule cart bears the body of Martin Luther King Jr. through Memphis on April 9, 1968. Courtesy of the Schomburg Center for Research in Black Culture.

Hispanics to Washington, D.C. in April 1968 to demonstrate for jobs for all Americans.

1968

February 29: The National Advisory Commission on Civil Disorders issues its report, warning that the nation "is moving toward two societies, one black and one white—separate and unequal." It recommends broad reforms in law enforcement, welfare, employment, housing and education.

April 4: Martin Luther King Jr., is assassinated in Memphis, Tennessee while trying to secure better employment conditions for the city's black sanitation workers. It precipitates massive rioting in more than 100 cities. A white man, James Earl Ray, is later arrested (June 8) and convicted of the murder.

April 9: Martin Luther King Jr. is buried after funeral services at Ebenezer Baptist Church and memorial services at Morehouse College, Atlanta. More than 300,000 people march be-

hind the coffin of the slain civil rights leader, which is carried through the streets of Atlanta on a farm wagon pulled by two Georgia mules. Scores of national dignitaries attend the funeral. Ralph Abernathy becomes president of the SCLC.

April 29–May 11: Poor People's Campaign begins; Abernathy leads a delegation of leaders representing poor whites, blacks, Indians and Hispanics to Washington, D.C. for meetings with cabinet members and congressional leaders.

June 5: Senator Robert F. Kennedy is assassinated in Los Angeles, California after addressing a rally celebrating his victory in the California Democratic presidential primary.

June 18: U.S. Supreme Court bans racial discrimination in the sale and rental of housing.

November 5: A record number of black men and the first black woman are elected to Congress. Richard M. Nixon wins the presidential election, defeating Hubert H. Humphrey in a close race.

1969

March 10: James Earl Ray pleads guilty to King's murder and is sentenced to 99 years in prison.

October 29: U.S. Supreme Court rules in *Alexander v. Holmes County Board of Education* that school systems must end segregation "at once" rather than "with all deliberate speed" and must "operate now and hereafter only unitary schools."

December 4: Two Black Panther leaders, Fred Hampton and Mark Clark, are killed in a Chicago police raid. Civil rights leaders charge that the men were murdered and that excessive violence was used.

1970

June 22: Nixon signs a bill extending the Voting Rights Act of 1965 to 1975.

1971

April 20: U.S. Supreme Court rules unanimously in *Swann v. Charlotte-Mecklenburg Board of Education* that busing is a constitutionally acceptable method of integrating public schools where de jure segregation has existed.

December 18: Jesse Jackson founds People United to Save Humanity (PUSH) in Chicago, Illinois.

1972

January 25: Congresswoman Shirley Chisholm begins her campaign for president of the United States, becoming the first black American to run for the presidency.

March 10–12: Three thousand delegates and 5,000 observers attend the first National Black Political Convention.

March 22: The Senate approves a constitutional amendment banning discrimination against women because of their sex and sends the measure to the states for ratification.

June 30: NAACP reports that the unemployment of "urban blacks in 1971 was worse than any time since the great depression of the thirties" and that more school desegregation occurred in 1971 than any other year since the 1954 *Brown* decision.

September 13: Two blacks, Johnny Ford of Tuskegee and A. J. Cooper of Prichard, are elected mayors in Alabama.

November 17: President Richard Nixon defeats Senator George McGovern (D, S.D.), carrying 49 of 50 states.

1973

May 29: Thomas Bradley is elected mayor of Los Angeles, California.

October 16: Maynard Jackson is elected mayor of Atlanta, Georgia.

November 6: Coleman Young is elected mayor of Detroit, Michigan.

1974

April: U.S. Department of Justice releases memos confirming that in the 1960s and early 1970s the FBI had waged a campaign designed to disrupt, discredit and neutralize black nationalist groups, including the Black Panthers.

October 3: Frank Robinson is named manager of the Cleveland Indians and becomes the first black manager in major league baseball.

1976

April 5: FBI documents, released in response to a freedom of information suit, reveal details about the government's campaign against the SCLC and SNCC in the 1960s.

November 2: Jimmy Carter, former governor of Georgia, is elected president, defeating President Gerald Ford.

November 6: Benjamin Hooks, Federal Communications Commission member, succeeds Roy Wilkins as NAACP executive director.

December 16: Congressman Andrew Young (D, Ga.) is named ambassador and chief delegate to the United Nations.

1977

February 11: Clifford Alexander Jr. is confirmed as the first black secretary of the U.S. Army.

November 19: Robert E. Chambliss, a former KKK member, is convicted of murder in the 1963 bombing of the Sixteenth Street Baptist Church, where four black girls were killed; he is sentenced to life imprisonment.

1978

June 28: U.S. Supreme Court rules in *University of California Regents v. Bakke* that the University of California Medical School at Davis' refusal to admit Allan P. Bakke constitutes reverse discrimination.

November 7: Five blacks are elected to Congress for the first time: William Gray III (Pennsylvania), Bennett Stewart (Illinois), Melvin Evans (Virgin Islands), Julian Dixon (California) and Mickey Leland (Texas).

1979

June 19: U.S. Census Bureau announces that black Americans still remain far behind white Americans in employment, income, health, housing and political power.

Andrew Young, president of the Security Council, United Nations, 1977. UN photo.

October 3: City Councilman Richard Arrington is elected the first black mayor of Birmingham, Alabama.

1980

November 4: Ronald W. Reagan, former governor of California, wins the presidential election in a landslide victory over incumbent Jimmy Carter.

1981

January 9: Labor Department reports that black unemployment is 14% compared with 7.8% for whites.

September 19: More than 300,000 demonstrators from labor and civil rights organizations protest the social policies of the Reagan administration in a "Solidarity" march in Washington, DC.

October 29: Andrew Young is elected mayor of Atlanta, Georgia.

1982

June 12: The Equal Rights Amendment for women is defeated after a 10-year struggle for ratification.

June 18–23: The Senate and House approve the extension of the Voting Rights Act of 1965 for 25 years.

1983

April 13: Congressman Harold Washington is elected mayor of Chicago, Illinois the first black to hold that office.

August 28: Commemorating the 20th anniversary of the historic March on Washington, 250,000 people reenact the 1963 march.

November 3: Jesse Jackson, head of Operation

PUSH, announces plans to run for the 1984 Democratic presidential nomination.

1984
May 2: Jackson wins the District of Columbia primary with 70% of the vote.
May 7: Jackson wins the Louisiana primary election with 43% of the vote.
July 12: Democratic presidential nominee Walter Mondale chooses Congresswoman Geraldine Ferarro (N.Y.) as his vice-presidential running mate. She is the first woman to run for that office.
July 17: Jesse Jackson addresses the Democratic National Convention; he calls for a "rainbow coalition" consisting of people from all races.
November 8: President Ronald Reagan defeats Walter Mondale in a landslide victory. Reagan wins 59% of the popular vote and 525 electoral votes.

1986
January 20: Martin Luther King Jr. Day is officially observed for the first time.

1987
September 8: Jesse Jackson announces that he will be a candidate for the Democratic presidential nomination in 1988.

1988
March 8: On "super Tuesday," Jackson wins primaries in Alabama, Georgia, Louisiana, Mississippi and Virginia.
June 29: In a unanimous decision, the Supreme Court rules that women and minorities need not prove intentional discrimination in hiring and promotion in cases where decisions by employers are based upon subjective criteria.
July 19: In a moving, fervent, 50-minute speech before the Democratic National Convention, Jesse Jackson implores the less fortunate to "keep hope alive."
July 21: In his second bid for the Democratic presidential nomination, Jesse Jackson comes

General Colin Powell, the first black chairman of the Joint Chiefs of Staff, gained national recognition during the Persian Gulf War. Powell calls on a reporter at a Pentagon press briefing. Courtesy of the National Archives.

in second behind the winner, Governor Michael Dukakis of Massachusetts.
August 27: Commemoration of the 25th anniversary of the August 1963 March on Washington; about 55,000 people attend, including Jesse Jackson and Governor Michael Dukakis.
November 8: Vice-President George Bush defeats Governor Michael Dukakis by 54% to 45% of the popular vote.

1989
February 10: Washington lawyer Ronald H. Brown is elected chairman of the Democratic National Committee. He is the first black chosen to lead a major American political party.
August 10: General Colin L. Powell becomes the first black chairman of the Joint Chiefs of Staff.

November 5: The Civil Rights Memorial in Montgomery, Alabama, designed by Vietnam Veterans Memorial artist Maya Lin, is dedicated. The monument honors the civil rights movement and those who died in the struggle for racial equality.

November 7: Douglas Wilder is elected governor of Virginia. Wilder, the grandson of a slave, a Bronze Star winner in the Korean War and a former member of the state senate, becomes the first elected black governor. David N. Dinkins is elected mayor of New York City, the first black to hold that office.

1990

July 13: Congress passes the Americans with Disabilities Act (ADA). It is the most sweeping antidiscrimination law passed since the Civil Rights Act of 1964. The ADA bans discrimination on the basis of physical or mental handicap in employment, public accommodations and transportation.

July 26: President Bush signs the ADA act.

1991

October 30: The Senate approves the 1991 civil rights bill by a vote of 95–5. The bill, overturning several Supreme Court decisions, makes it easier for employees to sue employers in job discrimination cases.

November 7: The House passes the 1991 civil rights bill by a vote of 381–38.

November 21: President Bush signs the Civil Rights Act of 1991.

1992

April 29: Rioting erupts in Los Angeles' South-Central district after four white police officers are acquitted by an all-white jury for using excessive force against Rodney G. King, a black motorist. (A vivid home video tape showing the officers striking King with batons was used as evidence in the trial). The rioting lasts for three days, and it is the worst urban disturbance in American history—51 people are killed, 2,000 are injured, 8,000 are arrested and $1 billion in property is damaged.

May 1: President Bush makes a special address to the nation and announces that he has ordered federal troops to Los Angeles and has ordered the U.S. Department of Justice to investigate the possible violation of Rodney King's civil rights. At a news conference, Rodney King asks, "Can we all get along?"

June 26: Thirty years after a court order forced the University of Mississippi to accept its first black student, James Meredith, the Supreme Court rules in *United States v. Fordice* that Mississippi must do more to dismantle the legacy of segregation in its eight public colleges and universities.

August 5: Four Los Angeles police officers acquitted in April 1992 for using excessive force against black motorist Rodney King are indicted by a federal grand jury for violating King's civil rights.

November 3: Governor Bill Clinton of Arkansas wins the presidential election in an Electoral College landslide victory over incumbent George Bush. Clinton wins 370 votes; Bush, 168. Carol Moseley Braun of Illinois is elected to the U.S. Senate. She becomes the first black woman senator. A record number of women are elected to Congress: 24 in the House of Representatives and four in the Senate.

1993

January 20: Bill Clinton becomes the 42nd president of the United States. In his inaugural address he states, "There is nothing wrong with America that cannot be cured by what is right with America." Maya Angelou, a black poet, delivers the inaugural poem.

January 24: Thurgood Marshall, pillar of the civil rights revolution, architect of the legal strategy that ended the era of official segregation and the first black Justice of the Supreme Court dies at the age of 84.

January 28: Millions of television viewers watch the memorial service for Justice Thurgood Marshall broadcast on several networks and some 4,000 people attend the service at the National Cathedral in Washington, D.C.

April 17: Two of the four white Los Angeles police officers acquitted (April 29, 1992) of using excessive force against black motorist Rodney King are convicted in a federal trial of violating King's civil rights.

1994

February 2: Byron De La Beckwith is convicted of the 1963 slaying of civil rights leader Medgar Evers in Mississippi, after two previous trials in the 1960s ended in hung juries.

October 21: Dexter Scott King, the youngest son of Martin Luther King Jr., is elected chairman of the Martin Luther King, Jr. Center for Nonviolent Social Change in Atlanta, Georgia. He succeeds his mother, Corretta Scott King, who headed the nonprofit center since its founding in 1968.

1995

May 14: The widow of slain civil rights leader Medgar Evers, Myrlie Evers-Williams, is sworn in as chairwoman of the NAACP.

1997

January: *Ghosts of Mississippi*, a feature film about the long struggle to bring white supremacist Byron De La Beckwith to justice for the 1963 shooting of Medgar Evers, is released. The film is directed by Rob Reiner and stars Whoopie Goldberg as Myrlie Evers-Williams.

June 12: President Bill Clinton forms a task force to advise him on race relations. The President's Commission on Race Relations is headed by renowned historian John Hope Franklin, author of *From Slavery to Freedom: A History of African Americans.*

September 25: In a ceremony commemorating the 40th anniversary of the desegregation of Central High School in Little Rock, Arkansas,

President Bill Clinton holds open the school's front doors for the original black students, known as the Little Rock Nine. Clinton says, "What happened here changed the course of our country forever."

1998

January 19: The New York Stock Exchange is closed for the first time in honor of Martin Luther King Jr. Day.

February 21: Julian Bond succeeds Myrlie Evers-Williams as chairman of the NAACP. In his acceptance speech, the veteran civil rights leader says he wants "to reach out to emerging Americans, Hispanics, Latinos, Native Americans, Asians, and white Americans."

1999

January 15: Rev. Jesse Jackson holds the Wall Street Project conference in New York City. The three-day event, sponsored by the Rainbow/PUSH Coalition, focuses on encouraging minority participation in the financial sector. Jackson tells conference attendees, including President Bill Clinton and black and white business leaders, "Sharecroppers are becoming shareholders. We have taken our battle from the picket line to the board room."

March 9: Congressman John Lewis of Georgia and a bipartisan congressional delegation reenact the 1965 voting rights march across the Edmund Pettus Bridge in Selma, Alabama.

June 7: Governor Jeanne Shaheen of New Hampshire signs a bill that recognizes statewide Martin Luther King Jr. Day. New Hampshire joins the rest of the country in honoring Dr. King with a holiday.

June 15: Rosa Parks is awarded the Congressional Gold Medal at a ceremony held at the Capitol and attended by President Clinton and Speaker J. Dennis Hastert. Parks says, "This will be encouragement for all of us to continue until all people have equal rights."

Eyewitness Testimony

The concept of "black power" is not a recent or isolated phenomenon: It has grown out of the ferment of agitation and activity by different people and organizations in many black communities over the years. In Lowndes County, for example, black power will mean that if a Negro is elected sheriff, he can end police brutality. If a black man is elected tax assessor, he can collect and channel funds for the building of better roads and schools serving black people—thus advancing the move from political power into the economic arena . . . Where Negroes lack a majority, black power means proper representation and sharing of control. It means the creation of power bases from which black people can work to change statewide or nationwide patterns of oppression through pressure from strength—instead of weakness.

Stokely Carmichael, SNCC chairman, in a
New York Review of Books *article of September 22, 1966.*

Well, I don't know what will happen now. But it really doesn't matter to me now. Because I've been to the mountaintop. I won't mind. Like anybody, I'd like to live a long life. Longevity has its place but I'm not concerned about that now. I just want to do God's will. And He's allowed me to go up to the mountain. And I've looked over and I've seen the Promised Land. I may not get there with you, but I want you to know tonight that we as a people will get to the Promised Land. So I'm happy tonight. I'm not worried about anything. I'm not fearing any man. "Mine eyes have seen the glory of the coming of the Lord."

Martin Luther King Jr., to about 2,000 supporters at the Mason Temple Church, Memphis, Tennessee, sermon of April 3, 1968. [This was King's last public address; he was assassinated the next day.]

The sixties were an exciting decade: loaded with ferment, freedom rides, sit-ins, marches. It was all here—from the strains of "We Shall Overcome," sung warmly with arms linked—to the penetrating cries of black power, with fists raised.

We buried some wonderful brothers and sisters who strode, like giants, across the decade, sweeping away injustice before them.

Martin Luther King Jr. Courtesy of the Lawrence Henry Collection, Schomburg Center for Research in Black Culture.

And for each murdered martyr, a half-million black soldiers took his place.

The '70s will be the decade of an independent black political thrust.

Its destiny will depend on us.

How shall we respond?

Will we walk in the unity or disperse in a thousand different directions?

Will we stand for principle or settle for a mess of pottage?

Will we act like free black men or timid shivering chattels?

Will we do what must be done?

These are the questions confronting this convention. And we—only we can answer them.

History will be our judge.

Mayor Richard Hatcher of Gary, Indiana, to the National Black Political Convention in Gary, Indiana, speech of March 11, 1972.

We had seen Watts rise up the previous year. We had seen how the police attacked the Watts community after causing the trouble in the first place. We had seen Martin Luther King come to Watts in an effort to calm the people, and we had seen his philosophy of nonviolence rejected. Black people had been taught nonviolence; it was deep in us. What good, however, was nonviolence when the police were determined to rule by force? . . . We had seen all this, and we recognized that the rising conscious- ness of Black people was almost at the point of explosion . . .

Out of this need sprang the Black Panther Party.

Huey P. Newton, co-founder of the Black Pan- *ther Party, in* Revolutionary Suicide *(1973).*

Our flag is red, white and blue, but our nation is a rainbow—Red, Yellow, Brown, Black and White— we're all precious in God's sight.

America is not like a blanket—one piece of unbro- ken cloth, the same color, the same texture, the same size. America is more like a quilt—many patches, many pieces, many colors, many sizes, all woven and held together by a common thread. The White, the Hispanic, the Black, the Arab, the Jew, the woman, the Native American, the small farmer, the business- person, the environmentalist, the peace activist, the young, the old, the lesbian, the gay and the disabled make up the American quilt.

Even in our fractured state, all of us count and fit somewhere. We have proven that we can survive without each other. But we have not proven that we can win and make progress without each other. We must come together.

Jesse Jackson, presidential candidate, to the *Democratic National Convention, speech of July* *17, 1984, in the* New York Times *(July 18,* *1984).*

Kids today, they're used to the way things are. Try as you can, you can't believe that white people once treated black people that way. It seems like some- thing that happened long, long ago.

Karyn Reddick, black student in Selma, Ala- *bama, statement of April 1985, in the* New *York Times (March 1, 1985).*

My right and my privilege to stand here before you has been won—won in my lifetime—by the blood and the sweat of the innocent . . . Dr. Martin Luther King, Jr. lies only a few miles from us tonight. Tonight he must feel good as he looks down upon us. We sit here together, a rainbow coalition—the

Jesse L. Jackson raises the arm of Rosa Parks as he honors the *heroine of the Montgomery bus boycott during his appearance* *before the Democratic National Convention in Atlanta, Georgia* *on July 19, 1988. Courtesy of AP/Wide World Photos.*

sons and daughters of slavemasters and the sons and daughters of slaves sitting together around a com- mon table, to decide the direction of our party and our country. His heart would be full tonight.

As a testament to the struggles of those who have gone before; as a legacy for those who will come after; as a tribute to the endurance, the patience, the courage of our forefathers and mothers; as an assur- ance that their prayers are being answered, their work has not been in vain, and hope is eternal, tomorrow night my name will be placed into nomi- nation for the presidency of the United States . . .

And I was not supposed to make it. You see, I was born of a teenage mother, who was born of a teenage mother. I understand. I know abandonment, and people being mean to you, and saying you're nothing and nobody can never be anything, I understand.

Wherever you are tonight, you can make it. Hold your head high. Stick your chest out. You can make it. It gets dark sometimes, but the morning comes. Don't you surrender. Suffering breeds character, character breeds faith, in the end faith with not disappoint.

You must not surrender. You may or may not get there but just know that you're qualified and you hold on and hold out. We must never surrender.

America will get better and better. Keep hope alive. Keep hope alive. Keep hope alive for tomorrow and beyond.

Jesse L. Jackson, presidential candidate, to the
Democratic National Convention, Atlanta,
Georgia, speech of July 19, 1988, in the New
York Times (July 20, 1988).

Today, we as a people, have come a long way, but
we have not yet arrived. Physically, we did move
from the back to the front of the buses. But some of
our minds, perhaps, are still in the back of the buses.
The racists are now more sophisticated, but the effects of racism on our people are not altogether
different. For example, the unemployment rate of
blacks almost doubles that of whites in America today.

From my perspective, a major aspect of the Civil
Rights Movement today is between the covers of our
books. We need brainpower, or a brain trust that can
understand the plight of our people; and through
this understanding, we will be able to pave new
directions and find solutions to our problems.

Dr. Robert L. Satcher Sr., academic dean and
provost of Fisk University and a Montgomery
bus boycott participant, in a Black Collegian
article of January/February 1989.

What I believe is most critical for the country to
understand, and particularly for blacks, is that the
Civil Rights Movement was not a phenomenon of
the 1960s, but has been an ongoing struggle for over
300 years. It began with the first protest of the slaves
in this country against their oppression, and it continues as each succeeding generation of blacks takes
up the battle against white supremacy and black
subordination.

Judge Robert L. Carter, U.S. district judge for
the Southern District of New York and former
NAACP Legal Defense Fund attorney, to the
author, 1991.

Ever since I first began considering the role of
blacks in shaping our national history, I have been
impressed by the profound influence they have exerted simply by being present, and this initially against
their will. They have constituted a challenge not only
to our moral standards but to our basic concepts of
governance. If the Americans who exercised power
usually managed to immunize their consciences against
the palpable injustices of the system, they kept running up against the high cost of subjugating a substantial portion of the population. Until the middle
of this century this presumably was offset by the fact

that holding blacks in thrall permitted their exploitation as a source of cheap labor. But this was no
longer the case. For a generation the unskilled had
been surplus population, a growing financial burden
rather than a benefit.

Harry S. Ashmore, author and former executive
editor of the Arkansas Democrat (1948–
1959), to the author, 1991 [quoting from his
book, Hearts and Minds: A Personal Chronicle of Race in America (1988)].

I believe there were two vital aspects of the movement, and the interaction between them helped deliver the successes of the 1960s. First, African
Americans themselves determined that oppressive
conditions and abuses of their rights were intolerable
and they mobilized to correct them. Second, white
Americans elevated moral considerations of justice,
fairness and equality above tradition and ideology
and joined the movement to overthrow segregation
and legal discrimination. I am hopeful that in the
1990s that spirit of cooperation in pursuit of a more
just society will be revitalized.

John E. Jacob, National Urban League president
and chief executive officer, to the author, 1991.

One of the factors of the civil rights movement that
often gets overlooked is that not only did it emanci-
pate blacks and give them equality under the law,
but it also resulted in a legal revolution for women,
for Hispanics, for other minorities, for the disabled
and for the aged. What you had was a total shift in
the legal system of America to protect those who
cannot protect themselves.

Joseph Rauh Jr., former general counsel for the
Leadership Conference on Civil Rights, to the
author, 1992.

During the 1950s and 1960s, America as a nation
was transformed because a large number of ordinary
people, black and white, had enough faith in this
country's founding principles that they were willing
to risk their lives to see those principles of freedom
and equality fulfilled.

Morris Dees, civil rights attorney and founder
of the Southern Poverty Law Center, to the author, 1992.

The presence of Black lawyers in many communities where the modern civil rights movement was
born gave added strength to parents who knew that
if their child was arrested, abused, or murdered,

while attempting to exercise their fundamental rights as citizens, that there was a Black lawyer to whom they could turn for help and upon whom they could depend to seek justice.

J. Clay Smith, Jr., professor of law, Howard University School of Law, to the author, 1992.

No legislative act growing out of the civil rights movement has done more to promote the cause of political equality for black Americans than the passage of the Voting Rights Act of 1965. While the 15th Amendment of the U.S. Constitution gave black Americans the right to vote, states and localities used a variety of methods to dilute the impact of votes cast by African Americans and in many instances prevented them from voting altogether. The Voting Rights Act, for the first time in the history of America, established a legal cause of action for private citizens and the government to challenge discriminatory voting practices and procedures . . . The Voting Rights Act, which was a direct result of the civil rights movement, represented an historic political victory for African Americans and for America.

Congressman Charles B. Rangel (D, N.Y.), member of the Black Congressional Caucus, to the author, 1992.

The most important legacy of the civil rights movement is the character of its participants: their commitment, their imagination, their incredible courage. Only someone who lived through it can understand what it took for a black person in Mississippi to try to register and vote in those days. The movement succeeded in changing the social and political structure of the South with the help of the Federal Government. That help was vital, but it came only because the effectiveness of the movement made a response by the Government unavoidable.

Anthony Lewis, New York Times columnist, who as a correspondent covered the U.S. Supreme Court from 1957 to 1964, to the author, 1992.

I believe the most important thing that Americans can learn from the civil rights movement is that we cannot depend on governmental authority to eliminate injustice, that democracy is not fulfilled by going through the "proper channels" of representative government, that democracy only comes alive when citizens unite to act together and create a *movement* which arouses the conscience of the society. Democracy is not fulfilled by going to the polls every few years and depending on officials to bring about change. It requires a ceaseless struggle, involving sacrifice and risk, but it is also a joyful and inspiring experience to be part of a community of activists united by a moral goal.

Howard Zinn, professor emeritus of political science at Boston University and a former SNCC activist, to the author, 1992.

The civil rights movement was started by miracle-workers who defied intellectual wisdom and risked everything for a cause we believed in. That spirit, part courage and part grace, needs renewal in every generation.

Tom Hayden, California assemblyman and a former SNCC activist, to the author, 1992.

The civil rights movement had many effects, most of them obvious from the written record of the time, the legislative product and the changed condition of black Southerners. For me, a white Mississippian, the effect was quite simple and quite direct: The movement freed me from the iron hand of Southern history, white conformity and white supremacy. It removed a burden which had weighed down the white South since the first slave arrived in Virginia. It did not produce utopia, but it brought us all out of a moral and political hell.

Hodding Carter III, journalist and former State Department press secretary during the Carter administration, to the author, 1992.

The Civil Rights Movement of the early 1960s was an integrated movement. It was, in the words of the movement hymn, "blacks and whites together." Until we remember that truth and act on it, we cannot hope to achieve the progress in race relations that the movement brought.

Claude F. Sitton, journalist who covered the civil rights movement in the early 1960s for the New York Times, to the author, 1992.

The most important thing we should understand and remember about the civil rights movement is that it cannot—and, indeed, *must* not—ever end. As the past dozen years have shown, civil rights can be rolled back instead of pushed forward. The legacy of the movement must be preserved and increased every day, if it is not to be lost.

Mayor David N. Dinkins of New York City, to the author, 1992.

The most important thing we should remember and understand about the civil rights movement is that it finally began the transformation of America into a more open and just society. By opening new doors of political, social, and economic opportunities, the movement dramatically increased the ability of African Americans to make major contributions in all walks of life. For the first time since the founding of the nation, America began to slowly understand that tapping into the tremendous intelligence, talent and skill in the African American community will make for a stronger future America.

Ronald H. Brown, secretary of commerce and labor and former Democratic National Committee chairman, to the author, 1992.

Despite the substantial achievements of the civil rights movement, for black as well as white Americans, the nation still cannot seem to shake its preoccupation with race as the basis for exclusion. Racial prohibitions have left a question that will haunt us forever: how much greater as a nation might we have been if we had not systematically excluded the abilities and talents of more than half the population on the basis of gender and race? In a rapidly growing and competitive world economy, obsession with race is an indulgence we can ill afford.

Joseph N. Boyce, a Wall Street Journal *senior editor and the first black reporter to work in the* Chicago Tribune *city newsroom in the 1960s, to the author, 1992.*

Slavery was our original sin, just as race remains our unresolved dilemma. The future of American cities is inextricably bound to the issue of race and ethnicity. By the year 2000, only 57 percent of the people entering the work force in America will be native-born whites. That means that the economic future of the children of white Americans will increasingly depend on the talents of nonwhite Americans. If we allow them to fail because of our penny-pinching or timidity about straight talk, America will become a second-rate power. If they succeed, America and all Americans will be enriched. As a nation, we will find common ground together and move ahead, or each of us will be diminished.

Senator Bill Bradley (D, N.J.), to the Senate, speech of March 26, 1992, in the Congressional Record *(1992).*

The civil rights movement was our democracy at its best and an example of the self-help ethic that has characterized black America's struggle for justice from Jamestown until today. It was successful because it was a mass movement, and not simply a series of highly publicized marches and protests led by famous figures. At its base was a faceless cadre of organizers, frequently unlettered and even today, largely unknown. Its lesson for our time is that a determined, nonviolent movement which appealed to fairness succeeded in eliminating legalized white supremacy in America; a similar movement today can remove racism's legacy.

Julian Bond, former Georgia state legislator and communications director for SNCC, to the author, 1992.

Though our challenges are fearsome, so are our strengths. Americans have ever been a restless, questing, hopeful people, and we must bring to our task today the vision and will of those who came before us. From our Revolution to the Civil War, to the Great Depression, to the Civil Rights movement, our people have always mustered the determination to construct from these crises the pillars of our history.

President Bill Clinton, inaugural address of January 20, 1993.

While *Brown* set the background for the whole racial struggle, it was understood years before that the voting arm of the fight was also important . . .

I . . . think that the focus was the movement of Martin Luther King and people in that category, the protest movement that seized upon the right to vote. Following that, the NAACP, headed by Clarence Mitchell, often called the 101st Senator because of his influence in the Congress of the United States, really spearheaded the drive for the Civil Rights Acts passed in the 1960s. It was those acts that got the right to vote. It was those acts that were used to increase the enrollment of blacks throughout the South, and that was important.

I realize that there was a change from the legal movement in the courts, to the protest movement in the streets, to the legislative halls, that brought about—to my mind—the registration and voting. To put your handle on exactly what was important, I think it's a conglomeration of all of them.

Supreme Court Justice Thurgood Marshall, from an interview conducted by the Columbia University Oral History Research Office (February, 1977; first released, January, 1993).

Under his leadership, the American constitutional landscape in the area of equal protection of the laws was literally rewritten . . . As a result of his career as a lawyer and as a judge, Thurgood Marshall left an indelible mark not just upon the law but upon his country. Inscribed above the front entrance to the Supreme Court building are the words "Equal justice under the law." Surely no one individual did more to make these words a reality than Thurgood Marshall.

Supreme Court Chief Justice William H. Rehnquist, from his eulogy delivered at the memorial service for Supreme Court Justice Thurgood Marshall at the National Cathedral in Washington, D.C., January 28, 1993.

Picture if you will the inescapable power of the beacon light Thurgood Marshall beamed into our cramped and constricted community. A community in which the law ordained that we should attend only segregated inferior schools; a community in which the law ordained that our parents be denied the right to vote; a community in which the law ordained segregation in the courtroom and the exclusion of our parents from the jury box.

It was Thurgood Marshall's mission to turn these laws against themselves, to cleanse our tattered constitution and our besmerched legal system of the filth of oppressive racism, to restore to all Americans a constitution and a legal system newly alive to the requirements of justice. By demonstrating that the law could be an instrument of liberation he recruited a new generation of lawyers who had been brought up to think of the law as an instrument of oppression.

Those of us who grew up under the heel of Jim Crow were inspired to set our sights on the law as a career; to try to follow him on his journey to justice and equality. So while all Americans are indebted to Thurgood Marshall's accomplishments, we who grew up in the sunlight of his deeds owe a special debt of gratitude. Farewell Mr. Civil Rights, farewell Mr. Justice Marshall. We thank you for all you have done . . .

Vernon E. Jordan Jr., former executive director of the National Urban League and civil rights attorney, from his eulogy delivered at the memorial service for Supreme Court Justice Thurgood Marshall at the National Cathedral in Washington, D.C., January 28, 1993.

Perhaps if more youth today knew and understood what we endured to get an education, they would have more appreciation for the opportunities presented to them today. I took their abuse because I wanted a future. They wanted Ernest Green to fail. I wouldn't let it happen. My mother wouldn't let it happen. Our community wouldn't let it happen. I became the first black student to graduate from Central High School. Martin Luther King, Jr. attended my graduation ceremony. It made all the suffering worth it.

Ernest Green, one of the Little Rock Nine, in We Wouldn't Give Up (The Crisis, October 1997).

The most important thing for us to remember is the phenomenal courage of the young people who marched and picketed and were made to suffer threats, intimidations, beatings, jailings and always the danger of death.

Martin Luther King was their leader—but it is clear that there were moments when they were alone and found the strength to follow leaders selected among themselves. Indeed, there were moments when Dr. King followed their lead—as in Montgomery during the Freedom Rides, and in Birmingham where grade school children participated in protests for the first time.

Their brave, non-violent self-discipline needs to be understood by succeeding generations of young people. Their bravery is a model for all generations for all times—particularly for moments when cynicism and self-interest undermine the national spirit.

John Seigenthaler, former editor/publisher of The Tennessean and aid to U.S. attorney general Robert F. Kennedy, to the author, 1999.

Our country is not officially divided on race. [Legal] racial discrimination is virtually nonexistent. Poverty is the challenge that Martin Luther King's "dream" leaves for us. Poverty is the moral equivalent of slavery and we can end it in the 21st century—in our lifetimes—like we ended slavery in the 19th century.

Andrew Young, former mayor of Atlanta, speech of January 30, 1999, at the Park Hill United Methodist Church in Denver, Colorado, in a Denver Post article of January 31, 1999.

Appendix A
List of Documents

1. The 13th Amendment, December 6, 1865.

2. The Civil Rights Act, April 9, 1866.

3. The 14th Amendment, July 9, 1868.

4. The 15th Amendment, February 3, 1870.

5. The Call, February 12, 1909.

6. The Formation of the NAACP, 1910.

7. Executive Order 8802, Establishing the President's Committee on Fair Employment Practices, issued by President Franklin Roosevelt, June 25, 1941.

8. Executive Order 9981, Barring segregation in the armed forces, issued by President Harry S Truman, July 26, 1948.

9. *Brown v. Board of Education*, May 17, 1954.

10. *Brown v. Board of Education* Supplemental Ruling, May 31, 1955.

11. Resolution of the Citizens' Mass Meeting, Montgomery, Alabama, December 5, 1955.

12. The Southern Manifesto, March 12, 1956.

13. The Civil Rights Act of 1957, September 9, 1957.

14. An Appeal for Human Rights, March 9, 1960.

15. The Civil Rights Act of 1960, May 6, 1960.

16. Student Nonviolent Coordinating Committee (SNCC) Statement of Purpose, May 14, 1960.

17. Letter from the Albany Movement to the Albany City Commission, January 23, 1962.

18. The Birmingham Manifesto, April 3, 1963.

19. The Birmingham Truce Agreement, May 10, 1963.

20. Marchers' Pledge, March on Washington for Jobs and Freedom, August 28, 1963.

21. Memorandum of Mississippi Summer Project, June 3, 1964.

22. The Civil Rights Act of 1964, July 2, 1964.

23. Federal Judge Frank M. Johnson's Opinion in *Williams v. Wallace,* March 17, 1965.

24. Petition to Alabama Governor George Wallace by Selma–to–Montgomery Marchers, March 25, 1965.

25. The Voting Rights Act of 1965, August 6, 1965.

26. Black Panther Party Manifesto, 1966.

27. The Report of the National Advisory Commission on Civil Disorders, February 29, 1968.

28. The Civil Rights Act of 1968 Provision for Open Housing, April 11, 1968.

29. *James E. Swann et al v. Charlotte-Mecklenburg Board of Education et al,* April 20, 1971.

30. The Civil Rights Act of 1991, November 21, 1991.

1. The 13th Amendment

Ratified December 6, 1865

Section 1. Neither slavery nor involuntary servitude, except as a punishment for crime whereof the party shall have been duly convicted, shall exist within the United States, or any place subject to their jurisdiction.

Section 2. Congress shall have power to enforce this article by appropriate legislation.

2. The Civil Rights Act

April 9, 1866

An Act to protect all Persons in the United States in their Civil Rights, and furnish the Means of their Vindication.

Be it enacted, That all persons born in the United States and not subject to any foreign power, excluding Indians not taxed, are hereby declared to be citizens of the United States; and such citizens, of every race and color, without regard to any previous condition of slavery or involuntary servitude, except as a punishment for crime whereof the party shall have been duly convicted, shall have the same right, in every State and Territory in the United States, to make and enforce contracts, to sue, be parties, and give evidence, to inherit, purchase, lease, sell, hold, and convey real and personal property, and to full and equal benefit of all laws and proceedings for the security of person and property, as is enjoyed by white citizens, and shall be subject to like punishment, pains, and penalties, and to none other, any law, statute, ordinance, regulation, or custom, to the contrary notwithstanding.

SEC. 2. *And be it further enacted,* That any person who, under color of any law, statute, ordinance, regulation, or custom, shall subject, or cause to be subjected, any inhabitant of any State or Territory to the deprivation of any right secured or protected by this act, or to different punishment, pains, or penalties on account of such person having at any time been held in a condition of slavery or involuntary servitude, except as a punishment for crime whereof the party shall have been duly convicted, or by reason of his color or race, than is prescribed for the punishment of white persons, shall be deemed guilty of a misdemeanor, and, on conviction, shall be punished by fine not exceeding one thousand dollars, or

imprisonment not exceeding one year, or both, in the discretion of the court.

SEC. 3. *And be it further enacted,* That the district courts of the United States . . . shall have, exclusively of the courts of the several States, cognizance of all crimes and offences committed against the provisions of this act, and also, concurrently with the circuit courts of the United States, of all causes, civil and criminal, affecting persons who are denied or cannot enforce in the courts or judicial tribunals of the State or locality where they may be any of the rights secured to them by the first section of this act . . .

SEC. 4. *And be it further enacted,* That the district attorneys, marshals, and deputy marshals of the United States, the commissioners appointed by the circuit and territorial courts of the United States, with powers of arresting, imprisoning, or bailing offenders against the laws of the United States, the officers and agents of the Freedmen's Bureau, and every other officer who may be specially empowered by the President of the United States, shall be, and they are hereby, specially authorized and required, at the expense of the United States, to institute proceedings against all and every person who shall violate the provisions of this act, and cause him or them to be arrested and imprisoned, or bailed, as the case may be, for trial before such court of the United States or territorial court as by this act has cognizance of the offence . . .

SEC. 8. *And be it further enacted,* That whenever the President of the United States shall have reason to believe that offences have been or are likely to be committed against the provisions of this act within any judicial district, it shall be lawful for him, in his discretion, to direct the judge, marshal, and district attorney of such district to attend at such place within the district, and for such time as he may designate, for the purpose of the more speedy arrest and trial of persons charged with a violation of this act; and it shall be the duty of every judge or other officer, when any such requisition shall be received by him, to attend at the place and for the time therein designated.

SEC. 9. *And be it further enacted,* That it shall be lawful for the President of the United States, or such person as he may empower for that purpose, to employ such part of the land or naval forces of the United States, or of the militia, as shall be necessary to prevent the violation and enforce the due execution of this act.

SEC. 10. *And be it further enacted,* That upon all questions of law arising in any cause under the provisions of this act a final appeal may be taken to the Supreme Court of the United States.

3. The 14th Amendment

Ratified July 9, 1868
Section 1. All persons born or naturalized in the United States and subject to the jurisdiction thereof, are citizens of the United States and of the State wherein they reside. No State shall make or enforce any law which shall abridge the privileges or immunities of citizens of the United States; nor shall any State deprive any person of life, liberty, or property, without due process of law; nor deny to any person within its jurisdiction the equal protection of the laws.

4. The 15th Amendment

Ratified February 3, 1870
Section 1. The right of citizens of the United States to vote shall not be denied or abridged by the United States or by any State on account of race, color, or previous condition of servitude.

Section 2. The Congress shall have power to enforce this article by appropriate legislation.

5. The Call

February 12, 1909
[Open letter published in the New York *Evening Post*. This was the basis for the National Negro Conference of 1909, which resulted in the formation of the National Association for the Advancement of Colored People (NAACP).]

To Discuss Means for Securing Political and Civil Equality for the Negro

The celebration of the centennial of the birth of Abraham Lincoln widespread and grateful as it may be, will fail to justify itself if it takes no note and makes no recognition of the colored men and women to whom the great emancipator labored to assure freedom. Besides a day of rejoicing, Lincoln's birthday in 1909 should be one of taking stock of the nation's progress since 1865. How far has it lived up to the obligations imposed upon it by the Emancipation Proclamation? How far has it gone in assuring to each and every citizen, irrespective of color, the equality of opportunity and equality before the law, which underlie our American institutions and are guaranteed by the Constitution?

If Mr. Lincoln could revisit this country he would be disheartened by the nation's failure in this respect. He would learn that on January 1st, 1909, Georgia had rounded out new oligarchy by disfranchising the negro after the manner of all the other Southern states. He would learn that the Supreme Court of the United States, designed to be a bulwark of American liberties, had failed to meet several opportunities to pass squarely upon this disfranchisement of millions by laws avowedly discriminatory and openly enforced in such manner that white men may vote and black men be without a vote in their government; he would discover, there, that taxation without representation is the lot of millions of wealth-producing American citizens, in whose hands rests the economic progress and welfare of an entire section of the country. He would learn that the Supreme Court, according to the official statement of one of its own judges in the Berea College case, has laid down the principle that if an individual State chooses it may "make it a crime for white and colored persons to frequent the same market place at the same time, or appear in an assemblage of citizens convened to consider questions of a public or political nature in which all citizens, without regard to race, are equally interested." In many States Lincoln would find justice enforced, if at all, by judges elected by one element in a community to pass upon the liberties and lives of another. He would see the black men and women, for whose freedom a hundred thousand of soldiers gave their lives, set apart in trains, in which they pay first-class fares for third-class service, in railway stations and in places of entertainment, while State after State declines to do its elementary duty in preparing the negro through education for the best exercise of citizenship.

Added to this, the spread of lawless attacks upon the negro, North, South and West—even in the Springfield made famous by Lincoln—often accompanied by revolting brutalities, sparing neither sex, nor age nor youth, could not but shock the author of the sentiment that "government of the people, by the people, for the people shall not perish from the earth."

Silence under these conditions means tacit approval. The indifference of the North is already responsible for more than one assault upon democracy, and every such attack reacts as unfavorably upon whites as upon blacks. Discrimination once permitted cannot be bridled; recent history in the South shows that in forging chains for the negroes, the white voters are forging chains for themselves. "A house divided against itself cannot stand"; this government cannot exist half slave and half free any better to-day than it could in 1861. Hence we call upon all the believers in democracy to join in a national conference for the discussion of present evils, the voicing of protests, and the renewal of the struggle for civil and political liberty.

Miss Jane Addams, Chicago
Ray Stannard Baker, New York
Mrs. Ida Wells-Barnett, Chicago
Mrs. Harriet Stanton Blatch, New York
Mr. Samuel Bowles, (*Springfield Republican*)
Prof. W. L. Bulkley, New York
Miss Kate Claghorn, New York
E. H. Clement, Boston
Prof. John Dewey, New York
Miss Mary E. Dreier, Brooklyn
Prof. W. E. B. Du Bois, Atlanta
Dr. John L. Elliott, New York
Mr. William Lloyd Garrison, Boston
Rev. Francis J. Grimke, Washington, D.C.
Prof. Thomas C. Hall, New York
Rabbi Emil G. Hirsch, Chicago
Rev. John Haynes Holmes, New York
Hamilton Holt, New York
William Dean Howells, New York
Rev. Jenkin Lloyd Jones, Chicago
Mrs. Florence Kelley, New York
Rev. Walter Laidlaw, New York
Rev. Frederick Lynch, New York
Miss Helen Marot, New York
Miss Mary E. McDowell, Chicago
Prof. J.G. Merrill, Connecticut
Mr. John E. Milholland, New York
Dr. Henry Moskowitz, New York
Miss Leonora O'Reilly, New York
Miss Mary W. Ovington, New York
Rev. Charles H. Parkhurst, New York
Rev. John P. Peters, New York
J. G. Phelps-Stokes, New York
Louis F. Post, Chicago
Dr. Jane Robbins, New York
Charles Edward Russell, New York
William M. Salter, Chicago

Joseph Smith, Boston
Mrs. Anna Garlin Spencer, New York
Judge Wendell S. Stafford, Washington, D.C.
Lincoln Steffens, Boston
Miss Helen Stokes, New York
Mrs. Mary Church Terrell, Washington, D.C.
Prof. W. I. Thomas, Chicago
President Charles F. Thwing, Western Reserve University
Oswald Garrison Villard, New York
Mrs. Henry Villard, New York
Miss Lillian D. Wald, New York
Dr. J. Milton Waldron, Washington, D.C.
William English Walling, New York
Bishop Alexander Walters, New York
Dr. William H. Ward, New York
Mrs. Rodman Wharton, Philadelphia
Miss Susan P. Wharton, Philadelphia
Horace White, New York
Mayor Brand Whitlock, Toledo
Rabbi Stephen S. Wise, New York
President Mary E. Wooley, Mt. Holyoke College
Rev. M. St. Croix Wright, New York
Prof. Charles Zueblin, Boston

6. The Formation of the NAACP

Report of 1910

TO THE NATIONAL NEGRO COMMITTEE:

Your Committee herewith submits the following plan of a permanent organization for your consideration:

ORGANIZATION:

The organization shall be known as The National Association for the Advancement of Colored People; its object to be equal rights and opportunities for all.

The National Association to be composed of a National Committee of 100 members, with an Executive Committee, to be elected from the members of the National Committee, of thirty members; 15 resident in New York City and 15 resident elsewhere; with an auxiliary membership as hereafter described.

The National Headquarters to be in New York City.

The Auxiliary Membership to be made up as follows:

(a) Members paying dues of $100 per year. Such members shall be entitled to receive, free of all other cost, the Proceedings, publications, and other literature published by the National Association. They shall have the privilege of voting at all elections and of attending all meetings, public and private, held under the auspices of the National Association;

(b) Members paying dues of $10 per year. Such members shall be entitled to receive, free of all other cost, the Annual Proceedings of the National Association. They shall have the privilege of voting at all elections, and of attending all public and private meetings held under the auspices of the National Association; and

(c) Members paying dues of $2 per year. Such members shall be entitled to receive, free from all other cost, the Annual Proceedings of the Association. They shall have the privilege of voting at all elections, and of attending all public meetings held under the auspices of the National Association.

ACTIVITIES:

It is recommended that the activities of the National Association be as follows:

(a) Public Meetings: A series of meetings to be held in the various cities in which the National Association is or shall be organized, at such intervals as may be determined at which Peonage, Public Education, Lynching, Injustices in the Courts, etc., will be presented and discussed; such meetings to be given the widest possible publicity and their Proceedings published by the National Association and widely circulated.

(b) Investigation: Your Committee deems it advisable that such department be instituted as soon as the funds can be secured; and that the whole time of at least one person be taken up with this work.

While the effort is being made to raise funds, it is proposed to undertake immediately a campaign involving a minimum of expense; i.e., simply the net cost of compiling such data as is already within easy reach of some of our members, or others who might be prevailed upon to undertake this work at cost. It is hoped that some of the members of the organization, and others outside, may have enough time to spare aside from their regular employments, to be willing to bring together for us as much data as can be readily collected, on the questions that interest us—such as Peonage, Public Education, Lynching, Injustice in the Courts, etc.—at cost to themselves in time and money. In this way it will not be necessary,

or desirable, to carry on any work of original investigation at the present moment, or until the funds are secured for a permanent investigator.

(c) Publicity: The same policy as above would apply to a permanent worker in this field, for the present. It is more than probable that a part of our collected material would be so novel and interesting that it could be sold to periodicals and newspapers, and in this manner compensate those of our members who should be disposed to write it up. It is recommended, however, that some individual from the Committee should be appointed especially to undertake at least a part of this work, and to secure the cooperation of others. All articles so appearing shall, on the approval of a Press Committee of the National Association, be given the widest possible circulation by the Committee.

As to the proposed Legal Aid Bureau, it is recommended that the work of the Constitution League be endorsed as filling the need in this direction at present.

The foregoing activities will necessitate a permanent headquarters and the services of a secretary to organize the membership, and there will also be expenses of postage, printing, etc.

It is recommended that our first effort be directed to securing funds for this purpose, and as many members as possible in those places where we have already secured a foothold—i.e. Boston, Philadelphia, Chicago, and Washington, in order that (a) meetings of our National Committee resident in those cities may be held, (b) a general meeting of members be arranged for those cities and (c) public meetings be held in these cities as well as New York City.

It is further recommended that the naming of the place of meeting for the coming year be left to the Executive Committee in order that it may be held in such place where the public interest seems to be most promising at that time.

Respectfully Submitted
Preliminary Committee on Permanent Organization
Oswald G. Willard
Edwin R. A. Seligman
W. E. B. Du Bois
Charles Edward Russell
John H. Milholland
William English Walling

7. Executive Order 8802, Establishing the President's Committee on Fair Employment Practices, issued by President Franklin Roosevelt

June 25, 1941
Reaffirming policy of full participation in the defense program by all persons, regardless of race, creed, color, or national origin, and directing certain action in furtherance of said policy.

Whereas it is the policy of the United States to encourage full participation in the national defense program by all citizens of the United States, regardless of race, creed, color, or national origin, in the firm belief that the democratic way of life within the nation can be defended successfully only with the help and support of all groups within its borders; and

Whereas there is evidence that available and needed workers have been barred from employment in industries engaged in defense production solely because of considerations of race, creed, color, or national origin to the detriment of workers' morale and of national unity:

Now, Therefore, by virtue of the authority vested in me by the Constitution and the statutes, and as a prerequisite to the successful conduct of our national defense production effort, I do hereby reaffirm the policy of the United States that there shall be no discrimination in the employment of workers in defense industries or government because of race, creed, color, or national origin; and I do hereby declare that it is the duty of employers and of labor organizations, in furtherance of said policy and of this order, to provide for the full and equitable participation of all workers in defense industries, without discrimination because of race, creed, color, or national origin;

And it is hereby ordered as follows:

1. All departments and agencies of the government of the United States concerned with vocational and training programs for defense production shall take special measures appropriate to assure that such programs are administered without discrimination because of race, creed, color, or national origin.

2. All contracting agencies of the government of the United States shall include in all defense contracts hereafter negotiated by them a provision obligating the contractor not to discriminate against any worker because of race, creed, color, or national origin.

3. There is established in the Office of Production Management a Committee on Fair Employment Practice, which shall consist of a chairman and four other members to be appointed by the President. The chairman and members of the committee shall serve as such without compensation but shall be entitled to actual and necessary transportation, subsistence, and other expenses incidental to performance of their duties. The committee shall receive and investigate complaints of discrimination in violation of the provisions of this order and shall take appropriate steps to redress grievances which it finds to be valid. The committee shall also recommend to the several departments and agencies of the government of the United States and to the President all measures which may be deemed by it necessary or proper to effectuate the provisions of this order.

8. Executive Order 9981, Barring segregation in the United States armed forces, issued by President Harry S Truman

July 26, 1948
Whereas it is essential that there be maintained in the armed services of the United States the highest standards of democracy, with equality of treatment and opportunity for all those who serve in our country's defense:

Now, therefore, by virtue of the authority vested in me as President of the United States, by the Constitution and the statutes of the United States, and as Commander in Chief of the armed services, it is hereby ordered as follows:

1. It is hereby declared to be the policy of the President that there shall be equality of treatment and opportunity for all persons in the armed services without regard to race, color, religion or national origin. This policy shall be put into effect as rapidly as possible, having due regard to the time required to effectuate any necessary changes without impairing efficiency or morale.

2. There shall be created in the National Military Establishment an advisory committee to be known as the President's Committee on Equality of Treatment and Opportunity in the Armed Services, which shall be composed of seven members to be designated by the President.

3. The Committee is authorized on behalf of the president to examine into the rules, procedures and practices of the armed services in order to determine in what respect such rules, procedures and practices may be altered or improved with a view to carrying out the policy of this order. The Committee shall confer and advise with the Secretary of Defense, the Secretary of the Army, the Secretary of the Navy, and the Secretary of the Air Force, and shall make such recommendations to the President and to said Secretaries as in the judgment of the Committee will effectuate the policy hereof.

4. All executive departments and agencies of the Federal Government are authorized and directed to cooperate with the Committee in its work, and to furnish the Committee such information or the services of such persons as the Committee may require in the performance of its duties.

5. When requested by the Committee to do so, persons in the armed services or in any of the executive departments and agencies of the Federal Government shall testify before the Committee and shall make available for the use of the Committee such documents and other information as the Committee may require.

6. The Committee shall continue to exist until such time as the President shall terminate its existence by Executive Order.

9. *Brown v. Board of Education,* the U.S. Supreme Court Opinion

May 17, 1954

THESE CASES [*Brown* v. *Board of Education, Briggs* v. *Elliott, Davis* v. *County School Board, Gebhart* v. *Belton*] come to us from the States of Kansas, South Carolina, Virginia, and Delaware. They are premised on different facts and different local conditions, but a common legal question justifies their consideration together in this consolidated opinion.

In each of the cases, minors of the Negro race, through their legal representatives, seek the aid of the courts in obtaining admission to the public schools of their community on a nonsegregated basis. In each instance, they have been denied admission to schools attended by white children under laws requiring or permitting segregation according to race. This segregation was alleged to deprive the plaintiffs of the equal protection of the laws under the Fourteenth Amendment. In each of the cases other than the Delaware case, a three-judge federal district court denied relief to the plaintiffs on the so-called "separate but equal" doctrine announced by this Court in *Plessy* v. *Ferguson,* 163 U.S. 537. Under that doctrine, equality of treatment is accorded when the races are provided substantially equal facilities, even though these facilities be separate. In the Delaware case, the Supreme Court of Delaware adhered to that doctrine, but ordered that the plaintiffs be admitted to the white schools because of their superiority to the Negro schools.

The plaintiffs contend that segregated public schools are not "equal" and cannot be made "equal," and that hence they are deprived of the equal protection of the laws. Because of the obvious importance of the question presented, the Court took jurisdiction. Argument was heard in the 1952 Term, and reargument was heard this Term on certain questions propounded by the Court.

Reargument was largely devoted to the circumstances surrounding the adoption of the Fourteenth Amendment in 1868. It covered exhaustively consideration of the Amendment in Congress, ratification by the states, then existing practices in racial segregation, and the views of proponents and opponents of the Amendment. This discussion and our own investigation convince us that, although these sources cast some light, it is not enough to resolve the problem with which we are faced. At best, they are inconclusive. The most avid proponents of the post-War Amendments undoubtedly intended them to remove all legal distinctions among "all persons born or naturalized in the United States." Their opponents, just as certainly, were antagonistic to both the letter and the spirit of the Amendments and wished them to have the most limited effect. What others in Congress and the state legislatures had in mind cannot be determined with any degree of certainty.

An additional reason for the inconclusive nature of the Amendment's history, with respect to segregated schools, is the status of public education at that time. In the South, the movement toward free common schools, supported by general taxation, had not yet taken hold. Education of white children was largely in the hands of private groups. Education of

Negroes was almost nonexistent, and practically all of the race were illiterate. In fact, any education of Negroes was forbidden by law in some states. Today, in contrast, many Negroes have achieved outstanding success in the arts and sciences as well as in the business and professional world. It is true that public school education at the time of the Amendment had advanced further in the North, but the effect of the Amendment on Northern States was generally ignored in the congressional debates. Even in the North, the conditions of public education did not approximate those existing today. The curriculum was usually rudimentary; ungraded schools were common in rural areas; the school terms was but three months a year in many states; and compulsory school attendance was virtually unknown. As a consequence, it is not surprising that there should be so little in the history of the Fourteenth Amendment relating to its intended effect on public education.

In the first cases in this Court construing the Fourteenth Amendment, decided shortly after its adoption, the Court interpreted it as proscribing all state-imposed discriminations against the Negro race. The doctrine of "separate but equal" did not make its appearance in this Court until 1896 in the case of *Plessy* v. *Ferguson, supra,* involving not education but transportation. American courts have since labored with the doctrine for over half a century. In this Court, there have been six cases involving the "separate but equal" doctrine in the field of public education. In *Cumming* v. *Board of Education of Richmond County,* 175 U.S. 528, and *Gong Lum* v. *Rice,* 275 U.S. 78, the validity of the doctrine itself was not challenged. In more recent cases, all on the graduate school level, inequality was found in that specific benefits enjoyed by white students were denied to Negro students of the same educational qualifications. *Missouri ex rel. Gaines* v. *Canada,* 305 U.S. 337; *Sipuel* v. *Board of Regents of University of Oklahoma,* 332 U.S. 631; *Sweatt* v. *Painter,* 339 U.S. 629; *McLaurin* v. *Oklahoma State Regents,* 339 U.S. 637. In none of these cases was it necessary to re-examine the doctrine to grant relief to the Negro plaintiff. And in *Sweatt* v. *Painter, supra,* the Court expressly reserved decision on the question whether *Plessy* v. *Ferguson* should be held inapplicable to public education.

In the instant cases, that question is directly presented. Here, unlike *Sweatt* v. *Painter,* there are findings below that the Negro and white schools involved have been equalized, or are being equalized, with respect to buildings, curricula, qualifications and salaries of teachers, and other "tangible" factors. Our decision, therefore, cannot turn on merely a compar-ison of these tangible factors in the Negro and white schools involved in each of the cases. We must look instead to the effect of segregation itself on public education.

In approaching this problem, we cannot turn the clock back to 1868 when the Amendment was adopted, or even to 1896 when *Plessy* v. *Ferguson* was written. We must consider public education in the light of its full development and its present place in American life throughout the Nation. Only in this way can it be determined if segregation in public schools deprives these plaintiffs of the equal protection of the laws.

Today, education is perhaps the most important function of state and local governments. Compulsory school attendance laws and the great expenditures for education both demonstrate our recognition of the importance of education to our democratic society. It is required in the performance of our most basic public responsibilities, even service in the armed forces. It is the very foundation of good citizenship. Today it is a principal instrument in awakening the child to cultural values, in preparing him for later professional training, and in helping him to adjust normally to his environment. In these days, it is doubtful that any child may reasonably be expected to succeed in life if he is denied the opportunity of an education. Such an opportunity, where the state has undertaken to provide it, is a right which must be made available to all on equal terms.

We come then to the question presented: Does segregation of children in public schools solely on the basis of race, even though the physical facilities and other "tangible" factors may be equal, deprive the children of the minority group of equal educational opportunities? We believe that it does.

In *Sweatt* v. *Painter, supra,* in finding that a segregated law school for Negroes could not provide them equal educational opportunities, this Court relied in large part on "those qualities which are incapable of objective measurement but which make for greatness in a law school." In *McLaurin* v. *Oklahoma State Regents, supra,* the Court, in requiring that a Negro admitted to a white graduate school be treated like all other students, again resorted to intangible considerations: ". . . his ability to study, to engage in discussions and exchange views with other students, and, in general, to learn his profession." Such considerations apply with added force to children in grade and high schools. To separate them from others of similar age and qualifications solely because of their race generates a feeling of inferiority as to their status in the community that may affect their hearts and minds in a way unlikely ever to be undone. The effect of this separation on their educational opportunities was well stated by a finding in the Kansas case by a court which nevertheless felt compelled to rule against the Negro plaintiffs:

Segregation of white and colored children in public schools has a detrimental effect upon the colored children. The impact is greater when it has the sanction of the law; for the policy of separating the races is usually interpreted as denoting the inferiority of the negro group. A sense of inferiority affects the motivation of the child to learn. Segregation with the sanction of law, therefore, has a tendency to [retard] the educational and mental development of Negro children and to deprive them of some of the benefits they would receive in a racial[ly] integrated school system.

Whatever may have been the extent of psychological knowledge at the time of *Plessy* v. *Ferguson*, this finding is amply supported by modern authority. Any language in *Plessy* v. *Ferguson* contrary to this finding is rejected.

We conclude that in the field of public education the doctrine of "separate but equal" has no place. Separate educational facilities are inherently unequal. Therefore, we hold that the plaintiffs and others similarly situated for whom the action have been brought are, by reason of the segregation complained of, deprived of the equal protection of the laws guaranteed by the Fourteenth Amendment. This disposition makes unnecessary any discussion whether such segregation also violates the Due Process Clause of the Fourteenth Amendment.

Because these are class actions, because of the wide applicability of this decision, and because of the great variety of local conditions, the formulation of decrees in these cases presents problems of considerable complexity. On reargument, the consideration of appropriate relief was necessarily subordinated to the primary question—the constitutionality of segregation in public education. We have now announced that such segregation is a denial of the equal protection of the laws. In order that we may have the full assistance of the parties in formulating decrees, the cases will be restored to the docket, and the parties are requested to present further argument on Questions 4 and 5 previously propounded by the Court for the reargument this Term. The Attorney General of the United States is again invited to participate. The Attorneys General of the states requiring or permitting segregation in public education will also be permitted to appear as *amici curiae* upon request to do so by September 15, 1954, and submission of briefs by October 1, 1954.

It is so ordered.

10. *Brown v. Board of Education*, U.S. Supreme Court's Supplemental Ruling

May 31, 1955

THESE CASES were decided on May 17, 1954. The opinions of that date declaring the fundamental principle that racial discrimination in public education is unconstitutional, are incorporated herein by reference. All provisions of federal, state, or local law requiring or permitting such discrimination must yield to this principle. There remains for consideration the manner in which relief is to be accorded.

Because these cases arose under different local conditions and their disposition will involve a variety of local problems, we requested further argument on the question of relief. In view of the nationwide importance of the decision, we invited the Attorney General of the United States and the Attorneys General of all states requiring or permitting racial discrimination in public education to present their views on that question. The parties, the United States, and the States of Florida, North Carolina, Arkansas, Oklahoma, Maryland, and Texas filed briefs and participated in the oral argument.

These presentations were informative and helpful to the Court in its consideration of the complexities arising from the transition to a system of public education freed of racial discrimination. The presentations also demonstrated that substantial steps to eliminate racial discrimination in public schools have already been taken, not only in some of the communities in which these cases arose, but in some of the states appearing as *amici curiae*, and in other states as well. Substantial progress has been made in the District of Columbia and in the communities in Kansas and Delaware involved in this litigation. The defendants in the cases coming to us from South Carolina and Virginia are awaiting the decision of this Court concerning relief.

Full implementation of these constitutional principles may require solution of varied local school problems. School authorities have the primary responsibility for elucidating, assessing, and solving these problems; courts will have to consider whether the action of school authorities constitutes good faith implementation of the governing constitutional principles. Because of their proximity to local conditions and the possible need for further hearings the courts which originally heard these cases can best perform this judicial appraisal. Accordingly, we believe it appropriate to remand the cases to those courts.

In fashioning and effectuating the decrees, the courts will be guided by equitable principles. Traditionally, equity has been characterized by a practical flexibility in shaping its remedies and by a facility for adjusting and reconciling public and private needs. These cases call for the exercise of these traditional attributes of equity power. At stake is the personal interest of the plaintiffs in admission to public schools as soon as practicable on a nondiscriminatory basis. To effectuate this interest may call for elimination of a variety of obstacles in making the transition to school systems operated in accordance with the constitutional principles set forth in our May 17, 1954, decision. Courts of equity may properly take into account the public interest in the elimination of such obstacles in a systematic and effective manner. But it should go without saying that the vitality of these constitutional principles cannot be allowed to yield simply because of disagreement with them.

While giving weight to these public and private considerations, the courts will require that the defendants make a prompt and reasonable start toward full compliance with our May 17, 1954, ruling. Once such a start has been made, the courts may find that additional time is necessary to carry out the ruling in an effective manner. The burden rests upon the defendants to establish that such time is necessary in the public interest and is consistent with good faith compliance at the earliest practicable date. To that end, the courts may consider problems related to administration, arising from the physical condition of the school plant, the school transportation system, personnel, revision of school districts and attendance areas into compact units to achieve a system of determining admission to the public schools on a nonracial basis, and revision of local laws and regulations which may be necessary in solving the foregoing problems. They will also consider the adequacy of any plans the defendants may propose to meet these problems and to effectuate a transition to a racially nondiscriminatory school system. During this period of transition, the courts will retain jurisdiction of these cases.

The judgments below, except that in the Delaware case, are accordingly reversed and the cases are remanded to the District Courts to take such proceedings and enter such orders and decrees consistent with this opinion as are necessary and proper to admit to public schools on a racially nondiscriminatory basis with all deliberate speed the parties to these cases. The judgment in the Delaware case—ordering the immediate admission of the plaintiffs to schools previously attended only by white children—is affirmed on the basis of the principles stated in our May 17, 1954, opinion, but the case is remanded to the Supreme Court of Delaware for such further proceedings as that Court may deem necessary in light of this opinion.

It is so ordered.

11. Resolution of the Citizens' Mass Meeting, Montgomery, Alabama

December 5, 1955

WHEREAS, there are thousands of Negroes in the city and county of Montgomery who ride busses owned and operated by the Montgomery City Lines, Incorporated, and

WHEREAS, said citizens have been riding busses owned and operated by said company over a number of years, and

WHEREAS, said citizens, over a number of years, and on many occasions have been insulted, embarrassed and have been made to suffer great fear of bodily harm by drivers of busses owned and operated by said bus company, and

WHEREAS, the drivers of said busses have never requested a white passenger riding on any of its busses to relinquish his seat and stand so that a Negro may take his seat; however, said drivers have on many occasions too numerous to mention requested Negro passengers on said busses to relinquish their seats and stand so that white passengers may take their seats, and

WHEREAS, said citizens of Montgomery city and county pay their fares just as all other persons who are passengers on said busses, and are entitled to fair and equal treatment, and

WHEREAS, there has been any number of arrests of Negroes caused by drivers of said busses and they are constantly put in jail for refusing to give white passengers their seats and stand.

WHEREAS, in March of 1955, a committee of citizens did have a conference with one of the officials of said bus line; at which time said official arranged a meeting between attorneys representing the Negro citizens of this city and attorneys representing the Montgomery City Lines, Incorporated and the city of Montgomery, and

WHEREAS, the official of the bus line promised that as a result of the meeting between said attorneys, he would issue a statement of policy clarifying the law with reference to the seating of Negro passengers on the bus, and

WHEREAS, said attorneys did have a meeting and did discuss the matter of clarifying the law, however, the official said bus lines did not make public statements as to its policy with reference to the seating of passengers on its busses, and

WHEREAS, since that time, at least two ladies have been arrested for an alleged violation of the city segregation law with reference to bus travel, and

WHEREAS, said citizens of Montgomery city and county believe that they have been grossly mistreated as passengers on the busses owned and operated by said bus company in spite of the fact that they are in the majority with reference to the number of passengers riding on said busses.

Be It Resolved As Follows:

1. That the citizens of Montgomery are requesting that every citizen in Montgomery, regardless of race, color or creed, to refrain from riding busses owned and operated in the city of Montgomery by the Montgomery City Lines, Incorporated until some arrangement has been worked out between said company and the Montgomery City Lines, Incorporated.

2. That every person owning or who has access to automobiles use their automobiles in assisting other persons to get to work without charge.

3. That the employers of persons whose employees live a . . . distance from them, as much as possible afford transportation to your own employees.

4. That the Negro citizens of Montgomery are ready and willing to send a delegation of citizens to the Montgomery City Lines to discuss their grievances and to work out a solution for the same.

Be it further resolved that we have not, are not, and have no intentions of using an unlawful means or any intimidation to persuade persons not to ride the Montgomery City Lines' busses. However, we call upon your consciences, both moral and spiritual, to give your whole-hearted support to this undertaking. We believe we have [a just] complaint and we are willing to discuss this matter with the proper officials.

12. The Southern Manifesto ("Declaration of Constitutional Principles")

March 12, 1956

[Denouncing the U.S. Supreme Court ruling on segregation in public schools, issued by 19 Southern senators and 82 members of the House of Representatives.]

THE UNWARRANTED DECISION of the Supreme Court in the public school cases is now bearing the fruit always produced when men substitute naked power for established law.

The Founding Fathers gave us a Constitution of checks and balances because they realized the inescapable lesson of history that no man or group of men can be safely entrusted with unlimited power. They framed this Constitution with its provisions for change by amendment in order to secure the fundamentals of government against the dangers of temporary popular passion or the personal predilections of public officeholders.

We regard the decision of the Supreme Court in the school cases as a clear abuse of judicial power. It climaxes a trend in the Federal judiciary undertaking to legislate, in derogation of the authority of Congress, and to encroach upon the reserved rights of the States and the people.

The original Constitution does not mention education. Neither does the 14th amendment nor any other amendment. The debates preceding the submission of the 14th amendment clearly show that there was no intent that it should affect the systems of education maintained by the States.

The very Congress which proposed the amendment subsequently provided for segregated schools in the District of Columbia.

When the amendment was adopted, in 1868, there were 37 States of the Union. Every one of the 26 States that had any substantial racial differences among its people either approved the operation of segregated schools already in existence or subsequently established such schools by action of the same lawmaking body which considered the 14th amendment.

As admitted by the Supreme Court in the public school case (*Brown* v. *Board of Education*), the doctrine of separate but equal schools "apparently originated in *Roberts* v. *City of Boston* . . . (1849), upholding school segregation against attack as being violative of a State constitutional guarantee of equality." This constitutional doctrine began in the North—not in the South, and it was followed not only in Massachusetts, but in Connecticut, New York, Illinois, Indiana, Michigan, Minnesota, New Jersey, Ohio, Pennsylvania, and other northern States until they, exercising their rights as States through the constitutional processes of local self-government, changed their school systems.

In the case of *Plessy* v. *Ferguson,* in 1896, the Supreme Court expressly declared that under the 14th amendment no person was denied any of his rights if the States provided separate but equal public facilities. This decision has been followed in many other cases. It is notable that the Supreme Court, speaking through Chief Justice Taft, a former President of the United States, unanimously declared, in 1927, in *Lum* v. *Rice,* that the "separate but equal" principle is "within the discretion of the State in regulating its public schools and does not conflict with the 14th amendment."

This interpretation, restated time and again, became a part of the life of the people of many of the States and confirmed their habits, customs, traditions, and way of life. It is founded on elemental humanity and commonsense, for parents should not be deprived by Government of the right to direct the lives of and education of their own children.

Though there has been no constitutional amendment or act of Congress changing this established legal principle almost a century old, the Supreme Court of the United States, with no legal basis for such action, undertook to exercise their naked judicial power and substituted their personal political and social ideas for the established law of the land.

This unwarranted exercise of power by the Court, contrary to the Constitution, is creating chaos and confusion in the States principally affected. It is destroying the amicable relations between the white and Negro races that have been created through 90 years of patient effort by the good people of both races. It has planted hatred and suspicion where there has been heretofore friendship and understanding.

Without regard to the consent of the governed, outside agitators are threatening immediate and revolutionary changes in our public-school systems. If done, this is certain to destroy the system of public education in some of the States.

With the gravest concern for the explosive and dangerous condition created by this decision and inflamed by outside meddlers:

We reaffirm our reliance on the Constitution as the fundamental law of the land.

We decry the Supreme Court's encroachments on rights reserved to the States and to the people, contrary to established law and to the Constitution.

We commend the motives of those States which have declared the intention to resist forced integration by any lawful means.

We appeal to the States and people who are not directly affected by these decisions to consider the constitutional principles involved against the time when they, too, on issues vital to them, may be the victims of judicial encroachment.

Even though we constitute a minority in the present Congress, we have full faith that a majority of the American people believe in the dual system of Government which has enabled us to achieve our greatness and will in time demand that the reserved rights of the State and of the people be made secure against judicial usurpation.

We pledge ourselves to use all lawful means to bring about a reversal of this decision which is contrary to the Constitution and to prevent the use of force in its implementation.

In this trying period, as we all seek to right this wrong, we appeal to our people not to be provoked by the agitators and troublemakers invading our States and to scrupulously refrain from disorders and lawless acts.

Signed by:
Members of the United States Senate: Walter F. George; Richard B. Russell; John Stennis; Sam J. Ervin, Jr.; Strom Thurmond; Harry F. Byrd; A. Willis Robertson; John L. McClellan; Allen J. Ellender; Russell B. Long; Lister Hill; James O. Eastland; W. Kerr Scott; John Sparkman; Olin D. Johnston; Price Daniel; J. W. Fulbright; George A. Smathers; Spessard L. Holland.

Members of the United States House of Representatives:

Alabama: Frank W. Boykin; George M. Grant; George W. Andrews; Kenneth A. Roberts; Albert Rains; Armistead I. Selden, Jr.; Carl Elliott; Robert E. Jones; George Huddleston, Jr.

Arkansas: E. C. Gathings; Wilbur D. Mills; James W. Trimble; Oren Harris; Brooks Hays; W. F. Norrell.

Florida: Charles E. Bennett; Robert L. F. Sikes; A. S. Herlong, Jr.; Paul G. Rogers; James A. Haley; D. R. Matthews; William C. Cramer.

Georgia: Prince H. Preston; John L. Pilcher; E. L. Forrester; John James Flynt, Jr.; James C. Davis; Carl

Vinson; Henderson Lanham; Iris F. Blitch; Phil M. Landrum; Paul Brown.

Louisiana: F. Edward Hébert; Hale Boggs; Edwin E. Willis; Overton Brooks; Otto E. Passman; James H. Morrison; T. Ashton Thompson; George S. Long.

Mississippi: Thomas G. Abernethy; Jamie L. Whitten; Frank E. Smith; John Bell Williams; Arthur Winstead; William M. Colmer.

North Carolina: Herbert C. Bonner; L. H. Fountain; Graham A. Barden; Carl T. Durham; F. Ertel Carlyle; Hugh Q. Alexander; Woodrow W. Jones; George A. Shuford; Charles R. Jonas.

South Carolina: L. Mendel Rivers; John J. Riley; W. J. Bryan Dorn; Robert T. Ashmore; James P. Richards; John L. McMillan.

Tennessee: James B. Frazier, Jr.; Tom Murray; Jere Cooper; Clifford Davis; Ross Bass; Joe L. Evins.

Texas: Wright Patman; John Dowdy; Walter Rogers; O. C. Fisher; Martin Dies.

Virginia: Edward J. Robeson, Jr.; Porter Hardy, Jr.; J. Vaughan Gary; Watkins M. Abbitt; William M. Tuck; Richard H. Poff; Burr P. Harrison; Howard W. Smith; W. Pat Jennings; Joel T. Broyhill.

13. The Civil Rights Act of 1957

September 9, 1957

Be it enacted by the Senate and House of Representatives of the United States of America in Congress assembled,

PART I—ESTABLISHMENT OF THE COMMISSION ON CIVIL RIGHTS

SEC. 101. (a) There is created in the executive branch of the Government a Commission on Civil Rights (hereinafter called the "Commission").

(b) The Commission shall be composed of six members who shall be appointed by the President by and with the advice and consent of the Senate. Not more than three of the members shall at any one time be of the same political party.

(c) The President shall designate one of the members of the Commission as Chairman and one as Vice Chairman. The Vice Chairman shall act as Chairman in the absence or disability of the Chairman, or in the event of a vacancy in that office . . .

Rules of Procedure of the Commission

SEC. 102. (a) The Chairman or one designated by him to act as Chairman at a hearing of the Commission shall announce in an opening statement the subject of the hearing.

(b) A copy of the Commission's rules shall be made available to the witness before the Commission.

(c) Witnesses at the hearings may be accompanied by their own counsel for the purpose of advising them concerning their constitutional rights.

(d) The Chairman or Acting Chairman may punish breaches of order and decorum and unprofessional ethics on the part of counsel, by censure and exclusion from the hearings.

(e) If the Commission determines that evidence or testimony at any hearing may tend to defame, degrade, or incriminate any person, it shall (1) receive such evidence or testimony in executive session; (2) afford such person an opportunity voluntarily to appear as a witness; and (3) receive and dispose of requests from such person to subpena additional witnesses.

(f) Except as provided in sections 102 and 105 (f) of this Act, the Chairman shall receive and the Commission shall dispose of requests to subpena additional witnesses.

(g) No evidence or testimony taken in executive session may be released or used in public sessions without the consent of the Commission. Whoever releases or uses in public without the consent of the Commission evidence or testimony taken in executive session shall be fined not more than $1,000, or imprisoned for not more than one year.

(h) In the discretion of the Commission, witnesses may submit brief and pertinent sworn statements in writing for inclusion in the record. The Commission is the sole judge of the pertinency of testimony and evidence adduced at its hearings . . .

(k) The Commission shall not issue any subpena for the attendance and testimony of witnesses or for the production of written or other matter which would require the presence of the party subpenaed at a hearing to be held outside of the State, wherein the witness is found or resides or transacts business . . .

Duties of the Commission

SEC. 104. (a) The Commission shall—

(1) investigate allegations in writing under oath or affirmation that certain citizens of the United States are being deprived of their right to vote and have that vote counted by reason of their color, race, religion, or national origin; which writing, under oath or affirmation, shall set forth the facts upon which such belief or beliefs are based;

(2) study and collect information concerning le-

gal developments constituting a denial of equal protection of the laws under the Constitution; and

(3) appraise the laws and policies of the Federal Government with respect to equal protection of the laws under the Constitution.

(b) The Commission shall submit interim reports to the President and to the Congress at such times as either the Commission or the President shall deem desirable, and shall submit to the President and to the Congress a final and comprehensive report of its activities, findings, and recommendations not later than two years from the date of the enactment of this Act.

(c) Sixty days after the submission of its final report and recommendations the Commission shall cease to exist . . .

PART II—TO PROVIDE FOR AN ADDITIONAL
ASSISTANT ATTORNEY GENERAL

SEC. 111. There shall be in the Department of Justice one additional Assistant Attorney General, who shall be appointed by the President, by and with the advice and consent of the Senate, who shall assist the Attorney General in the performance of his duties, and who shall receive compensation at the rate prescribed by law for other Assistant Attorneys General . . .

PART IV—TO PROVIDE MEANS OF FURTHER SECURING
AND PROTECTING THE RIGHT TO VOTE

SEC. 131. Section 2004 of the Revised Statutes (42 U.S.C. 1971), is amended as follows:

(a) Amend the catch line of said section to read, "Voting rights".

(b) Designate its present text with the subsection symbol "(a)".

(c) Add, immediately following the present text, four new sub-sections to read as follows:

"(b) No person, whether acting under color of law or otherwise, shall intimidate, threaten, coerce, or attempt to intimidate, threaten, or coerce any other person for the purpose of interfering with the right of such other person to vote or to vote as he may choose, or of causing such other person to vote for, or not to vote for, any candidate for the office of President, Vice President, presidential elector, Member of the Senate, or Member of the House of Representatives, Delegates or Commissioners from the Territories or possessions, at any general, special, or primary election held solely or in part for the purpose of selecting or electing any such candidate.

"(c) Whenever any person has engaged or there are reasonable grounds to believe that any person is about to engage in any act or practice which would deprive any other person of any right or privilege secured by subsection (a) or (b), the Attorney General may institute for the United States, or in the name of the United States, a civil action or other proper proceeding for preventive relief, including an application for a permanent or temporary injunction, restraining order, or other order. In any proceeding hereunder the United States shall be liable for costs the same as a private person.

"(d) The district courts of the United States shall have jurisdiction of proceedings instituted pursuant to this section and shall exercise the same without regard to whether the party aggrieved shall have exhausted any administrative or other remedies that may be provided by law.

"(e) Any person cited for an alleged contempt under this Act shall be allowed to make his full defense by counsel learned in the law; and the court before which he is cited or tried, or some judge thereof, shall immediately, upon his request, assign to him such counsel, not exceeding two, as he may desire, who shall have free access to him at all reasonable hours. He shall be allowed, in his defense to make any proof that he can produce by lawful witnesses, and shall have the like process of the court to compel his witnesses to appear at his trial or hearing, as is usually granted to compel witnesses to appear on behalf of the prosecution. If such person shall be found by the court to be financially unable to provide for such counsel, it shall be the duty of the court to provide such counsel."

PART V—TO PROVIDE TRIAL BY JURY FOR
PROCEEDINGS TO PUNISH CRIMINAL CONTEMPTS OF
COURT GROWING OUT OF CIVIL RIGHTS CASES AND
TO AMEND THE JUDICIAL CODE RELATING TO
FEDERAL JURY QUALIFICATIONS

SEC. 151. In all cases of criminal contempt arising under the provisions of this Act, the accused, upon conviction, shall be punished by fine or imprisonment or both: *Provided however,* That in case the accused is a natural person the fine to be paid shall not exceed the sum of $1,000, nor shall imprisonment exceed the term of six months: *Provided further,* That in any such proceeding for criminal contempt, at the discretion of the judge, the accused may be tried with or without a jury: *Provided further, however,* That in the event such proceeding for criminal contempt be tried before a judge without a jury and the sentence of the court upon conviction is a fine in excess of the sum of $300 or imprisonment in excess of forty-five days, the accused in said proceeding, upon demand therefor, shall be entitled to a trial de novo before a jury, which shall conform as near as may be to the practice in other criminal cases . . .

SEC. 152. Section 1861, title 28, of the United States Code is hereby amended to read as follows:
"§ 1861. Qualifications of Federal jurors
"Any citizen of the United States who has attained the age of twenty-one years and who has resided for a period of one year within the judicial district, is competent to serve as a grand or petit juror unless—.

"(1) He has been convicted in a State or Federal court of record of a crime punishable by imprisonment for more than one year and his civil rights have not been restored by pardon or amnesty.
"(2) He is unable to read, write, speak, and understand the English language.
"(3) He is incapable, by reason of mental or physical infirmities to render efficient jury service."

SEC. 161. This Act may be cited as the "Civil Rights Act of 1957".

14. An Appeal for Human Rights

March 9, 1960
[Paid advertisement in the *Atlanta Constitution*.]

We, the students of the six affiliated institutions forming the Atlanta University Center—Clark, Morehouse, Morris Brown, and Spelman Colleges, Atlanta University, and the Interdenominational Theological Center—have joined our hearts, minds, and bodies in the cause of gaining those rights which are inherently ours as members of the human race and as citizens of these United States . . .
. . . We want to state clearly and unequivocally that we cannot tolerate, in a nation professing democracy and among people professing Christianity, the discriminatory conditions under which the Negro is living today in Atlanta, Georgia—supposedly one of the most progressive cities in the South.
Among the inequalities and injustices in Atlanta and in Georgia against which we protest, the following are outstanding examples: .

(1) Education: In the Public School System, facilities for Negroes and whites are separate and unequal. Double sessions continue in about half of the Negro Public Schools, and many Negro children travel ten miles a day in order to reach a school that will admit them . . .
(2) Jobs: Negroes are denied employment in the majority of city, state, and federal governmental jobs, except in the most menial capacities.
(3) Housing: While Negroes constitute 32% of the population of Atlanta, they are forced to live within 16% of the area of the city . . .
(4) Voting: Contrary to statements made in Congress recently by several Southern Senators, we know that in many counties in Georgia and other southern states, Negro college graduates are declared unqualified to vote and are not permitted to register.
(5) Hospitals: Compared with facilities for other people in Atlanta and Georgia, those for Negroes are unequal and totally inadequate . . .
(6) Movies, Concerts, Restaurants: Negroes are barred from most downtown movies and segregated in the rest. Negroes must even sit in a segregated section of the Municipal Auditorium. If a Negro is hungry, his hunger must wait until he comes to a "colored" restaurant, and even his thirst must await its quenching at a "colored" water fountain.
(7) Law Enforcement: There are grave inequalities in the area of law enforcement. Too often, Negroes are maltreated by officers of the law. An insufficient number of Negroes is employed in the law-enforcing agencies. They are seldom if ever promoted. Of 830 policemen in Atlanta only 35 are Negroes.

15. The Civil Rights Act of 1960

May 6, 1960
Be it enacted by the Senate and House of Representatives of the United States of America in Congress assembled, That this Act may be cited as the "Civil Rights Act of 1960." . . .

TITLE II

Flight to avoid prosecution for damaging or destroying any building or other real or personal property; and, illegal transportation, use or possession of explosives; and, threats or false information concerning attempts to damage or destroy real or personal property by fire or explosives

Sec. 201. Chapter 49 of title 18, United States Code, is amended by adding at the end thereof a new section as follows:

"§ 1074. Flight to avoid prosecution for damaging or destroying any building or other real or personal property

"(a) Whoever moves or travels in interstate or foreign commerce with intent either (1) to avoid prosecution, or custody, or confinement after conviction, under the laws of the place from which he flees, for willfully attempting to or damaging or destroying by fire or explosive any building, structure, facility, vehicle, dwelling house, synagogue, church, religious center or educational institution, public or private, or (2) to avoid giving testimony in any criminal proceeding relating to any such offense shall be fined not more than $5,000 or imprisoned not more than five years, or both." . . .

Sec. 203. Chapter 39 of title 18 of the United States Code is amended by adding at the end thereof the following new section: "§ 837. Explosives; illegal use or possession; and, threats or false information concerning attempts to damage or destroy real or personal property by fire or explosives." . . .

"(b) Whoever transports or aids and abets another in transporting in interstate or foreign commerce any explosive, with the knowledge or intent that it will be used to damage or destroy any building or other real or personal property for the purpose of interfering with its use for educational, religious, charitable, residential, business, or civic objectives or of intimidating any person pursuing such objectives, shall be subject to imprisonment for not more than one year, or a fine of not more than $1,000, or both; and if personal injury results shall be subject to imprisonment for not more than ten years or a fine of not more than $10,000, or both; and if death results shall be subject to imprisonment for any term of years or for life, but the court may impose the death penalty if the jury so recommends." . . .

Sec. 204. The analysis of chapter 39 of title 18 is amended by adding thereto the following: "837. Explosives; illegal use or possession; and threats or false information concerning attempts to damage or destroy real or personal property by fire or explosives."

Title III

Federal Election Records

Sec. 301. Every officer of election shall retain and preserve, for a period of twenty-two months from the date of any general, special, or primary election

of which candidates for the office of President, Vice President, presidential elector, Member of the Senate, Member of the House of Representatives, or Resident Commissioner from the Commonwealth of Puerto Rico are voted for, all records and papers which come into his possession relating to any application, registration, payment of poll tax, or other act requisite to voting in such election, except that, when required by law, such records and papers may be delivered to another officer of election and except that, if a State or the Commonwealth of Puerto Rico designates a custodian to retain and preserve these records and papers at a specified place, then such records and papers may be deposited with such custodian, and the duty to retain and preserve any record or paper so deposited shall devolve upon such custodian. Any officer of election or custodian who willfully fails to comply with this section shall be fined not more than $1,000 or imprisoned not more than one year, or both.

Sec. 302. Any person, whether or not an officer of election or custodian, who willfully steals, destroys, conceals, mutilates, or alters any record or paper required by section 301 to be retained and preserved shall be fined not more than $1,000 or imprisoned not more than one year, or both.

Sec. 303. Any record or paper required by section 301 to be retained and preserved shall, upon demand in writing by the Attorney General or his representative directed to the person having custody, possession, or control of such record or paper, be made available for inspection, reproduction, and copying at the principal office of such custodian by the Attorney General or his representative. This demand shall contain a statement of the basis and the purpose therefor . . .

Title IV

Extension of Powers of the Civil Rights Commission

Sec. 401. Section 105 of the Civil Rights Act of 1957 (42 U.S.C. Supp. V 1975d) (71 Stat. 635) is amended by adding the following new subsection at the end thereof:

"(h) Without limiting the generality of the foregoing, each member of the Commission shall have the power and authority to administer oaths or take statements of witnesses under affirmation." . . .

Title VI

Sec. 601. That section 2004 of the Revised Statutes (42 U.S.C. 1971), as amended by section 131 of the

Civil Rights Act of 1957 (71 Stat. 637), is amended as follows: . . .

"The court may appoint one or more persons who are qualified voters in the judicial district, to be known as voting referees, who shall subscribe to the oath of office required by Revised Statutes, section 1757; (5 U.S.C. 16) to serve for such period as the court shall determine, to receive such applications and to take evidence and report to the court findings as to whether or not at any election or elections (1) any such applicant is qualified under State law to vote, and (2) he has since the finding by the court heretofore specified been (a) deprived of or denied under color of law the opportunity to register to vote or otherwise to qualify to vote, or (b) found not qualified to vote by any person acting under color of law. In a proceeding before a voting referee, the applicant shall be heard ex parte at such times and places as the court shall direct. His statement under oath shall be prima facie evidence as to his age, residence, and his prior efforts to register or otherwise qualify to vote. Where proof of literacy or an understanding of other subjects is required by valid provisions of State law, the answer of the applicant, if written, shall be included in such report to the court; if oral, it shall be taken down stenographically and a transcription included in such report to the court.

"Upon receipt of such report, the court shall cause the Attorney General to transmit a copy thereof to the State attorney general and to each party to such proceeding together with an order to show cause within ten days, or such shorter time as the court may fix, why an order of the court should not be entered in accordance with such report. Upon the expiration of such period, such order shall be entered unless prior to that time there has been filed with the court and served upon all parties a statement of exceptions to such report. Exceptions as to matters of fact shall be considered only if supported by a duly verified copy of a public record or by affidavit of persons having personal knowledge of such facts or by statements or matters contained in such report; those relating to matters of law shall be supported by an appropriate memorandum of law. The issues of fact and law raised by such exceptions shall be determined by the court or, if the due and speedy administration of justice requires, they may be referred to the voting referee to determine in accordance with procedures prescribed by the court. A hearing as to an issue of fact shall be held only in the event that the proof in support of the exception disclose the existence of a genuine issue of material

fact. The applicant's literacy and understanding of other subjects shall be determined solely on the basis of answers included in the report of the voting referee." . . .

"When used in the subsection, the word 'vote' includes all action necessary to make a vote effective, but not limited to, registration or other action required by State law prerequisite to voting, casting a ballot, and having such ballot counted and included in the appropriate totals of votes cast with respect to candidates for public office and propositions for which votes are received in an election; the words 'affected area' shall mean any subdivision of the State in which the laws of the State relating to voting are or have been to any extent administered by a person found in the proceedings to have violated subsection (a); and the words 'qualified under State law' shall mean qualified according to the laws, customs, or usages of the State, and shall not, in any event, imply qualifications more stringent than those used by the persons found in the proceeding to have violated subsection (a) in qualifying persons other than those of the race or color against which the pattern or practice of discrimination was found to exist."

(b) Add the following sentence at the end of subsection (c):

"Whenever, in a proceeding instituted under this subsection any official of a State or subdivision thereof is alleged to have committed any act or practice constituting a deprivation of any right or privilege secured by subsection (a), the act or practice shall also be deemed that of the State and the State may be joined as a party defendant and, if, prior to the institution of such proceeding, such official has resigned or has been relieved of his office and no successor has assumed such office, the proceeding may be instituted against the State." . . .

16. Student Nonviolent Coordinating Committee (SNCC) Statement of Purpose

May 14, 1960
[Written by James Lawson.]

We affirm the philosophical or religious ideal of nonviolence as the foundation of our purpose, the pre-supposition of our faith, and the manner of our action. Nonviolence as it grows from Judaic-Christian traditions seeks a social order of justice permeated by love. Integration of human endeavor represents the crucial first step towards such a society.

Through nonviolence, courage displaces fear; love transforms hate. Acceptance dissipates prejudice; hope ends despair. Peace dominates war; faith reconciles doubt. Mutual regard cancels enmity. Justice for all overthrows injustice. The redemptive community supersedes systems of gross social immorality.

Love is the central motif of nonviolence. Love is the force by which God binds man to himself and man to man. Such love goes to the extreme; it remains loving and forgiving even in the midst of hostility. It matches the capacity of evil to inflict suffering with an even more enduring capacity to absorb evil, all the while persisting in love.

By appealing to conscience and standing on the moral nature of human existence, nonviolence nurtures the atmosphere in which reconciliation and justice become actual possibilities.

17. Letter from the Albany Movement to the Albany City Commission

January 23, 1962
Gentlemen:

The Albany Movement came into being as a result of repeated denials of redress for inadequacies and wrongs, and finally, for the refusal to even consider petitions which have been presented to your group from as far back as 1957.

The first request was for sewage and paving relief in the Lincoln Heights area—nothing done. Next, the stoning of Negro ministers' houses, following an inflammatory editorial in the local press, caused a request to be sent by registered mail to the Mayor that a joint group try to stop the worsening conditions—no official acknowledgement of this request has ever been received by us. Again, a request that segregated polling places, which we felt were used to counteract the effect of our vote, was made from the top to the bottom—the refusal to attempt any kind of redress necessitated a successful suit to be waged in the Federal Court by us. Finally, it was the

refusal of Albany officials, through its police department, to comply with the ICC regulation which became effective last November 1, that made the creation of this body a necessity. Test rides were conducted throughout the entire state of Georgia. Atlanta, Savannah, Augusta, Macon, Columbus, Valdosta and Waycross all complied. Only Albany resisted.

Accordingly we staged further tests on November 22, which resulted in the initial arrests, trials, convictions and appeals. The cases were headed for higher courts and things would have proceeded in an orderly fashion to its conclusion, but for the arrests of the so-called "Freedom Riders."

This testing of the railroad's compliance with another ICC directive has been laid at our doors. Actually, we had absolutely nothing to do with this. It was the elaborately staged "infraction" and arrests of those people that caused us to rush to their defense. They were fighting for the same purpose as we and we could not abandon them to the wolves.

The mockery of fair play and justice which followed, in turn, caused the first planned "Marching Protest." The harsh, repressive measures employed caused further protests and further arrests. By now, the whole country, and the world for that matter, were aware of the unyielding, cruelly repressive measures used to combat our use of that First Amendment to the United States Constitution, "Freedom of Speech" through peaceful protest.

When an agreement was reached on December 18, one of the cardinal points was the privilege of substituting signature bonds in lieu of cash bonds. This agreement has not been kept by the city of Albany. Another agreement was that the police department would not interfere with the compliance of the bus company to the ICC order. This agreement has been only partly kept by the city of Albany.

The Albany Movement wishes to go on record, without reservation, of requesting the city of Albany to keep the faith by honoring its commitments.

We the members of the Albany Movement, with the realization that ultimately the people of Albany, Negro and white, will have to solve our difficulties; realizing full well that racial hostility can be the downfall of our city; realizing that what happens in Albany, as well as what does *NOT* happen in Albany, affects the whole free world, call upon you tonight to hear our position.

It is our belief that discrimination based on race, color or religion is fundamentally wrong and contrary to the letter and intent of the Constitution of the United States. It is our aim in the Albany Movement to seek means of ending discriminatory practices in public facilities, both in employment and in use. Further, it is our aim to encourage private businesses to offer equal opportunity for all persons in employment and in service.

Some of these ideals which are inherent in the Constitution of the United States of America are:

1. Equal opportunity to improve one's self by good education.
2. Equal opportunity to exercise freedom and responsibility through the vote and participation in governmental processes.
3. Equal opportunity to work and advance economically.
4. Equal protection under the law.
5. The creation of a climate in which the talents and abilities of the entire community may be used for the good of all, unfettered by considerations of race or class.

Before going into plans for implementation of these goals, we wish to ask of you, gentlemen, tonight to reaffirm in writing your oral agreement of December 18, 1961, that, (1) the bus and train station will be open at all times without interference from the police; (2) the cash bonds will be refunded in exchange for security bonds, at an early date, the date to be set tonight.

We submit as the next step the creation of a biracial planning committee . . . [to] be composed of 6 members, 3 of which shall be appointed by the Albany Movement and 3 by the City Commission. Because of the tremendous responsibilities that will be invested in this committee, we pledge ourselves, as we also urge the commission, to choose men of the highest integrity, good will and sincerity.

It is our hope that through negotiations and arbitrations, through listening and learning from each other, that we can achieve the purposes that will benefit the total community.

The problem of human rights belongs to us all, therefore, let us not falter in seizing the opportunity which almighty God has given to create a new order of freedom and human dignity. What is your pleasure gentlemen, in proceeding with the negotiations?

Respectfully Submitted,
For The Albany Movement

W. G. Anderson, President
M. S. Page, Executive Secretary

18. The Birmingham Manifesto (Alabama Christian Movement for Human Rights)

April 3, 1963
[This document was made public on April 3, 1963—the initial day of the nonviolent campaign in Birmingham, Alabama.]

The patience of an oppressed people cannot endure forever. The Negro citizens of Birmingham for the last several years have hoped in vain for some evidence of good faith resolution of our just grievances.

Birmingham is part of the United States and we are *bona fide* citizens. Yet the history of Birmingham reveals that very little of the democratic process touches the life of the Negro in Birmingham. We have been segregated racially, exploited economically, and dominated politically. Under the leadership of the Alabama Christian Movement for Human Rights, we sought relief by petition for the repeal of city ordinances requiring segregation and the institution of a merit hiring policy in city employment. We were rebuffed. We then turned to the system of the courts. We weathered set-back after set-back, with all of its costliness, finally winning the terminal, bus, parks and airport cases. The bus decision has been implemented begrudgingly and the parks decision prompted the closing of all municipally-owned recreational facilities with the exception of the zoo and Legion Field. The airport case has been a slightly better experience with the experience of hotel accommodations and the subtle discrimination that continues in the limousine service.

We have always been a peaceful people, bearing our oppression with super-human effort. Yet we have been the victims of repeated violence, not only that inflicted by the hoodlum element but also that inflicted by the blatant misuse of police power. Our memories are seared with painful mob experience of Mother's Day 1961 during the Freedom Ride. For years, while our homes and churches were being bombed, we heard nothing but the rantings and ravings of racist city officials.

The Negro protest for equality and justice has been a voice crying in the wilderness. Most of Birmingham has remained silent, probably out of fear. In the meanwhile, our city has acquired the dubious reputation of being the worst big city in race relations in the United States. Last Fall, for a flickering moment, it appeared that sincere community leaders from religion, business and industry discerned the inevitable confrontation in race relations approaching. Their concern for the city's image and commonweal of all its citizens did not run deep enough. Solemn promises were made, pending a postponement of direct action, that we would be joined in a suit seeking the relief of segregation ordinances. Some merchants agreed to desegregate their rest-rooms as a good faith start, some actually complying, only to retreat shortly thereafter. We hold in our hands now, broken faith and broken promises.

We believe in the American Dream of democracy, in the Jeffersonian doctrine that "all men are created equal and are endowed by their Creator with certain inalienable rights, among these being life, liberty and the pursuit of happiness."

Twice since September we have deferred our direct action thrust in order that a change in city government would not be made in the hysteria of a community crisis. We act today in full concert with our Hebraic-Christian tradition, the law of morality and the Constitution of our nation. The absence of justice and progress in Birmingham demands that we make a moral witness to give our community a chance to survive. We demonstrate our faith that we believe that the beloved community can come to Birmingham.

We appeal to the citizenry of Birmingham, Negro and white, to join us in this witness for decency, morality, self-respect and human dignity. Your individual and corporate support can hasten the day of "liberty and justice for all." This is Birmingham's moment of truth in which every citizen can play his part in her larger destiny. The Alabama Christian Movement for Human Rights, in behalf of the Negro community of Birmingham.

F. L. Shuttlesworth, President
N. H. Smith, Secretary

19. The Birmingham Truce Agreement

May 10, 1963
1. Within 3 days after close of demonstrations, fitting rooms will be desegregated.
2. Within 30 days after the city government is established by court order, signs on wash rooms, rest rooms and drinking fountains will be removed.

3. Within 60 days after the city government is established by court order, a program of lunchroom counter desegregation will be commenced.
4. When the city government is established by court order, a program of upgrading Negro employment will be continued and there will be meetings with responsible local leadership to consider further steps.

Within 60 days from the court order determining Birmingham's city government, the employment program will include at least one sales person or cashier.

Within 15 days from the cessation of demonstrations, a Committee on Racial Problems and Employment composed of members of the Senior Citizens' Committee will be established, with a membership made public and the publicly announced purpose of establishing liaison with members of the Negro community to carry out a program of up-grading and improving employment opportunities with the Negro citizens of the Birmingham community.

20. Marchers' Pledge, March on Washington for Jobs and Freedom

August 28, 1963
Standing before the Lincoln Memorial on the 28th of August, in the centennial year of emancipation, I affirm my complete personal commitment for the struggle for jobs and freedom for all Americans.

To fulfill that commitment, I pledge that I will not relax until victory is won.

I pledge that I will join and support all actions undertaken in good faith in accord with time-honored democratic tradition of nonviolent protest, or peaceful assembly and petition and of redress through the courts and the legislative process.

I pledge to carry the message of the March to my friends and neighbors back home and to arouse them to an equal commitment and an equal effort. I will march and I will write letters. I will demonstrate and I will vote. I will work to make sure that my voice and those of my brothers ring clear and determined from every corner of our land.

I will pledge my heart and my mind and my body, unequivocally and without regard to personal sacrifice, to the achievement of social peace through social justice.

21. Memorandum of Mississippi Summer Project

June 3, 1964
To: Members of the United States Congress
From: Council of Federated Organizations (COFO)

MISSISSIPPI RIGHTS DRIVE PLANNED; STATE OFFICIALS MOBILIZE FOR SUMMER

A massive education, community improvement, and voter registration drive is being launched in the State of Mississippi this summer by the Council of Federated Organizations (COFO), a civil rights coalition comprised of the Congress of Racial Equality, the National Association for the Advancement of Colored People, the Southern Christian Leadership Conference, and the Student Nonviolent Coordinating Committee. The National Council of Churches has joined the civil rights groups in this extensive drive. Hundreds of clergymen, students, teachers, lawyers and others will be going to Mississippi to volunteer for this project . . .

COFO is concerned about the physical safety of summer volunteers because of Mississippi's long record of violence against civil rights workers . . .

The State has passed five bills designed to halt demonstrations and has other proposals before it which would legalize the blatant harassment of our education and voter registration workers . . .

A powerful police force is being mobilized both locally and state-wide by Mississippi law enforcement officials in a response to the summer project . . .

PROPOSED ACTION TO PREVENT VIOLENCE AND MAINTAIN ORDER

In order to prevent possible violence and chaos—and to save lives—COFO is attempting to secure a federal presence in Mississippi *before* any tragic incidents occur. Public hearings before a panel of ten distinguished Americans are scheduled for June 8th at the National Theatre. Local Mississippians and Constitutional lawyers will testify as to the need for and legality of Federal action. Leaders of the COFO project are attempting to secure an appointment with President Johnson to confer on steps which should be taken . . .

ACTIONS REQUESTED OF MEMBERS OF CONGRESS

This briefing is an attempt to enlist your help. We are asking you to take the following steps:

1. Attend the June 8th hearings and plan to make a public statement on the basis of the testimony you hear that day.

2. In a few weeks, COFO will be sending you a list of the names of your constituents who will be working with us in Mississippi. We urge that you bring their presence in Mississippi to the attention of your colleagues and that you seek the aid of your colleagues in obtaining Federal protection for your constituents.

3. Contact the Justice Department, in writing, individually, or as a group, and urge that the Department take the following specific steps in order to insure that the Constitution is upheld in Mississippi this summer and that summer project volunteers are protected.

a. Assign several U.S. Marshals in every county or locality where there will be COFO projects designed to secure the constitutional rights for the Negro citizens of Mississippi. (The power of the Attorney General to do this is found under Section 549, Title 28, U.S. Code; and Section 3053, Title 18, U.S. Code.)

b. Set up a full-time branch office on a temporary basis in several key Mississippi cities, i.e., Greenwood, Hattiesburg, Jackson, and Batesville. (There are currently U.S. Attorney's offices in the first three cities. It is quite within reason to request that the Justice Department establish fully staffed operations in these cities, as well as Batesville, for the summer.)

c. Inform, by mail or otherwise, various Mississippi law enforcement officials both on the state and local level of Federal laws regarding intimidation and harm of citizens of the United States who are exercising their Constitutional rights and that the Attorney General make it clear to these officials that prosecution as well as the active use of Federal preventative force will be swift and sure.

d. Notify Governor Paul Johnson that the Justice Department intends to take whatever means are necessary to guarantee the Constitutional rights of U.S. citizens who are in the State of Mississippi this summer.

e. Recommend to President Johnson the immediate use of Section 332 of Title 10 of the U.S. Code since it is absolutely apparent that Constitutional rights cannot be currently enforced in any courts within the State of Mississippi and that such deprivations are going on in spite of any actions by the Federal courts. (Refer to Section 332 of Title 10 in the Appendix of the Legal Memo attached which refers, in part, to situations in which it is "impracticable to enforce the laws of the United States in any state or territory by the ordinary course of Judicial proceedings." The 1963 report of the Civil Rights Commission states: "The conclusion is inevitable that present legal remedies for voter discrimination are inadequate." One might cite, for example, *U.S. v. Lynd*, Forest County, Mississippi, instituted in 1960, which has yet to have a final effective decree allowing Negroes to freely register to vote.)

f. Meet with the leaders of the Mississippi civil rights project and recommend that President Johnson meet with them also.

4. Assign one person in your office to act as a liaison with COFO in the event that incidents similar to those which took place in Canton, Mississippi, this past week occur this summer. We would request that your office cooperate with the following procedure if and when incidents occur this summer.

a. The COFO office in Mississippi will phone the details of any incidents directly and immediately to the COFO office in Washington, D.C. COFO's legal advisers will determine under which statutes the Federal Government has the power to act in any given situation and will relate this information to your office.

b. With the attached legal memo to refer to, we would request your office to phone the Justice Department and urge that they take immediate action to bring relief to our volunteers and to resolve the situation.

c. The Justice Department will furnish you with a complete report. It has been the history of the Justice Department, in the majority of instances, to reply that they have insufficient information and/or power to act in a given situation. The COFO line to Mississippi should provide fast and accurate details on events in that State. We hope to point out to you, in the attached memo, that the Federal government has the power to act in Mississippi *before* any incidents occur; there is little doubt that the legal power exists under which the Justice Department may act in the event that Constitutional rights are violated.

d. If the Justice Department does not take swift and incisive action in the event of an incident in the State of Mississippi, COFO will request that your office make an additional inquiry upon receipt of the Justice Department report if it appears to be inadequate.

The Council of Federated Organizations sincerely hopes that it will not be necessary to use the above

procedure. However, because of our serious concern for the safety of summer project volunteers and because of our apprehension at the visible mobilization of the State of Mississippi in response to the project, we strongly urge you to develop the mechanisms within your own office to respond to our appeal if it is necessary.

It cannot be stated too many times that our basic goal is to obtain Federal preventative action *before* any more names are added to the list of civil rights martyrs. It is to this that we hope you will direct your efforts at this time by urging the Justice Department to take the steps we have outlined.

22. The Civil Rights Act of 1964

July 2, 1964

TITLE I—VOTING RIGHTS

Sec. 101 (2). No person acting under color of law shall—

(A) in determining whether any individual is qualified under State law or laws to vote in any Federal election, apply any standard, practice, or procedure different from the standards, practices, or procedures applied under such law or laws to other individuals within the same county, parish, or similar political subdivision who have been found by State officials to be qualified to vote; . . .

(C) employ any literacy test as a qualification for voting in any Federal election unless (i) such test is administered to each individual wholly in writing; and (ii) a certified copy of the test and of the answers given by the individual is furnished to him within twenty-five days of the submission of his request made within the period of time during which records and papers are required to be retained and preserved pursuant to title III of the Civil Rights Act of 1960 . . .

TITLE II—INJUNCTIVE RELIEF AGAINST DISCRIMINATION IN PLACES OF PUBLIC ACCOMMODATION

Sec. 201. (a) All persons shall be entitled to the full and equal enjoyment of the goods, services, facilities, privileges, advantages, and accommodations of any place of public accommodation, as defined in this section, without discrimination or segregation on the ground of race, color, religion, or national origin.

(b) Each of the following establishments which serves the public is a place of public accommodation within the meaning of this title if its operations affect commerce, or if discrimination or segregation by it is supported by State action:

(1) any inn, motel, or other establishment which provides lodging to transient guests, other than an establishment located within a building which contains not more than five rooms for rent or hire and which is actually occupied by the proprietor of such establishment as his residence;

(2) any restaurant, cafeteria, lunch room, lunch counter, soda fountain, or other facility principally engaged in selling food for consumption on the premises . . .

(3) any motion picture house, theater, concert hall, sports arena, stadium or other place of exhibition or entertainment . . .

(d) Discrimination or segregation by an establishment is supported by State action within the meaning of this title if such discrimination or segregation (1) is carried on under color of any law, statute, ordinance, or regulation; or (2) is carried on under color of any custom or usage required or enforced by officials of the State or political subdivision thereof . . .

SEC. 202. All persons shall be entitled to be free, at any establishment or place, from discrimination or segregation of any kind on the ground of race, color, religion, or national origin, if such discrimination or segregation is or purports to be required by any law, statute, ordinance, regulation, rule, or order of a State or any agency or political subdivision thereof . . .

SEC. 206. (a) Whenever the Attorney General has reasonable cause to believe that any person or group of persons is engaged in a pattern or practice of resistance to the full enjoyment of any of the rights secured by this title, the Attorney General may bring a civil action in the appropriate district court of the United States by filing with it a complaint . . . requesting such preventive relief, including an application for a permanent or temporary injunction, restraining order or other order against the person or persons responsible for such pattern or practice, as he deems necessary to insure the full enjoyment of the rights herein described.

. . . .

TITLE VI—NONDISCRIMINATION IN FEDERALLY ASSISTED PROGRAMS

SEC. 601. No person in the United States shall, on the ground of race, color, or national origin, be ex-cluded from participation in, be denied the benefits of, or be subjected to discrimination under any program or activity receiving Federal financial assistance.

23. Federal Judge Frank M. Johnson's Opinion in *Williams v. Wallace*

March 17, 1965
[Permitting the Selma–to–Montgomery march to take place and ordering Governor Wallace to supply necessary protection.]

Hosea WILLIAMS, John Lewis and Amelia Boynton, on behalf of themselves and others similarly situated, Plaintiffs, United States of America, Plaintiff-Intervenor,

v.

Honorable George C. WALLACE, as Governor of the State of Alabama, Al Lingo, as Director of Public Safety for the State of Alabama, and James G. Clark, as Sheriff of Dallas County, Alabama, Defendants.

March 17, 1965.

JOHNSON, District Judge.

The plaintiffs as Negro citizens and the members of the class they represent filed with this Court on March 8, 1965, their complaint, motion for temporary restraining order and motion for a preliminary injunction . . .

The defendant George C. Wallace is the Governor and chief executive officer of the State of Alabama. The defendant Albert J. Lingo is the Director of Public Safety of the State of Alabama, and the defendant James G. Clark, Jr., is the Sheriff of Dallas County, Alabama. The Governor as the chief executive officer of the State of Alabama is charged with the faithful execution of the laws of the State of Alabama and of the United States of America; in such capacity, the Governor controls and supervises the defendant Albert J. Lingo, and through the defendant Lingo the Governor controls and directs the activities of the Alabama Highway Patrol, also known as the Alabama State Troopers. The defendant Lingo as director is in the active control of the Alabama Highway Patrol.

The plaintiffs seek to have this Court guarantee their right to assemble and demonstrate peaceably for the purpose of redressing their grievances concerning the right to register to vote in the State of Alabama without unlawful interference.

Included in the rights plaintiffs seek and ask this Court to adjudicate is that of walking peaceably along the public highway in the State of Alabama between Selma and Montgomery. Plaintiffs also ask this Court to enjoin and restrain the defendants and all persons acting in concert with them from arresting, harassing, threatening, or in any way interfering with their peaceful, nonviolent march from Selma, Alabama, to Montgomery, Alabama, for the purpose of protesting injustices and petitioning their State government, particularly the chief executive officer—the Governor—for redress of grievances . . .

Under Alabama law, registration is prerequisite to voting in any election. In several counties in central Alabama, including Dallas County wherein Selma, Alabama, is located, fewer than 10% of the Negroes of voting age are registered to vote. For the purpose of obtaining better political representation for Negro citizens in these counties, the Negro communities, through local and national organizations, have conducted voter registration drives in recent years. These voter registration drives in Dallas and other central Alabama counties have been intensified since September, 1964. Public demonstrations have been held in these several counties, particularly in Dallas County, for the purpose of encouraging Negroes to attempt to register to vote and also for the purpose of protesting discriminatory voter registration practices in Alabama. The demonstrations have been peaceful. At the same time, cases have been filed in the United States District Courts in this district and also in the Southern District of Alabama; these cases are designed to secure to Negro citizens their right to register to vote in several central Alabama counties . . .

The efforts of these Negro citizens to secure this right to register to vote in some of these counties, have accomplished very little. For instance, in Dallas County, as of November, 1964, where Negro citizens of voting age outnumber white citizens of voting age, only 2.2% of the Negroes were registered to vote. In Perry County as of August, 1964, where the Negro citizens of voting age outnumber white citizens, only 7% of the Negroes were registered to vote. In Wilcox County as of December, 1963, where the Negro citizens of voting age outnumber white citizens over two to one, 0% of the Negro citizens were registered to vote as contrasted with the registration of 100% of the white citizens of voting age in this county. In Hale County, where Negro citizens of voting age outnumber white citizens, only 3.6% of these Negro

citizens have been registered to vote. The evidence in this case reflects that, particularly as to Selma, Dallas County, Alabama, an almost continuous pattern of conduct has existed on the part of defendant Sheriff Clark, his deputies, and his auxiliary deputies known as "possemen" of harassment, intimidation, coercion, threatening conduct, and, sometimes, brutal mistreatment toward these plaintiffs and other members of their class who were engaged in their demonstrations for the purpose of encouraging Negroes to attempt to register to vote and to protest discriminatory voter registration practices in Alabama. This harassment, intimidation and brutal treatment has ranged from mass arrests without just cause to forced marches for several miles into the countryside, with the sheriff's deputies and members of his posse herding the Negro demonstrators at a rapid pace through the use of electrical shocking devices (designed for use on cattle) and night sticks to prod them along. The Alabama State Troopers, under the command of the defendant Lingo, have, upon several occasions, assisted the defendant Sheriff Clark in these activities, and the State troopers, along with Sheriff Clark as an "invited guest," have extended the harassment and intimidating activities into Perry County, where, on February 18, 1965, when approximately 300 Negroes were engaged in a peaceful demonstration by marching from a Negro church to the Perry County Courthouse for the purpose of publicly protesting racially discriminatory voter registration practices in Perry County, Alabama, the Negro demonstrators were stopped by the State troopers under the command of the defendant Lingo, and the Negro demonstrators were at that time pushed, prodded, struck, beaten and knocked down. This action resulted in the injury of several Negroes, one of whom was shot by an Alabama State Trooper and subsequently died.

In Dallas County, Alabama, the harassment and brutal treatment on the part of defendants Lingo and Clark, together with their troopers, deputies and "possemen," and while acting under instructions from Governor Wallace, reached a climax on Sunday, March 7, 1965. Upon this occasion approximately 650 Negroes left the church in Selma, Alabama, for the purpose of walking to Montgomery, Alabama, to present to the defendant Governor Wallace their grievances concerning the voter registration processes in these central Alabama counties and concerning the restrictions and the manner in which these restrictions had been imposed upon their public demonstrations. These Negroes proceeded in an orderly and peaceful manner to a bridge near the south edge of the City of Selma on U.S. Highway 80 that leads to Montgomery, Alabama, which is located approximately 45 miles east of Selma. They proceeded on a sidewalk across the bridge and then continued walking on the grassy portion of the highway toward Montgomery until confronted by a detachment of between 60 to 70 State troopers headed by the defendant Colonel Lingo, by a detachment of several Dallas County deputy sheriffs, and numerous Dallas County "possemen" on horses, who were headed by Sheriff Clark. Up to this point the Negroes had observed all traffic laws and regulations, had not interfered with traffic in any manner, and had proceeded in an orderly and peaceful manner to the point of confrontation. They were ordered to disperse and were given two minutes to do so by Major Cloud, who was in active command of the troopers and who was acting upon specific instructions from his superior officers. The Negroes failed to disperse, and within approximately one minute (one minute of the allotted time not having passed), the State troopers and the members of the Dallas County sheriff's office and "possemen" moved against the Negroes. The general plan as followed by the State troopers in this instance had been discussed with and was known to Governor Wallace. The tactics employed by the State troopers, the deputies and "possemen" against these Negro demonstrators were similar to those recommended for use by the United States Army to quell armed rioters in occupied countries. The troopers, equipped with tear gas, nausea gas and canisters of smoke, as well as billy clubs, advanced on the Negroes. Approximately 20 canisters of tear gas, nausea gas, and canisters of smoke were rolled into the Negroes by these state officers. The Negroes were then prodded, struck, beaten and knocked down by members of the Alabama State Troopers. The mounted "possemen," supposedly acting as an auxiliary law enforcement unit of the Dallas County sheriff's office, then, on their horses, moved in and chased and beat the fleeing Negroes. Approximately 75 to 80 of the Negroes were injured, with a large number being hospitalized.

The acts and conduct of these defendants, together with the members of their respective enforcement agencies, as outlined above, have not been directed toward enforcing any valid law of the State of Alabama or furthering any legitimate policy of the State of Alabama, but have been for the purpose and have had the effect of preventing and discouraging Negro citizens from exercising their rights of citizenship, particularly the right to register to vote and the right to demonstrate peaceably for the purpose of protest-

ing discriminatory practices in this area. By these actions and by this conduct, the defendants, together with other members of their enforcement agencies, have intimidated, threatened and coerced Negro citizens in this section of Alabama for the purpose of interfering with citizens and preventing them from exercising certain of their basic constitutional rights— i.e., the right to register to vote, peaceably assemble, remonstrate with governmental authorities and petition for redress of grievances. The attempted march alongside U.S. Highway 80 from Selma, Alabama, to Montgomery, Alabama, on March 7, 1965, involved nothing more than a peaceful effort on the part of Negro citizens to exercise a classic constitutional right; that is, the right to assemble peaceably and to petition one's government for the redress of grievances . . .

The law is clear that the right to petition one's government for the redress of grievances may be exercised in large groups. Indeed, where, as here, minorities have been harassed, coerced and intimidated, group association may be the only realistic way of exercising such rights . . .

This Court recognizes, of course, that government authorities have the duty and responsibility of keeping their streets and highways open and available for their regular uses. Government authorities are authorized to impose regulations in order to assure the safety and convenience of the people in the use of public streets and highways provided these regulations are reasonable and designed to accomplish that end . . . As has been demonstrated above, the law in this country constitutionally guarantees that a citizen or group of citizens may assemble and petition their government, or their governmental authorities, for redress of their grievances even by mass demonstrations as long as the exercise of these rights is peaceful. These rights may also be exercised by marching, even along public highways, as long as it is done in an orderly and peaceful manner; and these rights to assemble, demonstrate and march are not to by abridged by arrest or other interference so long as the rights are asserted within the limits of not unreasonably interfering with the exercise of the rights by other citizens to use the sidewalks, streets and highways, and where the protestors and demonstrators are conducting their activities in such a manner as not to deprive the other citizenry of their police protection. As was stated in Kelly v. Page, supra, there must be in cases like the one now presented, a "constitutional boundary line" drawn between the competing interests of society. This Court has the duty and responsibility in this case of drawing the "constitutional boundary line." In doing so, it seems basic to our constitutional principles that the extent of the right to assemble, demonstrate and march peaceably along the highways and streets in an orderly manner should be commensurate with the enormity of the wrongs that are being protested and petitioned against. In this case, the wrongs are enormous. The extent of the right to demonstrate against these wrongs should be determined accordingly . . .

This Court finds the plaintiffs' proposed plan to the extent that it relates to a march along U.S. Highway 80 from Selma to Montgomery, Alabama, to be a reasonable one to be used and followed in the exercise of a constitutional right of assembly and free movement within the State of Alabama for the purpose of petitioning their State government for redress of their grievances. It is recognized that the plan as proposed and as allowed reaches, under the particular circumstances of this case, to the outer limits of what is constitutionally allowed. However, the wrongs and injustices inflicted upon these plaintiffs and the members of their class (part of which have been herein documented) have clearly exceeded—and continue to exceed—the outer limits of what is constitutionally permissible. As stated earlier in this opinion, the extent of a group's constitutional right to protest peaceably and petition one's government for redress of grievances must be, if our American Constitution is to be a flexible and "living" document, found and held to be commensurate with the enormity of the wrongs being protested and petitioned against. This is particularly true when the usual, basic and constitutionally-provided means of protesting in our American way—voting—have been deprived. It must never be forgotten that our Constitution is "intended to endure for ages to come, and consequently to be adapted to the various crises of human affairs." With an application of these principles to the facts of this case, plaintiffs' proposed plan of march from Selma to Montgomery, Alabama, for its intended purposes, is clearly a reasonable exercise of a right guaranteed by the Constitution of the United States . . .

24. Petition to Alabama Governor George C. Wallace by Selma–to–Montgomery Marchers

March 25, 1965

To the Honorable George C. Wallace, issue of God, citizen of the United States and Governor of the State of Alabama.

We as citizens of Alabama, citizens of many states in our United States, and as citizens of several foreign countries: come praying the blessing of God upon you and the many responsibilities that are yours to discharge.

We come petitioning you to join us, in spirit and in truth, in what is history's and America's movement toward The Great Society: A nation of justice where none shall prey upon the weakness of others; a nation of plenty where greed and poverty shall be done away; a nation of brotherhood where success is founded upon service, and not given for nobleness alone.

We have come to represent the Negro citizens of Alabama and freedom-loving people from all over the United States and the world. We have come not only five days and 50 miles, but we have come from three centuries of suffering and hardship. We have come to you, the Governor of Alabama, to declare that we must have our freedom NOW. We must have the right to vote; we must have equal protection of the law, and an end to police brutality.

We Must Appeal

When the course of human events so denies citizens of this nation the right to vote, a right to adequate education, an opportunity to earn sufficient income; and when legal channels for real change are both slow and costly, a people must turn to the rights provided by the First Amendment to the Constitution. We must appeal to the seat of government with the only peaceful and nonviolent resources at our command: Our physical presence and the moral power of our souls. Thus we present our bodies with this petition as a living testimony to the fact that we are deliberately denied the right to vote and constantly abused and brutalized by so-called law officers in this state.

We are here because for over 100 years now our constitutionally guaranteed right to vote has been abridged.

We are here because state troopers killed Jimmie Lee Jackson, because the psychotic climate of this state produced the men who savagely attacked and killed him.

We call upon you Governor Wallace, to declare your faith in the American creed; to declare your belief in the words of the Declaration of Independence, that "all men are created equal."

We call upon you to establish democracy in Alabama, by taking the steps necessary to assure the registration of every citizen of voting age and of sound mind, by repealing the poll tax in state elections, by opening the registration books at times which are convenient to working people—such as nights and Saturdays, by encouraging the cooperation of county officials in the democratic process, and by appointment of Negro citizens to boards and agencies of the state in policymaking positions.

We call upon you to put an end to police brutality and to assure the protection of the law to black and white citizens alike.

We call upon you to work to end the climate of violence and hatred which persists in this state, denouncing all who would use violence in the propagation of their beliefs, and by avoiding the perpetuation of racism through official statements and political addresses.

25. The Voting Rights Act of 1965

August 6, 1965

SEC. 2. No voting qualification or prerequisite to voting, or standard, practice, or procedure shall be imposed or applied by any State or political subdivision to deny or abridge the right of any citizen of the United States to vote on account of race or color.

SEC. 3. (a) Whenever the Attorney General institutes a proceeding under any statute to enforce the guarantees of the fifteenth amendment in any State or political subdivision the court shall authorize the appointment of Federal examiners by the United States Civil Service Commission in accordance with section 6 to serve for such period of time and for such political subdivisions as the court shall determine is appropriate to enforce the guarantees of the fifteenth amendment (1) as part of any interlocutory order if the court determines that the appointment of such examiners is necessary to enforce such guarantees or (2) as part of any final judgment if the court

finds that violations of the fifteenth amendment justifying equitable relief have occurred in such State or subdivision: *Provided*, That the court need not authorize the appointment of examiners if any incidents of denial or abridgement of the right to vote on account of race or color (1) have been few in number and have been promptly and effectively corrected by State or local action, (2) the continuing effect of such incidents has been eliminated, and (3) there is no reasonable probability of their recurrence in the future.

SEC. 4. (a) To assure that the right of citizens of the United States to vote is not denied or abridged on account of race or color, no citizen shall be denied the right to vote in any Federal, State, or local election because of his failure to comply with any test or device in any State with respect to which the determinations have been made under subsection (b) or in any political subdivision with respect to which such determinations have been made as a separate unit, unless the United States District Court for the District of Columbia in an action for a declaratory judgment brought by such State or subdivision against the United States has determined that no such test or device has been used during the five years preceding the filing of the action for the purpose or with the effect of denying or abridging the right to vote on account of race or color: *Provided*, That no such declaratory judgment shall issue with respect to any plaintiff for a period of five years after the entry of a final judgment of any court of the United States, other than the denial of a declaratory judgment under this section, whether entered prior to or after the enactment of this Act, determining that denials or abridgments of the right to vote on account of race or color through the use of such tests or devices have occurred anywhere in the territory of such plaintiff. (2) No person who demonstrates that he has successfully completed the sixth primary grade in a public school in, or a private school accredited by, any State or territory, the District of Columbia, or the Commonwealth of Puerto Rico in which the predominant classroom language was other than English, shall be denied the right to vote in any Federal, State, or local election because of his inability to read, write, understand, or interpret any matter in the English language, except that in States in which State law provides that a different level of education is presumptive of literacy, he shall demonstrate that he has successfully completed an equivalent level of education in a public school in, or a private school accredited by, any State or territory, the District of Columbia, or the Commonwealth of Puerto Rico in which the predominant classroom language was other than English.

SEC. 5. Whenever a State or political subdivision with respect to which the prohibitions set forth in section 4(a) are in effect shall enact or seek to administer any voting qualification or prerequisite to voting, or standard, practice, or procedure with respect to voting different from that in force or effect on November 1, 1964, such State or subdivision may institute an action in the United States District Court for the District of Columbia for a declaratory judgment that such qualification, prerequisite, standard, practice, or procedure does not have the purpose and will not have the effect of denying or abridging the right to vote on account of race or color, and unless and until the court enters such judgment no person shall be denied the right to vote for failure to comply with such qualification, prerequisite, standard, practice, or procedure . . .

SEC. 9. (a) Any challenge to a listing on an eligibility list prepared by an examiner shall be heard and determined by a hearing officer appointed by and responsible to the Civil Service Commission and under such rules as the Commission shall by regulation prescribe.

SEC. 10. (a) The Congress finds that the requirement of the payment of a poll tax as a precondition to voting (i) precludes persons of limited means from voting or imposes ·unreasonable financial hardship upon such persons as a precondition to their exercise of the franchise, (ii) does not bear a reasonable relationship to any legitimate State interest in the conduct of elections, and (iii) in some areas has the purpose or effect of denying persons the right to vote because of race or color. Upon the basis of these findings, Congress declares that the constitutional right of citizens to vote is denied or abridged in some areas by the requirement of the payment of a poll tax as a precondition to voting.

SEC. 11. (a) No person acting under color of law shall fail or refuse to permit any person to vote who is entitled to vote under any provision of this Act or is otherwise qualified to vote, or willfully fail or refuse to tabulate, count, and report such person's vote.

(b) No person, whether acting under color of law or otherwise, shall intimidate, threaten, or coerce, or attempt to intimidate, threaten or coerce any person for voting or attempting to vote, or intimidate, threaten, or coerce, or attempt to intimidate, threaten, or coerce any person for urging or aiding any person to vote or attempt to vote, or intimidate, threaten, or coerce any person for exercising any powers or duties under section 3 (a), 6, 8, 9, 10, or 12(e) . . .

. . . .

SEC. 14. (a) All cases of criminal contempt arising under the provisions of this Act shall be governed by section 151 of the Civil Rights Act of 1957 (42 U.S.C. 1995).

(b) No court other than the District Court for the District of Columbia or a court of appeals in any proceeding under section 9 shall have jurisdiction to issue any declaratory judgment pursuant to section 4 or section 5 or any restraining order or temporary or permanent injunction against the execution or enforcement of any provision of this Act or any action of any Federal officer or employee pursuant hereto.

(c)(1) The terms "vote" or "voting" shall include all action necessary to make a vote effective in any primary, special, or general election, including, but not limited to, registration, listing pursuant to this Act, or other action required by law prerequisite to voting, casting a ballot, and having such ballot counted properly and included in the appropriate totals of votes cast with respect to candidates for public or party office and propositions for which votes are received in an election.

. . . .

SEC. 16. The Attorney General and the Secretary of Defense, jointly, shall make a full and complete study to determine whether, under the laws or practices of any State or States, there are preconditions to voting, which might tend to result in discrimination against citizens serving in the Armed Forces of the United States seeking to vote. Such officials shall, jointly, make a report to the Congress not later than June 30, 1966, containing the results of such study, together with a list of any States in which such preconditions exist, and shall include in such report such recommendations for legislation as they deem advisable to prevent discrimination in voting against citizens serving in the Armed Forces of the United States.

26. Black Panther Party Manifesto

1966

1. We want freedom. We want power to determine the destiny of our Black Community.

We believe that black people will not be free until we are able to determine our destiny.

2. We want full employment for our people.

We believe that the federal government is responsible and obligated to give every man employment or a guaranteed income. We believe that if the white American businessman will not give full employment, then the means of production should be taken from the businessmen and placed in the community so that the people of the community can organize and employ all of its people and give a high standard of living.

3. We want an end to the robbery by the CAPITALIST of our Black Community.

We believe that this racist government has robbed us and now we are demanding the overdue debt of forty acres and two mules. Forty acres and two mules was promised 100 years ago as restitution for slave labor and mass murder of black people. We will accept the payment in currency which will be distributed to our many communities. The Germans are now aiding the Jews in Israel for the genocide of the Jewish people. The Germans murdered six million Jews. The American racist has taken part in the slaughter of over fifty million black people, therefore, we feel that this is a modest demand that we make.

4. We want decent housing, fit for shelter of human beings.

We believe that if the white landlords will not give decent housing to our black community, then the housing and the land should be made into cooperatives so that our community, with government aid, can build and make decent housing for its people.

5. We want education for our people that exposes the true nature of this decadent American society. We want education that teaches us our true history and our role in the present-day society.

We believe in an educational system that will give to our people a knowledge of self. If a man does not have knowledge of himself and his position in society and the world, then he has little chance to relate to anything else.

We believe that Black people should not be forced to fight in the military service to defend a racist government that does not protect us. We will not fight and kill other people of color in the world who, like black people, are being victimized by the white racist government of America. We will protect ourselves from the force and violence of the racist police and the racist military, by whatever means necessary.

6. We want all black men to be exempt from military service.

7. We want an immediate end to POLICE BRUTALITY and MURDER of black people.

We believe we can end police brutality in our black community by organizing black self-defense groups that are dedicated to defending our black community from racist police oppression and brutality. The Second Amendment to the Constitution of the United States gives a right to bear arms. We therefore believe that all black people should arm themselves for self-defense.

8. We want freedom for all black men held in federal, state, county and city prisons and jails.

We believe that all black people should be released from the many jails and prisons because they have not received a fair and impartial trial.

9. We want all black people when brought to trial to be tried in court by a jury of their peer group or people from their black communities, as defined by the constitution of the United States.

We believe that the courts should follow the United States Constitution so that black people will receive fair trials. The 14th Amendment of the U.S. Constitution gives a man a right to be tried by his peer group. A peer is a person from a similar economic, social, religious, geographical, environmental, historical and racial background. To do this the court will be forced to select a jury from the black community from which the black defendant came. We have been, and are being tried by all-white juries that have no understanding of the "average reasoning man" of the black community.

10. We want land, bread, housing, education, clothing, justice and peace. And as our major political objective, a United Nations-supervised plebiscite to be held throughout the black colony in which only black colonial subjects will be allowed to participate, for the purpose of determining the will of black people as to their national destiny.

When, in the course of human events, it becomes necessary for one people to dissolve the political bands which have connected them with another, and to assume, among the powers of the earth, the separate and equal station to which the laws of nature and nature's God entitle them, a decent respect to the opinions of mankind requires that they should declare the causes which impel them to the separation. We hold these truths to be self-evident, that all men are created equal; that they are endowed by their Creator with certain inalienable rights; that among these are life, liberty, and the pursuit of happiness. *That, to secure these rights, governments are instituted among men, deriving their just powers from the consent of the governed; that, whenever any form of government becomes destructive of these ends, it is the right of the people to alter or to abolish it, and to institute a new government, laying its foundation on such principles, and organizing its powers in such form, as to them shall seem most likely to effect their safety and happiness.* Prudence, indeed, will dictate that governments long established should not be changed for light and transient causes; and, accordingly, all experience hath shown, that mankind are more disposed to suffer, while evils are sufferable, than to right themselves by abolishing the forms to which they are accustomed. *But, when a long train of abuses and usurpations, pursuing invariably the same object, evinces a design to reduce them under absolute despotism, it is their right, it is their duty, to throw off such government, and to provide new guards for their future security.*

27. The Report of the National Advisory Commission on Civil Disorders

February 29, 1968

The summer of 1967 again brought racial disorders to American cities, and with them shock, fear, and bewilderment to the Nation.

The worst came during a 2-week period in July, first in Newark and then in Detroit. Each set off a chain reaction in neighboring communities.

On July 28, 1967, the President of the United States established this Commission and directed us to answer three basic questions:

What happened?

Why did it happen?

What can be done to prevent it from happening again?

To respond to these questions, we have undertaken a broad range of studies and investigations. We have visited the riot cities; we have heard many witnesses; we have sought the counsel of experts across the country.

This is our basic conclusion: Our Nation is moving toward two societies, one black, one white—separate and unequal.

Reaction to last summer's disorders has quickened the movement and deepened the division. Discrimination and segregation have long permeated much of American life; they now threaten the future of every American.

This deepening racial division is not inevitable. The movement apart can be reversed. Choice is still possible. Our principal task is to define that choice and to press for a national resolution.

To pursue our present course will involve the continuing polarization of the American community and, ultimately, the destruction of basic democratic values.

The alternative is not blind repression or capitulation to lawlessness. It is the realization of common opportunities for all within a single society.

This alternative will require a commitment to national action—compassionate, massive, and sustained, backed by the resources of the most powerful and the richest nation on this earth. From every American it will require new attitudes, new understanding, and, above all, new will.

The vital needs of the Nation must be met; hard choices must be made, and, if necessary, new taxes enacted.

Violence cannot build a better society. Disruption and disorder nourish repression, not justice. They strike at the freedom of every citizen. The community cannot—it will not—tolerate coercion and mob rule.

Violence and destruction must be ended—in the streets of the ghetto and in the lives of people.

Segregation and poverty have created in the racial ghetto a destructive environment totally unknown to most white Americans.

What white Americans have never fully understood—but what the Negro can never forget—is that white society is deeply implicated in the ghetto. White institutions created it, white institutions maintain it, and white society condones it.

It is time now to turn with all the purpose at our command to the major unfinished business of this Nation. It is time to adopt strategies for action that will produce quick and visible progress. It is time to make good the promises of American democracy to all citizens—urban and rural, white and black, Spanish-surname, American Indian, and every minority group.

Our recommendations embrace three basic principles:

To mount programs on a scale equal to the dimension of the problems;

To aim these programs for high impact in the immediate future in order to close the gap between promise and performance;

To undertake new initiatives and experiments that can change the system of failure and frustration that now dominates the ghetto and weakens our society.

These programs will require unprecedented levels of funding and performance, but they neither probe deeper nor demand more than the problems which called them forth. There can be no higher priority for national action and no higher claim on the Nation's conscience.

We issue this report now, 5 months before the date called for by the President. Much remains that can be learned. Continued study is essential.

As Commissioners we have worked together with a sense of the greatest urgency and have sought to compose whatever differences exist among us. Some differences remain. But the gravity of the problem and the pressing need for action are too clear to allow further delay in the issuance of this report . . .

The "typical" riot did not take place. The disorders of 1967 were unusual, irregular, complex, and unpredictable social processes. Like most human events, they did not unfold in an orderly sequence . . .

The President directed the Commission to investigate "to what extent, if any, there has been planning or organization in any of the riots." . . .

On the basis of all the information collected, the Commission concludes that:

The urban disorders of the summer of 1967 were not caused by, nor were they the consequence of, any organized plan or "conspiracy." . . .

In addressing the question "Why did it happen?" we shift our focus from the local to the national scene, from the particular events of the summer of 1967 to the factors within the society at large that created a mood of violence among many urban Negroes.

These factors are complex and interacting; they vary significantly in their effect from city to city and from year to year; and the consequences of one disorder, generating new grievances and new demands, become the causes of the next. Thus was created the "thicket of tension, conflicting evidence, and extreme opinions" cited by the President.

Despite these complexities, certain fundamental matters are clear. Of these, the most fundamental is the racial attitude and behavior of white Americans toward black Americans.

Race prejudice has shaped our history decisively; it now threatens to affect our future.

White racism is essentially responsible for the explosive mixture which has been accumulating in our cities since the end of World War II . . .

The causes of recent racial disorders are embedded in a tangle of issues and circumstances—social, economic, political, and psychological—which arise out of the historic pattern of Negro-white relations in America . . .

We describe the Negro's experience in America and the development of slavery as an institution. We show his persistent striving for equality in the face of rigidly maintained social, economic, and educational barriers, and repeated mob violence. We portray the ebb and flow of the doctrinal tides—accommodation, separatism, and self-help—and their relationship to the current theme of Black Power. We conclude:

The Black Power advocates of today consciously feel that they are the most militant group in the Negro protest movement. Yet they have retreated from a direct confrontation with American society on the issue of integration and, by preaching separatism, unconsciously function as an accommodation to white racism. Much of their economic program, as well as their interest in Negro history, self-help, racial solidarity and separation, is reminiscent of Booker T. Washington. The rhetoric is different, but the ideas are remarkably similar . . .

Although there have been gains in Negro income nationally, and a decline in the number of Negroes below the "poverty level," the condition of Negroes in the central city remains in a state of crisis. Between 2 and 2.5 million Negroes—16 to 20 percent—of the total Negro population of all central cities—live in squalor and deprivation in ghetto neighborhoods.

Employment is a key problem. It not only controls the present for the Negro American but, in a most profound way, it is creating the future as well. Yet, despite continuing economic growth and declining national unemployment rates, the unemployment rate for Negroes in 1967 was more than double that for whites . . .

A striking difference in environment from that of white, middle-class Americans profoundly influences the lives of residents of the ghetto . . .

Today, whites tend to exaggerate how well and quickly they escaped from poverty. The fact is that immigrants who came from rural backgrounds, as many Negroes do, are only now, after three generations, finally beginning to move into the middle class.

By contrast, Negroes began concentrating in the city less than two generations ago, and under much less favorable conditions. Although some Negroes have escaped poverty, few have been able to escape the urban ghetto . . .

One of the first witnesses to be invited to appear before this Commission was Dr. Kenneth B. Clark, a distinguished and perceptive scholar. Referring to the reports of earlier riot commissions, he said:

I read that report . . . of the 1919 riot in Chicago, and it is as if I were reading the report of the investigating committee on the Harlem riot of '35, the report of the investigating committee on the Harlem riot of '43, the report of the McCone Commission on the Watts riot.

I must again in candor say to you members of this Commission—it is a kind of Alice in Wonderland—with the same moving picture reshown over and over again, the same analysis, the same recommendations, and the same inaction.

These words come to our minds as we conclude this report.

We have provided an honest beginning. We have learned much. But we have uncovered no startling truths, no unique insights, no simple solutions. The destruction and the bitterness of racial disorder, the harsh polemics of black revolt and white repression have been seen and heard before in this country.

It is time now to end the destruction and the violence, not only in the streets of the ghetto but in the lives of people.

28. The Civil Rights Act of 1968, Provision for Open Housing

April 11, 1968
Discrimination in the Sale or Rental of Housing

Sec. 804. As made applicable by section 803 and except as exempted by sections 803(b) and 807, it shall be unlawful—

(a) To refuse to sell or rent after the making of a bona fide offer, or to refuse to negotiate for the sale or rental of, or otherwise made unavailable or deny, a dwelling to any person because of race, color, religion, or national origin.

(b) To discriminate against any person in the terms, conditions, or privileges of sale or rental of a dwelling, or in the provision of services or facilities in connection therewith, because of race, color, religion, or national origin.

(c) To make, print, or publish or cause to be made, printed, or published any notice, statement, or advertisement, with respect to the sale or rental of a dwelling that indicates any preference, limitation, or discrimination based on race, color, religion, or national origin, or an intention to make any such preference, limitation, or discrimination.

(d) To represent to any person because of race, color, religion, or national origin that any dwelling is not available for inspection, sale, or rental when such dwelling is in fact so available.

(e) For profit, to induce or attempt to induce any person to sell or rent any dwelling by representations regarding the entry or prospective entry into the neighborhood of a person or persons of a particular race, color, religion, or national origin.

29. James E. Swann et al v. Charlotte-Mecklenburg Board of Education et al.

Decided April 20, 1971
Mr. Chief Justice Burger delivered the opinion of the Court . . .

This case and those argued with it arose in States having a long history of maintaining two sets of schools in a single school system deliberately operated to carry out a governmental policy to separate pupils in schools solely on the basis of race. That was what *Brown* v. *Board of Education* was all about. These cases present us with the problem of defining in more precise terms than heretofore the scope of the duty of school authorities and district courts in implementing *Brown I* and the mandate to eliminate dual systems and establish unitary systems at once . . .

Nearly 17 years ago this Court held, in explicit terms, that state-imposed segregation by race in public schools denies equal protection of the laws. At no time has the Court deviated in the slightest degree from that holding or its constitutional underpinnings . . .

Over the 16 years since *Brown II*, many difficulties were encountered in implementation of the basic constitutional requirement that the State not discriminate between public school children on the basis of their race. Nothing in our national experience prior to 1955 prepared anyone for dealing with changes and adjustments of the magnitude and complexity encountered since then. Deliberate resistance of some to the Court's mandates has impeded the good-faith efforts of others to bring school systems into compliance. The detail and nature of these dilatory tactics have been noted frequently by this Court and other courts . . .

The central issue in this case is that of student assignment, and there are essentially four problem areas:

(1) to what extent racial balance or racial quotas may be used as an implement in a remedial order to correct a previously segregated system;
(2) whether every all-Negro and all-white school must be eliminated as an indispensable part of a remedial process of desegregation;
(3) what the limits are, if any, on the rearrangement of school districts and attendance zones, as a remedial measure; and
(4) what the limits are, if any, on the use of transportation facilities to correct state-enforced racial school segregation.

. . . We see therefore that the use made of mathematical ratios was no more than a starting point in the process of shaping a remedy, rather than an inflexible requirement. From that starting point the District Court proceeded to frame a decree that was within its discretionary powers, as an equitable remedy for the particular circumstances . . . A school authority's remedial plan or a district court's remedial decree is to be judged by its effectiveness. Awareness of the racial composition of the whole school system is likely to be a useful starting point in shaping a remedy to correct past constitutional violations. In sum, the very limited use made of mathematical ratios was within the equitable remedial discretion of the District Court . . .

The importance of bus transportation as a normal and accepted tool of educational policy is readily discernible . . . The District Court's conclusion that assignment of children to the school nearest their home serving their grade would not produce an effective dismantling of the dual system is supported by the record.

Thus the remedial techniques used in the District Court's order were within that court's power to provide equitable relief; implementation of the decree is well within the capacity of the school authority.

The decree provided that the buses used to implement the plan would operate on direct routes. Students would be picked up at schools near their homes and transported to the schools they were to attend. The trips for elementary school pupils average about seven miles and the District Court found that they would take "not over 35 minutes at the most." . . . In these circumstances, we find no basis for holding that the local school authorities may not be required to employ bus transportation as one tool of school desegregation. Desegregation plans cannot be limited to the walk-in school.

An objection to transportation of students may have validity when the time or distance of travel is so great as to either risk the health of the children or significantly impinge on the educational process . . . It hardly needs stating that the limits on time of travel will vary with many factors, but probably with none more than the age of the students. The reconciliation of competing values in a desegregation case is, of course, a difficult task with many sensitive facets but fundamentally no more so than remedial measures courts of equity have traditionally employed.

. . . On the facts of this case, we are unable to conclude that the order of the District Court is not reasonable, feasible and workable . . .

At some point, these school authorities and others like them should have achieved full compliance with this Court's decision in *Brown I* . . .

It does not follow that the communities served by such systems will remain demographically stable, for in a growing, mobile society, few will do so. Neither school authorities nor district courts are constitutionally required to make year-by-year adjustments of the racial composition of student bodies once the affirmative duty to desegregate has been accomplished and racial discrimination through official action is eliminated from the system. This does not mean that federal courts are without power to deal with future problems; but in the absence of a showing that either the school authorities or some other agency of the State has deliberately attempted to fix or alter demographic patterns to affect the racial composition of the schools, further intervention by a district court should not be necessary.

30. The Civil Rights Act of 1991

November 21, 1991
Be it enacted by the Senate and House of Representatives of the United States of America in Congress assembled,

SECTION 1. SHORT TITLE.
This Act may be cited as the "Civil Rights Act of 1991."

SEC. 2. FINDINGS.
The Congress finds that—
(1) additional remedies under Federal law are needed to deter unlawful harassment and intentional discrimination in the workplace;
(2) the decision of the Supreme Court in Wards Cove Packing Co. v. Atonio, 490 U.S. 642 (1989) has weakened the scope and effectiveness of Federal civil rights protections; and
(3) legislation is necessary to provide additional protections against unlawful discrimination in employment.

SEC. 3. PURPOSES.
The purposes of this Act are—
(1) to provide appropriate remedies for intentional discrimination and unlawful harassment in the workplace;
(2) to codify the concepts of "business necessity" and "job related" enunciated by the Supreme Court in Griggs v. Duke Power Co., 401 U.S. 424 (1971), and in the other Supreme Court decisions prior to Wards Cove Packing Co. v. Atonio, 490 U.S. 642 (1989);
(3) to confirm statutory authority and provide statutory guidelines for the adjudication of disparate impact suits under title VII of the Civil Rights Act of 1964 (42 U.S.C. 2000e et seq.); and
(4) to respond to recent decisions of the Supreme Court by expanding the scope of relevant civil rights statutes in order to provide adequate protection to victims of discrimination.

TITLE I—FEDERAL CIVIL RIGHTS REMEDIES

SEC. 101. PROHIBITION AGAINST ALL RACIAL DISCRIMINATION IN THE MAKING AND ENFORCEMENT OF CONTRACTS.
Section 1977 of the Revised Statutes (42 U.S.C. 1981) is amended—
(1) by inserting "(a)" before "All persons within"; and
(2) by adding at the end the following new subsections:
"(b) For purposes of this section, the term 'make and enforce contracts' includes the making, performance, modification, and termination of contracts, and the enjoyment of all benefits, privileges, terms, and conditions of the contractual relationship.

"(c) The rights protected by this section are protected against impairment by nongovernmental discrimination and impairment under color of State law."

SEC. 102. DAMAGES IN CASES OF INTENTIONAL DISCRIMINATION.
The Revised Statutes are amended by inserting after section 1977 (42 U.S.C. 1981) the following new section:

"SEC. 1977A. DAMAGES IN CASES OF INTENTIONAL DISCRIMINATION IN EMPLOYMENT.
"(a) Right of Recovery.—
"(1) Civil Rights.—In an action brought by a complaining party under section 706 or 717 of the Civil Rights Act of 1964 (42 U.S.C. 2000e-5) against a respondent who engaged in unlawful intentional discrimination (not an employment practice that is unlawful because of its disparate impact) prohibited under section 703, 704, or 717 of the Act (42 U.S.C. 2000e-2 or 2000e-3), and provided that the complaining party cannot recover under section 1977 of the Revised Statutes (42 U.S.C. 1981), the complaining party may recover compensatory and punitive damages as allowed in subsection (b), in addition to any relief authorized by section 706(g) of the Civil Rights Act of 1964, from the respondent.
"(2) Disability.—In an action brought by a complaining party under the powers, remedies, and procedures set forth in section 706 or 717 of the Civil Rights Act of 1964 (as provided in section 107(a) of the Americans with Disabilities Act of 1990 (42 U.S.C. 12117(a)), and section 505(a)(1) of the Rehabilitation Act of 1973 (29 U.S.C. 794a(a)(1)), respectively) against a respondent who engaged in unlawful intentional discrimination (not an employment practice that is unlawful because of its disparate impact) under section 501 of the Rehabilitation Act of 1973 (29 U.S.C. 791) and the regulations implementing section 501, or who violated the requirements of section 501 of the Act or the regulations implementing section 501 concerning the provision of a reasonable accommodation, or section 102 of the Americans with Disabilities Act of 1990 (42 U.S.C. 12112), or committed a violation of section 102(b)(5) of the Act, against an individual, the complaining party may recover compensatory and punitive damages as allowed in subsection (b), in addition to any relief authorized by section 706(g) of the Civil Rights Act of 1964, from the respondent.

"(3) Reasonable accommodation and good faith effort.—In cases where a discriminatory practice involves the provision of a reasonable accommodation pursuant to section 102(b)(5) of the Americans with Disabilities Act of 1990 or regulations implementing section 501 of the Rehabilitation Act of 1973, damages may not be awarded under this section where the covered entity demonstrates good faith efforts, in consultation with the person with the disability who has informed the covered entity that accommodation is needed, to identify and make a reasonable accommodation that would provide such individual with an equally effective opportunity and would not cause an undue hardship on the operation of the business.

"(b) Compensatory and Punitive Damages.—

"(1) Determination of punitive damages.—A complaining party may recover punitive damages under this section against a respondent (other than a government, government agency or political subdivision) if the complaining party demonstrates that the respondent engaged in a discriminatory practice or discriminatory practices with malice or with reckless indifference to the federally protected rights of an aggrieved individual.

"(2) Exclusions from compensatory damages.—Compensatory damages awarded under this section shall not include backpay, interest on backpay, or any other type of relief authorized under section 706(g) of the Civil Rights Act of 1964.

"(3) Limitations.—The sum of the amount of compensatory damages awarded under this section for future pecuniary losses, emotional pain, suffering, inconvenience, mental anguish, loss of enjoyment of life, and other nonpecuniary losses, and the amount of punitive damages awarded under this section, shall not exceed, for each complaining party—

"(A) in the case of a respondent who has more than 14 and fewer than 101 employees in each of 20 or more calendar weeks in the current or preceding calendar year, $50,000;

"(B) in the case of a respondent who has more than 100 and fewer than 201 employees in each of 20 or more calendar weeks in the current or preceding calendar year, $100,000; and

"(C) in the case of a respondent who has more than 200 and fewer than 501 employees in each of 20 or more calendar weeks in the current or preceding calendar year, $200,000; and

"(D) in the case of a respondent who has more than 500 employees in each of 20 or more calendar weeks in the current or preceding calendar year, $300,000.

"(4) Construction.—Nothing in this section shall be construed to limit the scope of, or the relief available under, section 1977 of the Revised Statutes (42 U.S.C. 1981).

"(c) Jury Trial.—If a complaining party seeks compensatory or punitive damages under this section—

"(1) any party may demand a trial by jury; and

"(2) the court shall not inform the jury of the limitations described in subsection (b)(3) . . .

SEC. 106. PROHIBITION AGAINST DISCRIMINATORY USE OF TEST SCORES.

Section 703 of the Civil Rights Act of 1964 (42 U.S.C. 2000e-2) (as amended by section 105) is further amended by adding at the end the following new subsection:

"(1) It shall be an unlawful employment practice for a respondent, in connection with the selection or referral of applicants or candidates for employment or promotion, to adjust the scores of, use different cutoff scores for, or otherwise alter the results of, employment related tests on the basis of race, color, religion, sex, or national origin." . . .

SEC. 110. TECHNICAL ASSISTANCE TRAINING INSTITUTE.

(a) Technical Assistance.—Section 705 of the Civil Rights Act of 1964 (42 U.S.C. 2000e-4) is amended by adding at the end the following new subsection:

"(j)(1) The Commission shall establish a Technical Assistance Training Institute, through which the Commission shall provide technical assistance and training regarding the laws and regulations enforced by the Commission.

"(2) An employer or other entity covered under this title shall not be excused from compliance with the requirements of this title because of any failure to receive technical assistance under this subsection.

"(3) There are authorized to be appropriated to carry out this subsection such sums as may be necessary for fiscal year 1992."

(b) Effective Date.—The amendment made by this section shall take effect on the date of the enactment of this Act . . .

TITLE II—GLASS CEILING

SEC. 201. SHORT TITLE.

This title may be cited as the "Glass Ceiling Act of 1991".

SEC. 202. FINDINGS AND PURPOSE.

(a) Findings.—Congress finds that—

(1) despite a dramatically growing presence in the workplace, women and minorities remain underrepresented in management and decisionmaking positions in business;

(2) artificial barriers exist to the advancement of women and minorities in the workplace;

(3) United States corporations are increasingly relying on women and minorities to meet employment requirements and are increasingly aware of the advantages derived from a diverse work force;

(4) the "Glass Ceiling Initiative" undertaken by the Department of Labor, including the release of the report entitled "Report on the Glass Ceiling Initiative", has been instrumental in raising public awareness of—

(A) the underrepresentation of women and minorities at the management and decisionmaking levels in the United States work force;

(B) the underrepresentation of women and minorities in line functions in the United States work force;

(C) the lack of access for qualified women and minorities to credential-building developmental opportunities; and

(D) the desirability of eliminating artificial barriers to the advancement of women and minorities to such levels;

(5) the establishment of a commission to examine issues raised by the Glass Ceiling Initiative would help—

(A) focus greater attention on the importance of eliminating artificial barriers to the advancement of women and minorities to management and decisionmaking positions in business; and

(B) promote work force diversity;

(6) a comprehensive study that includes analysis of the manner in which management and decisionmaking positions are filled, the developmental and skill-enhancing practices used to foster the necessary qualifications for advancement, and the compensation programs and reward structures utilized in the corporate sector would assist in the establishment of practices and policies promoting opportunities for, and eliminating artificial barriers to, the advancement of women and minorities to management and decisionmaking positions; and

(7) a national award recognizing employers whose practices and policies promote opportunities for, and eliminate artificial barriers to, the advancement of women and minorities will foster the advancement of women and minorities into higher level positions by—

(A) helping to encourage United States companies to modify practices and policies to promote opportunities for, and eliminate artificial barriers to, the upward mobility of women and minorities; and

(B) providing specific guidance for other United States employers that wish to learn how to revise practices and policies to improve the access and employment opportunities of women and minorities.

(b) Purpose.—The purpose of this title is to establish—

(1) a Glass Ceiling Commission to study—

(A) the manner in which business fills management and decisionmaking positions;

(B) the developmental and skill-enhancing practices used to foster the necessary qualifications for advancement into such positions; and

(C) the compensation programs and reward structures currently utilized in the workplace; and

(2) an annual award for excellence in promoting a more diverse skilled work force at the management and decisionmaking levels in business . . .

Appendix B
Biographies of Major Personalities

Abernathy, Ralph David (1926–1990)   Civil rights leader and a founder of the Southern Christian Leadership Conference (SCLC). Abernathy was one of Martin Luther King Jr.'s most trusted confidants and was with him when he was assassinated in Memphis on April 4, 1968. Born in Linden, Alabama, Abernathy, whose grandfather was a slave, was ordained a Baptist minister in 1948 and received a B.S. degree from Alabama State College in 1950 and an M.A. degree from Atlanta University in 1951. Soon thereafter, he met Martin Luther King Jr. and both became good friends while they were presiding over Baptist congregations in Montgomery, Alabama. Abernathy and King gained national prominence during the successful Montgomery bus boycott of 1955–1956. From this victory, Abernathy and King moved to mobilize the forces of black protest by forming the Southern Christian Leadership Conference (SCLC) in 1957, with King as its president and Abernathy as secretary-treasurer. The SCLC soon became the leading proponent of nonviolent direct action. As leaders of the SCLC, Abernathy and King frequently participated jointly in marches and demonstrations and went to jail together. Following King's assassination in April 1968, Abernathy assumed the presidency of the SCLC. He led the Poor People's Campaign on Washington, D.C. in the spring of 1968 and later organized SCLC's Operation Breadbasket, in which economic pressure by means of selective buying was brought against companies that had refused equal opportunities to blacks. He resigned from the SCLC in 1977 to run for the Atlanta seat in the U.S. House of Representatives that had been vacated by Andrew Young. After losing the election, Abernathy returned to serve as pastor of Atlanta's West Hunter Street Baptist Church. Abernathy's autobiography, *And The Walls Came Tumbling Down*, was published in 1989.

Ashmore, Harry Scott (1916–1998)   Executive editor of the *Arkansas Gazette*, 1948–1959. Ashmore won a Pulitzer Prize in 1958 for his editorials that gave support to integrating Little Rock's Central High school. In 1957, under Ashmore's direction, the *Gazette* denounced Arkansas Governor Orval E. Faubus for sending National Guardsmen to Little Rock to prevent nine black children from integrating Central High School and endorsed President Eisenhower's dispatch of federal troops to enforce the implementation of the court order desegregating the school. Born in Greenville, South Carolina, Ashmore began his journalism career with the Greenville *Piedmont*, and following wartime service, he was named associate editor of the Charlotte (N.C.) *News*, where he wrote editorials that advocated racial tolerance and the enfranchisement of blacks. In 1948 he became executive editor of the *Arkansas Gazette* and remained in that position until 1959, when he resigned to become director of the newly founded Center for the Study of Democratic Institutions. In 1967, on behalf of the center and with the authorization of the State Department, Ashmore and *Miami News* editor William C. Baggs visited North Vietnam. They had a rare two-hour talk with President Ho Chi Minh, who expressed a willingness to sit down to peace talks in return for the cessation of American raids on North Vietnam. The following year, he and Baggs published the book, *Mission to Hanoi*, which described their meeting with the North Vietnamese president and how their subsequent peace efforts were rebuffed by Washington. He is the author of several books, including *An Epitaph for Dixie* (1958) and *The Anatomy of Racism: From Roosevelt to Reagan* (1982).

Baker, Ella (1903–1986)   Civil rights activist. Born in Virginia, at the age of seven she moved with her

305

family to Littleton, South Carolina, where they settled on her grandparent's farm—land her grandparents had worked as slaves. She graduated from Shaw University in Raleigh in 1927 and by 1932 had become national director of the Young Negroes Cooperative League, a branch of the Works Progress Administration (WPA). In 1938 Baker became field secretary in the South with the National Association for the Advancement of Colored People (NAACP) and became president of the Manhattan NAACP in 1954. In the late 1950s, she returned to the South and joined the Southern Christian Leadership Conference (SCLC). In February 1960, Baker organized a youth leadership meeting for Easter weekend at her alma mater. Hundreds of black students attended, and out of this conference the Student Nonviolent Coordinating Committee (SNCC) emerged. Shortly thereafter, she quit the SCLC and became a key adviser to SNCC. During the struggle for voting rights in the South, she remained at the core of the movement, delivering a keynote address at the 1964 Jackson convention of the Mississippi Freedom Democratic Party (MFDP). She remained active well into the 1970s, and although then in her 70s and 80s, she campaigned for liberation in Africa, struggled against racial intolerance in America and worked for many organizations, especially in Harlem. In 1980 New York City held a tribute to Ella Baker, who was a source of wisdom for veteran civil rights activists and an inspiration for young people.

Barnett, Ida Wells　See WELLS-BARNETT, IDA BELL.

Barnett, Ross Robert (1898–1987) Governor of Mississippi, 1960–1963. As an ardent segregationist, Ross attempted to block the registration of James Meredith, a black student, at the University of Mississippi in September 1962. A federal district court had directed the University of Mississippi to admit Meredith, but Barnett vowed that no black person would attend the state's most prestigious white college. On September 30, after negotiations between federal and state officials failed, President Kennedy sent in federal troops to insure the safe enrollment of James Meredith. That evening, a riot ensued on the campus, and federal marshals, reinforced by the Army and federalized Mississippi National Guard troops, used tear gas to subdue a violent white mob. By night's end, two people were dead, including a French reporter, and nearly 200 people were arrested. The next day, Meredith, accompanied by federal marshals, successfully registered at the University of Mississippi. Born in Standing Pine, Mississippi, Barnett, the son of a Confederate veteran, graduated

from Mississippi College in 1922, graduated from the Mississippi School of Law in 1926 and soon thereafter went into private practice. After two unsuccessful attempts for the governorship of Mississippi in 1951 and 1955, Barnett, as a segregationist candidate and a member of the White Citizens' Council was elected in 1959. When violence broke out in Alabama in 1961 over protests against segregation on buses, he backed the Alabama authorities and jailed Freedom Riders entering Mississippi. When his term ended, Barnett returned to his private law practice. Barnett entered a 1967 Democratic gubernatorial primary, but he did not win the necessary amount of votes to qualify for the runoff.

Bates, Daisy Lee Gaston (1922–) Civil rights activist and president of the Arkansas NAACP, 1953–1961. Born in Huttig, Arkansas, Bates gained prominence in Little Rock, Arkansas when in 1941 she and her husband, news reporter C. L. Bates, organized what was to become one of the most widely read black weekly newspapers in the South, the *Arkansas State Press*. In 1957, as president of the Arkansas chapter of the National Association for the Advancement of Colored People (NAACP), Bates gained national recognition because of her active role in the effort to integrate Little Rock Central High School. She gave vital support to the nine black children who were to integrate the school, and in 1958 Bates and the "Little Rock Nine" were awarded the NAACP's Spingarn medal. She described her story in a book, *The Long Shadow of Little Rock* (1962). In 1972 Bates led an attack on President Nixon's decision to cut funds for economic opportunity programs in Mitcheville, Arkansas. She worked as publisher of the *Arkansas State Press* until she retired in 1987.

Bevel, James Luther (1936–) Civil rights activist and Southern Christian Leadership Conference (SCLC) organizer. Bevel was ordained a Baptist minister in 1959 and shortly thereafter became active in the civil rights movement. While studying at the American Baptist Theological Seminary in Nashville, he worked as an organizer for the Student Nonviolent Coordinating Committee (SNCC). In 1963 he joined the SCLC as Alabama's project coordinator. In April and May of 1963, Bevel helped organize the SCLC campaign to end segregation in Birmingham; in 1965 he helped direct the statewide drive to register black voters. The next year Bevel worked with the Mobilization to End the Vietnam War, and in 1967 he became head of the Spring Mobilization Committee to End the War in Vietnam. Returning to the SCLC in 1968, Bevel was one of the leaders of the Poor

People's Campaign in Washington. He subsequently worked as an aide for the late Ralph Abernathy, president of the SCLC. Bevel is now a church pastor in Chicago and works with the Nonviolent Human and Community Development Institute.

Blake, Eugene Carson (1906–1985) Civil rights activist; president, National Council of Churches of Christ in America, 1954–1957; executive director, Presbyterian Church in the U.S.A., 1951–1966; and general secretary, World Council of Churches, 1966–1972. Blake was one of the principal speakers at the March on Washington in August 1963. Born in St. Louis, Missouri, Blake graduated from Princeton in 1928 and from Princeton Theological Seminary in 1932. He held pastorates in New York City, Albany and Pasadena, California. During the 1950s, Blake publicly attacked McCarthyism for its infringement on human and civil rights. In the early 1960s, he sought interdenominational cooperation in support of the civil rights movement. During his tenure as the secretary-general of the World Council of Churches, he was an outspoken critic of the Vietnam War.

Bond, Horace Julian (1940–) Civil rights activist and communications director, Student Nonviolent Coordinating Committee (SNCC), 1961–1966. Bond was born in Nashville, Tennessee. While a student at Morehouse College in 1960, he cofounded the Committee on Appeal for Human Rights (COAHR), which organized a series of student sit-ins in Atlanta. In April 1960, he attended the conference at Shaw University (Raleigh, North Carolina) that formed the Student Nonviolent Coordinating Committee (SNCC), and in 1961, he became that organization's communications director. Bond edited its newspaper, *The Student Voice,* prepared radio and news releases for the press and supervised publicity for SNCC voter registration campaigns. Bond, as a Democrat, was elected to the Georgia State Assembly in 1965 but was barred by the legislature from taking office because of his opposition to the Vietnam War. As a result of a U.S. Supreme Court decision, Bond was seated by the Georgia house in January 1967. He was subsequently reelected several times to the Georgia Assembly, and in 1974 he was elected to the state senate. In 1986 Bond relinquished his state senate seat to run for representative of Georgia's Fifth Congressional District. He lost in the Democratic primary contest to John Lewis, a former chairman of SNCC who had been a longtime friend. Bond narrated the acclaimed PBS television documentary series produced by Henry Hampton, *Eyes on the Prize* (1987).

Since 1987, as a visiting professor, Bond has taught courses on the history of the civil rights movement at the University of Pennsylvania, Drexel University in Philadelphia, Harvard University, American University, Williams College and the University of Virginia. In 1998, he was named chairman of the NAACP.

Brown, Hubert Rap Geroid (1943–) Militant civil rights leader and chairman, Student Nonviolent Coordinating Committee (SNCC), 1967–1968. Brown grew up in Baton Rouge, Louisiana and enrolled at Southern University there in 1960. He withdrew from school in 1964, and after working for the Nonviolent Action Group (NAG), an affiliate of SNCC, he became an SNCC organizer in Greene County, Alabama in 1966. In 1967 Brown was elected as chairman of SNCC, replacing Stokely Carmichael. As SNCC chairman, Brown quickly captured the media's attention with his controversial remarks. He endorsed the ghetto riots and claimed that violence "is as American as cherry pie." In July 1967, he was arrested and later convicted for inciting to riot in Cambridge, Maryland. While released on bond pending his appeal, Brown served as the Black Panthers' minister of justice. In the spring of 1970, he was placed on the FBI's 10-most-wanted list after he failed to appear for trial. Brown was shot and captured by New York City police in 1971, and in 1973, he was found guilty of armed robbery in New York and was sentenced to a term of five to 15 years. Maryland dropped its riot charge against him after he pleaded to a lesser charge of failing to appear for trial in 1970. Brown was released from prison in 1977. He has since converted to the Black Muslim religion and is the head of a mosque in Atlanta, Georgia. He is the author of *Die Nigger Die* (1969).

Carmichael, Stokely [Kwame Ture] (1941–1998) Militant civil rights leader; chairman, Student Nonviolent Coordinating Committee (SNCC), 1966–1967; and prime minister, Black Panther Party, 1968–1969. Born in Trinidad, Carmichael came to the United States when he was 11. Raised in New York City, he attended the Bronx High School of Science and graduated from Howard University in 1964. In 1960 he joined the Congress of Racial Equality (CORE) in its efforts to integrate public accommodations in the South, and upon graduating from Howard, he joined the Student Nonviolent Coordinating Committee (SNCC). Carmichael became chairman of SNCC in 1966 and was instrumental in altering its orientation from peaceful integration to "black liberation." While leading the Meredith March Against Fear in Mississippi in June 1966, Carmichael coined the phrase "black power." He soon emerged as the foremost spokesman for the black power movement. Carmichael left SNCC in 1967 and briefly joined the Black Panther party. He resigned from the Black Panthers in July 1969, denouncing the organization for its "dogmatic" party line and its willingness to ally itself with white radicals. That same year, Carmichael and his wife, South African singer Mariam Makeba whom he married in 1968, moved to Guinea. He is the author of *Black Power: The Politics of Liberation in America* (1967), written with Charles V. Hamilton.

Carter, Robert Lee (1917–)　NAACP Legal Defense Fund attorney and federal judge. Carter received a B.A. degree from Lincoln University in 1937 and a law degree from Howard Law School in 1940. After serving in the Army Air Force, he joined the NAACP Legal Defense Fund in 1944. Carter was a member of Thurgood Marshall's staff and played a major role in several school desegregation cases, including *Brown v. Board of Education* (1954). By enlisting the support of sociologists and psychologists, among them Dr. Kenneth Clark, he presented to the Court evidence that suggested segregation causes irreparable damage to black children. In 1972 he was appointed a judge of the U.S. District Court for the Southern District of New York.

Chaney, James Earl (1943–1964)　Civil rights activist. One of the three civil rights workers killed by the Ku Klux Klan in Mississippi in June 1964. Born in Meridian, Mississippi, Chaney attended Harris Junior College, and in 1963, he became a CORE (Congress of Racial Equality) worker in Meridian. In January 1964, he helped Michael Schwerner and his wife, Rita, both CORE workers, open a field office in Meridian. Chaney and Schwerner attended the training session for Mississippi Freedom Summer Project volunteers at Western College for Women, Oxford, Ohio in early June 1964. At the conference, the two young men met Andrew Goodman, a volunteer from New York, and invited him to join the Meridian field office. On June 21, 1964, while driving back to Meridian after inspecting a torched black church in Philadelphia, Mississippi, Chaney, Goodman and Schwerner were pulled over by Deputy Sheriff Cecil Price and two carloads of Klansmen. The three young men were murdered, and their bodies were deposited at a nearby farm where an earthen dam was under construction. The disappearance of the civil rights workers sent shock waves throughout the nation, and within days the FBI began the biggest investigation ever conducted in Mississippi. An anonymous informer revealed the location of the bodies, and on August 4, 1964, the FBI uncovered the decomposed bodies of Chaney, Goodman and Schwerner. In December 1964, the FBI charged 21 men, most of them Klan members, including police officials, for conspiring to abduct and kill the three civil rights workers. In 1967 seven Klansmen, including Deputy Price, were found guilty of federal civil rights violations in the deaths of Chaney, Goodman and Schwerner. They were sentenced to prison terms ranging from three to ten years. The name of James Earl Chaney is one of 40 names engraved on the Civil Rights Memorial in Montgomery, Alabama.

Chisholm, Shirley Anita (1924–)　State legislator, U.S. congresswoman and educator. In 1968, Chisholm became the first black woman ever elected to the U.S. Congress. She was born and raised in the Bedford-Stuyvesant section of Brooklyn (the constituency that eventually elected her to Congress). Chisholm received a B.A. degree from Brooklyn College of the City of New York in 1946, and she received her M.A. degree from Columbia University in 1952. From 1946 until 1963 she worked in the day care and educational field and then in 1964 she began her political career as a member of the assembly in the New York state legislature. Chisholm was elected to Congress as a Democrat in 1968 and was subsequently reelected to several terms. In 1972, she ran in the New York Democratic primary for president of the United States, and although she lost, she had established another first for a black woman. Chisholm retired from Congress in 1982 and became a professor at Mount Holyoke College in Massachusetts, where she taught politics and womens studies until 1989. In 1993, citing failing eyesight, she declined President Clinton's offer of the ambassadorship to Jamaica.

Clark, Dr. Kenneth Bancroft (1914–)　Educator and psychologist. Born in the Panama Canal Zone, Clark earned a B.A. degree (1935) and an M.S. degree (1936) from Howard University and his Ph.D. degree from Columbia University in 1940. In 1939 and 1940, Clark and his wife, Mamie Philips, tested black children in Washington, D.C. and New York City to determine how children perceived themselves. Their black and white doll test revealed that the Washington students, who attended segregated schools, had lower self-esteem than the black children from New York's integrated schools. A study of their research was published in the *Journal of Experimental Education* in the spring of 1940. Fourteen years later, their doll test would become important evidence against segregation in *Brown v. Board of Education* (1954). Clark taught at the City University of New York from 1942 to 1975. He received the NAACP's Spingarn medal in 1961. He is the author of several books, including *Desegregation: An Appraisal of the Evidence* (1953), *Prejudice and Your Child* (1955) and *Dark Ghetto* (1965).

Connor, (Theophilus) Eugene Bull (1897–1973) Birmingham, Alabama commissioner of public safety, 1937–1953 and 1957–1963. As Birmingham's police chief in the early 1960s, Connor symbolized the harsh segregationist police officer of the Deep South—setting dogs on black demonstrators and ordering his men to use fire hoses to disperse crowds. Born in Selma, Alabama, Connor acquired a large following as a radio sports broadcaster in Birmingham in the 1920s and became known as "Bull" because of his deep voice. Elected to the state legislature for one term in the mid-1930s, he then won four consecutive terms as Birmingham's commissioner of public safety, serving from 1937 to 1953. He held that post again from 1957 to 1963. In the spring of 1962, during a series of publicized civil rights demonstrations led by Martin Luther King Jr. and Fred Shuttlesworth, Connor ordered his men to use dogs, nightsticks and pressure hoses against the protesters in an effort to crush their integration drive. Connor's strategy backfired. Responding to national and worldwide indignation against his tactics, the Kennedy administration exerted pressure on Birmingham's business community to negotiate with black leaders. In May 1963, Shuttlesworth and King announced an agreement that provided for the gradual desegregation of the city's major public accommodations and the hiring of blacks in some jobs previously held by whites. In 1964 Connor won a libel suit begun four years earlier against the *New York Times* over two articles that depicted him as a repressive force in Birmingham's racial politics. The judgment was ultimately overturned by the U.S. Supreme Court on freedom-of-the-press grounds.

Diggs, Charles Cole, Jr. (1922–1998)   Black United States congressman from Detroit, Michigan. Born in Detroit, Diggs studied at the University of Michigan for two years before transferring to Fisk University in 1942. He enlisted in the United States Army Air Corps in 1943 and rose to the rank of second lieutenant. After leaving the service in 1945, he was elected to the Michigan state legislature. In 1954 he became the first black in Michigan to be elected to the United States Congress, and he held his seat through 12 consecutive terms. In 1955 he traveled to Sumner, Mississippi to attend the trial of the two white men accused of killing Emmett Louis Till, a 14-year-old black boy from Chicago who had been visiting his relatives. That year, Diggs delivered a series of stirring speeches against racial discrimination in the South. He resigned from Congress in 1978 after he was convicted of improperly using his congressional office payroll. He left federal prison in 1981 and in 1983 became an undertaker in Maryland.

Doar, John (1921–) U.S. attorney for the civil rights division of the Department of Justice, 1960–1967. Born in Minneapolis, Doar received a B.A. degree from Princeton in 1944 and a law degree from the University of California at Berkeley in 1949. After practicing law in Wisconsin, he joined the civil rights division of the Justice Department in 1960, and in 1964, Doar became the assistant attorney general in charge of the division. He shepherded James Meredith through the first weeks at the University of Mississippi in 1962. Doar prosecuted several civil rights cases, including 30 Southern voting-rights cases and the murder of the three young civil rights workers, James Chaney, Andrew Goodman and Michael Schwerner, who were killed in Mississippi in June 1964. He was the government's chief representative during the 1965 Selma–to–Montgomery march for voting rights. Doar is now in private practice in New York City.

Douglass, Frederick A. (1818–1895) Abolitionist, journalist, orator, public official and often called the "father of the civil rights movement." He was born a slave in Tucahoe, Maryland. Sent to Baltimore in 1825 to be a house servant, he escaped 13 years later and settled in New Bedford, Massachusetts. A talent for public speaking led him into the organized abolitionist movement as an agent for the Massachusetts Anti-Slavery Society. In 1845 he published the *Narrative of the Life of Frederick Douglass,* a classic autobiographical account of his experiences as a slave. Two years later he founded the famous *North Star* newspaper in Rochester, New York. Through this, later called *Frederick Douglass' Paper,* he relentlessly fought slavery in the United States; he also lectured in Great Britain on slavery and its abolition. During the Civil War, he met with President Lincoln and assisted him in recruiting the celebrated 54th and 55th Massachusetts Negro regiments. In 1871, during the Reconstruction period, Douglass was appointed to the territorial legislature of the District of Columbia; in 1872 he served as one of the presidential electors-at-large for New York and, shortly thereafter, became secretary of the Santo Domingo Commission. In 1889 he was appointed by President Benjamin Harrison to the most important federal posts he was to hold—

minister resident and consul general to the Republic of Haiti and, later, chargé d'affairs for Santo Domingo. However, when he observed that Amerian businessmen were interested solely in exploiting Haiti, he resigned his post in 1891. Four years later he died at his home in Washington, D.C. In addition to his *Narrative* (1845), Douglass wrote two other autobiographies, *My Bondage and My Freedom* (1855) and *Life and Times of Frederick Douglass* (1881).

Du Bois, William Edward Burghardt (1868–1963) Historian, author, editor and a founder of the National Association for the Advancement of Colored People (NAACP). Du Bois is generally recognized as one of the foremost black intellectuals of the 20th century. Born in Great Barrington, Massachusetts, Du Bois received a bachelors degree from Fisk University in 1885 and went on to earn a second bachelors from Harvard College in 1890, graduating cum laude. After two years at the University of Berlin, he completed his dissertation at Harvard University and in 1895 received his Ph.D. degree, becoming the first American black to receive this degree from Harvard. He taught at Wilberforce University and the University of Pennsylvania before moving to Atlanta University to head the department of history and economics for 13 years. Here he wrote, for the *Atlanta Monthly, World's Work* and other magazines, articles that later were collected in *The Souls of Black Folk* (1903). One of the founders of the National Association for the Advancement of Colored People (NAACP) in 1909, Du Bois served as the organization's director of publications and editor of *Crisis* magazine until 1934. In 1944 he returned from Atlanta University to head the NAACP's special research department, a post he held until 1948. During the 1950s, he became involved in leftist causes and was subsequently shunned by his colleagues and harassed by federal agencies because of his alleged communist associations. In 1961 Du Bois immigrated to Ghana and became editor-in-chief of the *Encyclopedia Africana*, a compendium of information on Africans and peoples of African descent throughout the world. Shortly thereafter he joined the American Communist party and became a citizen of Ghana, where he died two years later at the age of 95.

Eastland, James O. (1904–1986) U.S. Senator from Mississippi, 1942–1978. Eastland was best known nationally as a symbol of Southern resistance to racial desegregation during most of his years in the Senate. Born in Doddsville, Mississippi, he attended the University of Mississippi, Vanderbilt University and the University of Alabama. After studying law, he was admitted to the Mississippi bar in 1927. A year later, at the age of 24, Eastland was elected to the state's house of representatives, serving there until 1932. After leaving the state legislature, he devoted his time to managing his huge cotton plantation but returned to politics when named to the U.S. Senate in 1942 to fill a vacancy created by the death of Senator Pat Harrison. In 1943, he was elected to the Senate and was subsequently reelected. Eastland became chairman of the Senate Judiciary Committee in 1956 and held that post until he retired from the Congress in 1978.

Elliot, Robert Brown (1842–1884) U.S. congressman during Reconstruction. Born in Boston, Massachusetts, Elliot studied law in England and moved to South Carolina after the Civil War. He was a member of the 1868 South Carolina constitutional convention and was twice elected in 1870 and 1872 to the U.S. House of Representatives. In 1872 Elliot was one of three blacks who addressed the Republican National Convention. Defeated in his bid for the Senate in 1872, he was then elected to the lower house of the state legislature and chosen speaker in 1875. In the post-Reconstruction period, Elliot resumed his law practice

Evers, Medgar Wiley (1925–1963) Civil rights leader. Born in Decatur, Mississippi, Evers graduated from Alcorn A & M College in 1952 and soon after joined the NAACP. In 1954 he became the NAACP's Mississippi field secretary. In his speeches, Evers spoke out against Mississippi's rigid system of school segregation, encouraged blacks to register to vote and advocated the boycotting of white merchants who discriminated against black workers and consumers. He became a symbol of leadership for the protection of the civil rights of blacks in the South and was a natural target for assassination by those who opposed them. On June 12, 1963, a few hours after President John F. Kennedy had delivered his strongest message on civil rights, Evers was killed outside his home from gunshots fired by Byron De La Beckwith, a charter member of the White Citizens' Council. As a World War II veteran, Medgar Evers was buried in Arlington National Cemetery on June 19, 1963. At the funeral, a military bugler played "Taps," and a crowd of 2,000 sang "We Shall Overcome." His death, which brought about new demonstrations and violence, was one of the factors that prompted President Kennedy to ask Congress to enact a comprehensive civil rights law. The life of Medgar Evers is described in *For Us the Living* (1967) by Myrlie Evers, the widow of the slain civil rights leader. The name of Medgar Evers is one of 40 names engraved on the Civil Rights Memorial in Montgomery, Alabama.

Farmer, James Leonard (1920–1999)   Civil rights leader and founder of the Congress of Racial Equality (CORE). Born in Marshall, Texas, Farmer earned a B.S. degree from Wiley College; he received a divinity degree in 1941 from Howard University but refused to be ordained when confronted with the fact that he would have to practice in a segregated ministry. In 1941 he accepted a post as race relations secretary of the Fellowship of Reconciliation, a pacifist group. The following year, he and a group of University of Chicago students organized CORE, the first American black protest organization that utilized the techniques of nonviolence and passive resistance advocated by the Indian revolutionary Mohandas Gandhi. In June 1943, CORE staged the first successful sit-in demonstration at a restaurant in the Chicago Loop. By 1944 CORE chapters had been formed in New York, Los Angeles, Philadelphia, Pittsburgh and Detroit. In 1961 Farmer became CORE's national director and soon after launched the Freedom Rides into the South, a protest that helped desegregate interstate transportation facilities. He served as cochairman of the 1963 March on Washington. Farmer left CORE in 1966 and for the next two years was a professor of social welfare at Lincoln University in Pennsylvania and an adjunct professor at New York University. He ran for the U.S. Congress in 1968 but was defeated by Shirley Chisholm. In 1969 President Richard M. Nixon appointed him assistant secretary of Health, Education and Welfare, a position he held until his resignation in 1970. During the 1970s Farmer gave lectures and for a while headed a "think tank" at Howard University. From 1977 until 1982 he was the executive director of the Coalition of American Public Employees in Washington, D.C. Farmer was a distinguished professor at Antioch University from 1983 until 1984, and from 1985 on was a visiting professor of history at Mary Washington College in Virginia. He was the author of *Freedom When* (1965) and an autobiography, *Lay Bare the Heart* (1985).

Faubus, Orval (1910–1994)   Governor of Arkansas, 1955–1967. In September 1957, Faubus attempted to block a federal court order to desegregate Central High School in Little Rock by having National Guard troops prevent nine black children from entering the building. His action precipitated a confrontation with President Eisenhower, who reluctantly dispatched federal troops to Little Rock to escort the nine black students into Central High. Following a 1958 Supreme Court decision, *Cooper v. Aaron*, that denied Faubus' claim that state officials have no duty to obey a federal court, he closed Little Rock's public schools. The schools remained closed throughout the 1958–59 academic year. Faubus also ran for governor in 1970, 1974 and 1986 but lost each time.

Forman, James (1929–)   Civil rights leader and executive secretary, Student Nonviolent Coordinating Committee (SNCC), 1961–1966. Born in Chicago, Forman graduated from Roosevelt University (Chicago, Ill.) with a degree in public administration and became a public school teacher in Chicago. In October 1961, he was elected to the post of executive secretary of SNCC. Forman participated in the demonstrations against segregation in Albany, Georgia in December 1961 and helped organize voter registration drives in Greenwood, Mississippi and in Selma, Alabama in 1963. In 1964 he helped plan the Mississippi Freedom Summer Project, a project to increase black voter registration and to establish freedom schools and community centers for blacks in the state. Forman accompanied the delegates of the Mississippi Freedom Democratic Party (MFDP) to the Democratic National Convention in Atlantic City in August 1964, where they challenged the seating of Mississippi's regular Democrats. Forman participated in voter registration drives in Selma, Alabama in 1965 and joined in the Selma-to-Montgomery march. In 1969 he presented a "Black Manifesto" at a Detroit conference on black economic development called by the Interreligious Foundation for Community Organization. The manifesto called for the creation of a permanent National Black Economic Conference (NBEC) and for white churches to give $500 million to the NBEC as reparations for the injustices suffered by blacks under slavery and capitalism. Forman is the author of several books, including *Sammy Young, Jr.: The First Black College Student to Die in the Black Liberation Movement* (1968) and *The Making of Black Revolutionaries: A Personal Account* (1972).

Garvey, Marcus (1887–1940)   Black nationalist leader. Born in Jamaica, British West Indies, Garvey served as an apprentice printer in his youth. From 1911 to 1914, he attended London University and traveled in Europe and North Africa. Believing that black independence—economic, military and political—was the only way by which black people could gain true equality with whites, he founded the Universal Negro Improvement Association (UNIA) in Jamaica in 1914. In 1916 Garvey came to the United

States where, in New York City's Harlem, he founded another branch of his organization and began to promote a "Back to Africa" movement. He recruited thousands into the UNIA and was able to start the newspaper *Negro World*. In 1919 he formed the Black Star Line, an international shipping company to provide transportation and encourage trade among the black businesses of Africa and the Americas. By 1922 the Black Star Line had suspended operations and his other enterprises were also failing. Three years later, Garvey was sentenced to a five-year jail term for mail fraud. After serving two years of his sentence, he was deported to Jamaica in 1927. Unable to reestablish the UNIA, he moved to London, where he died in 1940. Despite his downfall, Garvey's movement is widely recognized as the first black attempt to combine economic goals with mass organization.

Goodman, Andrew (1943–1964) Civil rights activist. One of the three civil rights workers killed by the Ku Klux Klan in Mississippi in June 1964. Born in New York City, Goodman came from an upper-middle-class background and had participated in civil rights marches in Washington when he was only 14. At age 16, he picketed a Woolworth's store in New York City in support of the Southern sit-ins. In his sophomore year at Queens College, he volunteered to participate in the Mississippi Freedom Summer Project of 1964. In early June 1964, while attending the training session at Western College for Women in Oxford, Ohio, he met CORE workers James Chaney and Michael Schwerner. Goodman accepted their invitation to join their CORE field office in Meridian, Mississippi. On June 21, 1964, while driving back to Meridian after inspecting a torched black church in Philadelphia, Mississippi, Goodman, Chaney and Schwerner were pulled over by Deputy Sheriff Cecil Price and two carloads of Klansmen. The three young men were murdered, and their bodies were deposited at a nearby farm where an earthen dam was under construction. The disappearance of the three civil rights workers sent shock waves throughout the nation, and within days the FBI began the biggest investigation ever conducted in Mississippi. An anonymous informer revealed the location of the bodies, and on August 4, 1964, the FBI uncovered the decomposed bodies of Goodman, Chaney and Schwerner. In December 1964, the FBI charged 21 men, most of them Klan members, including police officials, for conspiring to abduct and kill the three civil rights workers. In 1967 seven Klansmen, including Deputy Price, were found guilty of federal civil

rights violations in the deaths of Goodman, Chaney and Schwerner. They were sentenced to prison terms ranging from three to ten years. The name of Andrew Goodman is one of the 40 names engraved on the Civil Rights Memorial in Montgomery, Alabama.

Gray, Fred D. (1930–) Civil rights attorney. Born in Montgomery, Alabama, Gray received a B.A. degree from Alabama State University at Montgomery and an LL.B. degree from Case Western Reserve University (Cleveland, Ohio). After admission to the Ohio bar in 1954, Gray became involved in the famous 1955–1956 *City of Montgomery v. Rosa Parks* case, a lawsuit to determine whether a black woman had the right to refuse a bus seat to a white man. In February 1956, Gray filed suit in the United States District Court challenging the constitutionality of bus segregation. On June 5, 1956, the court ruled that segregation on bus lines was indeed unconstitutional. Throughout the 1950s and 1960s, Gray worked as an attorney for the National Association for the Advancement of Colored People (NAACP). He handled cases that won blacks admission into the University of Alabama and Auburn University. In 1970 he was elected to the Alabama state legislature. From 1985 to 1986, he was president of the National Bar Association. He is now a senior partner with the law firm of Gray, Langford, Sapp and Davis in Tuskegee, Alabama.

Greenberg, Jack (1924–) Civil rights attorney and director-counsel, NAACP Legal Defense and Education Fund, 1961–1984. Born and raised in New York City, Greenberg, after graduating from Columbia Law School, joined the NAACP Legal Defense and Education Fund in 1949. He argued two of the five cases that led to the Supreme Court's *Brown v. Board of Education* (1954) decision that held racial segregation in public schools to be unconstitutional. During the 1950s, he served as chief assistant to Thurgood Marshall, the fund's director-counsel, and in 1961 was selected as the new director-counsel when Marshall resigned. Under his direction, the fund successfully defended thousands of civil rights demonstrators and won court orders to desegregate several major Southern universities in the early 1960s. In 1965 he launched a fund campaign for the expansion of prisoners rights and for the abolition of capital punishment, and in 1967 he founded the National Office for the Rights of the Indigent (NORI), to assert the rights of the poor in court. From 1984 to 1993, Greenberg was dean of Columbia College. He is now a professor of law at Columbia Law School.

Hamer, Fannie Lou (1917–1977) Civil rights leader and vice-chairman, Mississippi Freedom Democratic Party (MFDP). The daughter of a sharecropper, Hamer was raised in rural Sunflower County, Mississippi. Hamer first became involved in the civil rights movement in 1962, when she led a group of 26 blacks in an unsuccessful attempt to register to vote in Ruleville, the county seat. She was jailed and beaten, and her family was evicted from the farm land they had worked for 18 years. Soon after, Hamer joined the Student Nonviolent Coordinating Committee (SNCC) and worked to register black voters in Mississippi. In 1964 she helped organize the Mississippi Freedom Summer Project, which included a massive voter registration drive sponsored by SNCC and other civil rights organizations. In the same year, Hamer also helped found the Mississippi Freedom Democratic Party (MFDP), an alternative to the state's white-run regular Democratic Party. At the 1964 Democratic National Convention, she gained national attention when she testified as an MFDP representative before the convention's credentials committee. Hamer stunned the convention when she described how Mississippi police had repeatedly beaten her in jail after her first attempt at voter registration. Although the MFDP received widespread support, the credentials committee voted to recognize only the regular Mississippi Democratic delegation. Four years later, at the 1968 Democratic Convention, Hamer attended as a delegate and received a standing ovation. Throughout the 1970s, Hamer remained active in Mississippi politics and spoke out on feminist and antiwar issues throughout the country.

Hicks, James L. (1916–1986) Newspaper reporter and editor. Hicks was a pioneer black American newspaper correspondent. Born in Akron, Ohio, he was educated at the University of Akron and Howard University. After serving in the U.S. Army during World War II, Hicks joined the *Afro-American* in Baltimore and later became the Washington bureau chief of the National Negro Press Association (NNPA). He was the first black sent to cover the Korean War, and in 1955 he covered for the *New York Amsterdam News* and for the NNPA the trial of the two white men accused of murdering Emmett Louis Till, a 14-year-old black boy from Chicago, who was killed while visiting his relatives in Mississippi. From 1955 to 1966 and from 1972 to 1977, Hicks served as the top editor of the *New York Amsterdam News* and helped build it into one of the country's largest and most influential black weeklies.

Hooks, Benjamin Lawson (1924–) Executive director of the National Association for the Advancement of Colored People (NAACP), 1977–1993. Born in Memphis, Hooks attended LeMoyne College and Howard University and received his law degree from DePaul University in 1948. He is a World War II veteran who served in the 42nd Infantry's Division campaign in Italy. As a lawyer in Memphis, he was an assistant public defender and later was the first black judge to serve in Shelby County (Memphis) Criminal Court. He succeeded the legendary Roy Wilkins as executive director of the NAACP in 1977. Under his leadership, the NAACP took a more aggressive position on U.S. policies toward South Africa and successfully fought against antibusing legislation. Hooks continued the NAACP's tradition of taking a stand against discrimination and fighting for the enforcement of civil rights laws. He also expanded the goals of the civil rights movement to include economic parity for black Americans, including full employment and minority ownership of businesses. He retired as executive director of the NAACP in 1993.

Hope, John (1868–1936) Educator. Born in Augusta, Georgia, Hope received a B.A. degree (1894) and an M.A. degree (1907) from Brown University. In 1906 he became president of Atlanta Baptist College, one of the first black Americans to head a black college established after the Civil War.

Houston, Charles Hamilton (1895–1950) Lawyer and educator. Houston is recognized as the architect and dominant force of the legal program of the National Association for the Advancement of Colored People (NAACP). Born in Washington, D.C., the son of a prominent Howard University professor, Houston received a B.A. degree and a Phi Beta Kappa Key at the age of 19 from Amherst College. After two years of teaching at Howard University and another two years in the armed forces, he entered Harvard Law School and became the first black elected to the editorial board of the *Harvard Law Review*. He received an LL.B. degree in 1922 and a D.J.S. degree in 1923. In 1924 he began a lifelong law partnership with his father under the firm name of Houston and Houston. Although his career took him away from the firm, he remained closely associated with his father. From 1924 to 1929, he was a law instructor at Howard University, and by 1929 he had become vice-dean of the School of Law. He served as special counsel to the NAACP from 1935 to 1940 and spearheaded the strategy that led to favorable U.S. Supreme Court decisions against restrictive real estate covenants and against discrimination in colleges. Although he did not live to see the fruit of his labors, Houston is credited with devising the legal strategy for the *Brown v. Board of Education* 1954 case in which the Supreme Court ruled that segregation in public schools is unconstitutional. His former student, Thurgood Marshall, who later became the first black Associate Supreme Court Justice, successfully argued the *Brown* case before the High Court. Houston was posthumously awarded the NAACP's Spingarn Medal.

Jackson, Jesse Louis (1941–)   Civil rights leader and politician. Born in Greenville, South Carolina, Jackson was raised in modest circumstances by a single mother. His success as a student and as an athelete led to a scholarship to the University of Illinois, but when he was not allowed to play quarterback, he transferred to North Carolina's all-black Agricultural and Technical College. Upon graduation, he enrolled in the Chicago Theological Seminary and was ordained as a Baptist minister in 1968. In 1965 Jackson began working with Martin Luther King Jr. and demonstrated his ability as an organizer when King assigned him to expand the Southern Christian Leadership Conference's (SCLC) operations in Chicago. He was present when King was assassinated in Memphis in April 1968. Jackson later became national director of Operation Breadbasket and then in 1971 became leader of his own organization, Operation PUSH (People United to Save Humanity). PUSH was formed to pressure large corporations to provide jobs and economic opportunities for blacks and other minorities. During the late 1970s, he founded PUSH-EXCEL, a program designed to motivate young school children to remain in school. In the 1980s, he ran two times for the Democratic presidential nomination. In 1984 his campaign was launched under an umbrella organization of minority groups, known as the "Rainbow Coalition." He attracted considerable media attention and managed to win primary contests in South Carolina, Louisiana and Washington, D.C. In his 1988 bid for the presidency, Jackson surprisingly gained support not only from many black voters but also from many whites. At the end of the Democratic primaries, Jackson had finished a strong second to Governor Michael Dukakis, winning 92% of the black vote and 20% of the white vote—6.6 million votes. Jackson changed forever the notion that a black president in America was inconceivable. He is president of the Rainbow/PUSH Coalition, a civil rights organization.

Jackson, Jimmie Lee (1938–1965)   Jackson was a civil rights marcher who was killed by state troopers in February 1965 in Marion, Alabama. The name of Jimmie Lee Jackson is one of the 40 names engraved on the Civil Rights Memorial in Montgomery, Alabama.

Johnson, Lyndon Baines (1908–1973)   Thirty-sixth president of the United States. As president, Johnson enacted more civil rights legislation than any other president in American history. Born in Stonewall, Texas, Johnson graduated from Southwest Texas State Teachers College in 1930, taught school in Houston, served as a congressional aide in Washington and became Texas director of the National Youth Administration, a New Deal agency. He was elected as a Democrat to the U.S. House of Representatives in 1938 and served four terms there. Elected to the U.S. Senate in 1948, he became Senate majority leader in 1953. As John F. Kennedy's vice-presidential running mate in 1960, Johnson helped his ticket to victory and became president when Kennedy was assassinated in November 1963. A few days after taking office, Johnson vowed to turn Kennedy's proposed comprehensive civil rights legislation into law. Using all of his political talents to the fullest, he secured approval of the Civil Rights Act of 1964, the first significant civil rights legislation since Reconstruction. After a landslide victory over Republican Barry Goldwater in the 1964 presidential election, Johnson continued his civil rights agenda by securing the passage of the Voting Rights Act of 1965. During his presidency, Johnson also enacted a wide range of Great Society programs, including Medicare (health insurance for the elderly), Medicaid (medical care for people who are unable to meet medical expenses), Headstart (preschool for underprivileged children), federally guaranteed college student loans and the creation of the National Endowment for the Arts and Humanities. However, these remarkable accomplishments were overshadowed by his involvement in the Vietnam War. In March 1968, Johnson stunned the nation by announcing that he would not seek a second term. He retired to his ranch in Texas in 1969, where he died on January 22, 1973, five days before the Paris Agreement on Ending the War and Restoring the Peace in Vietnam was signed.

Katzenbach, Nicholas deBelleville (1922–) U.S. Department of Justice attorney, 1962–1964, and U.S. attorney general, 1965–1966. Katzenbach directed the Justice Department's operations on the scene during the crisis over desegregation at the University of Mississippi in 1962 and at the University of Alabama in 1963. He graduated from Princeton University in 1945, received a law degree from Yale University in 1947 and then was a Rhodes Scholar at Oxford University for two years. Between 1952 and 1960, Katzenbach taught at Yale and the University of Chicago Law School. In January 1961, he was appointed an assistant attorney general in charge of the Justice Department's Office of Legal Counsel, and in 1962, he was named deputy attorney general, the second highest position in the Justice Department. He became acting attorney general when Robert Kennedy resigned in 1964 and was appointed to that post by President Johnson in 1965. In March 1965, he oversaw the Justice Department's role in ensuring that the state of Alabama did not interfere in the Selma–to–Montgomery march. Katzenbach also drafted the Johnson administration's voting rights bill, introduced in the Congress in March 1965, and then worked to attain its passage. As attorney general, he oversaw the enforcement of the Voting Rights Act and expanded the Justice Department's efforts to achieve school desegregation. In 1966 he was appointed undersecretary of state, and in 1969 he joined IBM as vice-president and general counsel. After leaving IBM in 1986, Katzenbach became a partner in the law firm of Riker, Danzig, Scherer, Hyland and Perretti in Morristown, New Jersey.

Kennedy, John Fitzgerald (1917–1963) Thirty-fifth president of the United States. Born in Brookline, Massachusetts, Kennedy graduated from Harvard University in 1940, served as an officer in the U.S. Navy during World War II and was elected to the House of Representatives in 1946 and to the Senate in 1952. While campaigning for the presidency in late October 1960, Kennedy called Mrs. Coretta Scott King to express his sympathy for her husband, Martin Luther King Jr., who was in jail for his participation in a mass sit-in in Atlanta, Georgia. Kennedy was promoted in the black community as the "Candidate with a Heart." It is believed that black voters contributed heavily to Kennedy's narrow victory over Vice-President Richard M. Nixon. (Kennedy won by a little more than 100,000 popular votes). At the age of 43, he became the youngest elected president in American history. At first Kennedy was reluctant to take any decisive stand on civil rights issues. His administration only began to act after civil rights activists such as James Farmer and Martin Luther King Jr. mounted nonviolent desegregation efforts in the South. In September 1962, Kennedy did indeed take a firm stand on enforcing a federal court order to permit James Meredith, a black student, to register at the University of Mississippi. Kennedy federalized

the Mississippi National Guard and dispatched federal marshals to Mississippi to escort Meredith to the university. On June 11, 1963, at the University of Alabama, Kennedy used federal troops to enforce a school desegregation order. That evening, in a televised address to the nation, Kennedy delivered his strongest message ever on civil rights and called on Congress to enact a comprehensive civil rights law. At the conclusion of the March on Washington (August 28, 1963), Kennedy met at the White House with the march's leaders, including Martin Luther King Jr., A. Philip Randolph, Whitney Young and John Lewis. Three months later, Kennedy was assassinated in Dallas, Texas.

Kennedy, Robert Francis (1925–1968) Attorney general of the United States and New York senator. Born in Brookline, Massachusetts, Kennedy graduated from Harvard College in 1948 and the University of Virginia Law School three years later. Kennedy first became involved in politics in 1952 as manager of his older brother John's successful campaign for the U.S. Senate. In 1953 Kennedy went to work for the Senate Subcommittee on Investigations, chaired by Senator Joseph McCarthy. He resigned six months later because he was disturbed with McCarthy's reckless accusations of disloyalty. He later gained a reputation as a skilled and relentless prosecutor while working as chief counsel for the Senate Rackets Committee in 1957–1959. In 1960 he managed his brother's successful campaign for the presidency. He became attorney general in 1961 and oversaw the Department of Justice's role in enforcing federal court orders to desegregate the Universities of Mississippi and Alabama. Kennedy believed that voting was the key to racial justice and proposed the most far-reaching civil rights statute since Reconstruction, the Civil Rights Act of 1964, which passed after President Kennedy's assassination. He resigned in August 1964 from the Johnson administration and was elected to the U.S. Senate from New York in November. Although Kennedy praised Johnson's Great Society programs, he increasingly disagreed with Johnson's foreign policy, especially concerning Vietnam. By 1968 Kennedy had emerged as a popular leader who was identified with caring for the dispossessed and powerless, including the poor, the young and racial minorities. After much hesitation, Kennedy declared his candidacy for the Democratic presidential nomination. When Martin Luther King Jr. was assassinated on April 4, 1968, Kennedy disregarded the advice of his advisers to avoid black neighborhoods and delivered a compassionate address to a mostly black crowd in Indianapolis. Two months later, Robert Kennedy fell to an assassin's bullet in Los Angeles.

King, Coretta Scott (1927–)   Civil rights leader. Born in Marion, Alabama, King received a B.S. degree from Antioch College in 1951 and a bachelor of music degree from the New England Conservatory of Music in 1954. While studying for her music degree, she met Martin Luther King Jr., then a graduate philosophy student at Boston University. She married King in 1953, and in 1954 the couple moved to Montgomery, Alabama, where he began his first pastorate at the Dexter Avenue Baptist Church. Mrs. King soon became deeply involved in her husband's civil rights activities, which began with the Montgomery bus boycott of 1955 and with the formation of the Southern Christian Leadership Conference (SCLC) in 1957. She marched beside him in demonstrations and accompanied him on speaking engagements in Europe and Asia. In April 1968, Mrs. King received national admiration for the dignity and fortitude with which she responded to her husband's assassination. The next month she participated in the Poor People's Campaign in Washington and delivered an address at the Lincoln Memorial, which focused on women uniting to fight against "the three great evils of racism, poverty and war." Soon after, she was elected to the executive bodies of both the SCLC and the National Organization for Women (NOW). In 1971 Mrs. King established the Martin Luther King Memorial Center for Nonviolent Social Change in Atlanta and is the author of *My Life with Martin Luther King* (1969).

King, Martin Luther, Jr. (1929–1968)   Civil rights leader, minister and author. King is recognized as one of the world's leading crusaders against the brutality of racism. As a well-known advocate of nonviolent direct action, he dedicated his life to the quest of securing equal rights for black Americans. The son and grandson of respected Baptist ministers in Atlanta, Georgia, King entered Moorehouse College at the age of 15 and received a B.A. degree in 1948. He then earned a divinity degree from Crozier Theological Seminary in 1951 and a Ph.D. degree in theology from Boston University in 1955. In early 1954, King accepted his first pastorate at the Dexter Avenue Baptist Church in Montgomery, Alabama. As president of the Montgomery Improvement Association (MIA) in 1955–1956, King led the black residents of Montgomery in their boycott of city buses. They were protesting the arrest of Rosa Parks, a black woman who was charged with violating Al-

abama's segregation laws. As a result of his involvement in the Montgomery bus boycott, King gained national prominence for his remarkable organizational and oratory skills. In January 1957, King founded the Southern Christian Leadership Conference (SCLC), one of the most powerful forces in the early civil rights movement. Although he traveled and spoke widely and committed the SCLC to Southern voter registration, King's major energies were absorbed from December 1961 to August 1962 in the Albany, Georgia desegregation movement. Following this, King participated in a well-publicized desegregation campaign in Birmingham (April–May 1963). Clashes between unarmed demonstrators and police with attack dogs and fire hoses generated newspaper headlines throughout the world. During these nonviolent demonstrations, King wrote his famous essay, *Letter from a Birmingham Jail.* In August 1963, King was one of the principals in the spectacular March on Washington that drew some 250,000 people, black and white, to demonstrate in behalf of the pending civil rights bill. At the steps of the Lincoln Memorial, King delivered his famous "I Have a Dream" speech. King was honored by the world community with the Nobel Peace Prize in December 1964. In 1965 he led the Selma–to–Montgomery march, which aided in bringing about the passage of the Voting Rights Act of 1965. After the march, King moved his campaign to Chicago. He returned to the South in 1966 after the ambush of James Meredith in order to continue Meredith's March Against Fear from Memphis to Jackson, Mississippi. In March 1968, King called for the Poor People's March on Washington to demonstrate the need for the federal government to launch a war on poverty. However, on April 4, 1968, while visiting Memphis on behalf of striking black sanitation workers, Martin Luther King Jr. was assassinated by James Earl Ray, a white sniper. His death caused rioting and a wave of disorder in more than 120 cities. Approximately 150,000 mourners, including several national dignitaries, attended his funeral in Atlanta, Georgia on April 9. Although death took the life of the symbolic leader of the civil rights movement, his message of nonviolence and commitment to freedom and equality continues to this day. Impatience with the denial of freedom and justice is King's special legacy. King was the author of *Stride Toward Freedom* (1958) and *Why We Can't Wait* (1964). In 1986 King's birthday, January 15, became a federal holiday. The name of Martin Luther King Jr. is one of the 40 names engraved on the Civil Rights Memorial in Montgomery, Alabama.

Lawson, James (1928–)   Civil rights leader. Born in Ohio, Lawson attended Oberlin College's theology school. He chose prison in the early 1950s as a conscientious objector during the Korean War. Paroled to the Methodist Board of Missions, Lawson spent three years as a missionary in India. In 1958, as a member of the Fellowship of Reconciliation, a pacifist group, he was sent to Nashville to lead a workshop in nonviolence for black civil rights activists. In 1959 he enrolled at Nashville's Vanderbilt University. As a divinity student there in 1960, he led hundreds of student volunteers in nonviolent protests against segregated stores in downtown Nashville. A few months before his graduation from Vanderbilt in 1960, Lawson was expelled because of his involvement in the Nashville student sit-in movement. In the spring of 1960, as a Southern Christian Leadership Conference (SCLC) representative, Lawson was a keynote speaker at the Shaw University, Raleigh, North Carolina conference that formed the Student Nonviolent Coordinating Committee (SNCC). He was chairman of the Memphis sanitation strike in 1968. Lawson is president of his local SCLC chapter and pastor of the Holman United Methodist Church in Los Angeles.

Lewis, John Robert (1940–)   Civil rights leader and chairman, Student Nonviolent Coordinating Committee (SNCC), 1963–1966. Born in Troy, Alabama, Lewis graduated from the American Baptist Theological Seminary (Nashville, Tenn.) in 1963. While a seminary student, he participated in the 1960 Nashville student sit-ins and the Freedom Rides of 1961. In 1963 he became chairman of SNCC and was the youngest speaker at the March on Washington (August 28, 1963). Lewis had prepared a strong speech in which he lashed out at the Kennedy administration and denounced the proposed civil rights bill as too little too late. March organizers asked Lewis to soften his criticism of the government, but at first he refused to compromise. Then, after meeting with A. Philip Randolph, the dean of the civil rights movement, Lewis agreed to tone down his speech. Even with modifications, which were made literally minutes before he was to deliver the address, Lewis' speech was one of the most powerful of the day. On March 7, 1965, along with the SCLC's Hosea Williams, he led the first march from Selma to Montgomery, Alabama, which was halted by some 200 state troopers at the Edmund Pettus Bridge. The marchers were attacked with tear gas and nightsticks, and Lewis suffered a concussion in the melee. He was a leader of the final march that went from Selma to Montgo-

mery on March 21. Lewis left SNCC in 1966 because of its increasing militancy and was replaced by Stokely Carmichael. For the next three years, he was director of community organization projects for the Southern Regional Council. In 1970 Lewis was named director of the Voter Education Project (VEP), another program of the council. By 1973 the VEP had registered nearly 3.5 million voters in 11 Southern states. In 1976 he was appointed by the Carter administration to a post with ACTION, the agency responsible for volunteer activities. Lewis returned to Atlanta in 1981 and was elected to the city council. In 1986 he was elected to the U.S. Congress, representing Georgia's Fifth Congressional District, which includes most of Atlanta and has since been reelected several times.

Liuzzo, Viola Gregg (1925–1965)   Civil rights activist. Viola Liuzzo, a white woman from Michigan, was killed by a group of Klansmen on March 25, 1965, while she was driving a few civil rights marchers back to Selma, Alabama from Montgomery following the five-day voting rights march. A mother of five and one of the few white members of the NAACP in Michigan, Viola Liuzzo drove by herself from Michigan to Selma after watching on television the film clips of state troopers attacking marchers on the Edmund Pettus Bridge in Selma during the first march earlier in the month. The name of Viola Gregg Liuzzo is one of the 40 names engraved on the Civil Rights Memorial in Montgomery, Alabama.

Lynch, John Roy (1847–1939)   U.S. congressman from Mississippi during Reconstruction and the first black to preside over a national convention of the Republican Party. Born into slavery in Louisiana, Lynch received some tutoring as a youth, and after emancipation he managed a successful photographic studio in Mississippi. In 1867 he was named a justice of the peace for Adams County, and in 1869 he was elected to the Mississippi state legislature. At the age of 24, he was elected speaker of the house, and in 1872 he was elected to the U.S. House of Representatives, where he served for two terms. On three occasions, Lynch was a delegate to the Republican Party's national convention, and he presided over it in 1884. He is known for his support of the 1875 Civil Rights Act that banned discrimination in public accommodations. Lynch wrote two books: *Facts of Reconstruction* (1913) and *Some Historical Errors of James Ford Rhodes* (1917).

McKissick, Floyd Bixler (1922–1991)   Civil rights leader and national chairman, Congress of Racial Equality (CORE), 1966–1968. Born in Asheville, North

Carolina, McKissick did undergraduate work at Morehouse College in Atlanta, Georgia and at North Carolina College at Durham. He graduated from the North Carolina Law School in 1951 and became the first black to receive a law degree from that institution. McKissick became well known throughout North Carolina as a civil rights attorney and, in addition to his private law practice, he served as counsel to CORE. In March 1966, he replaced James Farmer as national director of CORE. He joined Stokely Carmichael, chairman of the Student Nonviolent Coordinating Committee, in his cry for black power during the James Meredith March Against Fear in Mississippi in June 1966. In 1968 McKissick left CORE to launch Floyd B. McKissick Enterprises Inc., a corporation involved in organizing and financing businesses, including the development of Soul City, a new integrated community in North Carolina. However, Soul City ran into financial difficulties and was never developed. He is the author of *Three-Fifths of a Man* (1968).

Malcolm X (Al Hajj Malik Al-Sha-Bazz) (1925–1965) Civil rights leader, clergyman and orator; one of the most fiery and controversial black leaders of the 20th century. Born Malcolm Little in Omaha, Nebraska, Malcolm was the son of a Baptist preacher who was an avid supporter of Marcus Garvey's Universal Negro Improvement Association (UNIA). At an early age, Malcolm moved to Lansing, Michigan with his parents, both of whom were tragically lost to him in childhood. (His father was killed by a Klan-like hate group, and his mother was committed to a mental institution.) He dropped out of school after the eighth grade and made his way to New York City, where he soon became involved in a life of crime. In 1946, at the age of 21, Malcolm was sentenced to a 10-year prison term for burglary. While in jail, he was introduced to the Lost-Found Nation of Islam, the Black Muslim religion led by Elijah Muhammad, and changed his name to Malcolm X. Paroled from prison in 1952, Malcolm X became a minister and an outspoken defender of Muslim doctrines. He argued that for black people to ultimately survive, they must separate themselves in every way from the white culture. Threatened by Malcolm's increasing popularity, which was reaching into even the Student Nonviolent Coordinating Committee (SNCC), Elijah Muhammad suspended him from the Muslims in December 1963 after he characterized the assassination of President Kennedy as a case of the "chickens coming home to roost." A few months later, he traveled to Mecca and discovered that orthodox Muslims preach equality of the races, and this led him to

abandon his belief of separatism. In June 1964, he founded the Organization of Afro-American Unity and moved increasingly in the direction that the struggle for equality by blacks could be made with the help of world organizations, other black groups and even progressive white groups. On February 21, 1965, Malcolm X was assassinated by a dissenting Black Muslim group at a rally of his organization in Harlem. His *Autobiography of Malcolm X* as told to Alex Haley was published posthumously in 1965. Other works published after his death include: *Malcolm X Speaks* (1965); *The Speeches of Malcolm X at Harvard* (1968); and *By Any Means Necessary: Speeches, Interviews, and a Letter by Malcolm X* (1970). His life was the subject of a feature film, *Malcolm X* (1992), by screenwriter/director Spike Lee.

Marshall, Burke (1922–) U.S. assistant attorney general in charge of the Civil Rights Division, 1961–1964. A graduate of Yale University in 1943 and of Yale Law School in 1951, Marshall, a member of a Washington law firm throughout the 1950s, was named assistant attorney general in charge of the Justice Department's Civil Rights Division in 1961. Marshall played a major role in developing the Kennedy administration's civil rights policies. He had a major part in the federal government's handling of the 1961 Freedom Rides into the South and the spring 1963 demonstrations against segregation in Birmingham. Marshall was instrumental in negotiating a settlement between the leaders of the Birmingham demonstrators—Martin Luther King Jr. of the Southern Christian Leadership Conference (SCLC) and Fred L. Shuttlesworth of the Alabama Christian Movement for Human Rights (ACHMR) and Birmingham's business leaders. Birmingham's store owners agreed to begin desegregating downtown stores by hiring black sales clerks in return for an end to the mass demonstrations. In 1963 Marshall also helped draft President Kennedy's proposed civil rights bill, which was later passed into law as the Civil Rights Act of 1964. In 1965 he joined IBM as vice president and general counsel, and since 1970 he has taught at Yale Law School. Marshall edited the book *The Supreme Court and Human Rights* (1982).

Marshall, Thurgood (1908–1993) NAACP special counsel, U.S. solicitor general and the first black associate U.S. Supreme Court Justice (1967–1991). Arguing 32 cases before the Supreme Court and prevailing in 29 of them, Thurgood Marshall acquired the designation "Mr. Civil Rights." Born in Baltimore, Maryland, Marshall attended the city's racially segregated public schools, graduated from Lincoln

University (Pennsylvania) in 1930 and then graduated with high honors from Howard University Law School. He joined the NAACP's legal staff in 1934 and was an assistant to its special counsel, Charles Hamilton Houston. In 1938 he succeeded Houston as special counsel to the NAACP. Many of Marshall's cases established legal precedents for the civil rights of black Americans. He prepared the brief that led to the admission of a black student to the University of Missouri Law School in 1938; in *Smith v. Allwright* (1944), Marshall won the right for blacks to vote in primary elections in Texas; *Morgan v. Virginia* (1946) signaled the end of segregation on interstate passenger carriers in Virginia; *Shelley v. Kramer* (1948) held state enforcement of restrictive housing covenants to be unconstitutional; *Sweatt v. Painter* (1950) resulted in the admission of black students to the law school at the University of Texas; and *Brown v. Board of Education of Topeka* (1954) invalidated state-enforced racial segregation in public schools. In 1961 Marshall was appointed to the U.S. Court of Appeals for the Second Circuit by President Kennedy, and in 1965 President Johnson named him United States solicitor general. Two years later, Thurgood Marshall was appointed as an associate justice of the U.S. Supreme Court. In his 24-year tenure, he was an outspoken voice on a Court that became increasingly dominated by conservatives. Marshall voted to uphold racial affirmative action policies; dissented in every case in which the Court failed to overturn a death sentence; and dissented against all efforts to narrow or burden the right of women to obtain abortions. No other justice in American history has so consistently opposed the government's regulation of speech or sexual conduct or advanced the view that the Constitution places certain responsibilities on the role of government, including providing important benefits to the people (such as education, legal services and access to the courts by the poor). Marshall resigned from the Court in 1991 due to advancing age.

Meredith, James Howard (1933–) Civil rights activist. Meredith's application and subsequent admission to the University of Mississippi in 1961 was the event that initiated the desegregation of Ole Miss and led to the desegregation of other universities in the South. He was born in Kosciusko, Mississippi and served nine years in the air force. In the summer of 1960 he applied for admission to the University of Mississippi. At first he was refused admission because he was black, then in 1962 a federal court ordered Ole Miss to admit Meredith. In September 1962, after Governor Ross Barnett of Mississippi refused to comply with the order, President Kennedy dispatched a large force of federal marshals and troops to escort Meredith to the university. Upon the arrival of federal troops on September 30, rioting broke out on the campus. The next day, October 1, Meredith became the first black student to register at Ole Miss. After graduating with a B.A. in political science from Ole Miss in 1963, Meredith spent the next year studying in Nigeria, West Africa. When he returned to this country, he attended Columbia law school. In 1966, before completing his law studies, Meredith began a one-man "march against fear" from Tennessee Mississippi to publicize a drive for voter registration. On the second day of the march, he was wounded by a sniper. The march was later continued by Martin Luther King Jr., CORE's Floyd McKissick and SNCC's Stokely Carmichael. During this march, Carmichael's slogan of "black power" emerged. Following his graduation from law school, Meredith lectured on civil rights and worked in a stock brokerage firm. From 1989 to 1991, Meredith worked as a policy adviser to conservative Republican Senator Jesse Helms of North Carolina, who a decade earlier had nearly filibustered against a national holiday in memory of Martin Luther King Jr. Meredith is the author of the autobiographical account *Three Years in Mississippi* (1966).

Mitchell, Clarence M. (1911–1984) Chief lobbyist for the National Association for the Advancement of Colored People (NAACP) and the Leadership Conference on Civil Rights, 1950–1978. He played a prominent role in the passage of the Civil Rights Act of 1968. Mitchell became so influential among federal lawmakers that he was sometimes called the "101st Senator." Born in Baltimore, Maryland, Mitchell received an A.B. degree in 1932 from Lincoln College in Chester County, Pennsylvania and went on to graduate from the University of Maryland Law School. After working as a reporter for the *Afro-American* in Baltimore, he became executive secretary of the Urban League in St. Paul, Minnesota in 1937. In 1942 Mitchell became assistant director of the Negro Manpower Service in the War Manpower Commission and went on to hold other posts with the Fair Employment Commission, the War Production Board and other government organizations before joining the NAACP in 1945 as national labor secretary in the Washington office. He was awarded the NAACP's Spingarn medal in 1969 and was awarded the Medal of Freedom by President Jimmy Carter in 1980.

Moses, Robert (1935–) Civil rights leader. Born and raised in Harlem, Moses graduated from Harvard College in 1957 and began teaching the following year at Horace Mann, an elite private school in New York City. In the summer of 1960, he went to Atlanta as a volunteer for the newly organized Student Nonviolent Coordinating Committee (SNCC). The next year, Moses quit his teaching job and joined SNCC. He soon became an influential figure in the organization, especially in the area of voter registration. In July 1961, Moses set up SNCC's first voter registration project in Mississippi, and in 1962 he became project director of the Council of Federated Organizations (COFO), a voter registration group composed of several local civil rights groups in Mississippi and the forces of SNCC, CORE, the NAACP and the SCLC. Moses directed the 1964 Mississippi Freedom Summer Project, which brought over 1,000 student volunteers into the state to set up community centers, teach in "freedom schools" and encourage voter registration. That summer he also participated in organizing the Mississippi Freedom Democratic Party (MFDP), an alternative to Mississippi's segregationist regular Democratic Party. Moses accompanied the MFDP delegates to the National Democratic Convention in Atlantic City, where they challenged the seating of Mississippi's regular delegation. Although widely respected by many SNCC members and Mississippi blacks, Moses was reluctant to continue in that leadership role. He believed his goal was only to help local people organize so they would be able "to speak for themselves." Fearing that a cult was growing around his name, he changed it to Robert Parris in 1965 and shortly afterwards left Mississippi and SNCC. In 1982 he was the recipient of a MacArthur Foundation award, and he is now director of the *Algebra Project*, a nationwide mathematical literacy program aimed at minority youth.

Motley, Constance Baker (1921–) Civil rights attorney and federal judge. Born in New Haven, Connecticut, Motley earned a B.A. degree from New York University and her law degree from Columbia University School of Law in 1946. Even before her graduation from law school, she had joined the National Association for the Advancement of Colored People (NAACP) Legal Defense Fund and remained with it until 1965. From 1948 to 1956, Motley served as the organization's associate council. Between 1961 and 1964, she argued ten and won nine major civil rights cases before the U.S. Supreme Court, and in 1962 she represented James Meredith in his efforts to gain admission to the University of Mississippi. In 1964 Motley was elected to the New York State Senate, the first black American woman in the state's history elected to that office. She was elected president of the New York City Council in 1965, and a

year later President Johnson named her a judge of the United States District Court for the Southern District of New York. In 1982, Motley rose to chief judge. She held that position until 1986, when she retired from the bench.

Nabrit, James Madison, Jr. (1910–1998) Civil rights attorney and educator. Born in Atlanta, Georgia, Nabrit graduated from Morehouse College in 1923 and received his law degree from Northwestern University in 1927. After privately practicing law, he joined the Howard University law school faculty in 1936 and became Howard's president in 1960. In the early 1950s, as a staff member of the National Association for the Advancement of Colored People (NAACP) Legal Defense Fund, Nabrit developed the strategy of directly challenging the very concept of racial segregation in public schools. NAACP Legal Defense Fund attorneys used this approach when they successfully argued the *Brown v. Board of Education* (1954) case before the U.S. Supreme Court. In 1965 Nabrit was appointed United States deputy representative to the United Nations Security Council. Nabrit returned to Howard as president in 1968 and retired from the presidency of the university in 1969.

Newton, Huey Percy (1942–1989) Militant civil rights leader and a founder of the Black Panther Party for Self-Defense. Newton, the son of a Louisiana sharecropper, was illiterate when he graduated from high school, but he later taught himself to read and write and graduated from Merritt College (Oakland, California) in 1965. In 1966 he and Bobby Seale founded the Black Panther Party, a grass-roots organization in Oakland designed to protect ghetto residents from police brutality and harassment. In 1967 Newton was involved in a scuffle with Oakland police and was charged with killing a police officer. After his indictment for first-degree murder, Newton's case became a cause célèbre. "Free Huey" became a standard cry of black and white radicals throughout the country, who considered Newton a political prisoner. Newton claimed he had been shot by the police officer and was unconscious when the officer was killed. But he was convicted of voluntary manslaughter in 1968 and was sentenced to 2 to 15 years in prison. After spending two years in prison, Newton was released in 1970 after his conviction was overturned by the California Court of Appeals. In the ensuing years, Newton continued to become entangled with the law. In 1974, he was charged with murdering a 17-year-old prostitute, but the charges were dropped in 1979 after his trial ended in a mistrial with the jury deadlocked in favor of acquittal. Newton later earned a Ph.D. degree in social philosophy from the University of California at Santa Cruz. His dissertation was titled "War Against the Panthers: A Study of Repression in America." During the 1980s, Newton became involved in drug and alcohol abuse. He was shot to death in a drug-related shooting on an Oakland street in 1989. He was the author of *Revolutionary Suicide* (1973).

Nixon, Edgar Daniel (1900–1987)   Civil rights activist. In 1955 Nixon, a former NAACP Montgomery, Alabama chapter president and a Pullman porter who was a member of the Brotherhood of Sleeping Car Porters, was one of the principal organizers of the Montgomery bus boycott.

Parks, Rosa (1913–)   Civil rights activist and NAACP organizer. By refusing to give up her seat to a white man on a segregated city bus in Montgomery, Alabama on December 1, 1955, Parks set in motion the Montgomery bus boycott and in effect launched the nonviolent massive resistance movement. Born in Tuskegee, Alabama, Parks attended the laboratory school at Alabama State College, but after she was unable to find work commensurate with her education, she became a seamstress. In 1943 she became the secretary of the local NAACP chapter in Montgomery; in the late 1940s, Parks became the first secretary of the Alabama State Conference of NAACP Branches, and during this period she organized an NAACP Youth Council chapter in Montgomery. In the early 1950s, she organized members of the council to engage in some direct nonviolent action by attempting unsuccessfully to borrow books from the "white" library. In 1954 she attended an interracial civil rights meeting at Highlander Folk School in Tennessee. Shortly after her arrest for refusing to give up her seat on a segregated Montgomery bus in December 1955, Parks was fired from her job as a seamstress with a Montgomery department store. For over a year she remained without a steady job. Parks eventually moved to Detroit, where for more than 20 years she worked as a receptionist in the Michigan office of U.S. Congressman John Conyers. Since 1956 Parks has made regular appearances as an honored guest at many civil rights ceremonies. In 1988, at the Democratic National Convention in Atlanta, she was introduced by Jesse L. Jackson as "the mother of the civil rights movement."

Parris, Robert.   See MOSES, ROBERT.

Patterson, John Malcolm (1921–)   Governor of Alabama, 1959–1963. In May 1961, when the Congress of Racial Equality launched a series of Freedom Rides in an effort to integrate interstate bus facilities, Patterson refused to provide police protection for the riders. After the riders were attacked by white mobs in Anniston and Montgomery, President Kennedy ordered federal marshals to Montgomery, and Patterson reluctantly called out the Alabama National Guard to escort the riders to the Mississippi state line. Born in Goldville, Alabama, Patterson graduated from the University of Alabama in 1949 and soon thereafter joined his father's law firm. In 1954 he was elected state attorney general, and in 1958 he ran for governor on a segregationist platform and won. Patterson was succeeded in 1963 by George C. Wallace. He ran again for governor in 1966 but garnered only 4% of the vote in the Democratic primary. Since 1984, he has been an Alabama Court of Criminal Appeals judge.

Powell, Adam Clayton, Jr. (1908–1972)   U.S. Congressman, clergyman and civil rights leader. Born in New Haven, Connecticut, Powell graduated from Colgate University in 1930 and received an M.A. degree from Columbia University in 1932. In 1937 he succeeded his father as minister of the Abyssinian Baptist Church in New York City's Harlem, and in 1941 he was elected to the New York City Council. As a Democrat, Powell was elected to represent Harlem in the U.S. House of Representatives in 1944, a seat he retained for 11 successive terms. In 1960 he became chairman of the House Committee on Education and Labor. During his tenure, Powell helped guide through the House some of the major antipoverty and education bills of the Kennedy and Johnson administrations. Accused of misusing public funds, Powell was censured by Congress and lost his seat in 1967. However, he was seated again in 1969 but was stripped of his seniority. In 1970, Powell lost the Democratic congressional primary and retired to the Bahamas. Two years later he died of cancer on the island of Bimini.

Prinz, Joachim (1902–1988)   Civil rights activist. In 1963 Prinz, as president of the American Jewish Congress, was one of the principal organizers of the March on Washington (August 28, 1963). Born in Germany, he attended the University of Berlin and received a Ph.D. from the University of Giessen. He was ordained a rabbi at the Jewish Theological Seminary in Breslau in 1925. In 1937 he came to the United States after he was expelled from his native country for speaking out against the Hitler regime. Throughout the 1960s, Prinz took part in many demonstrations for civil rights causes in New York City and in the South.

Pritchett, Laurie (1925–)   Albany, Georgia police chief, 1959–1966. Pritchett played a major role in stifling the Albany Movement of 1961–62 by restraining his officers from using billy clubs or fire hoses against black demonstrators. He also prevented the protesters from filling up Albany's jails by securing jail space in nearby towns. Born in Griffin, Georgia, Pritchett worked in his hometown as a police officer for 12 years before becoming Albany's police chief in 1959. In 1966 he became police chief in High Point, North Carolina, and in 1974 he retired.

Rainey, Joseph Hayne (1832–1887)   U.S. congressman from South Carolina during Reconstruction. Rainey was the first black representative to be seated in the House of Representatives. Born into slavery in Georgetown, South Carolina, Rainey worked as a barber. When the Civil War began, he was conscripted to work on fortifications for the Confederate Army, but he escaped to the West Indies, where he remained until after the end of the war. After returning to South Carolina, Rainey became a delegate to the state constitutional convention in 1868 and to the state senate in 1870. In 1870 he was one of three black Republicans from South Carolina who were elected to the House of Representatives and served there until 1879.

Randolph, A. Philip (1889–1979)   Labor organizer and civil rights leader. Founder of the Brotherhood of Sleeping Car Porters (BSCP), a union of black porters who worked on the railroads, and a principal organizer of the "March on Washington" movement, which began in 1941. Born in Crescent City, Florida, Randolph was educated at Bethune-Cookman College in Daytona Beach, Florida, but because of his race, he was unable to find work commensurate with his background. Randolph became a train porter. In 1925 he organized his fellow workers into the Brotherhood of Sleeping Car Porters and obtained a charter for the union from the American Federation of Labor. In 1941 he planned a mass march on Washington to demand more jobs for blacks in the defense industries. Shortly before the day of the march, President Roosevelt issued an executive order declaring that there should be no discrimination in the employment of workers in the defense industries, and the march was canceled. Randolph was a leader of the Committee Against Discrimination in the Armed Forces, which helped influence President Truman to eliminate segregation in the armed forces. In 1958 he organized the youth march on Washington to demonstrate in favor of implementing the Supreme Court's school desegregation decision in *Brown v. Board of*

Education (1954). Randolph was one of the principal speakers at the largest civil rights demonstration in history, the August 1963 March on Washington for Jobs and Freedom. (More than 250,000 people, black and white, attended.) In 1964 he founded and became president of the A. Philip Randolph Institute, an organization that sponsors educational projects and campaigns for jobs in the skilled trades for blacks. Randolph died at the age of 90 in 1979.

Rapier, James Thomas (1837–1883)   U.S. congressman from Alabama during Reconstruction. Born in Florence, Alabama, Rapier was educated by private tutors and studied law in Canada, where he was admitted to the bar. After the Civil War, he returned to the South and worked for a brief time as a newspaper correspondent. In 1867 he became a delegate to the Alabama constitutional convention. He was elected to the U.S. House of Representatives in 1873 but failed to be reelected in 1874. After his defeat, Rapier took up farming in his home state and became quite successful. After Reconstruction, he remained active in politics, attending the 1880 Republican National Convention in Chicago.

Rauh, Joseph Louis, Jr. (1911–1992)   Civil rights attorney. For decades Rauh was one of the nation's leading champions of civil rights and civil liberties. Born in Cincinnati, Ohio, Rauh graduated from Harvard University in 1932 and Harvard Law School in 1935. He served as a law clerk to Supreme Court associate justices Benjamin N. Cardozo and Felix Frankfurter. While in private practice, Rauh became an important defender of civil liberties. Among his clients were the United Auto Workers Union, the Brotherhood of Sleeping Car Porters and a number of Americans accused of Communist affiliations. In 1947 Rauh was one of the founders of the Americans for Democratic Action (ADA), a liberal anti-Communist group that opposed what it regarded as the conservative orientation of both major political parties. Rauh was a regular participant at the Democratic National Convention, a role that in 1948 allowed him to make a milestone contribution to civil rights. That year he had a leading part in writing a strong civil rights plank that was adopted in the party's platform and provided a foundation for much of the federal rights legislation that would be enacted in the decades ahead. At the 1964 Democratic National Convention in Atlantic City, New Jersey, Rauh was counsel for the Mississippi Freedom Democratic Party (MFDP), an alternative to Mississippi's segregated regular Democratic Party. Although Rauh's presentation before the Credentials Committee won widespread support for the MFDP, it failed to unseat the regular Mississippi delegation. As general counsel for the Leadership Conference on Civil Rights, he and Clarence Mitchell of the NAACP were the chief lobbyists for the Civil Rights Act of 1964, the Voting Rights Act of 1965, the Fair Housing Act of 1968 and other civil rights legislation. Although Rauh had abandoned the practice of law in the 1980s, he kept an active schedule as a public speaker. He also continued to lobby strenuously against the Reagan and Bush administrations' conservative nominees to the Supreme Court. "I'm proud of our laws," he once said. "What our generation has done is bring equality in law. The next generation has to bring equality in fact."

Reeb, James J. (1927–1965)   Civil rights activist and clergyman. Reeb, a white man, was a civil rights activist who was beaten to death by a white gang in Selma, Alabama on March 11, 1965. Following the attack on black marchers at the Edmund Pettus Bridge on March 7, 1965, Reeb had flown to Selma from Boston to give his support to the demonstrators. Born in Casper, Wyoming, Reeb, the son of a well-to-do oil equipment distributor, graduated from Princeton Theological Seminary in 1953 and received a masters in theology from the Conwell School of Theology of Temple University in 1956. Following his graduation, he headed the youth division of the West Branch Young Men's Association in Philadelphia and was an assistant pastor of All Souls Unitarian-Universalist Church in Washington. In 1964 he moved to Boston to serve as director of the Metropolitan Boston Low-Income Housing Program, sponsored by the American Friends Service Committee. Reeb lived with his wife and three children at the edge of a Boston ghetto where he spent the last year of his life trying to improve slum conditions. The name of James Reeb is one of 40 names engraved on the Civil Rights Memorial in Montgomery, Alabama.

Revels, Hiram Rhodes (1822–1901)   First black U.S. senator. Born in Fayetteville County, North Carolina, Revels moved at a young age to a Quaker settlement in Indiana, where he acquired a basic education at a Quaker seminary. Later he attended Knox College in Galesburg, Illinois. Revels became a minister in the Methodist Episcopal Church and had pastorates in several border states. At the outbreak of the Civil War, he helped organize the first two black regiments raised in Maryland. After the war, Revels worked with the Freedmen's Bureau in Mississippi and was appointed military governor of the area. In 1869 he was elected to the Mississippi senate, and the follow-

ing year Revels was appointed to the United States Senate to fill the term vacated by Jefferson Davis. After his term in the Senate, he returned to Rodney, Mississippi to serve as president of Alcorn College, a black educational institution.

Robinson, Spottswood William, III (1916–1998)   NAACP special counsel for the southern region and federal judge. Robinson attended Virginia Union University and received his LL.B. degree with honors from Howard University School of Law in 1939. Following his graduation, he taught at Howard University and at the same time practiced law in Richmond, Virginia and also served as counsel for the NAACP. From 1960 to 1964, he served as dean of the Howard University School of Law. In 1964 he was named a judge of the U.S. District Court for the District of Columbia, and in 1966 he was appointed to the U.S. Court of Appeals for the District of Columbia. He retired in 1989.

Rustin, Bayard (1910–1987)   Civil rights leader. Rustin was an early adviser to Martin Luther King Jr., a founder of the Southern Christian Leadership Conference (SCLC) and deputy director of the March on Washington in 1963. Born in West Chester, Pennsylvania, Rustin attended Wilberforce University in Ohio and Cheney State College in Pennsylvania. In 1941 he joined the Fellowship of Reconciliation, a nonviolent antiwar group, and that same year he became a youth organizer for A. Philip Randolph's projected March on Washington to demand better job opportunities for blacks in the defense industry. During World War II, he was imprisoned as a conscientious objector and served about two-and-a-half years behind bars. In 1947 he was one of the organizers of the first Freedom Ride, the "journey of reconciliation," to test Southern compliance with antidiscriminatory interstate travel laws. Throughout the early 1950s, Rustin was involved with various pacifist and antiwar activities. In 1955 he began to work with Martin Luther King Jr., first on the Montgomery bus boycott and then in helping conceive and draw up plans for the Southern Christian Leadership Conference (SCLC). In the early 1960s, Rustin organized several civil rights demonstrations, the most notable of which was the March on Washington for Jobs and Freedom in 1963. In 1964 he became executive director of the newly formed A. Philip Randolph Institute, and he remained affiliated with the organization until his death in 1987. *Down the Line: The Collected Writings of Bayard Rustin* was published in 1971.

Schwerner, Michael (1939–1964)   Civil rights activist. One of the three civil rights workers killed by the Ku Klux Klan in Mississippi in June 1964. Born in New York City, Schwerner graduated from Cornell University in 1961. The next year he became a social worker at the Hamilton-Madison Settlement House on New York's Lower East Side. In January 1964, Schwerner and his wife, Rita, became CORE (Congress of Racial Equality) field staff workers, and they moved to Meridian, Mississippi to open a field office. Soon after they arrived in Meridian, James Earl Chaney, a young black CORE worker from Meridian, helped them get settled. In early June, while Schwerner and Chaney were attending a training session for the Mississippi Freedom Summer Project at the Western College for Women in Oxford, Ohio, they met Andrew Goodman, a volunteer from New York. Goodman accepted their invitation to join the Meridian CORE field office. On June 21, 1964, while driving back to Meridian after inspecting a torched black church in Philadelphia, Mississippi, Schwerner, Chaney and Goodman were pulled over by Deputy Sheriff Cecil Price and two carloads of Klansmen. The three young men were murdered, and their bodies were deposited at a nearby earthen dam under construction. The disappearance of the three civil rights workers sent shock waves throughout the nation, and within days the FBI began the biggest investigation ever conducted in Mississippi. An anonymous informer revealed the location of the bodies, and on August 4, 1964, the FBI uncovered the decomposed bodies of Schwerner, Chaney and Goodman. In December 1964, the FBI charged 21 men, most of them Klan members, including police officials, for conspiring to abduct and kill the three civil rights workers. In 1967 seven Klansmen, including Deputy Price, were found guilty of federal civil rights violations in the deaths of Schwerner, Chaney and Goodman. They were sentenced to prison terms ranging from three to 10 years. The name of Michael Schwerner is one of the 40 names engraved on the Civil Rights Memorial in Montgomery, Alabama.

Schwerner, Rita Levant (1941–)   Civil rights activist. Born in Mount Vernon, New York, Rita Schwerner attended the University of Michigan and graduated from Queens College in 1964. In 1962 she married Michael Schwerner. While attending Queens College, she performed volunteer work tutoring disadvantaged youth and was a practice teacher at a junior high school in Jamaica, Queens. Throughout the summer of 1964, she remained an outspoken critic of the federal government's investigation into the disappearance of her husband, Michael, and the two other young civil rights workers, James Earl Chaney and Andrew Goodman, in Mississippi. Rita Schwerner pointed out that if all three of the missing young men were black, the FBI and the national press would have most likely ignored their disappearance. At the 1964 Democratic National Convention in Atlantic City, she testified before the credentials committee on behalf of the Mississippi Freedom Democratic Party (MFDP).

Seale, Robert G. [Bobby] (1937–)   Militant civil rights leader and Black Panther Party founder. Born in Dallas, Texas, Seale served a three-year term with the U.S. Air Force, then attended Merritt College in Oakland, California, where he met Huey Newton. In 1966 he and Newton founded the Black Panther Party for Self-Defense. The Panthers were formed to combat police brutality in black ghetto neighborhoods. In 1969 Seale was indicted in Chicago, Illinois with seven others—a group that became known as the Chicago Seven—for conspiracy to disrupt the 1968 Democratic National Convention in Chicago. During a sensational trial, in which Seale's inflammatory behavior in the courtroom caused the judge to separate his case, Seale was sentenced to four years in prison for contempt of court. However, the government later requested that the charges against him be dropped. In 1973 Seale ran for mayor of Oakland as a Democrat and finished second among nine candidates with 43,710 votes. Since the mid-1980s, Seale has been affiliated with the Afro-American Studies Department at Temple University in Philadelphia. He is author of *Seize the Time: The Story of the Black Panther Party and Huey P. Newton* (1970).

Sherrod, Charles (1939–)   Civil rights activist. Sherrod helped organize the Albany movement of 1961–62. Born in Petersburg, Virginia, he graduated from Virginia Union University. In 1961 Sherrod became the Student Nonviolent Coordinating Committee's (SNCC) first field secretary. Sherrod was elected an Albany city commissioner in 1976.

Shuttlesworth, Fred Lee (1922–)   Civil rights leader; president, Alabama Christian Movement for Human Rights (ACMHR), 1956–1970; and secretary, Southern Christian Leadership Conference (SCLC), 1957–1970. Born in Mugler, Alabama, Shuttlesworth received a B.A. degree from Selma University and a B.S. degree from Alabama State Teachers College. From 1957 to 1960, he was the pastor of several Baptist churches, including the First Baptist Church in Birmingham (1957–1960). Shuttlesworth was one of the principal organizers of the demonstrations against segregation in Birmingham in the spring of

1963. He also helped organize the march from Selma to Montgomery, Alabama in March 1965 to protest voting discrimination in the state. Between 1958 and 1969, Shuttlesworth was a party in 10 Supreme Court cases involving civil rights. The Court overturned six of his 10 convictions resulting from his role in the 1961 Freedom Rides and in various Birmingham demonstrations. In *The New York Times v. Sullivan*, decided in March 1964, the Supreme Court reversed a $500,000 libel judgment against Shuttlesworth, three other black ministers and *The New York Times*. The suit had resulted from a March 1960 advertisement in *The Times* that criticized Alabama officials and sought to raise funds for civil rights causes. As a pastor of the Greater New Light Baptist Church in Cincinnati, Ohio and as a board member of the SCLC, Shuttlesworth continues to work for human rights. In 1988 Shuttlesworth established the Shuttlesworth Housing Foundation, which provides grants to help poor families in Cincinatti become homeowners.

Stevens, Thaddeus (1792–1868)   Radical Republican; an outspoken foe of slavery and champion of the equality of man. Born and educated in New England, Stevens moved as a young man to the Lancaster area of Pennsylvania, where he practiced law. Elected to Congress as a Whig in 1848, he served there until 1853 and was elected again in 1858. Stevens supported Lincoln in 1860 but was a critic of his lenient policy toward the South following the end of the Civil War. As a Republican floor leader, he shepherded to passage key measures of congressional Reconstruction, including the Civil Rights Act of 1866, the 14th Amendment and the Reconstruction Act of 1867.

Storey, Moorfield (1845–1929)   First president of the National Association for the Advancement of Colored People (NAACP), 1910–1929. Born in Roxbury, Massachusetts, Storey graduated from Harvard College in 1866 and from Harvard Law School in 1869. After serving as a private secretary to Massachusetts Senator Charles Sumner during Reconstruction, he went into private practice and became a distinguished Boston attorney. In 1909 Storey participated in the National Negro Conference that led to the formation of the NAACP, and he became its first president in 1910. On behalf of the NAACP, he argued several notable civil rights cases before the Supreme Court, including those involving voting rights and residential segregation. The victories won by Storey in the courtroom paved the way for the NAACP's eventual success in achieving the total

destruction of legally sanctioned segregation. Storey's efforts represented the culmination of the original abolitionist commitment, of Charles Sumner and his idea of "equality before the law."

Thurmond, Strom (1902–)   U.S. senator from South Carolina, since 1955. Thurmond was one of the leading opponents of civil rights legislation. The son of a South Carolina politician, he was elected governor after having served as a state senator and circuit court judge. In 1948, after the Democratic National Convention adopted a civil rights plank for its platform, Thurmond was chosen by the defecting States' Rights Party as its presidential candidate. Although he lost to President Truman, he carried five states in the Deep South and received a total of 39 electoral votes. Elected to the U.S. Senate in 1954, Thurmond transferred his allegiance from the Democratic to the Republican Party in 1964 so that he could work openly for the presidential candidacy of conservative Arizona Senator Barry M. Goldwater. He opposed President Johnson's voting rights bill of 1965 on the basis that it would usurp the constitutional authority of the states to establish voter qualifications and claimed that it would create a "totalitarian" federal government. As cochairman of the Senate Judiciary Committee, Thurmond has consistently supported the appointment of "strict constructionists" to the Supreme Court.

Truman, Harry S (1884–1972)   Thirty-third president of the United States. Elected to the U.S. Senate in 1939, Truman ran as Roosevelt's vice-presidential running mate in 1944 and succeeded him as president upon Roosevelt's death on April 12, 1945. Truman brought consternation to the ranks of Southern Democrats when in February 1948 he sent a message to Congress calling for a 10-point civil rights program to end religious and racial discrimination. Some Southern Democrats bolted from the party at the 1948 convention and formed the States Rights Party, also called the "Dixicrat" Party, that nominated Governor Strom Thurmond of South Carolina as their presidential candidate. With the Democratic party divided, public opinion polls predicted that the Republican candidate, Thomas E. Dewey, would win. Surprisingly, Truman was elected by a decisive margin. It was the greatest political upset in American history. In his second term, Truman, frustrated by Congress's refusal to enact civil rights legislation, used his executive power to increase black rights. He appointed a black to the federal judiciary and strengthened the Justice Department's civil rights division. Under his direction, the department filed amicus curiae briefs in support of efforts to end segregation in public schools and stop enforcement of restrictive covenants. Truman also accelerated the pace of desegregation in the armed forces.

Walker, Wyatt Tee (1929–)   Civil rights leader and executive director, Southern Christian Leadership Conference, 1960–1964. Walker played a key role in the planning and organization of the SCLC's desegregation campaign in Birmingham, Alabama in the spring of 1963. Born in Brockton, Massachusetts, he received his divinity degree from Virginia Union University and was pastor of a Petersburg, Virginia church. He was president of the NAACP in Virginia before joining the SCLC as executive director in 1960. In 1961 Walker joined the Freedom Rides, which challenged segregation in interstate facilities, and was a member of the Freedom Rides Coordinating Committee. He also helped direct the antisegregation drive in Albany, Georgia in 1961–62. Since 1964 Walker has been a pastor of Canaan Baptist Church in Harlem.

Wallace, George Corley (1919–1998)   Governor of Alabama. Throughout the 1960s and early 1970s, Wallace symbolized the segregationist cause in the South. In later years, he announced that he was wrong and begged blacks for forgiveness. Born in Clio, Alabama, Wallace received a law degree from Alabama Law School in 1942 and then served three years in the U.S. Air Force. Elected to the Alabama state legislature in 1947, he became a noted speaker and an effective promoter of various bills relating to trade, health and education. In the legislature he also fought against stemming the rising tide of integration. At the Democratic National Convention in 1949, Wallace began his struggle against the party's civil rights planks. Elected as governor of Alabama in 1962, Wallace unsuccessfully blocked the registration of black students at the University of Alabama in June of 1963. In September of that same year, Wallace also tried to prevent court-ordered desegregation of elementary and secondary schools in four Alabama cities. In both cases, integration was achieved after President Kennedy federalized the Alabama National Guard. In 1965 Wallace had a confrontation with President Johnson over his refusal to provide police protection to the Selma–to–Montgomery marchers. Wallace left Johnson with no choice but to federalize the Alabama National Guard. In 1968 Wallace ran for the presidency on an independent ticket and received 13% of the popular vote. While campaigning for the presidency in 1972, he was shot by Arthur Bremer and was partially paralyzed. Failing to win a presidential nomination in 1972 and 1976, Wallace again ran for governor of Alabama in 1982 and won reelection. He retired from office in 1987.

Warren, Earl (1891–1974)   Chief justice of the U.S. Supreme Court, 1953–1969. Warren is best known for leading the Court's unanimous decision in the epochal civil rights case, *Brown v. Board of Education* (1954). In delivering the Court's opinion, Warren stated that "the doctrine of 'separate but equal' has no place. Separate educational facilities are inherently unequal." This decision ended legally sanctioned segregation in the United States. Born in Bakersfield, California, Warren earned degrees in law at Berkeley in 1912 and 1914. During the 1920s, he held a number of district attorney posts, and in 1939, he became attorney general of California. Elected as governor in 1941, Warren went on to become the first governor of the state to be elected three times in succession. In 1953 he was appointed chief justice of the United States by President Eisenhower. In addition to the *Brown* decision, the Warren court made many other important decisions on civil rights, including those involving freedom of the press, the rights of the accused and voting. In 1964 Warren headed the committee that investigated the assassination of President Kennedy. The eponymous Warren Report named Lee Harvey Oswald as the lone assassin of the president. Warren retired from the Court in 1969.

Washington, Booker T. (1856–1915)   Black leader, educator and author. Washington is best known for promoting the philosophy of economic self-reliance. Born into slavery in Hale's Ford, Virginia, Washington graduated from Hampton Institute, one of the earliest freedmen's schools devoted to industrial education, in 1875. In 1881 Washington was appointed to head up the Tuskegee Institute, a black school in Alabama devoted to industrial and agricultural education and to the training of public school teachers. Under his direction, the institute went from two small frame buildings and 30 students to the foremost institute for vocational training of blacks in the country. In his Atlanta Exposition address, which he delivered at the Cotton States Exposition in 1895, Washington preached the doctrine of the separation of the races but stressed that blacks should be integrated into the economic life of the country. Soon after, Washington was denounced by a number of black intellectuals for forsaking equality in return for economic prosperity. W. E. B. Du Bois referred to Washington's address as the "Atlanta Compromise." Although not widely known at the time, Washington secretly worked against Jim Crow laws and racial violence by financing some of the earliest court cases against segregation and by protecting blacks from lynch mobs. He became a friend to the powerful and advised Presidents Theodore Roosevelt and William Howard Taft. In his classic autobiography, *Up From Slavery* (1901), Washington described his fascinating life and set forth his social and historical philosophy.

Wells-Barnett, Ida Bell (1862–1931)   Journalist, lecturer and civil rights leader. Born in Holly Springs, Mississippi, Wells began to teach in a country school at the age of 14. In 1884 she moved to Memphis, Tennessee, where she continued to teach while attending Fisk University during the summers. After losing a lawsuit involving her refusal to give up her seat in a railroad car designated for "whites only," Wells lost her teaching job and subsequently turned to journalism. For a time, she wrote for a local black newspaper, the *Living Word*, and in 1891 she became co-owner and editor of the *Memphis Free Speech*, a black weekly. In 1892, after revealing in the newspaper those responsible for the lynching of three Memphis black men, a mob of whites demolished her printing press and office. Wells fled to New York City, where she worked briefly for the *New York Age*, a black weekly, and then launched a nationwide antilynching lecture campaign. In 1898 she led a delegation to President William McKinley to protest lynchings, and that same year she became secretary of the national Afro-American Council, a forerunner of the NAACP. As chairman of the Anti-Lynching League, she was one of the two black women (Mary Church Terrell was the other) who signed "The Call" on February 12, 1909, the centential of Abraham Lincoln's birth, for a meeting "To Discuss Means for Securing Political and Civil Equality for the Negro." Wells was a member of the committee that led to the founding of the NAACP. In 1912 she began to devote most of her time to promoting suffrage for women. Her books, which documented facts about lynching, include *On Lynchings: Southern Horrors* (1892) and *A Red Record* (1895). Her autobiography, entitled *Crusade for Justice* and edited by her daughter Alfreda Duster, was published in 1970.

White, Walter Francis (1893–1955)   Civil rights leader and author. Walter White, who could have passed for white, was a relentless crusader in the fight to stamp out lynching in the United States, particularly after World War I. His most famous work was *Rope and Faggot: A Biography of Judge Lynch* (1929). Born in Atlanta, Georgia, White graduated from Atlanta University in 1916. While working for the Standard Insurance Company, he formed the Atlanta branch of the NAACP. In 1918 he became assistant to the chief administrative officer of the national NAACP, and in 1929 White became acting secretary of the NAACP. A year later White became secretary of the NAACP and began to direct campaigns for federal civil rights legislation in the form of antilynching laws. During World War II, he participated in the formation of the Committee on Fair Employment Practices. In 1945 and again in 1948, he served as a consultant to the U.S. delegations to the United Nations. Some of White's works include the novels *Fire in the Flint* (1924) and *Flight* (1926) and his autobiography, *A Man Called White* (1948).

Wilkins, Roy (1901–1981)   Executive director of the National Association for the Advancement of Colored People (NAACP), 1955–1977. Born in St. Louis, Missouri, Wilkins graduated from the University of Minnesota in 1923 and soon after joined the staff of the Kansas City *Call*, a leading black weekly. He rose to the position of managing editor. In 1931 he became a staff member of the NAACP, and from 1934 to 1949, he edited the organization's official magazine, *Crisis*. Wilkins was named executive director of the NAACP in 1955. He quickly established himself as one of the most articulate spokesmen in the civil rights movement. Wilkins testified before innumerable congressional hearings and conferred with presidents Kennedy, Johnson, Nixon, Ford and Carter. He was a strong believer in the progress of legislative reform, and he reacted strongly against the combative call for "black power," which was first raised by Student Nonviolent Coordinating Committee's Stokely Carmichael in 1966. Wilkin's moderate stand came under increasing attack by militant civil rights groups in the late 1960s and the 1970s, who derided the NAACP's reformist strategy as "outmoded." Despite criticism from civil rights leaders who espoused black power, Wilkins continued to provide financial and legal support for community action programs in northern ghettos. He retired from the NAACP in 1977 at the age of 76. He was the author of *Standing Fast: The Autobiography of Roy Wilkins* (1982).

Williams, Hosea (1926–)   Civil rights leader and project director, Southern Christian Leadership Conference (SCLC), 1963–1970. Williams, the son of a black sharecropper, was born in Attapulgus, Georgia. He worked as a fruit picker in Florida and served in the U.S. Army before studying at Morris Brown College in Atlanta, where he graduated in 1951. He worked briefly as a high school teacher and as a chemist with the U.S. Department of Agriculture before becoming a full-time project director for the

SCLC in 1963. Williams skill in grass-roots organizing soon made him one of the top assistants to Martin Luther King, president of the SCLC. In 1963 he led antisegregation demonstrations in Savannah, Georgia and St. Augustine, Florida, and in 1965 he was one of the organizers of the Selma–to–Montgomery march for voting rights. During the mid-1960s, Williams was jailed more than 40 times for his civil rights activities. Following King's assassination, he remained with the SCLC and supervised Resurrection City, an encampment of some 3,000 poor people and poverty workers who demonstrated in Washington in May 1968 for greater antipoverty spending. In 1970, as a leader of a radical faction in the SCLC, Williams rejected integration as a civil rights goal and adopted the philosophy of the black power movement. He emphasized, however, that black power meant self-respect and not violence. Williams was national executive director of the SCLC from 1969 to 1971 and again from 1977 to 1979. Since 1972 he has been pastor of the Martin Luther King Jr., People's Church of Love. In 1974 Williams was elected to the Georgia legislature and has since been reelected several times.

X, Malcolm. See Malcolm X.

Young, Andrew J., Jr. (1932–)   Civil rights leader, U.S. representative (1972–1977), U.S. ambassador to the United Nations (1977–1979) and mayor of Atlanta (1983–1989). Born in New Orleans, Louisiana, Young was educated at Dillard University in New Orleans, at Howard University and at Hartford Theological Seminary in Connecticut. From 1957 to 1961, Young served as associate director of the department of youth work for the National Council of Churches. As a Southern Christian Leadership Conference (SCLC)

staff member, Young played a major role in the 1963 Birmingham, Alabama demonstrations against segregation and in the 1965 Selma–to–Montgomery march for voting rights. From 1967 to 1970, he was executive vice-president of the SCLC, and in 1972 Young became the first black member of the Georgia delegation to the U.S. House of Representatives since Reconstruction. President Jimmy Carter named Young ambassador to the United Nations in 1977, and he held that post until 1979. In 1982 he was elected mayor of Atlanta and was subsequently elected to a second term. Young made a bid for the governorship of Georgia in 1990 but lost in the Democratic primary contest. He was appointed by President Bill Clinton in 1995 to establish small- and medium-sized businesses through South Africa. Young is the author of *An Easy Burden: The Civil Rights Movement and the Transformation of America* (1996).

Young, Whitney M. (1921–1971)   Civil rights leader and executive director of the National Urban League (1961–1971). Born in Lincoln Ridge, Kentucky, Young received his B.S. degree at Kentucky State College in 1941. He later did graduate work at the Massachusetts Institute of Technology and earned an M.A. in social work from the University of Minnesota in 1947. He served as dean of the Atlanta University of Social Work from 1954 to 1961. Young was named executive director of the National Urban League in 1961 and was among the organizers of the 1963 March on Washington. As a moderate civil rights leader, he urged blacks to work within the system and encouraged active participation by businesses, corporations and individual whites in the civil rights movement of the 1960s. Young died in Nigeria while attending a meeting with African leaders. He was the author of *To Be Equal* (1964) and *Beyond Racism* (1969).

Appendix C
Acronyms

ACMHR Alabama Christian Movement for Human Rights

BPP Black Panther Party

BSCP Brotherhood of Sleeping Car Porters

COHAR Committee on Appeal for Human Rights

COFO Council of Federated Organizations

CORE Congress of Racial Equality

MFDP Mississippi Freedom Democratic Party

MIA Montgomery Improvement Association

NAACP National Association for the Advancement of Colored People

NNPA National Negro Press Association

SCLC Southern Christian Leadership Conference

SNCC Student Nonviolent Coordinating Committee

UNIA Universal Negro Improvement Association

VEP Voter Education Project

Appendix D

Maps

1. Sites of the Civil Rights Movement

2. School Segregation: May 18, 1954

3. Route of the "Freedom Riders"

4. Protest Demonstrations in the South

1. Sites of the Civil Rights Movement

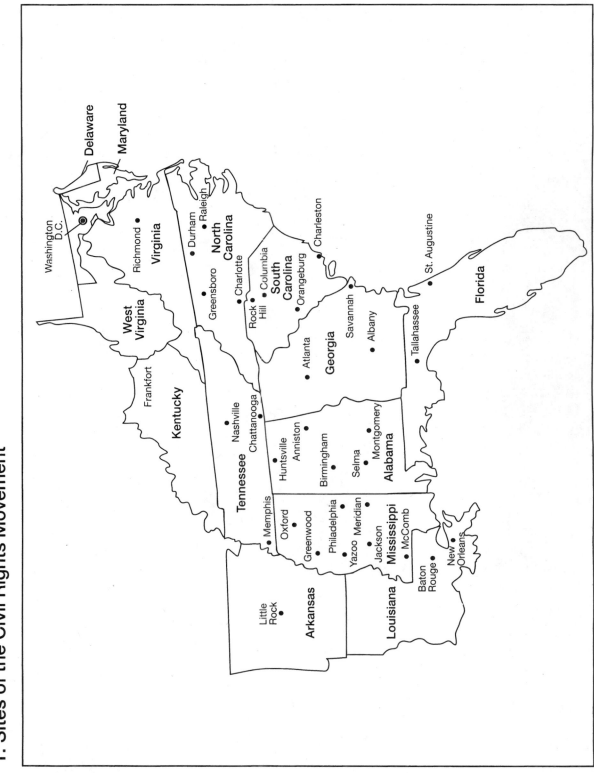

2. School Segregation: May 18, 1954

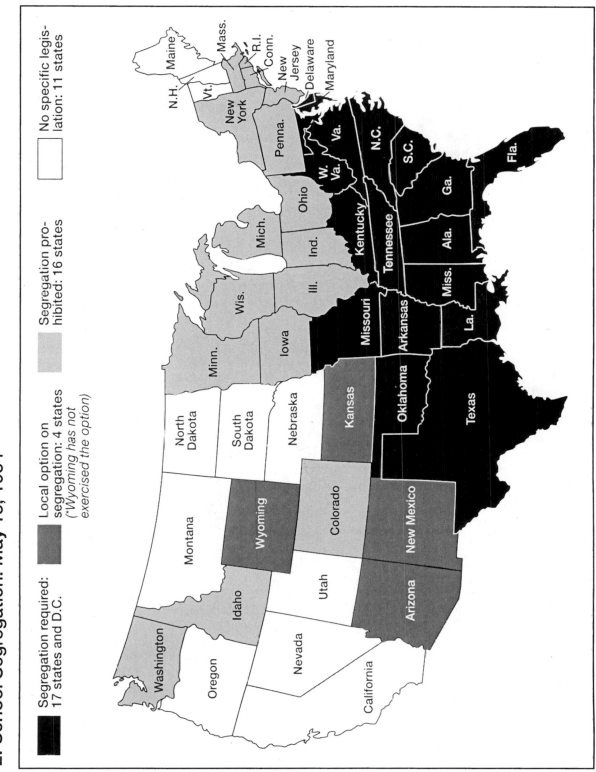

■ Segregation required:
  17 states and D.C.

▨ Local option on
  segregation: 4 states
  (*Wyoming has not
  exercised the option)

▨ Segregation pro-
  hibited: 16 states

□ No specific legis-
  lation: 11 states

3. Route of the "Freedom Riders"

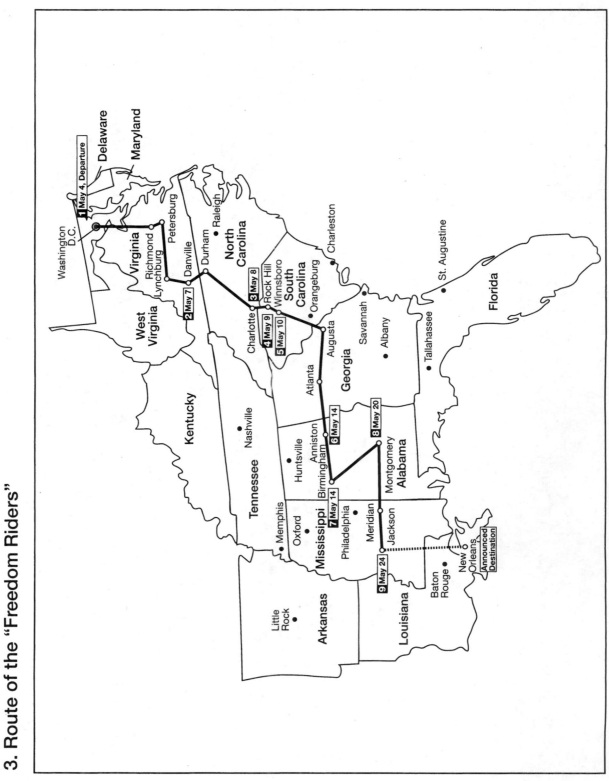

4. Protest Demonstrations in the South

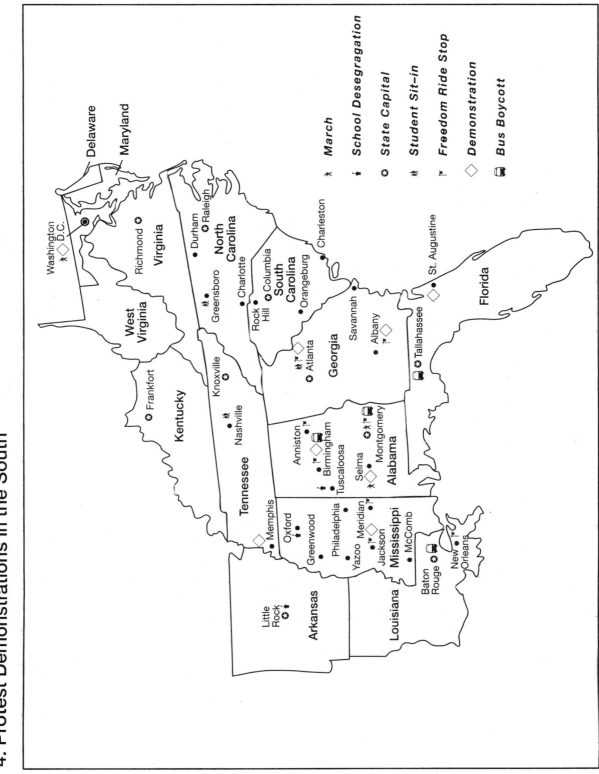

March — ⚐

School Desegragation — ⚐

State Capital — ✪

Student Sit-in — ⚐

Freedom Ride Stop — ⚐

Demonstration — ◇

Bus Boycott — ▣

Bibliography

Abernathy, Ralph, *And The Walls Came Tumbling Down*. New York: Harper and Row, 1989.

Adams, Olive A., *Time Bomb: Mississippi Exposed and the Full Story of Emmett Till*. N.p.: The Mississippi Regional Council of Negro Leadership, 1956.

Alabama Christian Movement for Human Rights, *Birmingham: People in Motion*. Birmingham, Ala.: Alabama Christian Movement for Human Rights, 1966.

Ahmann, Mathew, ed., *The New Negro*. Notre Dame, Ind.: Fides, 1961.

Allen, James S., *Reconstruction: The Battle for Democracy, 1865–1876*. New York: International Publishers, 1963.

Allen, Walter, *Governor Chamberlain's Administration in South Carolina*. New York: G. P. Putnam's Sons, 1888.

Anonymous, "I Saw It Happen in Little Rock," *U.S. News & World Report*, October 4, 1957.

Aptheker, Herbert A. (ed.), *A Documentary History of the Negro People*. New York: Citadel, 1974.

Baines, Lee E., *Birmingham, 1963: Confrontation Over Civil Rights*. B.A. thesis. Cambridge, Mass.: Harvard University, 1977.

Baker, Ella, "Bigger Than a Hamburger," *Southern Patriot*, June 1960.

Baker, Russell, "Capital Is Occupied by a Gentle Army," *The New York Times*, August 29, 1963.

Barrett, George, "Montgomery: The Testing Ground," *The New York Times Magazine*, December 16, 1956.

Barrett, Russell H., *Integration at Ole Miss*. Chicago: Quadrangle, 1965.

Bates, Daisy L., *The Long Shadow of Little Rock: A Memoir*. New York: David McKay, 1962.

Belfrage, Sally, *Freedom Summer*. New York: Viking, 1965.

Bennett, Lerone, Jr., *Before the Mayflower: A History of Black America*. New York: Penguin, 1984.

———, *Wade in the Water*. Chicago: Johnson, 1979.

Bernard, Joel, "Letter from a Freedom Worker," New York *Post*, August 9, 1964.

Blossom, Virgil, *It Has Happened Here*. New York: Harper, 1959.

Blumberg, Rhoda Lois, *Civil Rights: The 1960s Freedom Struggle*. Boston: Twayne, 1984.

Booker, Simeon, "50,000 March on Montgomery," *Ebony*, May 1965.

Branch, Taylor, *Parting the Waters: America in the King Years, 1954–1963*. New York: Simon and Schuster, 1988.

Breslin, Jimmy, "Changing the South," *New York Herald Tribune*, March 26, 1965.

Broderick, Francis L., and Meier, August (eds.), *Negro Protest Thought in the 20th Century*. New York: Bobbs-Merrill, 1965.

Broxton, Barbara Joan, "Jailhouse Notes," *Southern Patriot*, May 1960.

Cagin, Seth, and Dray, Philip, *We Are Not Afraid: The Story of Goodman, Schwerner, and Chaney and the Civil Rights Campaign for Mississippi*. New York: Bantam, 1988.

Carmichael, Stokely, "What We Want," *New York Review of Books*, September 22, 1966.

Carmichael, Stokely and Hamilton, Charles V., *Black Power: The Politics of Liberation in America*. New York: Vintage, 1967.

Carson, Clayborne et al. (ed.), *Eyes on the Prize: A Reader and Guide*. New York: Viking, 1987.

————, *In Struggle: SNCC and the Black Awakening of the 1960s*. Cambridge, Mass.: Harvard University Press, 1981.

Cassel, Louis, "A Hot Spot Revisited," *World Telegram & Sun*, December 28, 1957.

Chafe, William H., *Civilities and Civil Rights*. New York: Oxford University Press, 1980.

Clark, Kenneth B., *Dark Ghetto*. New York: Harper and Row, 1965.

————, *Desegregation: An Appraisal of the Evidence*. Boston: Beacon Press, 1955.

————, *Prejudice and Your Child*. New York: Harper and Row, 1965.

Coffin, Rev. William Sloan, Jr., "Why Yale Chaplain Rode: Christians Can't Be Outside," *Life*, June 2, 1961.

Cowan, Paul, "And Three Letters Home From Mississippi," *Esquire*, September 1964.

Demming, Barbara, "Notes After Birmingham," *Liberation*, Summer 1963.

DeMuth, Jerry, "Freedom Moves In to Stay," *The Nation*, September 14, 1964.

——, "I'm Tired of Being Tired," *The Nation*, June 1, 1964.

Diggs, Charles, "Emmett Trial Over But Negroes Should Never Forget Its Meaning," *Pittsburgh Courier*, October 8, 1955.

Douglass, Frederick, *Life and Times of Frederick Douglass, Written by Himself.* Boston: De Wolfe & Company, 1895.

——, *The Life and Writings of Frederick Douglass* ed. Philip S. Foner. New York: International, 1950–75.

——, *My Bondage and My Freedom.* Urbana, Ill.: University of Illinois Press, 1987; first published, 1855.

——, *Narrative of the Life of Frederick Douglass (Written by Himself).* New York: Signet, 1968; first published, 1845.

——, "Reconstruction," *Atlantic Monthly*, December 1866.

——, *Three Addresses on the Relations Between the White and Colored People of the United States.* Washington, D.C.: U.S. Government Printing Office, 1886.

——, "Mixed Schools," *The New National Era*, May 2, 1872.

Du Bois, William Edward Burghardt, *Black Reconstruction in America.* New York: Harcourt, Brace, 1936.

——, *Dusk of Dawn: An Essay Toward an Autobiography of a Race Concept.* New York: Harcourt, Brace, 1940.

——, *The Souls of Black Folks.* Chicago: McCurg, 1903.

Eckman, Fern Marja, "Freedom Rider's Journey—A Long, Lonesome Road." *New York Post*, May 18, 1961.

Eisenhower, Dwight D., *The Public Papers of the Presidents of the United States, 1957.* Washington, D.C.: U.S. Government Printing Office, 1958.

Evers, Myrlie, with William Peters, *For Us the Living.* Garden City, NY: Doubleday, 1967.

Fager, Charles E., *Selma 1965: The March That Changed the South.* Boston: Beacon Press, 1985.

Farmer, James, "Jailed in Mississippi," *CORE-lator*, August 1961.

——, *Lay Bare the Heart: An Autobiography of the Civil Rights Movement.* New York: Arbor House, 1985.

Finch, Minnie, *The NAACP: Its Fight for Justice*. Metuchen, N.J.: Scarecrow Press, 1981.

Fleming, Walter L., *Documentary History of Reconstruction*. New York: McGraw-Hill, 1906–07.

Forman, James, *The Making of Black Revolutionaries*. Seattle, Wash.: Open Hand, 1985.

———, *Sammy Young In: The First Black College Student to Die in the Black Liberation Movement*. New York: Grove Press, 1968.

Franklin, John Hope, *Reconstruction After the Civil War*. Chicago, Ill.: University of Chicago Press, 1961.

Friedman, Leon, *The Civil Rights Reader*. New York: Walker, 1967.

———, *Argument: The Oral Argument Before the Supreme Court in* Brown v. Board of Education of Topeka, *1952–1955*. New York: Chelsea House, 1969.

Garrow, David J., *Bearing the Cross: Martin Luther King, Jr. and the Southern Christian Leadership Conference*. New York: Morrow, 1986.

———, (ed.), *Birmingham, Alabama, 1956–1963: The Black Struggle for Civil Rights*. Brooklyn, N.Y.: Carlson, 1989.

———, *The FBI and Martin Luther King Jr.* New York: Penguin, 1983.

———, *Protest at Selma: Martin Luther King Jr. and the Voting Rights Act of 1965*. New Haven, Conn.: Yale University Press, 1978.

———, (ed.), *The Walking City: The Montgomery Bus Boycott, 1955–1956*. Brooklyn, N.Y.: Carlson, 1989.

Garvey, Marcus, *An Appeal to the Soul of White America*. Baltimore, Maryland: Soper Library, Morgan State University, 1923.

Gentile, Thomas, *March on Washington: August 28, 1963*. Washington, D.C.: New Day Publications, 1983.

Goldman, Peter, *The Death and Life of Malcolm X*. Urbana, Ill.: University of Illinois Press, 1979.

Goldstone, Robert, *The Negro Revolution*. New York: Macmillan, 1968.

Goodman, Andrew, "Corollary to a Poem by A. E. Houseman," *The Massachusetts Review*, Autumn–Winter, 1964–65.

Gove, Gene, "Where Are They Now? The 4 Original Sit-Ins," *Tuesday*, February 1966.

Grant, Joanne (ed.), *Black Protest: History, Documents, and Analyses, 1619 to the Present*. New York: Fawcett, 1968.

Green, Ernest, ". . . I'm Waiting to Go Back . . . ," *New York Post*, September 23, 1957.

Hamer, Fannie Lou, *To Praise Our Bridges: An Autobiography*. Jackson, Miss.: KIPCO, 1967.

Hamilton, Mary, Inghram, Louise, and others, *Freedom Riders Speak for Themselves*. Detroit, Mich.: News and Letters, 1961.

Hampton, Henry, and Fayer, Steve, *Voice of Freedom: An Oral History of the Civil Rights Movement*. New York: Bantam, 1990.

Herman, Susan, "I Went Because I Had To," *Southern Patriot*, June 1961.

Higginbotham, Julius, "Challenge Alabama Oppression in 50-mile Hike," *Pittsburgh Courier*, March 27, 1965.

Hinckle, Warren, and Welsh, David, "Five Battles of Selma," *Ramparts*, June 1965.

Hofstadter, Richard (ed.), *Great Issues in American History*. New York: Vintage, 1958.

Holt, Len, "Eyewitness: The Police Terror at Birmingham," *National Guardian*, May 16, 1963.

———, "So Few Can Do So Much," *Southern Patriot*, June 1961.

———, *The Summer That Didn't End*. London: William Heinemann, 1965.

Howe, M. A. DeWolfe, *Portrait of an Independent: Moorfield Storey, 1845–1929*. Boston: Houghton-Mifflin, 1932.

Huckaby, Elizabeth, *Crisis at Central High*. Baton Rouge, La.: Louisiana State University Press, 1980.

Hughes, Langston, *Fight for Freedom, the Story of the NAACP*. New York: Norton, 1962.

Johnson, Lyndon Baines, *The Public Papers of the Presidents of the United States, 1964–1969*. Washington, D.C.: U.S. Government Printing Office, 1964–69.

———, *The Vantage Point: Perspectives of the Presidency, 1963–1969*. New York: Holt, Rinehart and Winston, 1971.

Kempton, Murray, ". . . All the Saints," *New York Post*, March 6, 1956.

———, "He Went All the Way," *New York Post*, September 22, 1955.

Kennedy, John F., *The Public Papers of the Presidents of the United States: John F. Kennedy, 1961–1963*. Washington, D.C.: U.S. Government Printing Office, 1962–64.

King, Coretta Scott, *My Life with Martin Luther King, Jr.* New York: Holt, Rinehart and Winston, 1969.

King, Martin Luther, Jr., *A Testament of Hope: Essential Writings of Martin Luther King, Jr.*, ed. James Melvin Washington. San Francisco: Harper and Row, 1986.

——, "Civil Rights No. 1—The Right to Vote," *New York Times Magazine*, March 14, 1964.

——, *Stride Toward Freedom: The Montgomery Story*. New York: Harper, 1958.

——, "The Case Against Tokenism," *New York Times Magazine*, August 5, 1962.

——, "The Montgomery Story," *U.S. News & World Report*, August 3, 1956.

——, "The Social Organization of Non-Violence," *Liberation*, October 1959.

——, "The Time for Freedom Has Come," *New York Times Magazine*, September 10, 1961.

——, *Why We Can't Wait*. New York: Harper and Row, 1963.

King, Mary, *Freedom Song*. New York: Morrow, 1987.

Kluger, Richard, *Simple Justice: The History of* Brown v. Board of Education: *Black America's Struggle for Equality*. New York: Knopf, 1975.

Kumpa, Peter J., "Along the Road," *Baltimore Sun*, March 22–25, 1965.

Lau, James H., *Direct Action and Desegregation*, ed. David J. Garrow. Brooklyn, N.Y.: Carlson, 1989.

Lee, Bains, *Birmingham, 1963: Confrontation Over Civil Rights*. Senior thesis, Harvard College, 1977.

Leonard, George B., "Journey of Conscience—Midnight Plane to Alabama," *The Nation*, May 10, 1965.

Lerner, Max, "Bloody Road," *New York Post*, May 22, 1961.

Levine, Toby Kleban (managing ed.), *Eyes on the Prize: A Reader and Guide*, edited by Clayborn Carson, David J. Garrow, Vincent Harding and Darlene Clark Hine. New York: Penguin, 1987.

Lewis, Anthony, and *The New York Times, Portrait of a Decade: The Second American Revolution*. New York: Random House, 1964.

Lewis, David L., *King: A Critical Biography*. New York: Praeger, 1970.

Lincoln, Abraham, *Abraham Lincoln, Complete Works: Comprising His Speeches, Letters, State Papers and Miscellaneous Writings*, edited by John G. Nicolay and John Hay. New York: Century, 1920; first published, 1886–1906.

Lincoln, C. Eric, "The Strategy of A Sit-in," *Reporter*, February 5, 1961.

Loory, Stuart H., "Reporter Tails 'Freedom' Bus, Caught in Riot," *New York Herald Tribune*, May 21, 1961.

Lynch, John Roy, *Facts of Reconstruction*. New York: Neale Publishing Company, 1914; First published, 1913.

Lyons, Douglas C., "Selma: 25 Years Later," *Ebony*, March 1990.

McKissick, Floyd B. *Three Fifths of a Man*. New York: Macmillan, 1969.

Mahoney, William, "In Pursuit of Freedom," *Liberation*, September 1961.

Malcolm X, as told to Alex Haley, *Autobiography of Malcolm X*, New York: Grove Press, 1965.

———, *By Any Means Necessary: Speeches, Interviews, and a Letter by Malcolm X*, edited by George Breitman. New York: Pathfinder Press, 1970.

———, *Malcolm X Speaks*. New York: Grove Press and Merit Publishing, 1965.

March on Washington for Jobs and Freedom, *To March on Washington*. New York: March on Washington for Jobs and Freedom, 1963.

Mars, Florence, *Witness in Philadelphia*. Baton Rouge: Louisiana State University Press, 1977.

Marshall, Thurgood, "The Legal Attack to Secure Civil Rights," NAACP Papers, Library of Congress, July 13, 1944.

Massie, Robert, "What Next in Mississippi," *Saturday Evening Post*, November 10, 1962.

McAdam, Doug, *Freedom Summer*. New York: Oxford University Press, 1988.

McCord, William, *Mississippi: The Long Hot Summer*. New York: Norton, 1965.

McDonald, Jimmy, "A Freedom Rider Speaks His Mind," *Freedomways*, Summer 1961.

Meir, August and Rudwick, Elliot, *CORE: A Study in the Civil Rights Movement, 1942–1986*. New York: Oxford University Press, 1973.

Meltzer, Milton, *In Their Own Words: A History of the American Negro, 1865–1916*. New York: Crowell, 1965.

Meredith, James H., "I'll Know Victory or Defeat," *Saturday Evening Post*, November 10, 1962.

Mills, Nicolaus, *Like a Holy Crusade: Mississippi 1969– . The Turning Point in the Civil Rights Movement in America*. Chicago, Ill.: Ivan R. Dee, 1992.

———, *Three Years in Mississippi*. Bloomington: Indiana University Press, 1966.

Moody, Anne, *Coming of Age in Mississippi*. New York: Dial Press, 1968.

Moon, Henry Lee, *Balance of Power: The Negro Vote*. Garden City, N.J.: Doubleday, 1948.

Mosley, Ira L., "Written for the Post-Dispatch by a Teacher at Lincoln High School, Venicie, Illinois," *St. Louis Dispatch*, March 20, 1949.

National Association for the Advancement of Colored People (NAACP), *The Day They Changed Their Minds*. New York: NAACP, 1960.

————, Papers. Library of Congress, Washington, D.C.

————, *Speeches by the Leaders: The March on Washington for Jobs and Freedom, August 28, 1963*. New York: NAACP, n.d.

Newton, Huey P. *Revolutionary Suicide*. New York: Harcourt Brace Jovanovich, 1973.

Oates, Stephen B., *Let the Trumpet Sound: The Life of Martin Luther King, Jr.* New York: Harper and Row, 1982.

Ovington, Mary White, "How the National Association for the Advancement of Colored People Began," *Crisis*, August 1914.

Patillo, Melba, "Little Rock, Sept., 1957—The First Day," *New York Post*, September 26, 1957.

Paul, Irene, "A Day in the South: The Touchstone is Courage," *National Guardian*, July 25, 1964.

Peavy, Charles D. *Go Slow Now: Faulkner and the Race Question*. Eugene, Ore.: University of Oregon, 1971.

Peck, James, *Cracking the Color Line*. New York: Congress on Racial Equality, 1962.

————, *Freedom Ride*. New York: Simon and Schuster, 1962.

Pickens, William, "Jim Crow in Texas," *The Nation*, August 15, 1923.

Powledge, Fred, *Black Power/White Resistance*. New York: Simon and Schuster, 1967.

————, *Free At Last? The Civil Rights Movement and the People Who Made It*. Boston: Little, Brown, 1991.

Randolph, A. Philip, "Why Should We March?" *Survey Graphic*, November 1942.

Raines, Howell, *My Soul Is Rested: Movement Days in the Deep South Remembered*. New York: Putnam's, 1977.

Reagon, Bernice, "In Our Hands: Thoughts on Black Music," *Sing Out!*, January/February 1976.

Record, Wilson, and Record, Jane Cassels (eds.), *Little Rock, U.S.A.* San Francisco: Chandler, 1960.

Reddick, L. D., "The Southern Negro Speaks," *Dissent*, March 15, 1956.

Reed, Roy, "Alabama Police Use Gas and Clubs to Rout Negroes," *New York Times*, March 8, 1965.

Reston, James, "The White Man's Burden and All That," *New York Times*, August 28, 1963.

Richardson, James D. (ed.), *A Compilation of the Messages and Papers of the Presidents, 1789–1897*. Washington, D.C.: U.S. Government Printing Office, 1896–99.

Robinson, Jackie, "Marvelous March," *New York Amsterdam News*, September 7, 1963.

Robinson, Jo Ann Gibson, *The Montgomery Bus Boycott and the Women Who Started It*, ed. David J. Garrow. Knoxville: University of Tennessee Press, 1987.

Rustin, Bayard, *Down the Line: The Collected Writings of Bayard Rustin*. New York: Quadrangle, 1971.

——, "Montgomery Diary," *Liberation*, April 1956.

Satcher, Dr. Robert L., "Reflections on the Montgomery Bus Boycott," *Black Collegian*, January/February 1989.

Seale, Bobby, *Seize the Time: The Story of the Black Panther Party and Huey P. Newton*. New York: Random House, 1970.

Seeger, Pete. *Everybody Says Freedom: The Civil Rights Movement in Words, Pictures & Song*. New York: W. W. Norton, 1990.

Selby, Earl and Miriam, *Odyssey: Journey Through Black America*. New York: Putnam's, 1971.

Shuttlesworth, The Rev. Fred L., "Birmingham Revisited," *Ebony*, May 7, 1963.

Shelton, Robert, "Songs a Weapon in Rights Battle," *New York Times*, August 20, 1962.

Slappey, Sterling, "I Saw it Happen in Oxford," *U.S. News & World Report*, October 15, 1962.

Slater, Jack, "1954 Revisited," *Ebony*, May 1974.

Sitkoff, Harvard, *The Struggle for Black Equality, 1954–1980*. New York: Hill and Wang, 1981.

Southern Poverty Law Center, *Free at Last: A History of the Civil Rights Movement and Those Who Died in the Struggle*. Montgomery, Ala.: The Southern Poverty Law Center, 1989.

Stephens, Patricia, "Letter from a Jailed Student," *CORE-lator*, April 1960.

Smithsonian Institution Program in Black American Culture, *Voices of the Civil Rights Movement: Black American Freedom Songs, 1960–1966*. Washington, D.C.: Smithsonian Institution Program in Black American Culture, 1980.

Sugarman, Tracy, *Stranger at the Gates: A Summer in Mississippi*. New York: Hill and Wang, 1966.

Sumner, Charles, *The Works of Charles Sumner*. Boston: Lee and Shepard, 1883.

Sutherland, Elizabeth (ed.), *Letters from Mississippi*. New York: McGraw, 1965.

Swint, Henry L., *Dear Ones at Home*. Nashville, Tenn.: Vanderbilt University Press, 1966.

Thornbrough, Emma Lou (ed.), *Black Reconstructionists*. Englewood Cliffs, N.J.: Prentice-Hall, 1972.

Tobias, Dr. Channing, "Segregation Cases," *Crisis*, December 1953.

Torrance, Ridgely, *The Story of John Hope*. New York: Macmillan, 1948.

Truman, Harry S, *Public Papers of the Presidents of the United States: Harry S Truman, 1948*. Washington, D.C.: U.S. Government Printing Office, 1949.

Tuttle, William M., Jr., "Views of a Negro during the Red Summer of 1919," *Journal of Negro History*, July 1966.

U.S. Congress, *Report of the Joint Committee on Reconstruction*. Washington, D.C.: U.S. Government Printing Office, 1866.

———, *Report of the Joint Select Committee to Inquire into the Condition of Affairs in the Late Insurrectionary States*. 13 vols. Washington, D.C.: U.S. Government Printing Office, 1872.

———, *Report on the Alleged Outrages in the Southern States by the Select Committee of the Senate*. Washington, D.C.: U.S. Government Printing Office, 1871.

Viorst, Milton, *Fire in the Streets: America in the 1960's*. New York: Simon and Schuster, 1979.

Walton, Norman W., "The Walking City: A History of the Montgomery Boycott," *Negro History Bulletin*, October 6, 1956; November 20, 1956; February 20, 1957; April 20, 1957; and January 21, 1958.

Washington, Booker T., *Up From Slavery: An Autobiography*. New York: Doubleday, 1901.

Watters, Pat, *Down to Now: Reflections on the Southern Civil Rights Movement.* New York: Pantheon, 1971.

Webb, Sheyann, and Nelson, Rachel West, with Frank Sikora. *Selma, Lord, Selma: Girlhood Memories of the Civil-Rights Days.* Birmingham: University of Alabama Press, 1980.

Weisbrot, Robert, *Freedom Bound: A History of America's Civil Rights Movement.* New York: Norton, 1991.

Wells-Barnett, Ida B., *Crusade for Justice*, ed. Alfreda Duster. Chicago: University of Chicago Press, 1970.

————, *On Lynchings: Southern Horrors.* New York: Arno Press, 1969; first published, 1892.

Whalen, Charles, and Whalen, Barbara, *The Longest Debate: A Legislative History of the 1964 Civil Rights Act.* Cabin John, Md.: Seven Locks Press, 1985.

White, Theodore H., *The Making of a President: 1964.* New York: New American Library, 1965.

White, Walter F., *A Man Called White.* New York: Arno Press, 1969; first published, 1948.

————, *Rope and Faggot: A Biography of Judge Lynch.* New York: Alfred A. Knopf, 1929.

Whitfield, Stephen J. *A Death in the Delta: The Story of Emmett Till.* New York: The Free Press, 1988.

Wilkins, Roy, with Tom Mathews, *Standing Fast: The Autobiography of Roy Wilkins.* New York: Viking, 1982.

Williams, Juan, *Eyes on the Prize: America's Civil Rights Years, 1954–1965.* New York: Viking Penguin, 1987.

Wofford, Harris, *Of Kennedys and Kings: Making Sense of the Sixties.* New York: Farrar, Straus, and Giroux, 1980.

Wolff, Miles, *Lunch at the Five and Ten: The Greensboro Sit-ins.* New York: Stein and Day, 1970.

Woodley, Richard, "A Recollection of Michael Schwerner," *Reporter*, July 16, 1964.

————, "It Will Be a Hot Summer in Mississippi," *Reporter*, May 21, 1964.

Woods, Robin, "Trouble Was on the Outside," *New York Post*, September 24, 1959.

Wren, Chris, "Personal Terror in Mississippi," *Look*, September 8, 1964.

Young, Whitney, M. *Beyond Racism.* New York: McGraw-Hill, 1969.

———, *To Be Equal.* New York: McGraw-Hill, 1964.

Zinn, Howard, *Albany: A Study in National Responsibility.* Atlanta, Ga.: Southern Regional Council, 1962.

———, *SNCC: The New Abolitionists.* Boston: Beacon Press, 1964.

Credits

INDEX

Page numbers in **boldface** refer to biographical entries in Appendix B; numbers in *italics* refer to illustrations, captions and maps.

A

Aaron, John 93
Abernathy, Ralph 118, **305**
Albany Movement and 140, 141, 142, 148
Birmingham campaign and 162, 163, 164, 169, 171, 172
Montgomery bus boycott and 60, 69, 70, 75, 78, *81, 83*
Poor Peoples march and 251, 255
Selma-to-Montgomery march and 224, 237, *238, 249, 250*
Selma voting rights campaign and 217, 219, 229
Addams, Jane 9
Ahmann, Mathew 180, 188
Alabama Christian Movement for Human Rights (ACMHR) 162, 172
Alabama, University of 167, 169, 227
Albany, Georgia 137
Albany Movement xii, *122,* 137–143, 148, 150–154, 285–286
bus boycott 141
failure of 143, 161
marches and rallies 139, 140, 142, *150*
Alexander, Clifford 256
Alexander v. Holmes City Board of Education 255
Almond, J. Lindsay 96
American Disabilities Act (ADA) 259
Anderson, Candie 126
Anderson, William 138, *139,* 140, 142, 143, 151, 152, 153
Andrews, Notie B. 173
Angelou, Maya 259
Aninston, Alabama
Freedom Rides and 116–117, 122, 129

"Appeal for Human Rights, An" 111, 282
Arn, Edward F. 48
Arrington, Richard 257
Ashmore, Harry 87, 98, 263, 305
"Atlanta Compromise" (Booker T. Washington speech) 6–7, 15, 22
Atlanta, Georgia
sit-in movement in 111–112, 121
Azbell, Joe 70, 72

B

Baez, Joan 181, 225
Baker, Ella 112, *128,* 211, 305–306
Baker, Josephine 186
Baker, Russell 191
Bakke, Alan 256
Baldwin, James 182, *225*
Barnett, Ross 144, 145, 147, 148, 149, 154, 155, 156, 157, 306
Barrett, George 85
Bates, Daisy xii, 91, 92, 97, 103, 186, 306
Belafonte, Harry 96, 162, 170
Belfrage, Sally 211
Belton, Ethel Louise 41
Benner, Charles J. 207
Bennett, L. Roy 69, 77
Benston, Jim 233
Bernard, Joel 210
Bevel, James 164, 172, 218, 233–234, 240–241, 306–307
Billups, Charles 185
Birmingham, Alabama 161
Freedom Rides and 116, 118, 129, 130
Birmingham campaign xii, 143, 161–167, 169, 170–175, 178, 215, 186–287
Kennedy Administration and 164, 165, 166, 167, 169, 170, *174,* 175

media attention and *165, 171, 172, 173*
nonviolent resistance and 162–163, *164–165, 171*
police action in *165, 171, 173, 174*
Black Codes 2, 13
Black, Hugo 38, 144, 148
Black Panthers (Black Panther Party for Self-Defense) 246–247, 254, 255, 256, 261–262, 296–297
Black power movement 228, 243–247, 254, 261
SNCC and 246
Blair, Ezell Jr. 109, 123, *124*
Blake, Eugene Carson 180, 187, *191,* **307**
Blake, James 68
"Bloody Sunday" march (Selma, Alabama) 217–221, 229, 231–234
Blossom Plan 87–88
Blossom, Virgil T. 87–88, 97, 104
Bolden, Willie 233
Bolling v. Sharpe 35, 37, 41
Bond, Julian 129, 260, 265, **307**
Booth, John Wilkes 13
Boudwin, Jean 189
Boutwell, Albert 162, 167, 171–172
Boyce, Joseph N. 265
Boynton v. Virginia 114
Bradley, Bill (D.-N.J) 265
Bradley, Bill 238
Bradley, Thomas 256
Braton, Wiley 97
Braun, Carol Moseley 259
Breslin, Jimmy 240
Briggs, Harry 34, 40
Briggs v. Elliot 34, 35, 36, 37, 40, 41, 43
Brooke, Edward W. 254
Brotherhood of Sleeping Car Porters (BSCP) 10, 15, 177
Browder v. Gayle 77
Brown, H. Rap 254, **307**

Brown, Henry Billings 22
Brown, James 246
Brown, Linda 35, 40
Brown, Minniejean 92, 95, *105, 106*
Brown, Oliver 35, 40
Brown, R. Jes 199, 208
Brown, Robert Erving 88
Brown, Ronald H. 258, 265
Brown v. Board of Education xii, 6, 29–51, 89, 116, 137, 177, 228, 252, 256
as catalyst for civil rights movement 39
effects of 39, 47–50
implementation of 39, 42, 53, 61, 88, 94, 276–277
segregationists reaction to 39, 42, 47, 48, 49
U.S. Supreme Court and 36–39, 40, 41, 45–47, 53, 61, 87, 93, 274–277
Broxton, Barbara John 128
Bruce, Blanche 3
Bunche, Ralph 224
Bryant, Carolyn 55, 56, 61
Bryant, Ron 55, 57, 58, 59, 60, 61
Bulah, Shirley Barbara 41
Bush, George 258, 259
buses, segregation on 67–68
See also Montgomery bus boycott
busing 255–256
Butler, Richard C. 93
Byrd, Harry 48

C

"Call, The" 270–271
Carey, Gordon R. 129
Carmichael, Stokely **307–308**
Black power and 243–245, 246, 254, 261
Freedom Summer and 135
Carter, Hodding 158, 264
Carter, Jimmy 228, 256, 257

Carter, Robert L. 31, 35, 37, 43, 44, 263, **308**
Cassel, Louis 105–106
Center for Nonviolent Social Change 260
Chamberlain, Daniel H. 21
Chambliss, Robert E. 256
Chaney, Fannie Lee 212
Chaney, James Earl 199, *200*, 205, 206, 209, 211, 212, **308**
Chase, Lucy 17
Chicago
King and 254
Chisolm, Shirley 256, **308**
Civil Disobedience (Thoreau) 71
Civil Rights Act (1866) 3, 13, 269–270
Civil Rights Act (1875) 3–4, 14
Civil Rights Act (1957) 95, 195, 280–282
Civil Rights Act (1960) 282–284
Civil Rights Act (1964) 183, 205, 229, 259, 289–290
Johnson and 196–197, 210
lobbying for 196
passing of 196–197, 215
Civil Rights Act (1968) 299
Civil Rights Act (1991) 259, 300–303
Civil Rights Commission 13
Civil Rights Memorial *258*, 259
Civil War, U.S. xi, 1–2, 17, 29, 137, 216
Clarendon County South Carolina
school segregation and 33–35, 40, 43
Clark, Jim 216, 217, 219, 220, 236
Clark, Kenneth 34, 37, 40, 43, **308–309**
Clark, Mark 255
Clark, Robert 204
Clark, Tom 38
Clinton, Bill 259, 260, 265
Cloud, John 219, 221
Coffin, William Sloan 134
COFO *See* Council of Federated Organizations
COINTELPRO 247, 254
Collins, Leroy 121
Colored Farmers Alliance 5
Congress of Racial Equality (CORE) xi, 120, 127, 168, 178, 180, 197, 199, 203, 243, 245
Freedom Rides and 114–115, 117, 122, 129
Connor, Theophilus Eugene ("Bull") 117–118, 130, 161, 162, 163, 164, 165, 166, 171, 173, 174, 216, **309**
Cooper, A. J. 256

Cooper v. Aaron 93, 96, 107
Cothran, John 63
CORE *See* Congress of Racial Equality
Council of Federated Organizations (COFO) 197–198, 201, 206, 209–210
Cowan, Paul 210
The Crisis 9

D

Dallas County, Alabama 215, 126, 217, 228
Darrow, Clarence 26
Davies, Ronald N. 89, 90, 95, 98
Davis, Dorothy E. 36, 40
Davis, Jefferson 67, 225
Davis, John W. 37–38, 41, 45, 46
Davis v. County School Board 35, 36, 37, 40, 41, 44
Declaration of Independence vi
Dees, Morris 263
De La Beckwith, Byron 260
DeLaine, Joseph xii, 34, 40, 43
Demming, Barbara 173
Democratic National Convention (1968) 201–204, 205, 213–294
Democratic Party MFDP and 201–204, 213–214
Dennis, David 211
Dewey, John 9
Dewey, Thomas 11, 16
Dickinson, William J. 237
Diggs, Charles 58, 65, **309**
Dinkins, David 259, 264
Dirksen, Everett 196, 226
"Dixiecrats" 11, 13, 16, 27
Dixon, Julius 256
Doar, John 118, **309**
Douglass, Frederick 1, 14, *17, 18, 20, 21, 22, 309–310*
Dred Scott case 6
Du Bois, W. E. B. *8*, 23, 25, 35, 38, 137, 251, 310
Niagara movement and 9, 15, 24
Dukakis, Michael 252, 258
Dulles, Allen 201
Dylan, Bob 181

E

Eastland, James O. 39, 47, 119, 132–133, **310**
Eckford, Elizabeth 89, *90*, 94, 99, 105
Edmund Pettus Bridge, Alabama 218, *219*, 221, 229, 232, 260

Eisenhower, Dwight D. xii, 38, 41, 78, 81
Little Rock Central High School, Arkansas and 89, 90, 91, 92, 93, 95, 98–99, 100, 101, 102, 105
Elliot, Robert Brown 20–21, 310
Elliot, Roderick 34, 40
Emery, Jane 97
Equal Rights Amendment 257
Evans, Melvin 256
Evers, Medgar 169, 260, **310–311**
Evers-Williams, Myrlie 260
Executive Order 8802 10, 177, 273
Executive Order 9981 273–274

F

Fair Employment Practices Committee (FEPC) 10, 15, 177
Farmer, James *115*, 202, 204, 208, 227, 237, **311**
CORE and 114
Freedom Rides and 114–116, 119, 129, 134
March on Washington and 178, 180, 187
Faubus, Orval 88–90, 93, 95, 97, 98, 99, 100, 104, **311**
Faulkner, William 63
Federal Bureau of Investigation (FBI) 116, 117, 200, 205
black radical movement infiltrated by 247, 256
Ferraro, Geraldine 258
Fifteenth Amendment 14, 19, 270
Figgs, Robert 43
First Reconstruction Act (1867) 14
Fish, Hamilton 14
Folsom, James E. 82
Ford, Gerald 256
Ford, Johnny 256
Forman, James 199, 207, 221, 223, 225, **311**
Fourteenth Amendment 2, 3, 6, 15, 22, 29, 32, 44, 270
Frankfurther, Felix 45
Franklin, John Hope 260
Freedmens Bureau 2, 14, 18
Freedom Rides xii, 10, 114–119, 122, 129–135, 138, 148, 161, 228, 266, *334*
aim of 114–115
dangers of 116
federal protection of 116
imprisonment and 119, 122, 139–140

JFK and 116, 117, 118, 132, 134
John Lewis and 116, 117, 131, 132
mob violence and 116–117, 118, 122, 129–*130*, 131
Robert Kennedy and 117, 118, 119, 122, 131, 132, 133
Freedom Schools 201, *210*
Freedom Singers 209
Freedom songs 119, 133, 139, 151, 152, 153, 170, 173, 185, 209, 213, 231, 239
Freedom Summer 195–201, 205, 206–212, 214, 288–289
See also Mississippi Freedom Democratic Party (MFDP)

G

Gaines, Lloyd Lionel 31
Gandhi, Mohandes K. (Mohatma) 110, 123, 140, 153
Garvey, Marcus 26, **311–312**
Gayle, W. A. 73, 77, 81, 84
Gebhart, Francis B. 41
Gebhart v. Belton 35, 37, 41
Ghosts of Mississippi 260
Gleed, Robert 19
Goldwater, Barry 203, 212
Goodman, Andrew 199, *120, 201, 205, 206, 209, 211*, **312**
Goodman, Carolyn 209, 212
Goodman, Robert 211
Graetz, Robert 75, 78
Graham, Clarence 129
Gray, William III 256
Green, Ernest *91*, 92, 95, 100–101, 104, 266
Greenberg, Jack 35, 312
Greenwood, Tommy 189
Grimke, Francis J. 9
Greensboro, North Carolina
sit-ins and 109–*110*, 114, 120, 121, 123–125
Griswold, Erwin N. 48
Guihard, Paul 146, 155
Gunter, Roy 146

H

Hall, Grover C. 81
Hamer, Fannie Lou 202, 203, 204, 207, *213*, 313
Hampton, Fred 255
Harlan, John Marshall 6, 22
Harstfield, William B. 113
Hatcher, Richard 261
Hayden, Tom 264
Hayes, George E. 47
Hayes, Rutherford B. 5, 14
Henderson, Clarence *110*

Henry, Aaron 197, 198, 202, 203, *204*, 213
Herbert, Edward F. 48
Herman, Susan **134**
Hernandez, Mimi 211
Heschel, Abraham 224
Hibbler, Al 163
Hicks, James 64, 65, 100, **313**
Higginbotham, Julius 238
Highlander Folk School (Tenn.) 69
Hill, Elias 20
Hill, Joshua 20
Hill, Oliver 44
Holt, Len 133, 173
Hood, James 169
Hooks, Benjamin 256
Hoover, J. Edgar 247, 254
Hope, John 7, 22, **313**
Houston, Charles *30–32*, **313–314**
Huckaby, Elizabeth 104
Huddleston, George 130
Huff, William Henry 62, 63
Hughes, Langston 246
Huie, William Bradford 56, 61, 200
Humphrey, Hubert H. 190, 196, 203, 255
Hurley, Ruby 64, 151

I

"I Have A Dream" (King speech) 182, 184, 188–189
Ingalls, Luther 84
Ingram, Louise 135
Interstate Commerce Commission (ICC) 61, 114–115, 119, 122, 138, 139, 148

J

Jackson, Jesse *249*, 256, 260, **314**
  1984 political campaign and 252, 257–258, *262–263*
  1988 political campaign and 252–253, 258, *262*
Jackson, Jimmy Lee 218, 229, 231, 230, **314**
Jackson, Mahalia 182, 189
Jackson, Maynard 256
Jacob, John E. 263
James E. Swann et al. v. Charlotte-Mecklenburg Board of Education et al. 299–300
Javits, Jacob 189, 208–209, 220
Jayhawkers 4
Jefferson, Thomas vi
Jenkins, W. A. Jr. 163
Jim Crow Car Law 15

Jim Crow laws 5–6, 25–26, 29, 67, 70, 115
Johns, Barbara Rose 36
Johnson, Andrew 2, 14, 18
Johnson, Frank M. Jr. 223, 229, 290–293
Johnson, Lyndon Baines 184, *191*, 195–196, 202–203, 213–214, 217, 220, 221–222, 226, 228, 235, 237, 241, 253, 254, **314**
  Civil Rights Act (1964) and 196–197, 205, 206, 210
  Voting Rights Act (1965) and 222–223, 226–227
  Wallace and 221
Johnson, Marion *91*
Johnson, Paul 149
Jones, Charlie 154
Jones, Curtis 54, 56, 61
Jordan, Vernon E. Jr. 266
Journey of Reconciliation 115, 116
Judgement at Nuremberg 220

K

Katzenbach, Nicholas 145, 167, **314–315**
Kelly, Asa 142, 153
Kempton, Murray 64, 83
Kennedy, John F. **315**
  Albany Movement and 141, 153
  assassination of 184, 195
  Birmingham campaign and 165, 166, 169, 170, *174*
  civil rights position of 114, 167–168, 175–176, 196, 197, 206
  Freedom Rides and 116, 117, 118, 132, 134
  King and 113, 121–122
  March on Washington and 179–180, 182–183, 184, 185, 190–*191*
  University of Mississippi and 145, 146, 149, 155
Kennedy, Robert F. 113, 121–122, 205, **315–316**
  assassination of 251, 255
  Birmingham campaign and 164, 169, *174*, *175*
  on Kings death 250–251
  voting rights and 148, 237
  University of Mississippi and 145, 154, 155
Kerner Commission 248
  See also National Advisory Commission on Civil Disorders
Kilpatrick, James 125, 158

King, A. D. 163
King, Carleton J. 235
King, Coretta Scott 72, 74, *83*, *113*, *121*, *169*, *195*, *217*, *238*, 260, **316**
King, Dexter Scott 260
King, Edwin 198, 202, 203
King, Martin Luther Jr. xi, 60, 125, *126–127*, 128, 168, 177, 195, 203, 213, 258, 227, 243, 244, *249*, 253, 254, *261*, *265*, 266, **316**
  Abernathy as successor to 255
  Albany Movement and 140, 141, 142, 143, 148, 151–152, 153, 154, 161–162
  arrests and imprisonment of 74, 77, 112–113, 121, 122, 140, 141, 148, 163–164, 171, 217, 229
  assassination of 243, 248–251, 255
  belief in nonviolent resistance 110, 123, 142, 161
  Birmingham campaign and 161–164, 166, 167, 169, 170, 171, 172, 175
  Freedom Rides and 118–119, 135
  "I Have A Dream" and 182, *188–189*
  March on Washington and xii, 178, 180, 182, *188–189*, *191*, *194*
  Montgomery bus boycott and xi, 70–72, 73, 74, 75, 76, 77, 78, 80, *81*, 82, *83*, 84, 85
  philosophical influences of 71
  Nobel Peace Prize and 205, 214, 216
  rioting after death of 250, 255
  Robert Kennedy on death of 250–251
  Selma-to-Montgomery march and 224–225, 229, 237, *238*, 241
  Selma voting rights campaign and 215, 216–217, 218, 220–221, 222, 229, 231, 233, 234, 236
King, Martin Luther Sr. 113
King, Rodney 259, 260
King, Slater 142
Kirck, George W. 19
Ku Klux Klan (KKK) 4, 13, 19–20, 42, 53, 117, 118, 122,

166, 200, 205, 226, 229, 241, 251
Ku Klux Klan Act (1871) 14, 15
Kumpa, Peter J. 238–239

L

Lake, Clancy 130
Lange, Kathy 238
Lankford, Tom 232–233
Lawson, James 110, 127, **317**
Lee, Cage 238
Lee, George W. 53–54
Lee, Robert E. 2, 197
Leland, Mickey 256
Lemley, Harry J. 93, 95, 106
Leonard, George B. 237
Lerner, Max 132, 158
"Letter from a Birmingham Jail" (King) 163–164, 170–171, 217
Lewis, Anthony 264
Lewis, John *198*, *204*, 212, 213, 254, 260, **317**
  Freedom Rides and 116, 117, 118, 131, 132
  March on Washington and 178, 180, 182, 183, 187, *191*
  Selma-to-Montgomery march and *238*
  Selma voting rights campaign and *219*, 220, 223, 229, 231–232, 234
Leylveld, Arthur J. 212
Lincoln, Abraham 1, 13, 24, 180, 227
Lin, Maya 259
Little, Malcolm *See* Malcolm X
Little Rock, Arkansas 87, 92, 93
Little Rock Central High School, Arkansas desegregation of xii, 87–107
Little Rock Nine 89, 90, 91, 92, 95, *96*, 100, 101, 103, 104, 105, 106, 260
Little Rock Private School Corporation 93
Liuzzo, Viola 226, 229, **317**
Loeb, Harry 249
Long, Russell B. 39, 47
Lorraine Motel 250
Lorry, Stuart H. 131
Los Angeles riots (Watts) xii, 230, 248
Los Angeles riots (1992) 248, 259
Lucy, Autherin J. 77
Lynch, John Roy 21, 317
lynchings 9, 17, 23, 26, 27, 53
  See also Till, Emmett

M

McAllister, Paul D. 193–194
McCain, Franklin *109, 110,* 123, 124
McDonald, Jimmy 134
McGovern, George 256
McKissick, Floyd B. 187, 243, 244, 246, 254, **317–318**
McLaurin v. Oklahoma State Regents 32, 37, 40
McNally, Harold J. 43
McNeil, Joseph 109, *110,* 123, 124
McShane, James P. 146
Mahoney, William 133
Malone, Vivian 169, 227
Malcolm X 165, 175, 208, 214, *217, 218,* **318**
    assassination of 217, 229
Mandela, Nelson 253
Mann, Woodrow Wilson 91, 97
March Against Fear (1966) 243–246, 254
    See also black power movement
March on Washington (1941) 10, 15, 177, 178
March on Washington (1963) 168, 177–194
    idea and purpose of 177–178, 185
    "I Have A Dream" (King) and 182, 184, 188–189
    JFK and 179–180, 182, 183, 184, 185, *190–191*
    John Lewis and 178, 182, 183, 187, *191*
    King and xii, 178, 180, 182, 184, *186,* 194
    spirit of *180–181,* 182, 183, *184, 186, 187,* 190, 192
Margold Bible 29, 31, 32
Margold, Nathan 29
Marshall, Burke 118, 141, 165, 166, 175, 221, **318**
Marshall, Thurgood 26–27, 31, 40, 43, *44,* 82, 105, 228, 229, 254, 259–260, 265, **318**
    Brown and 32–*33,* 37, 39, 41, 45, *47,* 48
    eulogies of 266
Massie, Robert 156
Meany, George 235
Memphis, Tennessee
    King and 248–250
Meredith, James 319
    March Against Fear and 243–245, 254
    University of Mississippi and 122, 143–147, 148, *149,* 155, 156, *157, 158,* 159, 259

Meridian, Mississippi 199
MFDP *See* Mississippi Freedom Democratic Party
MIA *See* Montgomery Improvement Association
Milam, Juanita 55
Milam, J. W. 55, 56, 57, 58, 59, 60, 61
Military, segregation in 11, 16, 42
Mississippi
    Freedom Summer in 197–201
    Ku Klux Klan activities in 200
    voter registration in 197–199, 202
Mississippi Freedom Democratic Party (MFDP) 198, 201–204, 205, 207
    Democratic Party and 201, 213
    Johnson challenged by 202–203, 205
Mississippi Freedom Summer Project *See* Freedom Summer
Mississippi University of 144–147, 148, 149
Missouri v. Canada 31–32
Mitchell, Clarence 196, 265, **319**
Mize, Sidney C. 144
Mondale, Walter 235, 258
Montgomery, Alabama 215, 221, 223, 225, 226
    Freedom Rides and 118, 122, 131
Montgomery bus boycott xii, 60, 67–85, 178, 227, 228, 277–278
    beginnings of 69–70, 79–80
    Kings role in 70–72, 73, 74, 75, 76, 77, 80, 81, 82, 83, 84, 85
    See also Parks, Rosa
Montgomery Improvement Association (MIA) 70, 72, 73, 74, 77, 78, 80
Moody, Anne 62
Moon, Henry Lee 27
Morgan v. Virginia 114
Morin, Relman 100
Morse, Wayne 105, 190
Moses, Robert 197–198, 207, **319–320**
Mosley, Ira L. 27
Mothershed, Thelma *105*
Motley, Constance Baker 37, 39, 254, 320
Murphy, Curtis 127

Murphy, Timothy 239

N

NAACP *See* National Association for the Advancement of Colored People
NAACP Legal Defense Fund school desegregation and 32–39, 40, 41, 45, 46
    See also Brown v. Board of Education and Marshall, Thurgood
Nabrit, James M. Jr. 39, 45, *47,* **320**
Nash, Diane 117, 135
Nashville, Tennessee
    desegregation in 114
    sit-in protests in 110, 116, 120, *121, 125–126*
National Advisory Commission on Civil Disorders 248, 254, 255, 297–299
National Association for the Advancement of Colored People (NAACP) 8–10, 26, 67, 68, 75, 77, 88, 91, 93, 101, 120, 122, 138, 140, 161, 168, 177, 178, 196, 197, 260
    formation of 8–9, 15, 24–25, 271–272
National Grange 5
National Labor Convention of Colored Men 14
National Urban League 178, 188
Nelson, Rachel West 233
Neshoba County, Mississippi 199, 205
New Deal 29
Newton, Huey P. 246, 254, 261–262, **320–321**
Niagara Movement 9, 15, 24
    See also Du Bois, W. E. B.
Nineteenth Amendment 15
Nixon, E. D. 69, 74, 75, 77, 78, 79, 321
Nixon, Richard M. 113, 255
Nonviolent resistance
    Albany Movement and 138, 140, 150, 151, 153
    Birmingham campaign and 162–163, 164–*165, 169, 171,* 173
    Freedom Rides and 114–119, 129–135
    Kings belief in 123
    Selma voting rights campaign and 216–221, 231–234

sit-ins and 109–114, 123–127

O–P

Ovington, Mary White 25
Parchman State Penitentiary 119, 122, 135
Paris, Robert *See* Moses, Robert
Parker, Wheeler 62
Parks, Rosa xii, 227, 260, *262, 321*
Patterson, John 117, 118–119, 130, 131, **321**
Pattillo [Beals], Melba 100, 103, 104, *105*
Peck, James 116, 129
Peter, Paul and Mary 181
Philadelphia, Mississippi 199, 200, 201, 205, 211
Philips, Charles 173
Pickens, William 26
Plessy, Homer 6
Plessy v. Ferguson 15, 22, 29, 30, 32, 41
Poll tax 5, 26, 27
Poor People's Campaign (1968) 248, 254–255
    Abernathy and 251
Populists 5
Powell, Adam Clayton Jr. 8, 81, *128, 189,* **321**
Powell, Adam Clayton Sr. 8
Powell, Colin L. *258*
President's Commission on Race Relations 260
Price, Cecil 200, 201
Price, David 123
Prince Edward County, Virginia school segregation and 36
Prinz, Joachim 180, 188, *191,* **321**
Pritchett, Laurie 140, 141, 142, 151, 152, 154, **322**
Project C 162, 164
    See also Birmingham campaign

R

Rainbow/PUSH Coalition 260, 314
Rainey, Joseph H. *14,* **322**
Rainey, Lawrence 200, 201
Randolph, A. Philip 11, *26,* 65, *96,* 238, **322**
    March on Washington (1941) 10, 15, 177
    March on Washington (1963) 177–*178,* 180, 181–182

Rangel, Charles 264
Rapier, James 20, **322**
Rauh, Joseph L. Jr. 196, 201–202, 213, 263, **322–323**
Ray, Gloria *91, 105*
Ray, James Earl 251, 255
Reagan, Ronald 257, 258
Reagon, Bernice 150
Reagon, Cordell 138
Reconstruction xi, 1–5, 10, 13–14, 17–21, 92, 177, 254
Reddick, L.D. 83
Reeb, James J. 221, 222, 229, **323**
Reed, Roy 232
Reed, Stanley 38
Reed, Willis 58
Rehnquist, William H. 266
Reston, James 185
Resurrection City 251
    See also Poor People's Campaign
Reuther, Walter P. 180, 187, *191*
Revels, Hiram 3, *13*, 14, **323**
Richmond, David 109, 123, *124*
Ricks, Willie 244
Rioting 254
    Detroit xii, 248
    after Kings death 250, 255
    L.A. riots (1992) 248, 259
    Newark xii, 248
    Watts (1965) xii, 230, 248
Rivers, Hazel Mangie 189
Roberts, Torrence *105*
Robinson, Frank 256
Robinson, Jackie 15, 96, 193, *194*
Robinson, Jo Ann 69, 79, 83
Robinson, Marvin 175
Robinson, Spottswood 31, 36, 46, *323*
Rock, John 1, 13
Rogers, Willie 134
Roosevelt, Franklin 10, 15, 177
Roosevelt, Theodore 8
Russell, Richard B. 48, 104–105, 197
Rustin, Bayard 82, 176, *238*, 323
    March on Washington and *178, 179*, 180, 182, 183
Ryan, William Fitts 189–190

S

Salisbury, Harrison 161
Satcher, Robert L. 263
Saxton, Rufus 18
Schlesinger, Arthur Sr. 48
School desegregation
    Eisenhower and 89, 90, 91, 92, 93, 95, 98, 101, 102, 105
    NAACP and 29–39, 40, 41

Supreme Court and 38–39, 41, 42, 47, 53, 61, 87, 88, 93
white opposition to 39, 42, 47, 48, 49, 50, 53, 88–89, 91, 92, 93, 95, 96, 98, 100, 102, 104, 107
    See also Brown v. Board of Education; Little Rock Central High School; and Meredith, James
Schwerner, Anne 209, *212*
Schwerner, Michael 199, 200, 201, 205, 206, 207, 209, 211, 212, **324**
Schwerner, Rita 199, 202, 207, 209, 211, **324**
SCLC. *See* Southern Christian Leadership Conference
Scott, J. A. 21
Scottsboro Boys 15
Seale, Bobby 246, 254, **324**
Searles, A. C. 140
Seay, S. S. 84
Segregation xi, xiii, 6, 9, 12, 14, 137, 162, 228
    at bus terminals 115, 119, 122, 138, 148
    in schools. *See Brown v. Board of Education* and school desegregation
    Wallaces support for 167
    See also Albany Movement; Birmingham campaign; Freedom Rides; Montgomery bus boycott; and sit-in movement
Seigenthaler, John 117, 118, 266
Seitz, Collins 41
Selma-to-Montgomery march 223–226, 229, 237–241, 244, 293–294
    aim of 218
    hostility to 224
    Johnson and 223, 237
    King and 221, 224–226, 237, *238*, 241
    spirit of xii, 224–225, *238, 239, 240*
Selma voting rights campaign xi, xii, 215–221, 231–241
    "Bloody Sunday" march of 217–221
    Congressional reaction to 235
    John Lewis in *219*, 220, 229, 231–232, 234
    Johnson and 220, 221–223, 235, 236
    King and 216–217, 218, 220–221, 229, 231, 233, 234, 236

media attention of 216–217, 219
nonviolent resistance in 216–221, 231–234
police action in 219–220
SCLC and 217
SNCC and 217
state troopers in 220, 221, 231–234
"separate but equal" doctrine 6, 15, 27, 29, 31, 36, 38, 40, 41
Seward, William 14
Shaheen, Jeanne 260
Shelton, Robert 166
Sherrod, Charles 138, 150, 154, **324**
Shriver, Sargent 113
Shurz, Carl 18
Shuttlesworth, Fred 162, 163, 165–166, 172, 173–174, **324–325**
Simple Justice 38
Sims, B.J. 80
Sipuel v. Board of Regents of the University of Oklahoma 15
Sit-in movement xii, 109–114, 116, 120–121, 123–127, 138, 228, *332*
    in Atlanta 111–112
    in Greensboro 109, 114, *120*, 123–125
    King and 110, 121
    in Nashville 110, 114, 116, 120, *121*, 125–126
    origins and growth of 110
    SNCC and 112
    white hostility to 110, *111*
Sitton, Claude 156, 264
Sixteenth Street Baptist Church 104, 256
Slappery, Sterling 156
slavery xi, xii, 1, 2, 13, 17, 137, 215
Smiley, Glenn 75, 78
Smith, Billy *110*
Smith, Howard K. 129
Smith, J. Clay Jr. 263–264
Smith, Ledger 180
Smith, Robert B. 59, 64
Smith, Ruby Doris 131, 134–135
Smith, Sherill 238
Smitherman, Joel 236
SNCC *See* Student Nonviolent Coordinating Committee
Souls of Black Folk, The (Du Bois) 8–9, 137
Southern Christian Leadership Conference (SCLC) 112, 141, 143, 168, 178, 197, 199, 256
    Birmingham campaign and 161, 162, 163, 164, 169
    formation of 75, 78

Selma voting rights campaign and 216, 217
Southern Farmers Alliance 5
"Southern Manifesto" 77, 278–280
Speer, Hugh W. 35
States Rights Party 11, 16, 27
Stembridge, Jane 209
Stennis, John 208
Stephens, Patricia 127
Stevens, Thaddeus 17, **325**
Stevenson, Adlai 78
Stewart, Bennet 256
Stokes, Carl B. 254
Stokes, Louis 251
Storey, Moorfield 9, 25, **325**
Student Nonviolent Coordinating Committee (SNCC) 117, 122, 127, 168, 256
    Albany Movement and 138, 140, 141, 143, 148
    Black power and 243, 254
    formation of 112, 121, 128, 284–285
    Freedom Summer and 197, 199, 201, 203, 205
    Selma voting rights campaign and 216, 217, 221
Sugarman, Tracy 207
Sulzberger, C. L. 158
Sumner, Charles 1, 18–19, 20
Supreme Court, U.S. xii, 15, 22, 29, 114, 122, 148, 255, 256, 258, 259
    school desegregation and 36–39, 41, 42, 45, 47, 53, 61, 87, 88, 93, 96
    See also Brown v. Board of Education and specific cases
Swann v. Charlotte-Mecklenburg 255–256
Sweatt v. Painter 32, 37, 40

T

Talmadge, Herman 47, 105
Terrell, Mary Church 48
Thirteenth Amendment xi, 1, 2, 13, 269
Thomas, Henry 129
Thomas, Jefferson *105*
Thompson, Allen 199
Thompson, Estella 107
Thoreau, Henry David 71
Thurmond, Strom 189, 228, 325
    States Rights Party and 11, 16, 27
Tilden, Samuel 5
Till, Emmett 53–65, 142
    murder of xii, 56–57, 61

public reaction of 57–58, 59, 61, 62–65
Till, Louis 54
Till, Mamie Bradley 54, *55*, 57, *63*, 64, 65
Tobias, Channing H. 46, 47
Todd, Lucinda 40
Topeka, Kansas
school segregation and 35–36, 40
See also Brown v. Board of Education
Truman, Harry S. 325–326
civil rights program and 11–12, 16, 27
Turner, Henry MacNeal 18
Tuskegee Normal and Industrial Institute 6–7, 15

U

United States v. Fordice 259
Universal Negro Improvement Association 25
See also Garvey, Marcus
University of California Regents v. Bakke 256

V

VEP *See* Voter Education Project
Villard, Oswald Garrison 24
Voter Education Project (VEP) 148, 197–198
Voting rights 10, 29, 95, 138, 215, 252
intimidation and 27, 137, 197, 202, 216
legislation on 167, 222–223, 226–228, 231, 294–295

Selma campaign for. *See* Selma voting rights campaign
See also Voting Rights Act (1965)
Voting Rights Act (1965) 227–228, 229, 243, 252, 255, 257, 294–295
Johnson and 222–223, 226–227, 236, 241, 248

W

Walker, Edwin A. 101, 103–104
Walker, Wyatt T. **326**
Albany movement and 140–141, 148
Birmingham campaign and 162, 164, 170
Wallace, George 184, 208, 252, **326**
Birmingham campaign and 166, 174
Selma-to-Montgomery march and 218–219, 220, 221, 223, 226, 237
Selma voting rights campaign and 234, 235
University of Alabama and 167, 169, 227
Wallace, Mike 99
Walls, Carlotta *91, 105*
Warren, Earl 6, 38, 41, 47, 93, **326**
See also Brown v. Board of Education
Warting, T. R. 83
Washington, Booker T. 6, 7–8, 9, 15, 24, 326–327
"Atlanta Compromise" speech 7, 22

Watkins, Tom 145
Watts, California 230, 248, 261
Webb, Sheyann 233
Wells-Barnett, Ida B. 9, 22–23, **327**
Wells, Benjamin 142
"We Shall Overcome" 119, 135, 139, 181, 228, 244
Western College for Women 199, 207
White, Byron 118
White Citizens Council 42, 53, 73–74, 77, 83, 84, 144, 197, 216
White, George B. 23
White, Hugh 62
White, Walter 26, 40, 51, **327**
Whitten, John C. 59, 64
Wilder, Douglas 259
Wilkins, Roy 256, 327
Democratic National Convention (1968) and 202, 203, *204*
Emmett Till and 62
Little Rock Central High School and 101, 107
March Against Fear and 243, 244
March on Washington and 178, 180, 188, 189, *191*
Montgomery bus boycott and 82
Selma voting rights campaign and 235
Voting Rights Act (1965) and 227
Williams, Hosea *219*, 229, *249*, **327–328**
Williams v. Wallace 290–293
Wofford, Harris 113
Womens movement 251, 256

Womens Political Council 69, 79
Womens suffrage 16
Woodley, Richard 207
Woods, Anita 172
Woods, Robin 101
Woolworths lunch counter sit-ins in Greensboro, N.C. 109–*110*, *114*, *120*, *123*–*124*
See also sit-in movement
World War I 11, 25
World War II 10–11, 177
Wren, Chris 214
Wright, Mose 54, 55, 56, 57, 58, 60, 61, 62, 64
See also Till, Emmett

Y

Yarborough, Ralph 235
Young, Andrew 228, 256, 257, 266, **328**
Birmingham campaign and 162, 171
Selma voting rights campaign and 217
Young, Coleman 256
Young, Whitney M. Jr. **328**
Albany movement and 153
March Against Fear and 243, 244
March on Washington and 178, 180, 181, *191*

Z

Zinn, Howard 264
Zwerg, James 118, 132